Introduction to APL and Computer Programming

Edward Harms, Ph.D
Associate Professor
Fairfield University

Michael P. Zabinski Ph.D
Associate Professor
Fairfield University

JOHN WILEY & SONS

New York • Chichester • Brisbane • Toronto • Singapore

Library of Congress Cataloging in Publication Data

Harms, Edward.
  Introduction to APL and computer programming.

  Bibliography: p. 369
  Includes index.
  1. APL (Computer program language) 2. Elec-
tronic digital computers--Programming. I. Zabinski,
Michael P., joint author. II. Title.
QA76.73.A27H37   001.6'424   76-20587
ISBN 0-471-35201-2

Printed in the United States of America

10 9 8

TO OUR FAMILIES

    SHEILA, MICHAEL, BRYAN

    TOBY, ERIC, MARION

Preface

The computer language APL, short for A Programming Language, is based on a notation introduced by Kenneth E. Iverson in 1957. Since its implementation at IBM in the early 1960s, APL has gained wide acceptance in industry, research, and education. Its use continues to grow at a rapid rate. This book provides an introduction to APL, and through it, to some of the important concepts and applications of computer programming.

The reasons for the increased use of APL are many. It is a concise powerful language. The large number of functions supplied with the language and their natural use with arrays of data enable single APL instructions to perform procedures requiring many statements in other languages. This elimination of detail greatly decreases the amount of time spent in writing programs and removes many sources of error. Primitive functions supplied with the language make input-output instructions easy to write. Programming errors produce understandable error messages. These attributes, combined with good editing capabilities, make the language ideal for on-line use.

This book is directed at the beginning programmer. The features of APL that have led to its adoption as a practical programming language also make it an ideal educational tool. Only a brief introduction is required before meaningful tasks can be addressed. In this book we emphasize those parts of the language that are most frequently used, while more advanced topics are discussed in less detail or are included in the case studies or in the appendices. Many examples are included to explain the use of APL and illustrate the way in which practical problems may be solved with the language. They are supplemented by an abundance of exercises within and at the end of each chapter. Extended discussions are given of programming errors and debugging techniques.

The level of presentation and selection of material make this book suitable for a wide variety of readers. We assume no previous experience with computers and no mathematical background beyond the basic arithmetic skills. The examples chosen tend to deemphasize the purely mathematical aspects of computing and focus on a wide range of non-numerical applications. For example, character vectors are introduced early in the discussion and character data are used in many instances to illustrate the use of APL functions. Many of the illustrative examples and several of the case studies have been drawn from the business field. This reflects the increased use of APL in this area and the general familiarity of most readers with business problems. The case studies cover a range of subject matter and can be selectively chosen to suit different needs and interests.

Since APL is an ideal language for on-line use, the material is presented as it would appear when generated by using a terminal. A unique feature of this book is the inclusion of explanatory comments alongside the computer displays. These comments highlight and reinforce the text discussion, by pointing out new procedures and emphasizing important points. The reader is encouraged to work along with the text, trying out the illustrative examples on the computer, and experimenting with variations.

The book is divided into two parts: Part I, which includes Chapters 1 to 8, provides an introduction to the APL language. Part II consists of seven case studies that supplement the text material with examples of computer applications.

Chapter 1 introduces the student to the use of the APL terminal. Chapter 2 discusses numerical and character data and the use of variables to store information.

Chapter 3 introduces the basic arithmetic functions. The APL rules for working with single numbers as well as vectors are introduced, as is the right-to-left evaluation rule. The operation of reduction is also discussed. The basic procedures for writing and editing computer programs are described in Chapter 4. This chapter also contains material on program debugging and workspace management.

Chapter 5 covers logical data and their use with the logical, relational, and compression functions. A number of the special APL functions are presented in Chapter 6 with emphasis on their applications. A discussion of formatting techniques is also included in this chapter. Branching and looping are introduced in Chapter 7 in a form appropriate for APL, yet applicable to computer languages in general. Flowcharts are introduced to depict the algorithms. The trace control is used to elucidate the concept of looping. Matrices and their applications are discussed in Chapter 8.

The case studies in Part II of the book cover the topics of sorting, searching, simulation, graphing, payroll, and computer-assisted instruction. These case studies provide a wide cross section of areas of application.

The sorting case study investigates the comparator and bubble sort algorithms for sorting data and introduces techniques for comparing these methods. The search case study presents the linear and binary search algorithms. These two case studies describe the computations performed by the computer when the APL sort and search primitive functions are executed.

Simulation techniques are introduced in two case studies. The first simulation case study investigates the generation of random numbers and discusses their application in simulating random processes. The second, a financial model, develops the use of APL in a typical business problem. A report generator is presented as part of the case study.

The graphing case study presents a plotting function to display point and histogram plots. The payroll case study demonstrates a small payroll system. Programs are presented for entering, processing, and reporting payroll data. The CAI case study describes the computer's use in presenting topics in arithmetic and English grammar.

The appendices contain summary tables of error messages, system commands, and APL functions. Also included is a bibliography of texts and articles on APL and its applications. Solutions to selected exercises are provided at the end of the text. A complete set of solutions is contained in the Instructor's Manual, available from the publisher.

We are indebted to the many people who have contributed to the development of this book. Particular thanks are due to Fred Newpeck, University of New Mexico, Donald Reuther, Orange Coast College, Paul Heller, University of Pennsylvania, John Howland, Trinity University, and Ephraim McLean, University of California at Los Angeles, for reviewing the manuscript and providing numerous helpful suggestions. We also express our appreciation to Alan Rose of Scientific Time Sharing Corporation for his help and encouragement. Scientific Time Sharing Corporation's APL*Plus System was used to develop several of the text examples.

The final version of the book reflects the comments of many of our students at Fairfield University who used it in our classes. Gratitude is also expressed to Martin Ryan of the Fairfield Public Schools, who tested a portion of the book in his classroom.

Finally, we express special thanks to Mrs. Shirley Stengel for her careful attention to the enormous task of preparing preliminary versions of the book and the final copy for publication.

E. Harms

M. P. Zabinski

Contents

PART II   CASE STUDIES

List of Examples

Page

List of Tables and Figures

Page

TABLES

FIGURES

Introduction

The computer is one of the most powerful tools ever designed
by man and is certainly the most versatile. The raw material
for this machine consists of information of all kinds which it
manipulates and transforms flawlessly at an incredible speed.
In the few decades since the development of the first computer,
the "information machine" has become an integral component of
our way of life. The "computer revolution" will most likely
transform the society of man to as large an extent as have the
agricultural and industrial-technological revolutions of the
past and in a considerably shorter time period.

In view of the obvious accomplishments and potentialities
of the computer (no doubt many of these potentialities are
still undreamed of), many people are surprised to discover
that the computer itself has very little natural intelligence.
Its basic abilities consist of very simple operations such as
adding or subtracting two numbers, testing to see if a number
is one or zero, and reading and writing information.

For a computer to perform a task, the task must be described
in the most minute detail in terms of these basic operations.
This description is communicated to the computer by means of
its *machine language*, the set of instructions in the form of
numeric digits that the computer can recognize and act on.
This detailed and explicit set of instructions forms the end
result of the process of *computer programming*.

Fortunately, it is usually not necessary for the computer
programmer to write his programs using machine language. The
detailed step-by-step operation of the computer is far removed
from our usual manner of thinking , and writing a program in
machine language is a difficult and error-prone process. Most
computer programs today are written using one of several *user-oriented* languages of which *APL, A Programming Language* is one
example.

The vocabulary and structure of a user-oriented language is
designed to make writing computer programs simpler for people.
Since these languages are not understandable to the computer,
they must be translated into the computer's machine language.
In the case of APL, this is done by the *interpreter*, a computer
program that is written by experts familiar with machine language and that translates the instructions in a user's program
into a computer readable form.

THE COMPUTER

A computer is a machine capable of rapidly performing a large number of simple calculations and operations. However, this description by no means gives the complete picture. A computer is a device that can accept all types of information, process the information in a wide variety of ways and provide results. How can it do this? The computer has the ability to store vast quantities of information that can be made available to the user. Also, it can store a set of instructions; these may be necessary to process the stored information.

Let us consider the simple task of averaging the grades of a class of students. Although the procedure is straight-forward, the number of arithmetic operations associated with adding the grades (for example, 5 grades per student) and then averaging them for every student in a class of 30 students is large. A computer is suitable for this task. The information must be fed into the computer as *input*, for example via punched cards or a remote terminal.

The data is *stored* in the computer *memory*, available for use when required. Computer storage can be visualized as a set of post office boxes where each box is capable of holding a single number or instruction. The post office boxes are arranged in such a way that each can be identified so that its content is easily accessible. In our example the information, or data, consists of students' names and respective grades. According to the instructions contained in the computer program various arithmetic manipulations must be followed in the process of averaging. These instructions, in the form of machine language, are also stored in the computer memory.

The actual arithmetic calculations to determine the grade average for each student take place in the *arithmetic unit*. For this purpose, grades must be transferred from memory to the arithmetic unit. On completion of the calculations the results (average grades) are returned to storage.

The grades must now be retrieved from the computer in some meaningful way. This is done through an *output* device which, for example, may print or display a report on a computer terminal. The activities associated with the flow of data within the computer are coordinated by the *control unit*. The control unit examines each instruction and activates the appropriate unit of the computer. In the case of an instruction to add A to B, the control unit will cause the values of A and B to be placed in the arithmetic unit where the addition will take place. The result will then be transferred to memory for storage. In the case of an output instruction, it will transmit the results by printing them on the terminal. The following diagram illustrates the flow of information within a computer (solid lines) and the exercise of control (dashed lines).

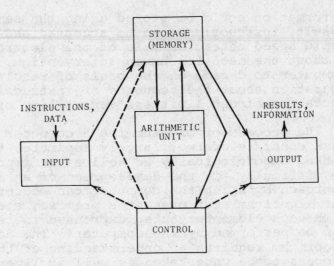

The APL system you will use is most likely operated under a
system of computer usage called *time-sharing*. In a
time-shared system, a number of different users are given
access to the computer simultaneously. The user communicates
with the system via a remote terminal which may be located
miles from the computer installation and connected to the
central computer by means of telephone lines.

In a time-shared system the computer serves each user in
rotation giving each one some fraction of its time. Since the
processing of information by the computer is so much more
rapid than the programmer's ability to enter information and
interpret the computer's response, the user has the impression
of having uninterrupted access to the computer.

Time-sharing provides for an interactive dialogue between
the programmer and the computer, with the computer checking
the validity of instructions *on-line*, allowing the programmer
to correct his program. The conversational aspects of time-
shared systems are also extremely important for the use of the
computer as an educational tool and hold great promise for
further extending the range of man-computer interaction.

COMPUTER PROGRAMMING

Computer programming plays an increasingly important role in
the use of computers. Rapid technological development in the
computer industry is quickly diminishing the restrictions
placed on computer systems by the limitation of the computer
devices themselves. More and more effort in the computer
field is focused on the development and improvement of the
programs necessary to utilize this machine.

The ability of a computer to store instructions as well as
data is crucial to its efficient operation. The stored
program concept is usually credited to John Von Neumann, a
mathematician, who demonstrated that both these forms of

information could be stored using the same language. As a
result, instructions can be accessed and executed with the
rapid speed characteristic of the electronic digital computer
without the need for human intervention. The ability of the
computer to decide on the basis of results obtained in its
operation about the sequence of instructions to follow produces the almost limitless versatility of this machine.

The process of programming a computer to perform a given
task consists of two, largely separate, steps. The first,
ranked chronologically as well as in importance and usually
in difficulty, is the development of an *algorithm* or method of
approach by which the computer can perform the task at hand.
The algorithm must present a precise, step-by-step procedure
with each elementary step expressed in terms of operations that
can be performed by the computer. The development of the
algorithm requires an understanding of the intricacies of the
process to be undertaken as well as liberal amounts of intelligence, ingenuity, and intestinal fortitude. This aspect of
computer programming lies largely outside the scope of this
book.

The second step in the development of a computer program
is the translation or *encoding* of the algorithm into a series
of instructions written in some language that the computer can
understand. This series of instructions is called the *computer
program*. If the rules of the language to be used are well
understood and the algorithm has been developed in sufficient
detail the translation should offer little difficulty. The
purpose of this book is to help you learn the basics of one
such language, APL. As you will see, the APL language has a
simple and easily learned structure, but is powerful enough to
be applicable to a wide class of algorithms.

Today the techniques of computer programming are in a
period of rapid transition. Improvements in our understanding
of the programming process have led to the introduction of a
series of new programming methods. These methods, which fall
under the heading of *structured programming*, have already produced substantial increases in programmer productivity and a
substantial decrease in the number of programming errors.

Structured programming is a manner of organizing and
writing programs that makes them easy to understand, edit, and
modify. Basically, the approach taken is to design the
algorithm and corresponding computer program to proceed from
the top to the bottom. In this process the overall algorithm
may be broken into individual fairly short program modules.

The APL language was originally developed by Kenneth
Iverson to provide a notation for expressing algorithms.
Since Iverson's first publication APL has undergone consider-
able further development, primarily at IBM. APL became
operational at the IBM Watson Research Center for the IBM
System/360 in 1966 as an experimental time-sharing system and

later became an IBM program product. Today APL is one of the
most concise and powerful languages, and is effective not only
in science and mathematics but also in business and the
liberal arts.

The original IBM product has been updated and modified by
IBM and by other computer manufacturers and time-sharing
services. At the present time the language is being used by
several universities and public school systems for student
instruction and research. Its use in business, engineering
and science has grown rapidly over the last 5 years and will
no doubt continue to grow as people gradually become aware of
and accept the power of that language "with all the funny
symbols."

Part I
The APL Language

Chapter 1
Using the APL Terminal

Time-sharing describes a processing system that has a number of simultaneously usable stations. Each station provides direct access to the central processing unit. The user communicates with the computer through a terminal that is either directly wired to the computer or connected to it by means of a telephone line. There are many types of terminal equipment available. The most common are typewriter terminals, machines similar in appearance to the electric typewriter but containing additional communications equipment. Also available are cathode ray tube (CRT) display terminals. These units look like small television sets that have a keyboard similar to a standard typewriter. Other examples include cash registers and accounting machines. Some terminals are as portable as a suitcase and can be connected to any telephone by means of an acoustic coupler.

The terminal serves as both an input and output device. The program and the input data are typed into the computer via the keyboard, and the output data are transmitted from the computer to the terminal where they are printed.

1.1 THE APL KEYBOARD

All computer languages use a certain set of characters to express the various statements in the language. The keyboard of a typical APL terminal (IBM Model 2741) containing the APL character set is shown in Figure 1.1. Your terminal may differ slightly.

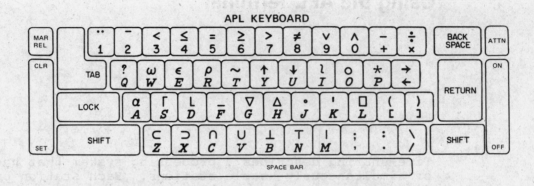

Figure 1.1   The APL keyboard

The keyboard has the usual alphabetic (A-Z), numeric (0-9), and arithmetic (+, -, ÷, etc.) characters. In addition, APL has a selection of special characters that are used to activate the large number of functions available for manipulating information. You will gain familiarity with the APL characters and their use as you proceed through this book.

On the APL keyboard the alphabetic and numeric characters are placed in the same position as on a standard typewriter. The keyboard has also been arranged to help you locate the special characters. For example, the sequence <, ≤, =, ≥, >, ≠ is located in this order over the numbers 3 through 8. The symbol ? is located over Q for Question Mark, producing a mnemonic connection between the two characters.   Similarly, the symbol ϵ is located over E making use of the relationship between the Greek symbol, epsilon, and its Roman counterpart.

Some symbols in the APL character set are formed from more than one character and are produced by typing one character, backspacing, and then typing the second character. For example, an exclamation point is produced by typing an apostrophe, backspacing, and then typing a period.

1.2   SIGN-ON AND SIGN-OFF PROCEDURE

Before beginning work at the terminal, it is necessary to make the connection with the computer. The following is a general outline of the steps necessary to sign on. Instructions are given for installations equipped with datasets or acoustic couplers. Directions may vary from terminal to terminal; it is suggested that you confirm the proper procedure at your computer center.

The procedure for using a dataset is:

1.   Turn on the on-off keyboard switch and put the COM-LCL switch in the COM position. Lift the telephone receiver, depress the TALK button, and dial the telephone number shown on the telephone.

2.   When you hear a high pitched tone, press the DATA button
     and replace the receiver.

3.   Once the keyboard is unlocked, enter a right parenthesis
     followed by your account number and your password (if
     any). Press the RETURN key. The computer then responds
     with system information including the date and the time.

4.   The terminal then indents six spaces before it allows you
     to type.

     The procedure with an acoustic coupler is:

1.   The same as above except, in addition, you must turn the
     coupler on-off switch to the off position.

2.   When you hear a high pitched tone, place the receiver in
     the acoustic coupler with the cord at the appropriate end.
     Then turn the coupler on-off switch to the on position.

3.   Once the keyboard is unlocked, enter a right parenthesis
     followed by your account number and your password (if
     any). Press the RETURN key. The computer then responds
     with system information including the date and the time.

4.   The terminal then indents six spaces before it allows you
     to type.

     Some computer terminals may be wired directly to the
computer. Sign-on procedures for these terminals do not
require use of a telephone. However, after connection with
the computer is made, steps 3 and 4 will be executed as
described above.

     A sample sign-on dialogue appears below:

```
)2555411:SHIRLEY
OPR:   LA USERS)LOAD 1 LA
121)   8.07.32 05/08/75 EAHARMS

     APL*PLUS SERVICE*
```

     The first line, which is typed by the user, identifies the
user by her account number followed by a password. The suc-
ceeding lines are the computer's response. A message from
the operator indicated by OPR: gives general information
about the system. This is followed by a line containing the
port number, 121 in the above example (the number of the
computer access port to which you are connected), the local
time, the date, and the user's name. The next line identifies
the APL system.

---

*$APL*PLUS$ is a servicemark of the APL system developed by
Scientific Time Sharing Corporation of Bethesda, Maryland.
Some of the examples in this book were executed on this
system.

To sign off, type the command)OFF and press RETURN. A
display similar to the following will be obtained.

```
     )OFF
121    10.09.42 05/08/75 EAHARMS
CONNECTED      2.02.10  TO DATE      8.57.16
CPU TIME       0.10.03  TO DATE      0.58.09
```

The first line shows the port number, the time and date of
sign-off, and the user's name. The second line lists the
connect time for this session and the accumulated connect time
to date. The last line gives the actual amount of time taken
by the central processing unit (CPU) to process the instructions entered during this session and the accumulated CPU time
to date.

1.3 COMMUNICATING WITH THE COMPUTER

Sending instructions or commands to the computer is done by
typing an appropriate statement on the keyboard. After the
entire statement has been entered, pressing the RETURN key
sends it to the computer where it will be acted upon. For
example, the following sequence illustrates the results of
adding two numbers

```
     3+2
5
     6+2
8
```

The instruction 3+2 is typed by the user and returned. The
result 5 is displayed by the computer on the next line starting ·at the left margin. The paper is then advanced one line
and the type element is indented to the seventh print position
where the computer awaits the next instruction. The second
addition, 6+2, is then entered and evaluated. The difference
in printing positions clearly distinguishes between instructions and displayed results. The positioning of the type
element is illustrated by the following example.

```
     4×3
12
     123456789
123456789
```

Throughout the textbook the input instructions and the
computer's response are displayed in the same manner as they
appear on your terminal. Explanatory comments are frequently
added alongside this dialogue.

COMMENTS

```
     3+2                    The sum of 3 and 2 is 5.
5
     6+2
8
```

___

If the computer does not understand the statement entered, a message such as *SYNTAX ERROR* will appear.

```
    2÷
SYNTAX ERROR
    2÷
    ^
```

This is one of several *error messages* that the computer uses to inform you of errors. Others will be discussed later. A complete list of error messages is tabulated in Appendix 1.

If you detect an error in the statement you are entering before pressing the RETURN key, it can be corrected by back-spacing to the first incorrect character and then striking the ATTENTION key. (Your terminal may require a slightly differ-ent procedure, such as striking the LINEFEED key.) This operation erases the incorrect character *and all characters to the right*. Now enter the correct character and continue entering the statement from that point.

For example, suppose we want to calculate the square of 3. In APL this can be done using the power function * (upper shift *P*) in the form 3*2. The following example demonstrates the steps necessary to correct the situation in which a *P* has been entered instead of *.

```
    3P2
    v
    *2
9
```

The line is typed incorrectly. Backspace to *P* and strike the ATTENTION key. The symbol v is displayed under the point at which the correction is made. This advances the paper and effectively erases *P*2. The correct symbols *2 are entered, RETURN is pressed, and the correct result is displayed.

Typing mistakes are not crucial and may be fixed readily. You should expect to make mistakes while learning APL. We encourage you to experiment at the terminal.

Chapter 2
Specifying Information

The vast power of computers lies in their ability to handle a large amount of information rapidly. We begin our study of APL by looking at some of the types of information that we can use and some of the ways this information can be organized.

The two types of information discussed in this chapter are numerical information and character information. A third type, logical information, will be taken up in Chapter 5. Other types of information with which you may be familiar are complex numbers or numbers using a base other than base 10. Current APL systems restrict themselves to handling numerical, character, and logical information, and this will suffice in most applications.

The way in which information is organized is equally as important as the type of information we are dealing with. For example, the single number

1984

could stand for a particular year. In APL terminology, single numbers such as this are called *scalars*. If we wanted to specify a particular day in the year we could use three numbers

6 11 1984

to represent the month, day, and year. In this case the information we want to express is given as a group of three values rather than a single numerical value. We will see many examples in which such sequences of numbers are the natural way to represent information. In APL these sequences are termed *vectors*.

Similarly, when handling character information, we may be interested in a single character,

'A'

More often, however, we are interested in several characters, for example a phrase

'A TIME FOR JOY'

or the contents of this book.

There are many other ways in which we can organize information. Examples of other frequently used forms are a multiplication table, a crossword puzzle, and a picture. These are illustrated in Figure 2.1. Such an arrangement of data is called a table or a *matrix* and will be discussed in detail in Chapter 8. This chapter and those that follow will concern themselves primarily with scalars and vectors.

2.1 NUMERICAL INFORMATION

Single numbers such as 21, 167, or 87 are called *numerical scalars*. These numbers can represent information of importance to you such as your age, weight, or your grade on your last exam. Decimal numbers are expressed in the usual manner, for example, 0.5 or 3.14159.

A negative number is specified by placing the *negative sign* (¯, upper shift 2) before it. Examples are ¯2 and ¯1.75. It is important to recognize the difference between the negative sign and the *minus sign* (-, upper shift +), which is used to perform subtractions. This will be discussed more fully when we deal with arithmetic expressions.

APL uses a modified version of *scientific notation* for representing very large numbers or very small numbers. Scientific notation breaks a number into two components, a number between 1 and 10 and an exponent of 10. For example, the age of the earth is about four and one half billion years which can be written as 4500000000 or in scientific notation as 4.5×10^9. In APL we can express the number as $4.5E9$, where E indicates that 9 is the exponent of 10. Additional examples are:

Number	Scientific Notation	APL
1574000	1.574×10^{6}	$1.574E6$
0.00036	3.6×10^{-4}	$3.6E^{-}4$

APL replaces *x10 to the* by *E*

In addition to considering single numbers, it is often useful to group numbers together to form *numerical vectors*. A numerical vector is a list of numbers specified by typing the numbers in the vector leaving a space between them. For example, the three numerical vectors

Multiplication Table

×	1	2	3	4	5
1	1	2	3	4	5
2	2	4	6	8	10
3	3	6	9	12	15
4	4	8	12	16	20
5	5	10	15	20	25

Crossword Puzzle

```
* * * * * * * *
* * F * * * * *
* PARTS * *
* * R * A * * *
* * MAP * * *
* * * * * * * *
```

Picture of the Authors
(Courtesy of Recreational Computer Systems, Atlanta, Georgia)

Figure 2.1 Information organized in matrix form

COMMENTS

```
     12.0 8.50 .99 5.19        Entering a numerical vector causes
12 8.5 0.99 5.19                it to be redisplayed.  Note that
     89 78 92 81 93             trailing zeros after the decimal
89 78 92 81 93                  point are dropped and a zero
     6 11 1984                  before the decimal point is added
6 11 1984                       for values less than one.
```

could represent the prices of items you bought at a store, the
grades on your exams for the semester, or the date. Each
number in the vector is called an *element*. The first element
in the first vector is 12.0, the second element is 8.50, and
so on. We refer to the number of elements in a vector as its
length. The first vector above has a length of four, the
second a length of five, and the third a length of three.

2.2   CHARACTER INFORMATION

In addition to numerical scalars and vectors, APL also allows
for the use of single *characters* such as

   'A', 'B', 'C', '2', '3', '*', '!'

or *character vectors* (strings) such as

   'ABC', '23', '*!+-'

Characters are entered as follows:

COMMENTS

```
      'A'                       On input, character data are indi-
A                               cated by apostrophes.  On output,
      '2'                       the characters are displayed
2                               without the apostrophes.
      '*'
*
      'MNOP'
MNOP
      '∘O0◊'
∘O0◊
```

The character '2' and the numerical scalar 2 have different
meanings. In particular, the numerical scalar 2 can be added
to another numerical scalar while characters cannot be added.

```
      ¯2+2
4
      '2'+'2'
DOMAIN ERROR
      '2'+'2'
        ∧
```

The error message *DOMAIN ERROR* is displayed since the process
of addition is not defined for character information. The
caret (∧) points to the location of the error.

The following example illustrates some additional features
of character information.

    'PLEASE DON''T EAT THE DAISIES'
PLEASE DON'T EAT THE DAISIES

Notice that to produce an apostrophe in this character vector,
we typed two successive apostrophes. The first element in the
character vector is a *P*, the seventh is a blank space. In all
there are 28 elements: 23 letters, 4 blanks, and one
apostrophe.

If the RETURN key is accidentally pressed before the final
apostrophe in a character vector is typed, the computer's
response will depend on the APL implementation at your
installation. Two types of responses are typical. On some
systems the paper will advance one line and the type element
will move to the left margin and no further execution will be
accomplished until the final apostrophe is entered. On other
systems the paper is advanced and the computer automatically
types the closing quote. The user must then press the RETURN
key.

The following examples illustrate some features of the types
of information we have discussed.

		COMMENTS
	1	A numerical scalar.
1		
	'1'	A character, the numeral one.
1		
	123	A numerical scalar.
123		
	'123'	A character vector containing three numerals.
123		
	1 2 3	A numerical vector having three elements.
1 2 3		
	'1 2 3'	A character vector containing five elements, three numerals and two blanks.
1 2 3		

2.3   A WAY TO THINK ABOUT THINGS

The reader should be sure that he is able to make the distinction between the different types of data we have discussed,
that is character and numerical, and the different ways in
which these data can be organized, as scalars, vectors or
matrices. In APL the term *shape* is often used to refer to the
organization of data. This term corresponds to a convenient
pictorial way of representing and thinking about the different
forms of data organization. Thus, for example, we can think
of the shape of a vector as that of a line of boxes, such as

       [ ] [ ] [ ] [ ] [ ] [ ] [ ] [ ]

In this way of thinking about vectors, the shape is determined
by giving the number of boxes in the vector, that is by its
length. Each box would contain a single numerical or
character value

        [A] [B] [C] [D] ... [Z]

Matrices on the other hand can be pictured as a rectangular
arrangement of boxes, such as

        [1] [2] [3] [4]
        [2] [4] [6] [8]
        [3] [6] [9] [12]
        [4] [8] [12] [16]
        [5] [10] [15] [20]

The actual shape is determined by the number of horizontal rows
and vertical columns present. Once again, each box is thought
of as holding a single numerical value or character. A scalar
has only one value

        [A]

and can be thought of as a point. Throughout this book, we
will use pictures like these to help you understand and
visualize the way in which APL processes data.

2.4 VARIABLES

The previous sections introduced different types of information; thus far it has been necessary to enter information
from the keyboard. We often run into situations in which we
want to store information for later use. This capability is
provided through the use of *variables*. A variable is a name
that represents data stored in the computer. The data may be
one or more numbers or one or more characters. It is not
fixed but may be changed before or during program execution.

If we are to write a program that will average student
grades, we need to have available the number of exams taken
by each student. Since this number will, in general, not be
known in advance (we, for example, want to write a program
that can be used for any course), we may assign a name to
this quantity, for example N. The quantity N is called a
variable. In a class in which exams are frequent, N may have
the value 10 while for another class in which exams are
infrequent, N might be 3. Thus N will not always stand for
the same number but the number represented by N will always
be the number of exams taken by each student. The same
program might use another variable to stand for the student's
name.

Variable names are formed from alphabetic characters
(including the Δ character, upper shift H), underlined alphabetic characters, or numerals. Variable names can be up to
77 characters in length in most APL implementations, and must

start with a letter or underlined letter. Underlined letters
are formed by entering the letter, backspacing, and then
striking upper shift *F*. Examples of valid variable names are:

> *A*, *A̲*, *A*1, *GRADE*, *GRA̲DE*

Examples of invalid variable names are:

> 1*A*   variable name must start with a letter
>
> *A**   variable name may not contain special
>   characters
>
> *A1̲*   numerals may not be underlined

It is useful to select variable names that are easily
associated with the items they represent. For example, the
variable name for test grades could be *GRADE* rather than the
name *G*, or even worse, *X*.

2.5 ASSIGNMENT

The procedure by which we specify the value of a variable is
called assignment. Assignment is indicated by a left arrow
($\leftarrow$). To assign the value 1 to the variable *A* we use the
instruction

> *A*$\leftarrow$1

Enter *A*, the left arrow, and 1. Then press the RETURN key.
From this point on *A* has the value 1 unless its value is
changed by a subsequent assignment statement. No display is
returned by the computer following the assignment statement.
To have the computer tell us the current value of any variable,
we enter the variable name. For example, to retrieve the
value just assigned to *A* we type *A* and press RETURN.

> *A*
>
> 1

If we enter the letter *B*, however, we find the error message
VALUE ERROR, indicating that *B* has not been assigned any
value.

> *B*
>
> *VALUE ERROR*
> *B*
> ∧

When the computer encounters the assignment statement
A$\leftarrow$1, it places the value 1 in a storage location in its memory
and associates this storage location with the variable name *A*.
When the value of the variable is to be displayed, the computer recognizes the variable name *A* and displays the information
contained in the storage location assigned to *A*. Displaying
the value of *A* does not change its value in storage.

  COMMENTS

        A
1
        A   The value of *A* is still 1.
1

    A variable can be assigned any type of information:

                                        COMMENTS

        GRADE←70 80 90   Storing a numerical vector.
        GRADE
70 80 90

        LETTER←'A'   Storing a character.
        LETTER
A

        RHO←'ρ'
        RHO
ρ

        SINGER←'TOM JONES'   Storing character vectors.
        SINGER
TOM JONES

        ARROWS←'↑←→↓'
        ARROWS
↑←→↓

    A variable can be assigned a new value, but in the process
the old value is lost. The variable *GRADE* contains grades
70 80 90. To change these grades we can use a second assignment statement.

                                        COMMENTS

        GRADE   Old grades.
70 80 90
        GRADE←80 90 100 95   Assign new grades.
        GRADE
80 90 100 95   Old grades are lost.

    A variable name can be used in place of the information it
represents.

                                        COMMENTS

        SINGER
TOM JONES
        PERSON←*SINGER*   The variable *PERSON* is now assigned
        PERSON   the same value as *SINGER*.
TOM JONES

COMMENTS

	A	*A* has the value 1.
1		
	A+2	The value of *A* is used in the addition.
3		
	A	*A* is unchanged.
1		

Variable names currently in use may be ascertained with the *system command*)*VARS* (for VARiableS).

```
     )VARS
A    ARROWS    GRADE    LETTER    PERSON    RHO    SINGER
```

The sign-on and sign-off procedures are examples of other system commands. Such commands have a right parenthesis as their first character. A complete list of system commands is given in Appendix 2.

A variable name is removed using the system command)*ERASE*.

COMMENTS

)*ERASE SINGER*	Variable *SINGER* erased.
)*ERASE ARROWS LETTER*	Variables *ARROWS* and *LETTER* are erased.
)*VARS*	
A GRADE PERSON RHO	Remaining variables are displayed.
ARROWS	Variable *ARROWS* is no longer specified.
VALUE ERROR	
ARROWS	
∧	
GRADE	Variable *GRADE* remains unchanged.
80 90 100 95	

EXERCISES

While you are doing these exercises keep a record of the errors you make and the error messages you receive. Before you enter instructions, record the result you anticipate in the column <u>Anticipated Display</u>. If the actual display differs from the anticipated display, record the result in the column <u>Display</u> with an explanation.

If necessary, before submitting information to the computer, edit the text.

1.   Practice signing on and off the terminal. What happens if you enter an incorrect command?

2.   Enter two single numbers (enter means type a number, then press the RETURN key). Record your results.

	Instruction	Anticipated Display	Display
a.			
b.			

3.   Enter two vectors of numbers.

	Instruction	Anticipated Display	Display
a.			
b.			

4. Enter the following:

	Instruction	Anticipated Display	Display
a.	123456789123		
b.	⁻0.000076		
c.	⁻0.076		

Try other examples to determine the range of numbers for which your computer system returns the values in scientific notation.

5. Enter the following, record the result, and explain.

	Instruction	Anticipated Display	Display
a.	$1E2$		
b.	$A \leftarrow 1E^{-}1$		
	A		
c.	$15E2$		
d.	$0.15E3$		
e.	$^{-}77E^{-}3$		

6. Enter the following, record the result, and explain.

	Instruction	Anticipated Display	Display
a.	$'A'$		
b.	A		
c.	$'MY\ NAME'$		
d.	$MY\ NAME$		
e.	$'*|('$		

	Instruction	Anticipated Display	Display

f. `1234567`

g. `'1234567'`

h. `'123,456'`

i. `''''`

j. `''''''`

7. Assign your name to a variable *NAME*, your home address to a variable *ADDRESS* and your telephone number to a variable *PHONE*. Store the information as character vectors. Display the three variables.

8. Specify and display:

   a. A character vector that will display the digits 1 through 9, separated by spaces.
   b. A character vector that will display the digits without spaces between them.
   c. Two numerical quantities that will do the same as a. and b.

9. Store and display the APL special characters in a variable *CHARAC*.

10. Enter the following instructions. If you anticipate an error indicate the source of that error.

	Instruction	Anticipated Display	Display

a. *VECTOR1*←1 2 3 *A*

b. 6*SCALAR*←6

c. *SCALAR6*←6

d. *NUMBER*←'SIX'

e. *I DO NOT*←'NOT'

f. *HAPPY*←*I LIKE APL*

g. *FIRST*←'LAST'

h. *VARIABLE*←2 3 4

i. *ONE*+*ONE*←1+1

j. *A1*←10

11. The vector *GRADE* contains the old grades from last
    semester, for example, 80 90 95 85. How could you assign
    GRADE the grades for this semester, 85 80 95 100 90 while
    retaining the grades from last semester? (HINT: introduce
    a new variable *OLDGRADES*.)

12. We assume that two variables *A* and *B* have been assigned
    values (for example *A*←10, *B*←20). Find a sequence of
    instructions to interchange the values of *A* and *B* without
    referring to these values explicitly. This sequence
    should work for any values that *A* and *B* may have. (HINT:
    the statements *A*←*B*, *B*←*A* will not suffice. Why not? Try
    using a third variable, *C*.)

13. a. After completing these exercises use the)*VARS* command
       to display the names of all defined variables in the
       workspace.
    b. Erase all the variables using the)*ERASE* command.
    c. Check part b. by using the)*VARS* command.

14. a. Find the largest N for which 10^N does not exceed the
       limit for a constant on your computer. (HINT: in
       scientific notation, enter successively increasing
       numbers of the form 1*E*2, 1*E*10, and so on.)
    b. How does your system indicate when a number is too big
       to be used? (This is termed *overflow*.)
    c. Try entering successively smaller numbers, such as
       1*E*¯2, 1*E*¯10, and so on. What happens?

15. Suppose a given numerical vector contains elements some
    of which when displayed by themselves would appear in
    scientific notation while others would not; what form
    does the display of the entire vector take?

16. How many spaces are placed between the elements in a
    numerical vector when they are displayed by the computer?

17. Do you know last year's Gross National Product (GNP)?
    Assign its value to the variable *GNP* and display it.

Chapter 3
Arithmetic Functions

The previous chapter deals with the manner in which information is represented and stored in the APL language. We now begin to study the different tools at our disposal for using that information. One of the unique features of APL is the abundance of these tools.

This chapter discusses the arithmetic functions. They are a group of functions that are supplied as part of the standard APL language and that permit manipulation of numerical information. They include the familiar addition, multiplication, subtraction, and division functions as well as some other important but less familiar ones.

In addition to introducing these other arithmetic functions, in this chapter we describe some general features of APL functions and the rules that are followed when using them. In particular we introduce the all-important right-to-left evaluation rule.

3.1 DYADIC AND MONADIC FUNCTIONS

Arithmetic functions fall into two groups. With the first group, the *dyadic* functions, the function symbol (+, -, ×, ...) is placed between two numerical quantities indicating that the function is to be performed using both of these quantities. The second group consists of the *monadic* functions in which one numerical quantity is placed to the right of the function symbol. The quantities adjacent to the function symbol are called its *arguments*. A dyadic function has two arguments; a monadic function has one argument.

                              COMMENTS

          6÷3   dyadic division
    2
          ÷2   monadic division (reciprocal)
    0.5

In the first example the division function is dyadic since it has two arguments, 6 and 3. The result is obtained in the usual manner, 6 divided by 3, or 2. In the second example the division symbol is used monadically and the resulting function is called *reciprocal*. It has one argument, 2, and the result

is 1 divided by 2 or 0.5. In this case the monadic and dyadic
uses of the ÷ symbol are closely related. This will not
always be true.

Numerical information can be stored as scalars, vectors, or
matrices and all shapes are valid arguments for arithmetic
functions. This freedom gives considerable versatility to APL
and removes the need for much of the detailed work required in
other languages. In this chapter we will restrict our attention to scalars and vectors and give the rules that are
followed for combining these data shapes. In Chapter 8 we
will see that these rules extend in a natural way when we deal
with matrices.

3.2   DYADIC FUNCTIONS BETWEEN TWO SCALARS

Using two scalars as the arguments of an arithmetic function
causes that function to be performed with these two arguments:

COMMENTS

	1+2	The instruction 1+2 is entered.
3		The sum is displayed.
	1+¯2	Note the difference between the
¯1		negative sign (¯) indicating ¯2
	1-¯2	is a negative number and the minus
3		sign (-) indicating subtraction.
	A←3	
	4-A	The arguments may be constants,
1		variables, or any combination.
	B←5	
	A×B	
15		
	6÷A	
2		

The instruction 1+2 differs from the following:

```
      '1'+'2'
DOMAIN ERROR
      '1'+'2'
       ∧
```

The *DOMAIN ERROR* arises since '1' and '2' are characters
having no numerical value and are therefore outside of the
domain over which the addition function is defined.

3.3   DYADIC FUNCTIONS BETWEEN A SCALAR AND A VECTOR

If one of the arguments of the dyadic function is a scalar and
the other is a vector, the function is performed with the
scalar and each element of the vector. The result is a vector
with the same number of elements (same shape) as the argument
vector.

COMMENTS

```
      1+2 4 ¯6
3 5 ¯5
```

1 is added to each element of the
vector 2 4 ¯6.

```
      ¯2 2 5-1
¯3 1 4
```

1 is subtracted from each element
of the vector ¯2 2 5.

```
      C←1 2 3
      5×C
5 10 15
```

Either or both of the arguments may
be variables. The vector may
appear on either side of the
function symbol.

```
      D←4 5 6
      B
5
      D÷B
0.8 1 1.2
```

Assign a value to D.
Display the current value of B.

Example: Computing Sales Tax

The following example illustrates the calculation of the sales
tax and total price of a series of purchased items.

COMMENTS

```
      RATE←0.06
      NET←50 10 35
      TAX←NET×RATE
      TAX
3 0.6 2.1
      GROSS←NET+TAX
      GROSS
53 10.6 37.1
```

6% sales tax.
Three items purchased.
Compute the tax on each item. TAX
is the product of the vector NET
and the scalar RATE.

Price of each item including sales
tax.

The calculation of GROSS involves the addition of two vectors,
an operation which is discussed in the next section.

3.4 DYADIC FUNCTIONS BETWEEN TWO VECTORS

Both arguments of the dyadic function may be vectors. In this
case both vectors must have the same length. The result is a
vector of the same length as the argument vectors. The first
element in the result is obtained by taking the first element
of each of the argument vectors and performing the indicated
arithmetic function on them. Similarly, the second element of
the result vector is obtained by combining the second elements
of the argument vectors, and so on.

COMMENTS

```
      1 2 3+4 5 6
5 7 9
```

1+4=5;2+5=7;3+6=9

The arguments and the result are vectors of length 3. The
first element in the result, 5, is obtained by taking the
first element in the left argument, 1, and adding it to the
first element in the right argument, 4. The second element in
the result, 7, is obtained by adding together the second elements, 2 and 5, of the argument vectors.

Other examples:

```
      3 2 2×4 5 6
12 10 12
      6 10 12÷3 5 6
2 2 2
```

If the two arguments of a dyadic function are vectors, they
must be of equal length or a *LENGTH ERROR* occurs.

```
      1 2×3 4 5
LENGTH ERROR
      1 2 × 3 4 5
       ∧
```

Here the left argument has two elements while the right argument has three, resulting in a *LENGTH ERROR*.

Example: Inventory Evaluation

At the end of each quarter the manager of a small business
takes inventory. In one of his departments he finds on hand
the following quantities of four different items.

```
      QUANT←320 45 22 90
```

The original cost per unit for these items was

```
      COST←1.20 33.20 19.15 0.55
```

The value of the inventory at its original cost is

```
      INVCOST←COST×QUANT
      INVCOST
384 1494 421.3 49.5
```

When sold at retail the fractional markup is

```
      MARKUP←0.2 0.3 0.24 0.5
```

and on these items the store may expect to make a profit of

```
      INVCOST×MARKUP
76.8 448.2 101.112 24.75
```

Pictorially, the combination of two scalars using a dyadic function can be represented by

```
A           [3]
+            +
B           [2]
↓            ↓
C           [5]
```

where we have used the addition function as an example.

The combination of a scalar and a vector is given by

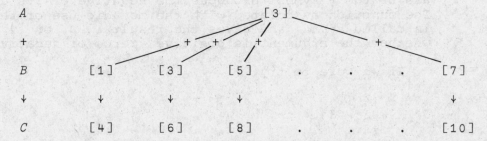

```
A                           [3]

+             +    +    +              +

B     [1]    [3]   [5]   .   .   .    [7]

↓      ↓      ↓     ↓                  ↓

C     [4]    [6]   [8]   .   .   .   [10]
```

The final result C has the same shape as the argument vector B. Elements in the result vector are obtained by combining the scalar with each element in the argument vector and storing the result in the corresponding position in the result vector.

Combining two vectors we have

```
A     [6]    [5]   [3]    .    .    .    [8]
       |      |     |                     |
+      +      +     +                     +
       |      |     |                     |
B     [1]    [2]   [3]    .    .    .    [1]

↓      ↓      ↓     ↓                     ↓

C     [7]    [7]   [6]    .    .    .    [9]
```

The shapes of the argument vectors are the same as that of the result. Corresponding elements in the arguments are combined and the result is stored in the corresponding position in C.

3.5 MONADIC FUNCTIONS

Both scalar and vector arguments may be used for a monadic function. If the argument is scalar, the calculation is performed on that single value. With a vector argument, the function is applied to each element in the vector, and the result is a vector of the same length as the argument vector.

```
        A←3 0 ⁻2
        A
3 0 ⁻2
        +A
3 0 ⁻2
        -A
⁻3 0 2
        ×A
1 0 ⁻1
```

When used monadically, the + symbol is called the *additive identity* and produces no change in its argument. The monadic use of the - symbol produces the negative of its argument. The function associated with the monadic use of the × symbol is called *signum* and gives the result 1, 0, or ⁻1 depending on whether the argument is positive, zero, or negative.

If we were to try

```
        ÷A
DOMAIN ERROR
        ÷A
        ∧
```

we run into trouble because the monadic ÷ called *reciprocal*, is equivalent to 1÷A. One element of A is zero.

```
        1÷0
DOMAIN ERROR
        1÷0
         ∧
```

Division by zero is undefined, resulting in a *DOMAIN ERROR*. However,

```
        ÷2 4 5
0.5 0.25 0.2
```

gives the expected results.

3.6 ADDITIONAL ARITHMETIC FUNCTIONS

Thus far we have discussed arithmetic functions with the elementary operations +, -, ×, and ÷. A number of other arithmetic functions are available. Some of these are listed in Tables 3.1 and 3.2 with their definitions. We only discuss the more essential functions and introduce others in problems at the end of the chapter. A complete list of all APL functions and their definitions is given in Appendix 3.

3.7   POWER ($A*B$)

This operation raises A to the power B.

                                              COMMENTS

        10*¯1 0 1 2   Powers of 10.
0.1 1 10 100

        0 4 9 16*.5   Square roots.
0 2 3 4

        2 3*3 2   Two cubed and three squared.
8 9

Example: Compound Interest

As an example of the use of the power function, suppose your grandparents deposited $1000 in a savings account for you at your birth. Assuming the money is compounded once a year and earns an annual rate of 5 percent, after one year there would be

        1000×1.05
1050

in the account. After two years there would be

        1000×(1.05*2)
1102.5

Watching the money grow until you are 21 is just as easy

        YEAR←6 11 16 21
        1000×(1.05*YEAR)
1340.095641 1710.339358 2182.874588 2785.96259

3.8   MAXIMUM ($A\lceil B$) AND MINIMUM ($A\lfloor B$)

These functions return the larger, for maximum, and smaller, for minimum, of arguments A and B. These symbols are upper shift S and D on the keyboard.

                                              COMMENTS

        7⌈5   Maximum returns the larger of its
7   arguments.
        7⌊5   Minimum returns the smaller of its
5   arguments.

In this case both arguments are scalars.

Table 3.1 Dyadic Arithmetic Functions

Function	Result	Function Name
$A + B$	the sum of A and B	Add
$A - B$	the difference between A and B	Subtract
$A \times B$	the product of A and B	Multiply
$A \div B$	the quotient of A divided by B	Divide
$A * B$	A raised to the power B	Power
$A \lceil B$	the larger of A and B	Maximum
$A \lfloor B$	the smaller of A and B	Minimum
$A \mid B$(*)	the remainder left after dividing B by A	Residue
$A \circledast B$ (o backspace *)	the logarithm of B to the base A, $\log_A B$	Logarithm
$A ! B$(*) (' backspace .)	number of combinations of B things taken A at a time	Combinations

(*)The given result is for positive integers
A and B; a more general definition is given
in Appendix 3.

Table 3.2   Monadic Arithmetic Functions

Function	Result	Function Name
$+ A$	A	Additive identity
$- A$	$\bar{1} \times A$ (additive inverse)	Negation
$\times A$	1, 0, or $\bar{1}$ depending on whether A is positive, zero, or negative	Signum
$\div A$	the reciprocal of A $(1 \div A)$	Reciprocal
$* A$	the base of the natural logarithm, e, raised to the power A	Exponential
$\lceil A$	the smallest integer greater than or equal to A	Ceiling
$\lfloor A$	the largest integer less than or equal to A	Floor
$\mid A$	the absolute value of A	Magnitude
$\circledast A$	the natural logarithm of A	Natural logarithm
$! A$ [*]	the product of all integers from 1 to A $(1 \times 2 \times 3 ... \times A)$	Factorial.
$? A$	a random integer chosen from the integers 1 to A	Roll

[*] The given result is for integer A; a more general definition is given in Appendix 3.

We can also evaluate a famous comparison.

```
    6⌈(.5×12)
6
    6⌊(.5×12)
6
```

Six of one, half-a-dozen of the other!

Example: Billing with a Minimum Charge

If the purchases made in a parts department are

```
PURCHASE←2.35 5.87 15.50
```

but there is a minimum charge for each purchase

```
MINIMUM←3.00
```

then the amount billed is

```
BILL←MINIMUM⌈PURCHASE
BILL
3 5.87 15.5
```

In this case the scalar *MINIMUM* is compared with each element of the vector *PURCHASE*, and at each comparison the larger value is taken. The result, *BILL*, is a vector of the same length as *PURCHASE*.

As with all arithmetic functions the arguments of maximum and minimum can both be vectors. Suppose H and W refer to the ages of husbands and wives, respectively.

		COMMENTS
	H←23 44 33 19	Husbands' ages.
	W←18 47 33 16	Wives' ages.
	$H⌈W$	Ages of older spouses.
23 47 33 19		
	$W⌈H$	Order of arguments is not important.
23 47 33 19		
	$H⌊W$	Ages of younger spouses.
18 44 33 16		
	18⌊W	One wife cannot vote.
18 18 18 16		

3.9   CEILING (⌈A) AND FLOOR (⌊A)

These functions round off decimal numbers to integer numbers; the ceiling function rounds off to the smallest integer, which is greater than or equal to A; while the floor function rounds off to the largest integer, which is smaller than or equal to A.

                                              COMMENTS

        $\lceil 5.5$ Rounds to 6, the next highest
6   integer.
        $\lceil ^-5.5$ The next integer greater than $^-5.5$
$^-5$ is $^-5$.
        $\lceil 5$ An integer argument remains the same.
5
        $\lfloor 8.3 \ 0 \ ^-0.1$
8 0 $^-1$

A power tool rents at a rate of \$5 per hour or a fraction
thereof. If the time used is

    $USE \leftarrow 4.5 \ 7 \ 3.25$

the hours charged are

    $CHARGE \leftarrow \lceil USE$
    $CHARGE$
5 7 4

and the cost is

    $5 \times CHARGE$
25 35 20

Example: Truncation

The ceiling and floor functions can be used to round off to
values other than integers. For example, we can truncate a
value by dropping all parts smaller than one hundredth.

                                              COMMENTS

    $DOLLARS \leftarrow 1.30 \ 2.6333$ The values to be truncated.
    $CENTS \leftarrow 100 \times DOLLARS$ Multiply by 100.
    $CENTS$
130 263.33
    $CENTS \leftarrow \lfloor CENTS$ Drop fractional parts.
    $CENTS$
130 263
    $DOLLARS \leftarrow CENTS \div 100$ Divide by 100.
    $DOLLARS$
1.3 2.63

In this example truncating to hundredths is equivalent to
dropping fractional cents.

3.10 RESIDUE (OR MODULUS) $(A|B)$

For integer A this function gives the remainder left after
dividing B by A.

```
        3│0  1  2  3  4  5
0  1  2  0  1  2
```

```
        3│0.5  1.5  2.5  3.5  4.5  5.5
0.5  1.5  2.5  0.5  1.5  2.5
```

A particular case which is often of use is the *1 residue*. This gives the fractional part of a number.

```
        1│0  1  2  3  4  5
0  0  0  0  0  0
```

```
        1│0.7  1.2  3.6  4.85
0.7  0.2  0.6  0.85
```

Example: Stock Dividends

Company ABC declares a stock dividend of 0.06 shares of stock for each share held. Four shareholders have the following numbers of shares:

```
    SHARES←10  75  180  275
```

Their dividends would be

```
    DIV←0.06×SHARES
    DIV
0.6  4.5  10.8  16.5
```

Whole shares are redeemed in stock

```
    STOCK←⌊DIV
    STOCK
0  4  10  16
```

while fractional shares

```
    FRACT←1│DIV
    FRACT
0.6  0.5  0.8  0.5
```

are redeemed in cash at the current market value of the stock, $75 per share.

```
    CASH←75×FRACT
    CASH
45  37.5  60  37.5
```

3.11 MAGNITUDE (│A)

The function │ (upper case M for <u>M</u>agnitude) gives the absolute value of A.

                                            COMMENTS

        | ‾10 ‾.1 0 1 10   Negative values change sign; zero
      10 0.1 0 1 10   or positive values are
                                      unaffected.

3.12   FACTORIAL (!A)

For A, a positive integer, the function ! (upper shift K
backspace period) gives the product of all the integers less
than or equal to A. For A equal to zero it gives the value 1.

                                            COMMENTS

          !4 $1 \times 2 \times 3 \times 4$
      24
          !0   Zero factorial is 1.
      1

3.13   ROLL (?)

Random numbers may be generated using the roll function ?
(upper shift Q for Question). Used in the form $?N$ where N is
a positive integer, roll generates a random integer between 1
and N inclusive.

                                            COMMENTS

          ?6   An integer is chosen at random from
      1   1 2 3 4 5 6.
          ?6
      5
          ?6   The results are random.
      3
          ?6 6 6   The argument may be a vector.
      4 2 1
          ?6 6 6
      5 5 6

As will be discussed in detail in the case studies, the roll
function provides the capability to simulate many real-life
situations. For instance, the above examples could be interpreted as a simulation of the throwing of dice. Note in
the last example that the numbers obtained may be duplicates
of one another.

EXERCISES

Before executing the instructions shown, fill in what you
anticipate the display will be. Add an explanation for any
error you make.

1.   Assume $A \leftarrow 2$
             $B \leftarrow {}^-4$
             $C \leftarrow 1 \ 3 \ 5$
             $D \leftarrow 2 \ {}^-3 \ 4$

Instruction	Anticipated Display	Display
a. $A + B$		
b. $A + C$		
c. $C + D$		
d. $A - B$		
e. $A - C$		
f. $C - D$		
g. $A \times B$		
h. $A \times C$		
i. $C \times D$		
j. $A \div B$		
k. $A \div C$		
l. $C \div D$		
m. $A * B$		
n. $A * C$		
o. $C * D$		
p. $- A$		
q. $- C$		
r. $\div A$		
s. $\div D$		
t. $! A$		
u. $! C$		
v. $\times D$		

2.   Assume $A \leftarrow 2$
          $B \leftarrow {}^-4$
          $C \leftarrow 1\ 3\ 5$
          $D \leftarrow 2\ {}^-3\ 4$

Instruction	Anticipated Display	Display
a. $2\lceil C$		
b. $B\lceil D$		
c. $0\lfloor D$		
d. $A\lceil C$		
e. $\mid B$		
f. $\mid A$		
g. $\lfloor D$		
h. $\lceil B$		
i. $1\ 3\ \lceil\ 2\ 2$		
j. $3\mid {}^-3\ {}^-2\ {}^-1\ 0\ 1\ 2\ 3$		
k. $D\mid 15$		

3.   In the following problems let:

    $SCALAR \leftarrow 100$
    $VECTOR1 \leftarrow 1\ 2\ 3\ 4\ 5$
    $VECTOR2 \leftarrow 10\ 20\ 30\ 40\ 50$
    $STRING1 \leftarrow$ 'I AM FREE'

Perform the given operations and note the results.

Instruction	Anticipated Display	Display
a. $VECTOR1 + VECTOR2$		
b. $VECTOR2 - VECTOR1$		
c. $SCALAR + VECTOR1$		
d. $SCALAR + STRING1$		
e. $)VARS$		

4. Locate the error(s) in each of the following instructions.

    Instruction

    a. 1 2 3÷¯1 0 1

    b. ¯4 0 4*.5

    c. 3 2 1×.5 .25

    d. !2 1 0 ¯1

5. Compute the squares, cubes, square roots, and cube roots
    of the integers from 1 through 10.

6. When using the power function, $A*B$, if A is zero, what are
    the permissible values for B?

7. Find the largest integer N such that $N*N$ does not exceed
    the limit for a constant on your computer.

8. Find the largest integer N such that $!N$ does not exceed
    the limit for a constant on your computer.

    In the following an attempt should be made to formulate
    APL expressions that solve the problems for any numerical
    values and not just the given values.

9. Reduce the number 12311.237 to the next lowest 1000, 10,
    1/10, and 1/100.

10. How could you determine if a number N is odd or even?
    Integral or nonintegral?

11. Three stores, A, B and C sell the same four items but at
    different prices. The prices in each store are given by

        A←15 2.50 3.99 1.99

        B←16 2.75 3.89 1.19

        C←14.89 2.25 3.99 1.19

    Find the difference between the highest and lowest prices
    charged for each of these items.

12. The unit price of four items in store A is

        $COSTA$←2.45 9.99 1.32 0.95

    In store B these same items cost

        $COSTB$←2.87 9.79 1.30 1.15

A shopper wishes to purchase the following quantities of these four items

    $QUANT \leftarrow 3$ 1 2 4

a. What will be the amount spent on each class of items in store A? in store B?
b. How much will the shopper save on the purchase of each class of items, if the items are bought at the lowest available price? (Compare the lowest price available with the price charged in each store.)
c. How much more will the shopper spend if the higher available price is paid? Once again give an answer for each store.

13. Suppose $1000 is deposited in a bank account with interest compounded annually at a rate of R percent. The rule of 72 says that the number of years required to double this amount is $72 \div R$. For example, at 5% it would take $72 \div 5 = 14.4$ years.

   a. Test the rule for several interest rates.
   b. Does this rule apply for any initial amount deposited?

14. Examine the definition of residue in Appendix 3 and evaluate $A|B$ for A and B assuming positive, negative integral, and nonintegral values.

3.14 EVALUATING EXPRESSIONS CONTAINING MORE THAN ONE FUNCTION

Up to this point we have usually only considered expressions which contain one function. However, even simple calculations often require several successive function evaluations in one expression. This section discusses the way in which these expressions are interpreted in the APL language.

   To convert a height given in feet and inches, say 5'10", to inches, we perform the calculation

    $5 \times 12 + 10$

Without some conventions on how to interpret this expression, it is ambiguous. Do we first multiply 5 × 12 and then add 10 (result 70), or add 10 to 12 and then multiply by 5 (result 110)? According to the usual conventions, multiplication has preference over addition, so the multiplication is performed first and then the addition. In this case the correct result is 70. If we wish to perform the addition first, parentheses would be used to specify the order of evaluation as

    $5 \times (12+10)$

   In APL, expressions containing a series of calculations are evaluated according to the following rule. Given an expression containing more than one function, the computer chooses the *rightmost* function and performs the appropriate computation. It then goes to the next rightmost function and, using the result from the previous function, performs the indicated computation. This continues until there are no more functions to be executed. The procedure described is referred to as the *right-to-left evaluation rule*.

The reason for this rule is that APL provides a large number of functions for the processing of data. Any attempt to introduce a hierarchy among these functions would result in a complex and rather unnatural ordering. The choice has been made then to avoid this difficulty by treating all functions as equivalent. The order in which they are evaluated depends only on their location within an expression.

We illustrate the use of the right-to-left rule with a number of examples. Each step shows the status of the expression after executing the rightmost function. Study the examples carefully until you understand them.

    9×8-2

    9×6

    54

The rightmost function is the subtraction. Subtracting 2 from 8 gives the result 6. This is then multiplied by 9. If we had mistakenly worked from left to right in this example we would have obtained 70 as an answer (72-2=70).

    3+¯2+7

    3+5

    8

Note that the negative sign on ¯2 is part of this number. Contrast this with

    3+-2+7

    3+-9

    3+¯9

    ¯6

In this case the negation is performed after the rightmost addition.

A helpful procedure for guaranteeing the proper use of the right-to-left rule is to use your finger or a slip of paper to cover the parts of the expression to the left of and including the second rightmost function. The part of the expression that is exposed is evaluated first. This procedure is continued, moving to the left until the entire expression is evaluated.

Let's try this procedure on the following example:

```
‾9⌈2 3×4
```

We first cover the entire expression with a slip of paper

```
‾9⌈2 3×4
```

The paper is moved to the left until two functions are visible

```
‾9⌈2 3×4
```

The second function is covered once again, leaving the expression to be evaluated exposed to view.

```
‾9⌈2 3×4
    8 12
```

It is now clear that the first evaluation is a multiplication between the vector 2 3 and the scalar 4. We have written the result below the original expression. Continuing in the same manner, we uncover the maximum function and the - symbol and then recover the - symbol.

```
‾9⌈2 3×4
‾9⌈8 12
  9 12
```

For clarity we write in ‾9⌈ on the second line and then evaluate the exposed expression. Finally we uncover the - symbol. Since it is at the end of the expression, it is being used to invoke the negation function. The final result is

```
‾9⌈2 3×4
‾9⌈8 12
‾9 12
‾9 ‾12
```

where once again we have written in symbols on the lower lines for the sake of clarity.

As you become more experienced in the use of APL you will be able to use the right-to-left rule without the aid of this procedure. While learning the language, however, it is a convenient method for guaranteeing the proper use of this rule.

It is important to note that the right-to-left rule determines the order in which functions in an expression are evaluated but does not modify the way in which they are interpreted. For example, in the expression 4+6-2, the right-to-left rule indicates that the subtraction is to be performed before the addition. The subtraction performed is six minus two and not two minus six.

Parentheses, ( ), may be used to modify the order in which expressions are evaluated. When parentheses are encountered in an expression, that part of the expression inside of the parentheses will be executed first. If more than one function is present inside the parentheses, the usual right-to-left rule holds. After the expression inside the parentheses is evaluated the order of execution will once again follow the usual right-to-left rule.

```
5-(3×¯7)+10
5-¯21+10
5-¯11
16
```

The addition cannot be performed until the expression in parentheses is evaluated. The expression in parentheses is completed first, and then the entire expression is evaluated from right to left.

```
10×(6÷2)+5-2
10×(6÷2)+3
10×3+3
60
```

Scanning this expression from right to left, we can evaluate the subtraction first, but to perform the addition the expression within the parentheses must be calculated.

```
((40+2)÷6)-3
(42÷6)-3
7-3
4
```

Here we have parentheses inside parentheses. The expression within the innermost parentheses is evaluated first.

There must always be the same number of left parentheses as right parentheses, that is, the parentheses must balance.

```
      (42÷(2+4)-3
SYNTAX ERROR
      (42÷(2+4)-3
       ∧
```

This example has two left parentheses and one right parenthesis, resulting in a *SYNTAX ERROR*.

The rules given above also apply to expressions containing variables and vectors. The only requirement is that at each step in the calculation the arguments of the function are permissible arguments. For example (2 3+1) ÷ 1 2 3 is not permitted, since after the quantity in parentheses is evaluated, we are left with division of a vector of length 2 by one of length 3.

```
      (2 3+1)÷1 2 3
LENGTH ERROR
      (2 3+1)÷1 2 3
      ∧
```

If you have difficulty following the right-to-left rule, you may find the quad function □ (upper shift *L* for L̲ook) helpful. This function may be used to display the value of a variable.

```
      □←S←'DOG'
DOG
```

This has the same result as

```
      S←'DOG'
      S
DOG
```

The quad function allows us to specify *S* and display its value in the same line.

After the values assigned to the quad function have been displayed, they are still available for use. Thus the quad function can be used to display intermediate results within a complex expression.

COMMENTS

```
      3×□←4 7⌊5              The intermediate result
4 5                              4 7⌊5=4 5 is displayed.
12 15
```

Repeating an earlier example we note the intermediate results

COMMENTS

```
      10×□←(□←8÷2)+□←5-2
3                              5-2=3
4                              8÷2=4
7                              4+3=7
70                             10×7=70
```

Example: Rounding to the Nearest Penny

As a practical example let us consider how to round a dollar amount to the nearest penny. If the fractional cent is less than one half, it is dropped; otherwise, the quantity is rounded upwards to the next penny. Following the procedure we used in the previous section, we convert dollars

```
      DOLLARS←3.80 2.6333 3.755 4.928
```

to cents

```
        CENTS←100×DOLLARS
        CENTS
380 263.33 375.5 492.8
```

To round off to the nearest penny we add 0.5 cents to these
values and then truncate with the floor function

```
        CENTS←⌊0.5+CENTS
        CENTS
380 263 376 493
```

which gives the desired result. To convert back to dollars we
divide by 100

```
        CENTS÷100
3.8 2.63 3.76 4.93
```

This entire procedure can be combined into a single expression

```
        (⌊0.5+100×DOLLARS)÷100
3.8 2.63 3.76 4.93
```

or

```
        0.01×⌊0.5+100×DOLLARS
3.8 2.63 3.76 4.93
```

Example: Regular and Overtime Pay

A worker receives a normal pay rate of $4 per hour

```
        RATE←4
```

with time-and-a-half for all hours over 35 in one week.
Assuming the following hours worked

```
        HOURS←30 35 40
```

regular hours are obtained from

```
        REGULAR←35⌊HOURS
        REGULAR
30 35 35
```

with overtime hours calculated as

```
        OVERTIME←0⌈HOURS-35
        OVERTIME
0 0 5
```

The total pay is obtained from

```
        PAY←(RATE×REGULAR)+1.5×RATE×OVERTIME
        PAY
120 140 170
```

The entire calculation can be performed in the single
expression

$$PAY \leftarrow RATE \times (35 \lfloor HOURS) + 1.5 \times 0 \lceil HOURS - 35$$

Example: Evaluating a Polynomial

The value of a polynomial written in conventional notation as

$$5 - 3X + 2X^2 - X^3$$

can be calculated as follows

                                           COMMENTS
        $X \leftarrow 0$ 1 2 3   Assign a value to X.
        $5 + (^{-}3 \times X) + (2 \times X * 2) - X * 3$ The APL expression for the
                                               polynomial.
   5 3 $^{-}$1 $^{-}$13   The polynomial evaluated at 0,
                                               1, 2, and 3.

The parentheses are necessary here to insure the proper
sequence of operations. The minus sign in the second term is
incorporated in the $^{-}$3 requiring only additions to be performed.

Another way of writing a polynomial is the so called *nested*
form. In conventional notation the polynomial would appear as

$$5 + X(-3 + X(2 - X))$$

In APL this takes the form

        $5 + X \times ^{-}3 + X \times 2 - X$
   5 3 $^{-}$1 $^{-}$13

The right-to-left rule eliminates the need for parentheses.

Example: Multiple Assignments

An expression can contain more than one assignment. The
evaluation of such expressions also follows the right-to-left
rule.

        $TEN \leftarrow 4 + SIX \leftarrow 4 + TWO \leftarrow 2$
        TWO
   2
        SIX
   6
        TEN
   10

Going from right to left, the variable TWO is assigned the
value 2. We then add 4 giving the numerical value 6, which is
assigned to the variable SIX. Again adding 4 gives TEN, the
value 10.

3.15   REDUCTION

Frequently it is necessary to combine the elements of a
vector to obtain, for example, their sum or product. The
operation of reduction presents a convenient way of representing such multiple calculations. Reduction takes the form

     function/A

where function may be any of the dyadic functions we have
considered so far. The result of this process is to place the
function between the elements of A and then to perform the
resulting sequence of evaluations using the right-to-left rule.

	COMMENTS
+/1 2 3 4	Equivalent to 1+2+3+4.
10	
×/1 2 3 4	The same as !4 or 1×2×3×4.
24	
-/1 2 3 4	
¯2	

The minus reduction is illustrated in the last example. In
conventional notation this is equivalent to the alternating
sum. The minus reduction

     -/1 2 3 4

is equivalent to

     1-2-3-4

in APL notation, and is equivalent to

     1-2+3-4   or   1-(2-(3-4))

in conventional notation.

   We are given a number of different coins and wish to determine their total value. This calculation can be performed
readily with the reduction operation. The number of coins of
each type (quarters, dimes, nickels, and pennies) are
contained in the variable $COINS$.

     $COINS$←3 2 4 2

The value of each coin is given by

     $VALUE$←25 10 5 1

and the total amount of each type of coin is given by

     $CENTS$←$COINS$×$VALUE$
     $CENTS$
75 20 20 2

The total value of all the coins is obtained from the plus reduction

```
    +/CENTS
117
```

The largest element in a vector of numbers can be determined by performing a reduction with the maximum function.

```
    ⌈/3 7 1 5
7
```

In more detail

                                    COMMENTS

```
    ⌈/3 7 1 5         The maximum is inserted between all
    3⌈7⌈1⌈5              the elements and the expression
    3⌈7⌈5               is evaluated from right to left.
    3⌈7
    7
```

The minimum function can be used to find the smallest number in a string of numbers

```
    A←3 7 1 5
    ⌊/A
1
```

Example: Determining the Number of Elements in a Vector

We can also use plus reduction to determine the number of elements in a numerical vector.

```
    VEC←87 23.1 93 1.3 11
    +/1+0×VEC
5
```

Proceeding from right to left, each element is multiplied by zero giving a vector with the same number of elements as *VEC* but all elements equal to zero. Adding one changes all elements to one. The plus reduction then sums the ones giving the number of elements in the vector. Another way of determining the number of elements in a vector is discussed in Chapter 6.

We can observe the process by inserting quads.

                                    COMMENTS

```
    +/□←1+□←0×VEC     Quad is used to display intermediate
                          steps.
0 0 0 0 0             The result of 0×VEC.
1 1 1 1 1             The result of adding 1.
5                     The number of terms.
```

Example: Calculating Elementary Statistics

Let the variable *GRADE* contain the semester grades of a
student. With the reduction operation, we can obtain useful
statistical information about these grades.

	COMMENTS
GRADE	Display *GRADE*.
70 87 80 93 90 95 73	
MAX←⌈/GRADE	The highest grade is obtained with
MAX	the "max" reduction.
95	
MIN←⌊/GRADE	The lowest grade is obtained with
MIN	the "min" reduction.
70	
RANGE←MAX-MIN	The range is defined as the
RANGE	difference between the highest
25	and lowest grades.

The average grade can be obtained from the following
calculation

        AV←(+/GRADE)÷N←+/1+0×GRADE
        AV
84
        N
7

Proceeding from right to left, the variable *N* is assigned a
value equal to the number of elements in *GRADE*. This
procedure was described in the previous example. *N* is divided
into the sum of all the grades, the result being the average
grade.

The range gives a measure of the spread of grades around
the average value. Other frequently used measures of spread
are the average deviation and standard deviation.

	COMMENTS
DEV←GRADE-AV	The deviations are differences
DEV	between the grades and the
¯14 3 ¯4 9 6 11 ¯11	average.
AVDEV←(+/|DEV)÷N	The average deviation is the
AVDEV	average of the absolute value
8.285714286	of the deviations.

The standard deviation is the square root of the average of
the squares of the deviations.

        *STDEV←((+/DEV*2)÷N)*0.5*
        STDEV
9.102589898

In computing the above averages, the reduction was enclosed in parentheses forcing the sum to be computed before the division took place. This requires fewer machine computations. Why?

EXERCISES

1. Evaluate the following expressions; be sure you understand how each result is obtained.

Instruction	Anticipated Display	Display
a. 2×1 + 1×2		
b. (2×1) + 1×2		
c. 1×2 + 1×2		
d. 1×2 + (1×2)		
e. 6⌈ 3-2+7		
f. 6⌈ 3+⁻2+7		
g. 3÷4 2÷3		
h. -2×4 6 -5		
i. -2 1⌈3-4		
j. 2 1 + 5 + ⁻3 2 1		
k. 3×2+4		
l. (3×2)+4		
m. 4+(6÷3)+1		
n. 4+6÷3+1		
o. 8 2 4÷1 2 4		
p. ⌊/4 ⁻1 6		
q. +/4 ⁻1 6		
r. -/4 ⁻1 6		
s. 4÷(3+5)÷6		

t. $A \leftarrow 1$
      $A \leftarrow B \leftarrow C \leftarrow A \leftarrow 1 + C \leftarrow A$
      A
      B
      C

	Instruction	Anticipated Display	Display

u. $A \leftarrow 3$
   $C \leftarrow A + B \leftarrow 2 \ ^-3 \ 5$
   A
   B
   C

v. $A \leftarrow 2 \ 4$
   $B \leftarrow 1 \ 3$
   $C \leftarrow 5$
   $C + A \ B$
   $\lfloor / A \ B \ C$

2. In each case below, pick from the list of expressions to the right of the colon the expression(s) that is (are) equivalent to the expression before the colon.

   a. $-(2+3)$: $\quad -2-3$ or $^-2+^-3$ or $-2+3$

   b. $\div(A \div B)$: $\quad \div A \times B$ or $B \div A$ or $A \div B$ or $\times B \times A$

   c. $A \div B \div C$: $\quad A \div B \times C$ or $A \times B \div C$ or $A \times C \div B$

   d. $|A$: $\quad A$ or $\times A$ or $A \times \times A$ or $A \div \times A$

   e. $M \times X + B$: $\quad M \times (X+B)$ or $(M \times B) + X$

   f. $A \star 2 + 2$: $\quad 2 + (A \star 2)$ or $A \star 4$ or $2 \times A \star 2$

3. Distinguish between the following: (V is a vector.)

   a. $\lfloor V$ and $\lfloor / V$

   b. $\times V$ and $\times / V$

   c. V and $V \times \times V$

4. What is the meaning of the result of the following expressions? (V is a vector.)

   a. $+/V$

   b. $+/\times V$

   c. $\times / |V$

   d. $+/0 \lceil V$

   e. $\times / \times V$

   f. $\times / V$

5. Which of the following pairs of expressions are equivalent? (V is a vector.)

   a. $\div / V$ and $\div \times / V$

b. $|+/V$ and $+/|V$

c. $|×/V$ and $×/|V$

d. $+/×V$ and $×/+V$

e. $1++/V$ and $+/1+V$

f. $⌈/V$ and $÷⌊/÷V$

g. V and $÷÷V$

h. V and $V××V$

i. V and $(|V)××V$

j. $(|V)$ and $V××V$

6. On your APL system what is the value of

a. $0÷0$

b. $0*0$

c. $!0$

7. a. In a list of numbers find the smallest and the largest numbers as well as their differences.
    b. Compute the sum of the first 12 even integers.

8. Mr. Smith has joined the programmer's union and now earns $6.60 per hour for a 40-hour week and overtime at a rate of 1 1/2 times his normal rate ($9.90) for any hours worked beyond 40 hours. Compute the weekly total gross pay, the 40-hour gross pay, and the overtime gross pay (if any) for the following hours worked in four successive weeks: 40, 37, 45, 56.5 hours.

9. As N gets larger, what value does the following expression take on:

$$(1 + \frac{1}{N})^N = ?$$

Let $N = 10, 100,$ and 1000.

10. Using the right-to-left rule, write APL expressions to solve problems 11 to 13 of the previous set of exercises. Attempt to give as concise an expression as possible.

11. Rates for telephone calls from city A to B are 70 cents for the first three minutes and 20 cents for each additional minute or fraction thereof. Give an APL expression that will calculate the charge for a call of any length. Verify your expression for calls of 1.5, 2, 3, 3.5, 5, and 7.5 minutes.

12. Use the residue, ceiling, and floor functions to solve the following problems.

   a. You are given an amount of money, A, with which to buy as many units as possible of an item costing C dollars per unit. How many units can you buy? How much money will be left? Try to get a general solution, then use it to solve the case in which $A \leftarrow 35\ 15.75$ and $C \leftarrow 11\ 3.25$.

   b. A warehouse stacks cartons containing TV sets in a single row several layers high. Assuming that each layer is completely filled before cartons are stacked on a higher level, how would you determine the number of layers needed if there are N sets altogether and R sets can be stacked per layer? How many cartons will be in the top layer?

13. Given the daily high and low outside temperatures for a period of one week, compute daily degree days as well as their sum (degree day = 65-0.5 × (high temp - low temp).) Test your expressions for the following daily temperature data.

   a. $HI \leftarrow 47\ 50\ 30\ 28\ 15$
      $LO \leftarrow 12\ 18\ 16\ 5\ {}^{-}2$

   b. $HI \leftarrow 83\ 75\ 65\ 40$
      $LO \leftarrow 65\ 64\ 50\ 28$

   NOTE: degree days are always positive or zero.

14. A more accurate approach to computing degree days is to use the formula degree day = 65-(average outside temp), where the average temperature is based on 24 hourly readings. Suppose we are given the hourly temperatures for a certain day.

   a. Write an APL expression to compute the degree days for:

      $TEMP \leftarrow 34\ 34\ 33\ 33\ 34\ 34\ 34\ 33\ 35\ 37\ 38\ 39\ 40\ 40\ 42\ 40\ 40$
      $\qquad 40\ 36\ 35\ 34\ 32\ 32\ 30$

   b. Compute the degree day value for $TEMP$ using the day's high-low temperatures (see procedure outlined in previous problem) and compare the result to a. of this problem.

   NOTE: degree days are always positive or zero.

15. XYZ Company owns shares of stock in five other enterprises. The number of shares in each is given by

      $SHRS \leftarrow 75\ 200\ 50\ 150\ 180$

   The original cost of a share of stock in each enterprise was

      $COST \leftarrow 125\ 117.50\ 280\ 98.50\ 212$

___

The current market value of a share is

$MKT \leftarrow 121\ 137\ 250\ 98.50\ 216$

Find the total value of the stock owned by XYZ under the following conditions.

a. The shares of stock are valued at their original cost.
b. The shares of stock are valued at the current market value.
c. The shares of stock are valued by taking the *lower* of the original cost and the market value for each share.
d. What would be the loss in value over the original cost if shares are evaluated as in c?

16. A new bus company plans to build its fleet of buses over a five-year period. The number of buses to be purchased in each of these years is

$P \leftarrow 25\ 15\ 15\ 10\ 5$

a. What will be the total cost of these buses if each bus costs $20,000?
b. What will be the total cost of these buses if a 10 percent discount is given on each bus over 10 purchased during any one year?

17. The amount of the monthly payment necessary to pay off a home mortgage is given (in conventional notation) by

$$P\ =\ A \times I \times \frac{(1+I)^n}{(1+I)^n - 1}$$

where A is the amount of the mortgage, I is the monthly interest rate (as a decimal) and n is the number of monthly payments. Give an APL expression that is equivalent to this formula. Assuming A has the value $30,000, evaluate this expression for

a. a lifetime of 20 years at (yearly) interest rates of 7.5, 8.0, and 8.5 percent.
b. an interest rate of 8.5 percent and a lifetime of the mortgage of 20, 25, and 30 years.

SUPPLEMENTARY EXERCISES

1. Write a minimal (as few characters as possible) APL expression for the following:

Conventional Notation	APL Notation

a. $(A+B)-C$

b. $C \times (A-Y)$

c. $(A \times B)-C$

<u>Conventional Notation</u>   <u>APL Notation</u>

d. $A \times (B-C) \times A$

e. $C - \dfrac{B}{3} - D$

f. $\dfrac{A \times B - C \times (A-B)}{B-A} - (A \times C)$

2. Convert the following from APL notation to conventional notation:

a. $X \div Y - Z$

b. $Z \times Y - Z \times X$

c. $Z \div X + Y + X$

d. $X \times Y - X \times Y$

e. $(X \times T) \times (Z+X) \div X - Y$

f. $X + Y$

3. Find the numbers represented by the following expressions:

a. $((3) \times (-4) + (3+4))$

b. $(4 \times 5) - (4 \times (-2))$

c. $4 \times (-3 + -7)$

d. $(-2) \times (-4 - (-5))$

e. $(+5) \times (-8 + (+2))$

f. $((-12) - (-3)) \times (-4)$

g. $(12 + (-4)) \times (-2)$

h. $(-25 \times 4) - (-12 + (+3))$

i. $(5 + -8) + (5 \times (-2))$

j. $((-12) \times (-4)) + (3 \times (-4))$

4. What is the result of the following APL expressions:

a. $3 - 2 \div 4 + 2 - 6 + 1 \times 2 \div 4$

b. $3 - 2 \div 4 \div 2 - 6 + 1 \times 2 \div 4$

5. Find all the groups of equivalent expressions in the list below and evaluate the result of each group.

a. $10 \times 8 + 3 \times 9$

b. `(10×8)+3×9`

c. `(10×8+3×9)`

d. `((10×8)+3)×9`

e. `10×(8+(3×9))`

f. `10×(8+3)×9`

g. `(((10×8)+3)×9)`

h. `(10×((8+3)×9))`

i. `10×8+(3)×9`

j. `10×8+(3×9)`

6. Compute the interest on $24 compounded annually at 3 percent since 1627, the year Manhattan was bought for $24 from the Indians. (The bank balance at the end of N years is $P×(1+I)*N$ where I represents the annual interest rate and P the initial bank deposit.)

7. Compare your bank balances every other year for 20 years if you deposit $1000 in bank A paying 6 percent compounded annually and another $1000 in bank B paying 5 3/4 percent compounded monthly.

8. Compute the total amount you would have by letting $1000 accumulate for 12 years at an interest rate of 6 percent compounded: (a) yearly; (b) quarterly; (c) monthly; (d) weekly; (e) daily; (f) hourly; (g) every second.

9. Let X be a numerical vector; what is the result of `100⌊X`?

10. Suppose that X is a numerical vector. What will be the result of the following instruction?

    `1⌈10⌊X`

    (HINT: how does this affect values less than 1, greater than 10, and between 1 and 10?)

11. Let A, B, and C be numerical vectors.

    a. Under what conditions will `⌈/A⌈B⌈C` give the largest number in any of these?
    b. Give an expression that will give the largest element in these vectors for arbitrary A, B, and C.

12. You are given a time duration T in minutes. Give APL expressions to express this in hours and minutes.

13. Give an expression that will replace all positive elements in a numerical vector by zeros.

14. A workman buys 6 two-by-fours for $2.67 apiece, 3 sheets of plywood for $13.50 apiece, a box of nails for $1.50, and 10 boxes of tile for $6.75 a box. Create vectors N and C giving the number of each item and the cost of each item purchased. Evaluate the following:

    a. The total cost of each item.
    b. The total cost of all items.
    c. The sales tax on each item, assuming a rate of 6 percent.
    d. The price of each item including tax.
    e. The total cost of all items including tax.
    f. The cost of each item assuming the workman gets a discount of 25 percent before tax.

15. The contents of a piggy bank are expressed as a five element numerical vector. The elements in the vector correspond to the number of half dollars, quarters, dimes, nickels, and pennies in the bank. Find:

    a. The total number of coins.
    b. Their total value in cents.
    c. Their total value in dollars.

16. Determine all numbers between 40 and 60 such that if the final digit is deleted, the original number is divisible by the new.

17. Give a sequence of expressions that will compute the sum of the cubes of the digits of a three-digit number.

18. Hero's formula for the area of a triangle is

$$\text{Area} = \sqrt{S(S-A)(S-B)(S-C)}$$

    where A, B, and C are the lengths of the three sides of the triangle and S is one half of the perimeter. Give APL expressions to evaluate Hero's formula assuming

    a. The lengths of the sides of the triangle are stored in the variables A, B, and C.
    b. The lengths are stored in the three element vector $SIDES$.

19. The positions of points on a graph are given in terms of their X (horizontal) and Y (vertical) coordinates. For each point these can be stored as a two element numerical vector, the first element being the X coordinate and the second being the Y coordinate.

    a. Give an APL expression to determine the slope of a straight line passing between two points whose coordinates are stored in the variables A and B. The slope of the line is given as the ratio of the difference in their Y coordinates to the difference in their X coordinates.

b. Give an expression to determine the distance between the two points. The distance is given by

$$((X_A-X_B)^2+(Y_A-Y_B)^2)^{1/2}$$

20. Let S be a vector of scores and W be a vector of weights. The weighted average of the scores in S is given (in conventional notation) by

$$AV \leftarrow (\sum_{i=1}^{N} S_i W_i) \div \sum_{i=1}^{N} W_i$$

where N is the number of weights and the number of scores. Give an APL expression to evaluate this average.

21. An example in this chapter showed how to truncate a value to hundredths. Generalize this procedure to truncate to any value of the form $10*N$.

22. In the previous problem, what will be the result of $(10*N)|NUMBER$, where $NUMBER$ has been truncated to $10*N$?

23. In using the power function $A*B$, for what values of B can A be negative?

Chapter 4
Computer Programs

We have learned how to use a number of the functions available in APL. Often a set of functions will be used several times over, and it may be desirable to save this set of functions rather than to reenter them every time. This can be done by creating a *computer program*.

In the previous chapter, we used a series of statements to extract from a vector of five grades the highest grade, the lowest grade, and the average grade. To perform these calculations we stored the grades in a vector and then executed additional statements. Suppose we want to obtain this information for the grades of more than one student. In that case we would have to enter the same series of statements along with a set of grades for each student. For a class of 25 students this task would be rather lengthy. We could simplify matters considerably if we stored the instructions in the computer for future use. To do this we combine the statements into a computer program.

4.1 WRITING A PROGRAM

To illustrate how to write a program, let us formulate a series of statements to convert a person's height given in feet and inches to inches. We will store the person's height, say 5 ft. 10 in., in a two element vector $HEIGHT \leftarrow 5\ 10$. The first element gives the number of feet, the second the number of inches. The calculation can be done as follows:

	COMMENTS
$HEIGHT \leftarrow 5\ 10$	The person's height is stored in a two component vector, $HEIGHT$.
$INCHES \leftarrow 12\ 1 \times HEIGHT$ $INCHES$ 60 10	Multiplying $HEIGHT$ by the vector 12 1 converts feet into inches.
$INCHES \leftarrow +/INCHES$	The reduction gives the total height in inches; 5 ft. 10 in. equals 70 in.
$HEIGHT$ 5 10	Display the height in feet and inches.
$INCHES$ 70	Display the height in inches.

The variable *INCHES* is used to store an intermediate calculation and a final result. Note how its value varies during the calculation.

We want to show how to save some of the above instructions in a computer program so that they do not have to be reentered every time we wish to make a conversion. The computer operates in one of two modes. In performing calculations so far the computer has been in the *execution mode* or *desk calculator mode*. In this mode of operation any instructions you type are immediately executed and are not stored. When we sign onto the terminal the computer is in the execution mode.

To store a set of instructions, that is enter a program, we must change the mode of operation to the *definition* or *programming mode*. This is done using the symbol ∇ ("del", upper shift *G*). The ∇ symbol indicates that the instructions to follow are to be stored and not immediately executed. Along with the symbol ∇, we enter a *program name* that will be used to identify the stored instructions and to retrieve them again when we wish to use them.

We will use *CONVERT* as the name of a program to perform the height calculation. The rules for selecting program names are the same as for variable names.

The first step in writing the program is to enter ∇ followed by the program name *CONVERT*.

```
      ∇CONVERT
[1]
```

The computer is informed that we are about to enter a program called *CONVERT*. The ∇ puts us into the definition mode. The computer's response is to type the numeral 1 enclosed in brackets [1]. We now enter the first instruction next to *line number* [1].

```
[1]    INCHES←12 1×HEIGHT
[2]
```

After we return this instruction, the computer types the number [2] and we may enter our second instruction. This continues until all of our instructions have been entered. When we are finished we type the ∇ once again, indicating that all instructions have been entered. The second ∇ returns us to the execution mode. As typed at the terminal, the program appears as follows:

		COMMENTS
	∇CONVERT	Enter the programming mode.
[1]	INCHES←12 1×HEIGHT	Convert feet to inches.
[2]	INCHES←+/INCHES	Calculate total inches.
[3]	HEIGHT	Display height in feet and inches.
[4]	INCHES	Display height in inches.
[5]	∇	Return to the execution mode.

Compare the sequence of instructions in this program with those used at the beginning of this section to carry out the conversion in the execution mode.

To run the program *CONVERT* we assign a value to the variable *HEIGHT*. We may give it any value we want. We then execute *CONVERT* by entering its name.

COMMENTS

```
    HEIGHT←5 10            Specify a person's height.
    CONVERT               Execute program CONVERT.
5 10                      The height in feet and inches.
70                        The height in inches.
```

The stored instructions are executed exactly as though we had entered them one at a time and the desired results are displayed. At this point we may convert any person's height to inches by specifying *HEIGHT* and executing the program.

COMMENTS

```
    HEIGHT←6 5            Specify HEIGHT.
    CONVERT               Execute the program.
6 5                       Person's height in feet and inches.
77                        Person's height in inches.
```

In writing this program we have stored four instructions and named them *CONVERT*. The stored instructions are retrieved and executed by entering the name of the program. These instructions are executed in the order that they appear in the program, exactly as though we entered them in the execution mode. Any instruction that can be executed in APL can be stored in a program.

The variable *HEIGHT* must have a value before *CONVERT* can be executed. To see what happens when *HEIGHT* does not have a value, consider:

COMMENTS

```
    )ERASE HEIGHT

    CONVERT               Execute the program.
VALUE ERROR               An error appears on line [1].
CONVERT[1] INCHES← 12 1×HEIGHT
                  ^
```

After we erase *HEIGHT* it no longer has a value and the *VALUE ERROR* results. The computer indicates that the error occurs in line [1] of *CONVERT* and points to the position where an error occurred in evaluating the expression.

Example: The Pythagorean Theorem

According to the Pythagorean theorem, the length c of the hypoteneuse of a right triangle is given by the expression

$$c = (a^2 + b^2)^{1/2}$$

where a and b are the lengths of the other two sides. An APL
program to perform this calculation is shown below

```
        ∇ HYP
[1]     C←((A*2)+B*2)*0.5∇
```

The program is used as follows:

                                        COMMENTS

```
    A←3 12 1                Assign A and B values.
    B←4  5 1

    HYP                     Execute the program.
    C                       Display the result.
5 13 1.414213562
```

Note that no display was produced by the program since it
merely stored the result in the variable C.

4.2 DISPLAYING MESSAGES

It is often useful to display messages along with the
numerical results of a calculation. For example, this helps
us to recall what the results mean. We can display messages
by displaying a character vector as a step in our program. For
example,

```
[4]    'HEIGHT IN INCHES'
```

will cause the message HEIGHT IN INCHES to be printed when
line [4] is reached. This instruction acts the same as if we
had entered it in the execution mode, since entering a character vector causes the computer to display it.

A sequence of values can be printed on the same line by
placing semicolons between them. For example:

```
[4]    'HEIGHT IN INCHES ';INCHES
```

causes the message and the value of INCHES to be shown on the
same line.

On some newer systems, notably IBM's VS APL system, this
form of output is not available. The same results may be
achieved by using the format function ⍕ (upshift N, backspace
upshift J) in the form

```
[4]    'HEIGHT ',(⍕INCHES)
```

How this statement works will be discussed in more detail in
Chapter 6. In the text we will continue to use the semicolon
display form.

We might wish to modify *CONVERT* as follows (how to make such a modification will be discussed in the next section):

```
     ∇ CONVERT
[1]    INCHES← 12 1×HEIGHT
[2]    INCHES←+/INCHES
[3]    'HEIGHT IN FEET AND INCHES ';HEIGHT
[4]    'HEIGHT IN INCHES ';INCHES
     ∇
```

Executing the program we obtain:

COMMENTS

```
    HEIGHT← 4 11                  Execute the program.
    CONVERT                       The results are displayed
HEIGHT IN FEET AND INCHES 4 11    with the accompanying
HEIGHT IN INCHES 59               explanatory messages.
```

The character vectors and numerical values are displayed on the same line. Note that the space between the letters and the numerals must be included as part of the character vector as is done in lines [3] and [4].

Example: Kepler's Third Law of Planetary Motion

Kepler's third law of planetary motion expresses a relationship between the average distance of a planet from the sun and the time it takes for the planet to make a complete trip around the sun. The law states that the ratio of the square of the period of a planet's orbit divided by the cube of its average distance from the sun is a constant which is the same for all the planets.

The function *KEPLER* can be used to verify this law.

```
     ∇ KEPLER
[1]    '*** PERIODS ***'
[2]    PERIOD
[3]    ' '
[4]    '*** AVERAGE DISTANCES ***'
[5]    DISTANCE
[6]    ' '
[7]    '*** RATIOS ***'
[8]    (PERIOD*2)÷DISTANCE*3
     ∇
```

Lines [1] to [3] and [4] to [6] display the periods and average distances. These data are stored in the variables *PERIOD* and *DISTANCE* respectively. A blank line is produced by lines [3] and [6] improving the readability of the output. Lines [7] and [8] calculate and display the ratio specified by Kepler's law.

Data for the periods and distances of the planets are stored in the variables *TP* and *DP* respectively. To use the program, we transfer these data to the variables *PERIOD* and *DISTANCE*.

```
    PERIOD←TP
    DISTANCE←DP
```

and then execute the program.

```
    KEPLER
*** PERIODS ***
0.2408 0.6152 1 1.881 11.86 29.46 84.01 164.8 248.8

*** AVERAGE DISTANCES ***
0.3874 0.7228 1 1.523 5.202 9.541 19.19 30.09 39.51

*** RATIOS ***
0.9977 1.002 1 1.001 0.9992 0.9991 0.9987 0.9971 1.004
```

The periods are given in years and the distances in multiples
of the earth's distance from the sun. The displayed ratios
are constant to within a few tenths of a percent. (A)DIGITS
setting of 4 was used in this example. See Appendix 2.)

4.3   EDITING COMPUTER PROGRAMS

In the process of writing computer programs we frequently make
errors that need to be corrected for the program to operate
properly. At other times we may wish to alter programs to do
additional calculations or the same calculation in a different
way. In this section we discuss methods for *editing* computer
programs.

A program called Z has been written to assign the values 1
and 5 to the variables A and B and then compute and display
their sum. We will use this program to illustrate various
editing instructions.

The command $\nabla Z[\Box]$ will display this program. As usual, ∇
puts us into the definition mode, and Z specifies the program
name. The group of symbols $[\Box]$ displays the program.

```
      ∇Z[□]
    ∇ Z
[1]   A←1
[2]   A←5
[3]   'THE SAM OF A AND B IS ';A+B
    ∇
[4]
```

After the program is displayed the first unused line number
[4] is shown.

The quad $\Box$, upper shift L, permits us to Look at the
program. The entire program is displayed followed by the next
unused line number. Additional program statements may now be
entered.

There are two errors in this program. Line [2] should read
B←5, and *SAM* in line [3] should be *SUM*. We will correct line
[2] by replacing the entire line. This form of editing is
accomplished by typing next to [4], the numeral 2 enclosed in
brackets followed by the correct statement for line [2].

```
[4]     [2]B←5
[3]
```

By typing the [2] we inform the computer that line [2] rather
than line [4] is to be entered. The instruction following is
the new contents of line [2]. After returning this instruction
line [2] is corrected and, if desired, a new line [3] can be
entered.

It is possible to display the new line [2] with the command
[2□].

```
[3]     [2□]
[2]     B←5
[2]
```

Line [2] has its new form. The computer is now ready to
accept input for line [2]. In general, the instruction [*N*□]
where *N* is a line number causes the display of line *N*.

The next correction is to change *SAM* to *SUM*. Line [3] may
be changed by typing [3] followed by the desired expression.
However, since the line is long and only one character is
incorrect, we will use the *line editing* capability to change
[3]. To do this, we type a left bracket, followed by 3□ and
then followed by an estimate of the position in line [3] of
the error. Finally, we type a closing right bracket.

```
[2]     [3□10]
[3]     'THE SAM OF A AND B IS ';A+B
          ↑
```

Line [3] is displayed and the type element stops under *E*
(the type-element position here is indicated by ↑), which is
in the tenth position.

We want to delete the *A* in *SAM* and replace it by *U*. To do
this we space over three spaces to the *A* and type a slash, /.
This will cause the deletion of the *A*. To leave space for the
U we next type 1 under the *M*, instructing the computer to
leave one space in front of the *M*.

```
[3]     'THE SAM OF A AND B IS ';A+B
             /1
[3]     'THE S M OF A AND B IS ';A+B
```

The editing instruction /1 deletes the *A* above the / and
leaves one space before the *M*.

After this instruction is returned, line [3] is redisplayed
with the *A* deleted, one space left before the *M*, and the type
ball backspaced to the blank. We then type *U* in the blank
space, completing the editing of this line.

[3]   '*THE SUM OF A AND B IS* ';*A+B*
[4]

To display the current version of the program, we enter [□].

[4]   [□]
    ∇ *Z*
[1]   *A←1*
[2]   *B←5*
[3]   '*THE SUM OF A AND B IS* ';*A+B*
    ∇
[4]   ∇

We enter ∇ on line [4] to leave the definition mode and are
ready to execute the program. Note that ∇ may be typed on any
line without changing its content. Thus, if there were an APL
statement on line [4] and ∇ entered when [4] was displayed as
in the previous case, we would return to execution mode and
the content of line [4] would not be changed.

We execute *Z* and obtain the expected result.

    Z
THE SUM OF A AND B IS 6

As in the last example, the line editing procedure has
three steps. In the definition mode we enter a command of the
form [*N*□*M*]. The entry of this instruction causes line *N* to be
displayed and the type ball to stop on the next line at
position *M*. This position is usually taken to be an estimate
of the location of the first correction to be made.

Editing instructions are then entered. A slash under a
character causes that character to be deleted. Typing an
integer, 1 to 9, under a character causes that many blanks to
be inserted in front of the character. More than 9 blanks can
be inserted by typing a letter. Typing *A* causes 5 blanks to
be inserted, *B* causes 10 blanks, *C* 15 and so on. After this
instruction is entered, the edited line is displayed with
blanks inserted and the type ball is automatically backspaced
to the first inserted blank. The editing is completed by
typing in the correct characters. Generally there is no problem with inserting extra blanks during line editing as the APL
system will remove them once the corrected line is returned.
An exception to this is inserting blanks in character vectors.
Here, all inserted blanks are retained.

To illustrate another editing technique, we will modify *Z*
so that the product of *A* and *B* is calculated and displayed
before the sum. This requires the *insertion* of an additional
statement after line [2]. To do this we first return to the
definition mode by typing a ∇ followed by the program name *Z*.

COMMENTS

```
       ∇Z                         Switch into the definition mode to
[4]                              change Z.  First unused line
                                 number is displayed.
```

In this case we did not type the [□] after the program name
and only the first unused line number is printed rather than
the entire program. The new line is now inserted.

```
[4]    [2.1]'THE PRODUCT OF A AND B IS ';A×B
[2.2]
```

In general, we insert a line after line [N] by typing [N.I]
where I is a positive integer. Another line can then be
inserted by typing it next to [2.2]. Instead we enter [□] and
display the program. We include a ∇ to return us to the execution mode after the display.

```
[2.2] [□]∇
    ∇ Z
[1]    A←1
[2]    B←5
[2.1] 'THE PRODUCT OF A AND B IS ';A×B
[3]    'THE SUM OF A AND B IS ';A+B
    ∇
```

Observe that the new line [2.1] has been inserted properly,
and its line number is unchanged. The final ∇ returns us to
the execution mode. Note that the display instruction was
entered in line [2.2] . Editing instructions can be entered at
any time and do not change the contents of that line.

   If we now display Z once again we find the lines renumbered.

```
    ∇Z[□]∇
    ∇ Z
[1]    A←1
[2]    B←5
[3]    'THE PRODUCT OF A AND B IS ';A×B
[4]    'THE SUM OF A AND B IS ';A+B
    ∇
```

Note the form of the display instruction used here. This instruction displays the program but because of the final ∇
leaves us in the execution mode. Executing Z we find

```
    Z
THE PRODUCT OF A AND B IS 5
THE SUM OF A AND B IS 6
```

The final editing command to be introduced allows us to delete
a line. We will remove lines [1] and [2] in Z so that A and B
can be given any value before executing Z and these values will
then be used in the program. We delete a line by typing the
line number enclosed in brackets and then striking the
ATTENTION (or LINEFEED) and RETURN keys.

COMMENTS

	∇Z	Enter the definition mode to change Z.
[5]	[1]	Line [1] is deleted by typing its
	∨	number and then hitting ATTENTION (or LINEFEED) and then the
[2]		RETURN key.
	∨	Line [2] is deleted using the same procedure.
[3]	∇	Return to the execution mode. Line [3] is unaffected by the ∇.

We now display Z.

```
      ∇Z[□]∇
    ∇ Z
[1]    'THE PRODUCT OF A AND B IS ';A×B
[2]    'THE SUM OF A AND B IS ';A+B
    ∇
```

The two lines have been removed and successive lines renumbered. We assign values to A and B

```
      A←¯7 11
      B←3 4
```

and execute the program

```
      Z
THE PRODUCT OF A AND B IS ¯21 44
THE SUM OF A AND B IS ¯4 15
```

To ascertain the names of programs that we have defined, we can use the system command)FNS (for FuNctionS).

```
      )FNS
CONVERT Z
```

The two programs present are *CONVERT* and *Z*. Lines within a program as well as the program name may be edited. For this purpose the name is referred to as line [0]. Thus, to change the name of program *Z* we would proceed as follows

```
      ∇Z
[3]    [0]MODZ
[1]    [□]∇
    ∇ MODZ
[1]    'THE PRODUCT OF A AND B IS ';A×B
[2]    'THE SUM OF A AND B IS ';A+B
    ∇
```

In line [1] we request a display of the program and return to the execution mode. The name of the program has now been changed from *Z* to *MODZ*.

COMMENTS

```
      )FNS
CONVERT MODZ
      Z
VALUE ERROR
      Z
      ^
```

Display the names of the functions
   present.
Program *Z* is no longer with us.

Functions can be erased using the *)ERASE* system command.

COMMENTS

```
      )ERASE MODZ
      )FNS
CONVERT
```

MODZ has been erased and the only
   remaining function is *CONVERT*.

A complete list of editing instructions is given in Table 4.1.

Table 4.1 Editing Instructions

Instruction	Result
I. Display Instructions (*)	
[□]	Display entire program.
[N□]	Display line [N].
[□N]	Display all lines from line [N] to the end of the program.
II. Numbering Instructions (*)	
[N]	Specify statement number to be entered.
[N.1]	Insert statement after line N.
III. Line Editing Instructions	
[N□M] (*)	Line N is to be edited after it is displayed; type element stops on the next line at position M.

The following symbols are placed below the character in the line to be edited.

/	Deletes character above.
1,2,3,...9	Inserts 1,2,...9 blanks in front of the character above.
A,B,C,...	Inserts 5 (if A), 10 (if B), blanks in front of the character above.
IV. Deleting a Line (*)	
[N] ∨	Statement N is deleted by hitting the ATTENTION (or LINEFEED) key and then RETURN.

(*) These instructions can be entered in the form ∇PROGNAME[---] or while in the definition mode.

4.4 FLOWCHARTS

When faced with a problem to be solved by a computer, a programmer must first break down the solution method into component steps that can be understood by the computer. Of course, not all programs are as simple as the examples considered in the previous sections. It is often convenient to have a pictorial way of displaying the steps to be used in the computer program solution of the problem. The flowchart is the usual means for doing this. For complicated programs the use of a flowchart is a necessity whereas for simpler programs this is not always true. However, the habit of using a flowchart for all programs is a good one to develop. The drawing of the flowchart during the design of your program helps you organize your thoughts and avoid major errors. A clear flowchart is then readily translated into an APL program.

The symbols to be used here for flowcharts are shown in Table 4.2. There is no universally accepted set of symbols, although the ones used here appear frequently.

Two flowcharts for the program *CONVERT* developed in section 2 are shown in Figure 4.1

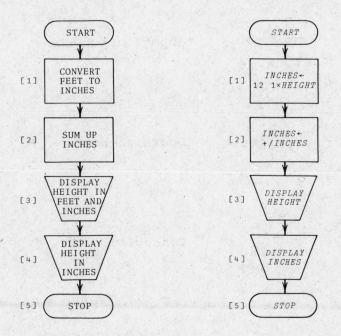

Figure 4.1 Flowcharts of the program *CONVERT*

Table 4.2   Flowchart Symbols

Symbol	Symbol Name	Type of Instruction
	Processing box	Processing of data
	Predefined process box	Use of predefined program
	Terminal box	Starting or stopping execution
	Input/Output box	Input or output of information
	Decision box	Decision for conditional transfers
	Connector	Connects flowchart segments
	Flow lines	Indicate direction of program flow

The two flowcharts are equivalent. Prior to the execution
of the program the variable *HEIGHT* is assigned a value. The
beginning of the program is indicated by the start box. The
algorithm on the right is in a more APL-oriented form. In
line [1] we convert feet to inches and assign the values to
INCHES. In the next step we then sum up the inches and assign
the sum to *INCHES*. These instructions represent the processing of data and are shown in rectangular boxes. Lines [3] and
[4] are contained in output boxes and display *HEIGHT* (feet and
inches) and *INCHES* respectively. The end of the program is
shown by the terminal stop box.

4.5 KEYBOARD RESPONSE

In using the program *CONVERT* we have emphasized the need for
specifying the variable *HEIGHT* prior to execution. It is
possible to have a program obtain information that will be
entered from the keyboard while the program is executing.
This is done by putting the quad function ($\square$) to the right of
the assignment function.

We edit *CONVERT* to make provision for entering a person's
height during execution by inserting 2 lines between the
header, the line containing the program name, and line [1].
First we enter the definition mode indicating that we wish to
insert lines between line [0], the header, and line [1]. We
enter the 2 new lines and return to the execution mode.

```
      ∇CONVERT[0.1]
[0.1] 'ENTER HEIGHT IN FEET AND INCHES'
[0.2] HEIGHT←□∇
```

Displaying the edited program we note that the two lines have
been inserted and all lines have been renumbered from [1] to
[6]. The first inserted line displays a message indicating
the desired input. The second line serves to obtain this
input and store it in *HEIGHT*.

```
      ∇CONVERT[□]∇
    ∇ CONVERT
[1]   'ENTER HEIGHT IN FEET AND INCHES'
[2]   HEIGHT←□
[3]   INCHES← 12 1×HEIGHT
[4]   INCHES←+/INCHES
[5]   'HEIGHT IN FEET AND INCHES ';HEIGHT
[6]   'HEIGHT IN INCHES ';INCHES
    ∇
```

When this program is executed it displays the message of
line [1] followed on the next line by a quad and a colon,
indicating input is to be entered from the keyboard. The keyboard is then released so that the person's height may be
entered by typing a numerical vector and returning it. The
program then executes lines [3] through [6]. We now execute
this function.

```
      CONVERT
ENTER HEIGHT IN FEET AND INCHES
□:
      6 0
HEIGHT IN FEET AND INCHES 6 0
HEIGHT IN INCHES 72
```

Frequently the data to be entered from the keyboard is a character vector, for example, someone's name. In this case the symbol ▯, quote-quad, (□ backspace ') is used. When the keyboard is released, the response typed on the keyboard is treated as a character vector. *Apostrophes need not be used in the keyboard response.* For example, in the following program

```
      ∇HELLO[□]∇
    ∇ HELLO
[1]   'HI! WHAT IS YOUR NAME?'
[2]   N←▯
[3]   'HELLO ';N
[4]   'MY NAME IS APL'
    ∇
```

when the keyboard is released in line [2], the type element moves to the left-most carriage position and the keyboard is unlocked. The person operating the program then enters her name without apostrophes.

COMMENTS

```
      HELLO
HI! WHAT IS YOUR NAME?
TOBY
HELLO TOBY
MY NAME IS APL
```

Program execution is requested.

No apostrophes are necessary to enter the character vector, *TOBY.*

```
      HELLO
HI! WHAT IS YOUR NAME?
'SHEILA'
HELLO 'SHEILA'
MY NAME IS APL
```

The apostrophes are part of the character vector.

Example: Supply and Demand

A central warehouse fills parts orders sent to it by surrounding repair shops. If the total demand for parts is less than the available supply, all orders can be filled. If not, the warehouse ships in proportion to the amount requested.

```
        ∇ALLOCATE[□]∇
      ∇ ALLOCATE
[1]     'ENTER NUMBER OF UNITS IN STOCK'
[2]     SUPPLY←□
[3]     'ENTER NUMBERS OF UNITS REQUESTED'
[4]     DEMAND←□
[5]     SHIP←DEMAND⌊SUPPLY×DEMAND÷+/DEMAND
[6]     SHIP←⌊SHIP
[7]     ''
[8]     'SHIPMENTS . . . . . . . ';SHIP
[9]     'UNITS LEFT IN STOCK . . ';SUPPLY-+/SHIP
      ∇
```

On line [5] the shipments are calculated as the smaller of
the units requested or the corresponding fraction of the units
available. If supply exceeds demand, the actual demand will
be the smaller but if supply does not meet the demand the
proportional supply will be the smaller. Line [6] insures that
only whole units are shipped. In line [9] the units remaining
in stock are calculated as the original supply minus the total
units shipped.

```
    ALLOCATE
ENTER NUMBER OF UNITS IN STOCK
□:
    150
ENTER NUMBERS OF UNITS REQUESTED
□:
    40 75 20

SHIPMENTS . . . . . . 40 75 20
UNITS LEFT IN STOCK . . 15
```

Here the demand was less than the supply.

```
    ALLOCATE
ENTER NUMBER OF UNITS IN STOCK
□:
    150
ENTER NUMBERS OF UNITS REQUESTED
□:
    25 40 65 90

SHIPMENTS . . . . . . . 17 27 44 61
UNITS LEFT IN STOCK . . 1
```

In this case demand exceeds supply. Why does one unit remain?

4.6   COMMENTS

It is important that a program be written in a way that is
easily understood by the reader. The most important factor
determining the clarity of a program is its organization or
structure. A good program is one that proceeds smoothly and
logically from beginning to end. Calculations should proceed
in a manner that is, in some sense, natural for the task being
performed. A good program, therefore, requires good planning.

Another factor influencing the readability of a program is the complexity of the APL expressions that are used. Because of the large number of functions that are available in the language and the ability to chain these functions together, some rather amazing calculations can be accomplished within one line of code. Generally, however, these "one-liners" as they are called are very difficult to understand and should be avoided. The argument that such expressions execute more rapidly is not really relevant if the milliseconds of saved computer time are gained at the expense of minutes or hours of programmer time.

Program clarity is also enhanced by the appropriate choice of variable and program names and the use of explanatory comments within the program. Comments are indicated by the symbol ⍝ (upper shift J backspace upper shift C). The symbol is then followed by the comment.

Example: Mortgage Payments

As an example of the use of comments, we give a program to calculate the monthly payments necessary to pay off a mortgage. In standard notation the payment is specified by the formula

$$P = A \times I \times \frac{(1+I)^M}{(1+I)^M - 1}$$

where P is the monthly payment, A is the amount of the mortgage, I is the monthly interest rate, and M is the number of monthly payments. Several comments outline the procedure.

```
        ∇MORTGAGE[□]∇
      ∇ MORTGAGE
[1]   ⍝THIS PROGRAM CALCULATES MONTHLY MORTGAGE PAYMENTS
[2]    'ENTER THE AMOUNT OF THE MORTGAGE'
[3]    AMOUNT←□
[4]    'ENTER THE ANNUAL INTEREST RATE IN PERCENT'
[5]    INT←□
[6]    'ENTER THE DURATION OF THE MORTGAGE IN YEARS'
[7]    TIME←□
[8]   ⍝CALCULATE THE MONTHLY INTEREST AS DECIMAL FRACTION
[9]    INT←0.01×INT÷12
[10]  ⍝CONVERT MORTGAGE DURATION FROM YEARS TO MONTHS
[11]   TIME←TIME×12
[12]  ⍝CALCULATE MONTHLY PAYMENT
[13]   TEMP←(1+INT)*TIME
[14]   PAY←AMOUNT×INT×TEMP÷TEMP-1
[15]  ⍝ROUND TO THE NEAREST PENNY
[16]   PAY←0.01×⌊0.5+PAY×100
[17]   'THE MONTHLY PAYMENT IS ';PAY
      ∇
```

The first comment appearing in line [1] describes the purpose of the program. The ⍝ symbol is displayed beginning one position to the left of other lines. The input section of the program requires no comments, since it is quite adequately described by the messages displayed when requesting input. Comments are then used to indicate the steps taken to evaluate the payments. Note that results are rounded to the nearest penny, a procedure discussed in Chapter 3.

EXERCISES

The display and input procedures presented in this chapter can be used in execution mode as well as within programs. This is illustrated in the following problems. Record your inputs, the computer outputs, and your explanation of what occurs.

1. Give the display you expect from executing the following examples. Check your results by entering the expressions while in the execution mode. Be careful to observe the positions of the blanks in these expressions.

Instruction	Anticipated Display	Display
a. 1;2;3;4		
b. 1 ;2 ;3 ;4		
c. 1;'2';3;'4'		
d. 1;' 2 ';3;' 4'		
e. 1;' ';2;' ';3		
f. 'A';'B';1		
g. 'A ';'B';1		
h. 'TIME';3;':';40		
i. 'TO';'BE'		
j. 'FOUR';4		
k. 'FOUR ';4		
l. 1 2 3;4 5		
m. A←11 12 46 'DATE';A		

2. The variables M, D, and Y are used to store today's date. M has the month (1-12), D has the day, and Y has the year. Give an APL expression which will express the date as

$$\_ \_/\_ \_/\_ \_$$

    where the blanks are to be filled in by the values of M, D, and Y respectively. (Thus, Halloween would be shown as 10/31/75.)

3. While in execution mode type

    $X \leftarrow \square$

   What happens? Now type 1+1. Display X. What can you
   infer from this? Try other examples.

4. While in the execution mode type

    $X \leftarrow \boxed{!}$

   What happens? Now type 1+1. Display X. What can you
   infer from this? Try the same thing, but enter $DON'T$.
   Try other examples. Is this a convenient way to enter
   character data?

   The following problems illustrate the techniques you have
   learned in the preceding sections. Some of the problems
   below require you to write simple programs. When answer-
   ing these problems, you should be sure the program works
   properly. Work out some test examples by hand and compare
   them with the computer results. Take the time to organize
   your output displays into an easily readable format.

5. Which of the following are valid program names?

    a. *FOUR*   f. $A\Delta$

    b. *FOR*   g. $A\nabla$

    c. 4   h. $1RUN$

    d. $I2$ i. $RUN1$

    e. $H*$ j. P

6. a. Write a program to compute the maximum, minimum, and
      average grade. Assume the grades are contained in the
      vector G, which is specified prior to executing the
      program.
   b. Modify the program of a. to display the maximum,
      minimum, and average grade with appropriate descriptive
      text, such as *THE MAXIMUM GRADE IS....*
   c. Modify the program to input the vector of grades during
      execution. A message requesting the grades should be
      displayed.

7. a. Write a program to calculate the area of a rectangle.
      The base of the rectangle, B, and the height, H, should
      be obtained from the keyboard during execution.
      Display the base, the height, and the area with appro-
      priate labeling of values. (Area of rectangle equals
      base times height.)

b. Modify the program of question a. to calculate and display the perimeter of the rectangle as well as the area. (Perimeter equals two times the sum of the base and the height.)

8. You have been hired to automate the estimation of charge for a rug company. A rectangular rug has the following costs:

   COST OF MATERIAL = AREA OF RUG × COST PER SQUARE FOOT
   COST OF BINDING THE EDGES = PERIMETER OF RUG × 15 CENTS
       PER FOOT
   DELIVERY CHARGE = $3.00

   Modify the program of the previous problem to get the required information from the keyboard and display each individual cost and the total cost of the rug. Include descriptive messages to identify the numerical output.

9. a. Modify program *MORTGAGE* of Section 4.6 to calculate the total of all payments made over the life of the mortgage and display the result along with the appropriate message.
   b. Use program *MORTGAGE* as modified in a. to investigate the monthly payment and total amount paid for a 20-year $50,000 mortgage financed at annual interest rates of 7, 8.5, and 10 percent.
   c. Repeat b. for an interest rate of 8.5 percent and lifetimes of 20, 25, and 30 years.

10. a. Write a program to obtain your name and social security number from the keyboard and then display them. (Should your social security number be obtained as a numerical vector or a character vector?)
    b. Edit the program of a. to obtain your age and home address and display them with the other information at the end of the program.

11. a. Write a program to obtain an employee name, hours worked, and hourly pay from the keyboard. Display the employee's name and his gross pay.
    b. Modify the program of a. to include overtime pay. Assume time-and-a-half for hours worked in excess of 35 hours per week. Prior to printing the gross pay the program should output the regular and overtime earnings.
    c. Edit the program in b. to display the employee's name, gross pay, and net pay. (Net pay equals gross pay minus 20 percent of gross pay.)

12. A time interval is given in minutes and contained in the variable T. Write a program *TIME* that expresses this time interval in hours and minutes. Store the hours in the variable H and the minutes in the variable M. The display should appear in the form __:__ where the blanks are filled in with the value of H and T. For example,

```
        T←263
        TIME
    4:23
```

13.   Use the line editing feature to convert the program
      OLDPROGRAM shown below to the program *NEWPROGRAM*.
      Execute the program to be sure no errors are present.

```
        ∇ OLDPROGRAM
[1]   'I''M SAD'
[2]    'LOVE IS A SPLENDID TING'
[3]    5÷÷ 2 10 50
[4]    (305)×3-7÷2
[5]    'FOR YEARS'
[6]    FIVE←4+ONE←1
        ∇
```

```
        ∇ NEWPROGRAM
[1]    'I''M HAPPY'
[2]    'LOVE IS A SPLENDID THING'
[3]    5× 2 10 50
[4]    (3+5)×(3-7)÷2
[5]    'FOUR SCORE AND SEVEN YEARS'
[6]    FIVE←2+THREE←2+ONE←1+ZERO←0
        ∇
```

14.   You have just executed a program *M*. The program
      executed completely but you detected an erroneous result.
      Show the steps you would use for displaying the current
      form of line [4] in *M*, replacing this line by the
      instruction *P←A+B+C* and returning to the execution mode.

15.   Lines [10] and [11] in a program *G* have the following
      form

```
[10]   'THE RESULT IS'
[11]   R
```

      a. Assuming *R* has the value 10 15 17 when we reach line
         [10], what will the display produced by these lines
         look like?
      b. Indicate the *editing procedure* you would use to make
         the display appear as

         THE RESULT IS 10 15 17

         with two blank spaces between *IS* and the first
         displayed digit.
      c. Using the original form for *G*, indicate the editing
         instructions you would use to produce the following
         display.

         THE RESULT IS

         10 15 17

         Note the skipped line. Use the most efficient editing
         procedure you can.
      d. How would you edit the original version of program *G*
         to display the result indented five spaces?

16. A program L operates in the following manner.

        L (User types the program name.)
    ENTER A VECTOR OF NUMBERS
    ☐:
        11 5 2   (This is the user's input.)
    THE PRODUCT IS
    110

    Write a program that will reproduce this display, giving the correct product for any vector of numbers typed in by the user.

17. An APL function F has been defined and contains 15 lines.

    a. What is the result of the expression ∇F?

    For b. through f., assume you have just executed the instruction ∇F and the result of a. has occurred. Give the command you would use to do the following:

    b. Display line [7].
    c. Insert the expression $N←$☐ between lines [5] and [6].
    d. Replace line [2] by the expression $M←\lfloor M$.
    e. Display the function from line [10] to the end and return to the execution mode.
    f. Add the expression '*THE END*' to the end of the program and return to the execution mode.

18. Consider the following program:

        ∇ *NOS*
    [1]   '*FIRST*'
    [2]   '*SECOND*'
    [3]   '*FOURTH*'
    [4]   '*THIRD*'
        ∇

    Use the line editing procedure to rearrange the lines into the proper order by editing the line numbers, that is, edit the values in brackets. Insert line [4] between lines [2] and [3]. Then remove the old line [4]. This is a useful procedure for rearranging lines in a program without retyping them.

19. a. Create a program with the name V. Try to execute $V←3$. What happens?
    b. Execute $P←7$. Then try to define a program P by typing ∇P. What happens?

4.7   MORE ON PROGRAMS, FUNCTIONS, AND VARIABLES

The following program will calculate the sum of a vector of numbers.

```
      ∇SUM[☐]∇
    ∇  SUM
[1]    RESULT←+/VECTOR
    ∇
```

We execute it as follows:

                              COMMENTS

```
VECTOR←7 3 11          Assign a value to VECTOR.
SUM                    Execute the program.
RESULT                 Display RESULT.
```
21

   While this is a simple program, would you remember one week from today that the input had to be stored in the variable VECTOR and that the result would be stored in the variable RESULT? Probably not. We could overcome this difficulty by requesting the input from the keyboard and displaying the results, but what if we wanted the result to be stored in TOTAL rather than RESULT or if the input information resulted from a previous calculation and was stored in a variable other than VECTOR?

   The problem here is that the variables RESULT and VECTOR are hidden from view. In order to determine what variable name should be used to store the input information and what variable will contain the computed result, we must display the function. When using the primitive APL functions, these problems did not occur. Calculations using the primitive functions could be performed on any variable and the result of the calculation could either be displayed or stored in any other variable. In this section, we consider other forms that programs can assume. We will see that some of these can be executed in the same way as primitive APL functions.

   Consider the following program ASUM:

                              COMMENTS

```
      ∇ASUM[☐]∇              Display the program ASUM.
    ∇  ASUM VECTOR           The program header.
[1]    RESULT←+/VECTOR
    ∇
```

The calculation on line [1] is the same as in SUM. However, the *header*, the line containing the program name, is different. A program defined in this manner with a header of the form

      ∇PROGRAMNAME VARIABLE

uses an explicit input argument in the same manner as a monadic function. In program headings of this form *PROGRAMNAME* is the program name and *VARIABLE* is the name of the variable which contains input data. To execute the program, we type the program name followed by the data to be used.

We execute *ASUM*.

COMMENTS

        ASUM 8 9 3   Execute *ASUM* for the input data
        RESULT   8 9 3.
20   The sum of these numbers.

        X←¯1 2 3
        ASUM X   Execute *ASUM* with the input *X*.

        RESULT
4   The sum of the elements in *X*.

The program *ASUM* obtains input information in the same manner as a standard monadic function. To execute the program we typed the program name followed by the input information. This information can be any numerical vector or variable. No explicit reference need be made to *VECTOR*.

We must provide *ASUM* with an argument.

        ASUM
SYNTAX ERROR
        ASUM
        ʌ

Example: The Rule of 72

A deposit left in the bank to accumulate interest will eventually double in value. The *rule of 72* states that the number of years needed for the money to double is approximately equal to 72÷I where *I* is the annual interest rate in percent. This is only approximately true. The exact doubling time can be obtained from the APL expression

        YR←(1+R)⍟2

This calculates the logarithm of 2 to the base 1+R where *R* is the interest rate expressed as a decimal fraction. For example, for a 6 percent interest rate, R←0.06. It is easy to see why the much simpler rule of 72 is useful.

The following program compares the results calculated for the time to double using both the rule of 72 and the exact formula.

```
     ∇RULEOF72[☐]∇
  ∇ RULEOF72 I
[1]    ' '
[2]    'RULE OF 72    ';⌈72÷I
[3]    'EXACT RESULT ';⌈(1+I÷100)⍟2
     ∇
```

The interest rate to be used in the program is the argument *I*. After skipping a line, the program calculates the result of the rule of 72 on line [2] and the exact result on line [3]. The division by 100 on line [3] converts the percent interest rate to a fractional rate. The ceiling function is used in both calculations to round the results to full years.

To execute this program, we type its name followed by the interest rates for which the doubling time is to be computed.

COMMENTS

        *RULEOF*72 1 3 5 7   Execute the program for interest
                                                    rates of 1, 3, 5 and 7 percent.
RULE OF 72   72 24 15 11
EXACT RESULT 70 24 15 11

        RATE←10 15 20 25   The input data can be stored in any
        *RULEOF*72 *RATE*   variable. The variable name is
                                                    typed after the program name.
RULE OF 72   8 5 4 3
EXACT RESULT 8 5 4 4

From the above examples we see that the rule of 72 is quite accurate over a large range of interest rates. Note that in using this program in these examples no explicit reference to the argument variable *I* was necessary.

Returning to our previous discussions, let's display *VECTOR*.

    VECTOR
7 3 11

The value of *VECTOR* is the same as when we executed *SUM* and has not been changed by executing *ASUM*.

This is unexpected. To study this further, let's edit *ASUM* to display the value of *VECTOR* during its execution.

COMMENTS

        ∇*ASUM*   The first unused line is [2].
[2]   '*VECTOR*= ';*VECTOR*∇   Modify *ASUM* to display *VECTOR*. The
                                                    final ∇ returns us to the execu-
                                                    tion mode.

    VECTOR←'*START***'   Assign a value to *VECTOR*.

    ASUM 7 8 9   Execute *ASUM* for the input 7 8 9.
VECTOR= 7 8 9   *VECTOR* has the expected value.
    RESULT   *RESULT* is displayed by typing its
24   name. It has the expected value.

    VECTOR   *VECTOR* has the value *START***
*START***   assigned above *before* the
                                                    execution of *ASUM*.

To understand the behavior of *VECTOR*, we need to introduce a new concept. In APL there are two different types of variables. When we are in the execution mode and assign a value to a variable, we are creating what is called a *global variable*. In executing the program *SUM*, we used the global variables *VECTOR* and *RESULT* to enter the input information and to store the result. These variables had the same value after the execution of *SUM* as they did during the execution.

On the other hand, when the variable *VECTOR* was used in the program *ASUM*, it behaved differently. During the execution of *ASUM* it had the value 7 8 9, but after the execution it had its original value *START**.

When a variable name appears in the header of a function, the variable acts as a *local* or *dummy* variable. If as in the case of *VECTOR* in *ASUM* the variable acquires a value during the execution of the program, *it retains this value only during the program execution*. After the execution is complete, the value of the variable reverts to the value it had prior to execution. If the variable did not have a global value before execution, it is undefined after the execution.

Example: An Automated Check Book

Most applications of computers require more than one program. A system of programs to maintain the balance in a checkbook is shown below.

COMMENTS

```
    ∇BALANCE[□]∇
  ∇ BALANCE
[1]  'BALANCE ';∆BAL
  ∇
```
Displays the current balance contained in the global variable ∆BAL.

```
    ∇CHECK[□]∇
  ∇ CHECK X
[1]  ∆BAL←∆BAL-+/X
[2]  'DEDUCT        ';X
[3]  'NEW BALANCE ';∆BAL
  ∇
```
A monadic program to calculate the new balance after writing a group of checks X. Line [1] adds up the checks and subtracts the total from the current balance.

```
    ∇DEPOSIT[□]∇
  ∇ DEPOSIT X
[1]  ∆BAL←∆BAL++/X
[2]  'DEPOSIT       ';X
[3]  'NEW BALANCE ';∆BAL
  ∇
```
A monadic program to add the total of the deposits in its argument X to the balance.

```
    ∇SETBALANCE[□]∇
  ∇ SETBALANCE X
[1]  ∆BAL←X
[2]  'NEW BALANCE ';∆BAL
  ∇
```
Changes the balance to whatever value is specified by X.

These programs are used as follows:

                                        COMMENTS

        SETBALANCE 100   Open the account with $100.
NEW BALANCE 100

        CHECK 75   A check is written for $75. The
DEDUCT   75   amount of the check and the new
NEW BALANCE 25   balance are displayed.

        DEPOSIT 450   A $450 deposit is made. The amount
DEPOSIT   450   of the deposit and the new
NEW BALANCE 475   balance are displayed.

        CHECK 65 125 245   Due to the plus reduction in line
DEDUCT   65 125 245   [1] of *CHECK* (and *DEPOSIT*) a
NEW BALANCE 40   vector of checks may be used.
                                        The total of the checks is
                                        subtracted.
        BALANCE   Display the current value of ΔBAL,
BALANCE 40   the checkbook balance.

In this example it is important to note the interplay between
the programs and the global variable ΔBAL which stores the
balance.

    Now consider the function *BSUM*.

                                        COMMENTS

        ∇*BSUM*[□]∇   Display the function *BSUM*.
        ∇ *RESULT←BSUM VECTOR*   The header of this function.
[1]   *RESULT←+/VECTOR*   The calculation to be performed.
        ∇

        BSUM 3 5 9   The sum of 3 5 9 is displayed.
17
        TOTAL←BSUM 3 5 9   The sum of 3 5 9 is stored in
        TOTAL   *TOTAL*.
17

The function *BSUM* takes an argument and returns a result in
exactly the same manner as a monadic APL function. No explicit
reference is made to the variables *VECTOR* or *RESULT* when the
function is used.

    Since they appear in the header, the variables *RESULT* and
VECTOR are local variables when used in *BSUM*.

```
                           COMMENTS
       RESULT←'*GLOBAL*'     Initialize RESULT.
       )ERASE VECTOR         VECTOR is now undefined.
       BSUM 3 5 7            Execute BSUM with the input 3 5 7
15                               giving the correct answer.
       RESULT               The global value of RESULT is
*GLOBAL*                         unchanged.
       VECTOR               VECTOR is still undefined.
VALUE ERROR
       VECTOR
       ^
```

These variables have the expected value during the calculation
in *BSUM* but after the execution is completed their values
revert to the values they had prior to execution.

Although they are frequently used interchangeably, it is
convenient to make a distinction between the terms *function*
and *program*. A function such as *BSUM* or any of the standard
APL functions return an *explicit result*. A program does not.
For a standard function, the result returned is the usual
result obtained by performing the indicated operation. In a
defined function such as *BSUM*, the header will contain a variable name to the left of the assignment arrow. For example,
it may be of the form

       ∇RESULTVAR←FUNCNAME INPUTVAR

The result returned is the *last* value assigned to *RESULTVAR*
during the execution of the function. Other forms for
function headers will be presented shortly.

Consider the function *FCONVERT*, which is a defined monadic
function that performs the conversion from feet and inches to
inches.

```
       ∇FCONVERT[□]∇
     ∇ INCHES←FCONVERT HEIGHT
[1]    INCHES← 12 1 ×HEIGHT
[2]    INCHES←+/INCHES
     ∇
```

This function performs the same calculations as the program
CONVERT but obtains the input height as an argument and
returns the converted height as an explicit result. When the
function is executed

```
       FCONVERT 6 5
77
```

the result is the final value of *INCHES* as determined in line
[2] rather than the intermediate value in line [1].

Results that we wish to save after the execution of a
program must be stored in global variables. If we try to use
the program *ASUM* in the same manner as the function *BSUM*, we
get into trouble.

COMMENTS

$X \leftarrow BSUM$ 4 6 8	Assign a value to X using the function $BSUM$.
X	Display X.

18

$X \leftarrow ASUM$ 4 6 8	Try to assign a value to X.

VALUE ERROR
    $X \leftarrow ASUM$ 4 6 8
     ∧

$ASUM$ does not return an explicit result so that there is no value to assign to X.

A *function* can be combined in APL expressions with primitive APL functions or other user-defined functions.

COMMENTS

$BSUM$ 7 3 4	Execute the function $BSUM$.

14

$3 \times BSUM$ 7 3 4	The right-to-left rule is observed.

42

$3 \times BSUM$ 7 3 4+1 2 3

60

Now the last example in more detail:

    7 3 4+1 2 3
8 5 7
    $BSUM$ 8 5 7
20
    3×20
60

Example: Evaluating an Infinite Series

The value of the fraction $X \div 1 - X$ (or $X \div (1-X)$ in conventional notation) can be expressed as the sum of the infinite series

$$(X*1)+(X*2)+(X*3)+(X*4)+...$$

for values of X less than one in magnitude. While this series has an infinite number of terms, the terms continue to decrease in value and the entire sum gives a finite result.

We can use the computer to try to verify the equivalence of the series and the fraction $X \div 1 - X$

COMMENTS

$X \leftarrow .5$ $X \div 1 - X$	For X equal to 0.5 the fraction has the value 1.

1

$S \leftarrow +/X*1$ 2 S	Form the sum of the first two terms.

0.75

COMMENTS

```
        S←S++/X*3 4                  Add on the sum of the third and
        S                               fourth terms.  The value is
0.9375                                  approaching 1.
```

We could continue in this way but the calculations can be done more easily if we write some functions to help us. The function T sums terms in the series. The terms to be summed are specified by the vector N, the argument of the function.

COMMENTS

```
        ∇T[□]∇                       The result $Z$ is the sum of the
     ∇  Z←T N                           terms obtained by raising $X$ to
[1]     Z←+/X*N                         the powers in $N$.
     ∇
```

```
        S←T 1 2 3 4                  $S$ is the sum of the first four
        S                               terms.
0.9375
```

```
        T 5 6 7                      The sum of terms five, six and
0.0546875                              seven.
```

```
        S←S+T 5 6 7                  $S$ is now the sum of the first seven
        S                               terms.
0.9921875
```

Introducing the program ADD simplifies the calculations further.

COMMENTS

```
        ∇ADD[□]∇                     The program adds to $S$ the sum of
     ∇  ADD N                           the terms $X*N$.  This sum is
[1]     S←S+T N                         calculated using the function $T$.
[2]     S                           The new $S$ value is displayed.
     ∇
        S                           The sum of seven terms.
0.9921875
        ADD 8 9 10                  The sum through 10 terms.
0.9990234375
        ADD 11 12 13 14 15
0.9999694824
        ADD 16 17 18 19 20          Adding additional terms causes the
0.9999990463                          sum to get closer and closer to
        ADD 21 22 23 24 25            1.
0.9999999702
        ADD 26 27 28 29 30
0.9999999991
        ADD 31 32 33 34 35          The sum of the first 35 terms in
1                                     the series is 1 with 10 figures
                                      of accuracy.
```

As in this example, whenever we have a repetitive set of calculations to perform, the use of functions can eliminate considerable effort.

Previous examples illustrated monadic functions. We may
also define dyadic functions. For example, the function *AREA*
will calculate the area of a rectangle given the length of its
base (*B*) and its height (*H*).

```
      ∇AREA[□]∇
   ∇  A←B AREA H
[1]    A←B×H
   ∇
```

This function takes two arguments, *B* and *H*, and returns a
result. It is executed as follows:

	COMMENTS
`3 AREA 5`	The area is 15.
`15`	
`RESULT←3 AREA 4`	The area is stored in *RESULT*.
`RESULT`	
`12`	

If carpeting sells for $14.50 per square yard, a 12 by 15 ft
rug would cost

	COMMENTS
`14.50×4 AREA 5`	Calculate the area of the rug in
`290`	yards and multiply by cost per
	square yard.

Another expression to calculate the cost is

```
      14.50×(12 AREA 15)÷ 3 AREA 3
290
```

From right to left we calculate the number of square feet in
one square yard and divide the result into the area of the rug
in square feet. The resulting area in square yards is then
multiplied by the cost of the rug per square yard. Note the
use of the function *AREA* in this expression. The function
AREA is a dyadic function that behaves the same as ×.

The variables *A*, *B*, and *H* are all local to *AREA*.

	COMMENTS
`)ERASE A B H`	
`10 AREA 20`	Execute *AREA* again.
`200`	
`A`	None of the variables *A*, *B*, or *H*
`VALUE ERROR`	are defined.
`    A`	
`    ∧`	
`B`	
`VALUE ERROR`	
`    B`	
`    ∧`	

H
VALUE ERROR
H
∧

These variables were used in the calculation of the area but after the function was executed they have no value. They appear in the header of the function *AREA* and are local to that function. After the execution of the function, they are undefined since they were undefined before the execution.

Example: The Distance Between Two Points

On a graph, points are indicated by giving their horizontal or X position and their vertical or Y position. A point 3 units in the horizontal direction and 4 in the vertical direction can be represented by a two element vector 3 4. The first element gives the X position and the second gives the Y position. Similarly 7 1 represents a point 7 units in the X direction and 1 unit in the Y direction.

The length of the line connecting these two points is given by (in conventional notation)

$$d = ((X_1 - X_2)^2 + (Y_1 - Y_2)^2)^{1/2}$$

It is the square root of the sum of the squares of the differences between the X and Y positions of the two points.

An APL function to calculate the distance is given below.

COMMENTS

∇*DIST*[□]∇ ∇ *Z←PT1 DIST PT2* [1]　*Z←(+/(PT1-PT2)*2)*0.5* ∇	The vectors *PT1* and *PT2* each contain two elements, the X and Y positions of point one and point two.
3 4 *DIST* 7 1 5	Calculate the distance between the point (3,4) and the point (7,1).
*S←*7 1 *DIST* 3 4 *S* 5	The result can be stored in a variable using the same procedure as with a primitive function.

We can specify additional variables to be local to a function by using the form

∇*PROGNAME*; *VARIABLENAME*; *VARIABLENAME*;...

The names of additional local variables are separated from other header information by a semicolon. If there is more than one additional local variable, the names are separated by semicolons.

As an example consider the following programs:

```
    ∇TYPE1[□]∇
  ∇ TYPE1
[1]   'X IS A ';X
  ∇
```

and

```
    ∇TYPE2[□]∇
  ∇ TYPE2;X
[1]   X←'LOCAL VARIABLE'
[2]   'X IS A ';X
  ∇
```

In *TYPE2* X is local while in *TYPE1* it is global.

COMMENTS

X←'GLOBAL VARIABLE' TYPE1	We create the global variable X.
X IS A GLOBAL VARIABLE TYPE2	The global value of X is used.
X IS A LOCAL VARIABLE X	The local value of X is used.
GLOBAL VARIABLE	The global value of X remains after the program execution.

A list of the basic function forms is given in Table 4.3.

Table 4.3 Basic Function Types

Header	Type
1. ∇P; *LOCAL VARIABLES*	Niladic, no explicit result
2. ∇Z←F; *LOCAL VARIABLES*	Niladic, returns explicit result
3. ∇P A; *LOCAL VARIABLES*	Monadic, no explicit result
4. ∇Z←F A; *LOCAL VARIABLES*	Monadic, returns explicit result
5. ∇B P A; *LOCAL VARIABLES*	Dyadic, no explicit result
6. ∇Z←B F A; *LOCAL VARIABLES*	Dyadic, returns explicit result

In the above, P stands for a permissible program name and F for a function name. Result variables are designated by Z and arguments by A and B. Result and argument variables are always local to the function. Additional local variables can be specified by using semicolons to separate them from previous parts of the header and from one another.

Let's examine what we have done from another point of view. The APL language provides us with a number of functions that are represented by symbols in the APL character set and that can be executed by typing the appropriate symbol. These functions are referred to as the *standard* or *primitive* functions. Some of these functions have already been introduced, and others will be introduced later. Since there are so many calculations that people will want to perform, only the most frequently used calculations can be supplied as part of the standard language.

The programming capability allows us to construct our own functions to perform calculations not supplied in the language. As we have just seen, these functions can be used in the same manner as the standard APL functions. This ability to construct functions with the same syntax as the standard functions gives great power to the APL language. In effect, users are able to create their own language extending APL to solve the problems facing them.

There are other advantages to using programs. In the solution of lengthy problems it is frequently advantageous to break up the task into several shorter subtasks. Each of these subtasks would then be performed by separate programs. The process of breaking a program into a number of smaller segments is called *modularization* or *segmentation*. An example of this division in an application is to write separate programs to input the data, process the data, and finally output the results. These three programs are then used by the "main" program.

```
      ∇MAIN[□]∇
   ∇ MAIN
[1]    INPUT
[2]    PROCESS
[3]    OUTPUT
   ∇
```

The *INPUT* program not only accepts the data, but may also display instructions, check the input data for errors, allow for correcting the data, and prepare the data for processing. The *PROCESS* program then takes the input data and performs the necessary calculations to extract the desired information. The information is then displayed by the *OUTPUT* program. Possible forms of output include graphic displays, reports, or storage of data in a file on a disk.

Modularization helps in organizing programs and improves their readability. When properly used it helps to eliminate errors and facilitates the checking of a program's operation. This topic will be discussed further in the case studies.

Another advantage of programs is their transportability. In the process of solving a problem it is possible to take advantage of programs that have already been written by yourself or some other person. Thus a social scientist interested in

analyzing a questionnaire may use statistical programs written
by a statistician. Substantial libraries of these programs
are generally available at your computer center. Later in
this chapter you will learn how to gain access to these
libraries.

4.8   THE TRACE AND STOP CONTROLS

One of the main tasks of the programmer is to be sure the program is operating correctly. For complex programs, this is
often quite difficult since many calculations will be performed and much of the operation of the program is hidden from
view. Only the results of a program are normally available to
the user. Intermediate results are not.

   To check on the execution of a program, the *trace* control
($T\Delta$) can be used. It takes the form

   $T\Delta PROGNAME \leftarrow LINEA, LINEB, \ldots$

   Here *PROGNAME* is the name of the program or function whose
execution is to be traced. The lines to be traced are specified by a numerical vector of line numbers. This instruction
causes the display of the *final* result in each line indicated.

   As an example, let's trace the execution of the function
FCONVERT

```
        ∇FCONVERT[□]∇
      ∇ INCHES←FCONVERT HEIGHT
[1]     INCHES← 12 1×HEIGHT
[2]     INCHES←+/INCHES
      ∇
```

We trace lines [1] and [2] . The result of line [1] is not
seen in the normal execution.

                               COMMENTS

```
    T∆FCONVERT←1 2          Put a trace on lines [1] and [2].
    FCONVERT 6 1
FCONVERT[1] 72 1           The results of lines [1] and [2]
FCONVERT[2] 73                are displayed along with the
73                           normal output.
```

To remove the trace option from *FCONVERT*, we set the trace
control to zero.

```
    T∆FCONVERT←0
    FCONVERT 5 10
70
```

The trace has been removed.

The function *FCONVERT* is simple enough, and we have used it frequently enough that we would be very surprised if it contained a bug, but in fact it does. Suppose we use this function to get the height of Tom Thumb, who is 5 inches high. We might try to do this as follows:

    FCONVERT 5
65

Surprise! The result 65 inches is clearly incorrect. We will use another program checking technique, the *stop* control, to determine what has happened here.

The stop control allows us to halt the execution of a program at any line we wish. To invoke this control, we use the form:

    SΔPROGNAME←LINEA,LINEB,...

Here *PROGNAME* is the name of the program whose execution is to be stopped. The lines at which execution is to halt are specified by a numerical vector of line numbers. Execution interrupts *prior* to executing each of the specified lines. In *FCONVERT* we will stop execution before lines [1] and [2].

                              COMMENTS

    SΔCONVERT←1 2   Set stop control to interrupt exe-
                                 cution prior to lines [1] and
                                 [2].
    FCONVERT 5   Execute *FCONVERT* with the trouble-
                                 some input.
FCONVERT[1]   Execution interrupts prior to exe-
                                 cuting line [1].

The interruption in execution is indicated by the display of the function name and the line number at which it is suspended.

One reason for using the stop control is that it allows us to look at local variables within a function. The two local variables here are *HEIGHT* and *INCHES*.

                              COMMENTS

    HEIGHT   *HEIGHT* is the input variable and
5   has the correct value.
    INCHES   At this point in the function
VALUE ERROR   *INCHES* has not yet received a
    INCHES   value.
    ^

Everything looks all right so far.

To resume execution we use the right arrow, →. This symbol can be interpreted as "go to." Followed by a function line number, it causes execution to resume at that line. The use of this symbol to control the flow of execution in a program will be discussed in detail in Chapter 7. The instruction →1 causes the program to resume execution at line [1].

                                   COMMENTS

        →1   Execution to resume at line [1].

FCONVERT[2]   The function stops prior to
                                      executing line [2].
        HEIGHT   HEIGHT is unchanged.
5
        INCHES   The bug: 12 1×5 yield 60 5.
60 5

We forgot that the function assumes that the input is a vector
with two elements. It will accept a scalar input but then
gives incorrect results. The proper input for a height of five
inches is the vector 0 5.

                                   COMMENTS

    FCONVERT 0 5

FCONVERT[1]   Execution interrupts before line
                                      [1].

The stop control is still in effect. To remove it we type
SΔCONVERT←0. Executing FCONVERT again gives the correct
result.

        FCONVERT 0 5
5

    We now introduce an additional system command, the *state
indicator*. This command is invoked by)SI. Executing this
command we find

)SI
FCONVERT[1] *
FCONVERT[2] *

When the execution of a program is interrupted, due to an
error or the use of the stop control, the system keeps track
of this interruption. The)SI command is used to access this
information. The result displayed here indicates that the
execution of FCONVERT was suspended prior to lines [1] and [2]
and not allowed to proceed to completion. The suspension at
line [1] occurred when we inadvertently tried to execute the
program without removing the stop control. The suspension at
line [2] occurred when we detected the error. Note that, in
displaying the state indicator, the most recent suspension
appears first. One way to remove the suspension is to continue execution of the function by transferring to the point
of suspension. Suspensions are removed one at a time beginning with the most recent. Thus we transfer to line [1].

        →1
5

The function resumes execution and gives the expected result since in the most recent suspension the input was 0 5. To assure ourselves that the suspension has been removed, we display the state indicator.

```
    )SI
FCONVERT[2] *
```

We can also remove the suspension by typing a single right arrow. This removes the most recently suspended function without causing any further execution or display.

```
    →
    )SI
```

The suspensions have been removed and the state indicator is now clear. It is a good idea to remove suspensions when they occur, since in keeping track of suspensions, the system can use considerable amounts of storage space.

4.9 TESTING THE PROGRAM

A program is ready to be executed once it has been entered into the computer and all known mistakes have been corrected using the editing features. The program must now be tested. Experience has shown that more often than not a program will not run as planned the first time and that, when a program fails to run properly, it is usually the program and not the computer that is to blame. Indeed, a major portion of program development time is normally devoted to isolating and correcting errors and testing programs, a process called *debugging*. It is consequently important to become acquainted with the common types of errors made and the general approach taken in their detection and correction.

Given the numerous different errors that can be made (and that you *will* make), it is not possible to give unambiguous classifications for them all. Two frequently used distinctions are to classify errors as *language errors* or *logical errors*. The two types of errors differ in that language errors are detected by the computer while logical errors are not. When the program is executed for the first time the computer will interpret each line and list the language errors in the form of diagnostic messages. Here the computer is most helpful as it points to the location of the error within the instruction using the caret (∧). The error messages are classified by the computer; examples of such errors are the syntax errors, the domain errors, length errors, and so on. A complete list of these error messages is given in Appendix 1.

Once all mistakes have been corrected the program will generally begin to produce answers. Our joy at receiving results may be shortlived if we find the answers make no sense. In this case we have probably made an error in the logic of the program. For example, perhaps we are inadvertently calculating the sum of two variables instead of their ratio, or are using

an incorrect formula in our financial model. Clearly, logical
errors are more difficult to detect than language errors. A
more systematic approach must be taken to isolate them and
test the program so that we can be reasonably sure that it is
free of bugs.

One useful procedure is to run the program with test data
for which we know the answers. If the computer answers for the
test do not agree with the known answers, we may wish to display intermediate results at a number of key points in the program. The trace and stop controls are useful for this purpose.
In this context it is important to realize that complex and
very lengthy instructions are difficult to debug even with the
aid of the trace control, since the trace does not display intermediate results.

Once the logical errors have been corrected and the program
yields the correct answers for the test cases, we are ready to
make a run with the actual data. If you are using a large
amount of data as is true in almost all business data processing, your program itself should check for the reasonableness
of the data. Don't let an age of 550 years instead of 55 slip
by, or the weekly hours worked be 95 instead of 45 hours. A
data validity check built into the program will help detect
such errors and avoid erroneous results.

The process of debugging lengthy programs is eased somewhat
if variable names suggest their meaning and if comments are
inserted at key points to describe the execution of your
program. Also, a well-organized program that calculates the
quantities of interest in an orderly sequential fashion will be
easier to debug. In any case, you should recognize that
logical errors are inescapable in computer programming. We
must, however, attempt to minimize their occurrence and write
our programs in such a way as to make the debugging process as
straightforward as possible.

As an example of the debugging process, let's consider the
program *STATISTICS*, which takes a numerical vector as its argument and calculates some simple statistics.

```
      ∇STATISTICS[□]∇
    ∇ STATISTICS VECT
[1]   A**DETERMINE THE NUMBER OF ELEMENTS
[2]    'NUMBER OF ELEMENTS: ';N←+/0×VEC+1
[3]   A**CALCULATE MEAN
[4]    'MEAN: ';MEAN←(+/VEC)÷N
[5]   A**CALCULATE STANDARD DEVIATION
[6]    STDV←+/(VEC-MEAN*2)
[7]    'STDV; ':STDV←(STDV÷N)*0.5
[8]   A**CALCULATE MAX, MIN AND RANGE
[9]    'MAX: ';⌈VEC
[10]   'MIN: ';⌊VEC
[11]   'RANGE:' RANGE←MAX-MIN
    ∇
```

Line [2] in the program determines the number of elements in the input vector. This is done by multiplying each element in the input by zero and then adding one. The resulting vector will have a one for each element. The plus reduction adds these ones together to give the number of elements. This is then used to calculate the mean and standard deviation of the values. The maximum and minimum values, and the range of values are also calculated.

To generate some test data with which to check the program, we run through a calculation using the values 1, 2, and 3.

```
     MEAN←+/1 2 3
     MEAN←MEAN÷3
     MEAN
2
```

The standard deviation is obtained by first computing the difference between the input values and the mean.

```
     STDV←1 2 3-MEAN
```

We then square the differences and add them together

```
     STDV←+/STDV*2
```

Finally we divide by the number of elements present and take the square root.

```
     STDV←STDV÷3
     STDV*.5
0.8164965809
```

Clearly, the maximum value for this set of data is 3, the minimum is 1, and the range is 2.

There are a number of errors present in the program *STATISTICS*; in fact, more than you might normally expect to find in such a short program. They are, however, typical of the types of errors most frequently made. See how many you can detect before continuing.

To test the program we try to execute it using simple trial data, a vector of three 1's. In this case we expect the mean, the maximum, and the minimum to be one and the standard deviation and range to be zero.

```
     STATISTICS 1 1 1
VALUE ERROR
STATISTICS[2] 'NUMBER OF ELEMENTS: ';N←+/0×VEC+1
                                           ∧
```

We immediately get an error and a surprising one at that. Since the error suspends the execution of the function,

```
     )SI
STATISTICS[2] *
```

we can attempt to look at the local variable *VEC*, which seems
to be causing the trouble.

```
        VEC
VALUE ERROR
        VEC
        ∧
```

That is where the problem is, but why? Sometimes when
debugging a program you really have to be a detective, and it
might take a while to realize that the trouble here is in the
header.

```
        ∇STATISTICS[0□]
[0]     STATISTICS VECT
[0]
```

The argument is written as *VECT*, with a *T*, while throughout
the program *VEC* is used.

   This is corrected by retyping the header as

```
[0]     STATISTICS VEC∇
SI DAMAGE
```

The ∇ puts us back in the execution mode. To see what the
message *SI DAMAGE* means, we display the state indicator:

```
     )SI
     *
     →
```

The name of the program no longer appears. Whenever a change
is made to the header of a suspended function, the suspension
information is destroyed. We completely remove the suspension
by typing the right arrow.

   We are now ready to try the program again.

```
     STATISTICS 1 1 1
NUMBER OF ELEMENTS: 0
DOMAIN ERROR
STATISTICS[4] 'MEAN: ';MEAN←(+/VEC)÷N
                              ∧
```

The computer has detected another error. The only candidate
for the error here is *N*.

```
     N
0
```

The error results from an attempt to divide by zero. We could
also have detected this error from the first line of the output, which indicates no elements present when it should show
3. The error arises when we calculate *N* in line [2]. The
error and its correction are shown below.

```
        ∇STATISTICS[2□40]
[2]     'NUMBER OF ELEMENTS: ';N←+/0×VEC+1
                                  2     //
[2]     'NUMBER OF ELEMENTS: ';N←+/1+0×VEC
[3]     ∇
```

The problem was one that occurs frequently: the incorrect
use of the right-to-left rule. Instead of multiplying by zero
and then adding one, the expression actually first adds 1 and
then multiplies by zero. The corrections are made by editing
line [2].

The function is now suspended at line [4].

```
        )SI
STATISTICS[4] *
```

We could exit from the suspension and start again but a more
direct procedure is to use the right arrow to begin at line
[1].

```
        →1
NUMBER OF ELEMENTS: 3
MEAN: 1
SYNTAX ERROR
STATISTICS[7] 'STDV; ':STDV←(STDV÷N)*0.5
                    ∧
```

The number of elements and the mean are now computed
correctly. Line [7] contains a typing error. The colon should
be inside the parentheses and the semicolon outside.

```
        ∇STATISTICS[7□10]
[7]     'STDV; ':STDV←(STDV÷N)*0.5
             /1 /1
[7]     'STDV: ';STDV←(STDV÷N)*0.5
[8]     ∇
```

While the program is suspended at line [7], we may as well
check that STDV is being calculated correctly thus far.

```
        STDV
0
```

It is.

Now that the error in line [7] has been corrected, we can
use the right arrow to direct the program to resume execution
at that line without starting all over from line [1]. This
ability to correct a program at the point of an error and then
to continue execution from that point is very handy, particularly when correcting errors near the end of a long program.

```
       →7
STDV: 0
MAX: 1 1 1
MIN: 1 1 1
VALUE ERROR
STATISTICS[11] 'RANGE:' RANGE←MAX-MIN
                              ∧
```

The system has detected another error. This time it indicates that the value of *MIN* is undefined. We can check this
for ourselves.

```
       MIN
VALUE ERROR
       MIN
       ∧
```

Actually, if we had been watching the output as it was displayed during the execution of the program, we would have
detected an error as soon as the results for *MAX* were displayed. Here we obtain a vector when we expected only one value.
If we check the value of *MAX* we find

```
       MAX
VALUE ERROR
       MAX
       ∧
```

and *MAX* is not defined either.

To see what has happened, we display the parts of the program that calculate the maximum and minimum. The editing code
[□8] displays *STATISTICS* from line [8] to the end.

```
       ∇STATISTICS[□8]
[8]    ⍝**CALCULATE MAX, MIN AND RANGE
[9]    'MAX: ';⌈VEC
[10]   'MIN: ';⌊VEC
[11]   'RANGE:' RANGE←MAX-MIN
[11]
```

Inspection reveals that there are two errors. First we
forgot the slash for calculating the max and min reductions;
thus lines [9] and [10] apply the ceiling and floor functions
to *VEC* rather than extracting the maximum and minimum values.
This explains why the results are vectors. Second, although
we display the results of lines [9] and [10] and label them
correctly, we forgot to store them in the variables *MAX* and
MIN.

Note that there were two errors present here. It would have
been very easy, and very tempting, after finding one of them to
immediately correct it and then try to run the program again.
When you detect an error in the results of a program and then
find a mistake in the program, you should always verify that
the mistake in the program would in fact cause the erroneous
results. If not, or if it would produce only part of the errors,
then there are other bugs to be found.

___

We correct the errors we have located by replacing lines
[9] and [10].

```
[11]   [9]'MAX: ';MAX←⌈/VEC
[10]   'MIN: ';MIN←⌊/VEC∇
```

The program is still suspended.

```
      )SI
STATISTICS[11] *
```

Everything seems alright in the program prior to the calculation of *MAX*, so we restart execution at that point.

```
      →9
MAX: 1
MIN: 1
SYNTAX ERROR
STATISTICS[11] 'RANGE:' RANGE←MAX-MIN
                        ∧
```

The maximum and minimum values are computed correctly but
we forgot the semicolon for displaying *RANGE*.

```
      ∇STATISTICS[11□5]
[11]   'RANGE;' RANGE←MAX-MIN
              1
[11]   'RANGE:'; RANGE←MAX-MIN
[12]   ∇
```

It was not really necessary to insert a blank in front of
RANGE since there was one there already. The advantage of
doing so is that the system automatically positions the type
ball for the correction. Line [11] should work correctly now.

```
      →11
RANGE:0
```

All statements in the program have executed correctly.
Let's try the entire program again.

```
      STATISTICS 1 1 1
NUMBER OF ELEMENTS: 3
MEAN: 1
STDV: 0
MAX: 1
MIN: 1
RANGE:0
```

The results are correct; however, there is a slight inconsist-
ency in the form of the output. For all displays except *RANGE*
a blank is present between the colon and the first displayed
digit. It is a simple matter to insert the necessary blank.

```
        ∇STATISTICS
[12]    [11□10]
[11]    'RANGE:';RANGE←MAX-MIN
             1
[11]    'RANGE: ';RANGE←MAX-MIN
[12]    ∇
```

Errors associated with the arrangement of output displays
are most easily detected after a program has been run. In
fact, it is often difficult to visualize the best output form
ahead of time. For example, in this program it might be better
to align the output by inserting extra spaces in the lines displaying *MAX* and *MIN*. So don't spend excessive amounts of time
planning the exact form of your output since you are likely to
change it anyway. As a general rule, first get the program to
work, and then make the output look pretty.

At this point the program seems to be free from syntax
errors, but we still cannot be sure it is correct since the
input data we have used thus far is very simple. Another
simple set of input data seems to work well also.

```
        STATISTICS 0 0 0
NUMBER OF ELEMENTS: 3
MEAN: 0
STDV: 0
MAX: 0
MIN: 0
RANGE: 0
```

For the next test we use the vector 1 2 3 as input. Recall
that we did hand calculations for this example. We expect a
mean of 2, a standard deviation of about 0.816, and a max, min,
and range of 3, 1, and 2 respectively.

```
        STATISTICS 1 2 3
NUMBER OF ELEMENTS: 3
MEAN: 2
DOMAIN ERROR
STATISTICS[7] 'STDV: ';STDV←(STDV÷N)*0.5
                  ∧
```

The new data have located a problem that was not detected in
previous runs. To determine the cause of the error, we display
the variables in question.

```
        STDV
⁻6
        N
3
```

STDV is negative and the *DOMAIN ERROR* arises because we are
trying to take the square root of a negative number. A negative value for *STDV* should never occur here, since at this
point in the program *STDV* is supposed to be the sum of the
squares of differences between *VEC* and *MEAN*. To investigate
the difficulty we must check line [6] which represents the first
step in calculating *STDV*.

```
        ∇STATISTICS[6□]
[6]     STDV←+/(VEC-MEAN*2)
[6]
```

By inspection we note that the right-most parenthesis is out
of order, so that only *MEAN* is being squared and the result is
then subtracted from *VEC*.

```
[6]     [6□20]
[6]     STDV←+/(VEC-MEAN*2)
                        1 /
[6]     STDV←+/(VEC-MEAN)*2
[7]     ∇
```

Note that although the error here was detected in line [7],
the mistake in the program actually occurred prior to this
point in line [6].

   We execute the program again.

```
        STATISTICS 1 2 3
NUMBER OF ELEMENTS: 3
MEAN: 2
STDV: 0.8164965809
MAX: 3
MIN: 1
RANGE: 2
```

Everything looks all right. *STDV* agrees with the value we calculated by hand before. As another test we run the program
with negative numbers.

```
        STATISTICS ¯1 ¯2 ¯3
NUMBER OF ELEMENTS: 3
MEAN: ¯2
STDV: 0.8164965809
MAX: ¯1
MIN: ¯3
RANGE: 2
```

Once again, everything looks fine. The final correct version
of program *STATISTICS* is:

```
        ∇STATISTICS[□]∇
      ∇ STATISTICS VEC
[1]    ⍝**DETERMINE THE NUMBER OF ELEMENTS
[2]     'NUMBER OF ELEMENTS: ';N←+/1+0×VEC
[3]    ⍝**CALCULATE MEAN
[4]     'MEAN: ';MEAN←(+/VEC)÷N
[5]    ⍝**CALCULATE STANDARD DEVIATION
[6]     STDV←+/(VEC-MEAN)*2
[7]     'STDV: ';STDV←(STDV÷N)*0.5
[8]    ⍝**CALCULATE MAX, MIN AND RANGE
[9]     'MAX: ';MAX←⌈/VEC
[10]    'MIN: ';MIN←⌊/VEC
[11]    'RANGE: ';RANGE←MAX-MIN
      ∇
```

4.10   WORKSPACE MANAGEMENT

While we have learned how to store instructions in programs,
we have not indicated how these programs can be saved for
future use. If we sign off the terminal, any programs we may
have written are lost. This inconvenience is resolved in APL
systems by providing the means for saving programs on the computer's auxiliary storage facilities, thus preserving them.

The basic organizational unit of most APL systems is the
workspace. A workspace can be thought of as a portion of
memory where programs, data, and system information are
stored. All communications with the computer are carried out
utilizing the *active workspace*. After all entries have been
made into the active workspace, a user may, if desired,
instruct the computer to save the contents of the workspace.
The saved workspace is identified by a name chosen by the user
and the entire or partial contents of a saved workspace may
later be retrieved and used in the active workspace.

Saved workspaces are stored in *libraries*. The workspaces
in the user's *private library* are associated with the user's
sign-on number. In addition to their private libraries, users
have access to *public libraries*. The programs and functions
contained within these libraries are of general interest to
users. These libraries may contain all purpose programs for
inventory control, solution of mathematical equations, graphical display of data, text editing, and so on.

In this section we discuss the systems commands used to
manipulate workspaces. We begin by first signing on at the
terminal.

```
)2555411:SHIRLEY
121) 14.54.16 05/24/75 EAHARMS

    APL*PLUS SERVICE
```

When we are signed on, the computer assigns us a *clear*
active workspace. The system command)*WSID* (WorkSpace
IDentification) displays the name of the active workspace

```
    )WSID
CLEAR WS
```

A clear workspace contains no functions or variables

```
    )FNS
    )VARS
```

We first enter some functions and variables into the active
workspace.

```
BOXES←'□▣▩'
ARROWS←'↑↓←→↡↟'

    ∇Z←X PLUS Y
[1]   Z←X+Y∇
```

```
        ∇Z←THREE
[1]     Z←3∇


        )FNS
PLUS    THREE
        )VARS
ARROWS  BOXES
```

The system command)*SAVE* allows us to save the contents of the active workspace for future use. To be able to retrieve the workspace we must give it a name. In this case we name the workspace *ONE*

```
        )SAVE ONE
   15.03.20 05/24/75
```

This command causes a copy of the current active workspace to be stored on disk under the name *ONE*.

To verify that the contents of our workspace have indeed been saved, we clear the active workspace and retrieve the contents of workspace *ONE* into the now clear active workspace. The system command)*CLEAR* erases the contents of the active workspace.

```
        )CLEAR
CLEAR WS
        )WSID
CLEAR WS
        )FNS
        )VARS
```

The contents of workspace *ONE* are retrieved using the)*LOAD* command

```
        )LOAD ONE
SAVED  15.03.20 05/24/75
```

The active workspace now contains a *duplicate* of workspace *ONE*

```
        )WSID
ONE
        )FNS
PLUS    THREE
        )VARS
ARROWS  BOXES
```

The original copy of the workspace is still retained on disk.

At this point we can add new functions and variables to the workspace, for example

```
        ∇Z←FIVE
[1]     Z←5∇


        EIGHT←FIVE PLUS THREE
        EIGHT
8
```

```
        )FNS
FIVE    PLUS    THREE
        )VARS
ARROWS  BOXES   EIGHT
```

This new version of workspace *ONE* is now saved

```
        )SAVE
   15.06.36 05/24/75 ONE
```

This action replaces the old version of *ONE* on disk by the new version. Locking a workspace will prevent other users from accessing its contents. We apply a lock to the workspace by adding to the)*SAVE* command a colon followed by a password

```
        )SAVE ONE:TOBY
   15.07.13 05/24/75
```

Workspace *ONE* is now locked and can only be accessed knowing the password *TOBY*

```
        )LOAD ONE
WS LOCKED
```

To access a locked workspace we add a colon and the password to the normal)*LOAD* command

```
        )LOAD ONE:TOBY
SAVED   15.07.13 05/24/75
        )WSID
ONE
```

A user will normally have more than one saved workspace. The collection of all workspaces saved by the user form a personal library. The names of the workspaces contained within the library are displayed by the command)*LIB*

```
        )LIB
APL
CONTINUE
ONE
```

At this point, let us increase our library by saving the contents of the active workspace as a new workspace called *TWO*.

```
        )SAVE TWO
   15.08.27 05/24/75
        )LIB
APL
CONTINUE
ONE
TWO
```

The new workspace *TWO* has been added to the library and now forms the active workspace.

```
        )WSID
TWO
```

Another important system command for manipulating the contents of workspaces is the)COPY command. The workspace APL in the library contains several functions that appeared previously in the book. We use the)COPY command to place a copy of the function CONVERT from workspace APL into the active workspace.

```
     )COPY APL CONVERT
SAVED  17.10.06 05/21/75
     )FNS
CONVERT FIVE     PLUS THREE
```

A copy of the function CONVERT has been added to the active workspace.

We add the contents of the active workspace to our library as workspace THREE.

```
     )SAVE THREE
  15.12.01 05/24/75
     )LIB
APL
CONTINUE
ONE
THREE
TWO
```

The)DROP command deletes a workspace from the library:

```
     )DROP ONE
  15.12.34 05/24/75
     )LIB
APL
CONTINUE
THREE
TWO
```

Workspace ONE has been dropped and cannot be loaded:

```
     )LOAD ONE
WS NOT FOUND
```

Another workspace in our library is CONTINUE. This workspace provides protection against accidental interruption of the terminal-computer connection. In the event of such an interruption the computer will place a replica of the active workspace prior to the interruption into the CONTINUE workspace. When the connection is reestablished, the CONTINUE workspace is automatically placed into the active workspace.

To demonstrate this feature we first drop CONTINUE from the library.

```
     )DROP CONTINUE
  15.13.58 05/24/75
     )LIB
APL
THREE
TWO
```

We next define a new function in the active workspace.

```
     ∇Z←X MINUS Y
[1]   Z←X-Y∇
```

Before saving the active workspace and before signing off, we interrupt the connection.

COMMENTS

    ÷∩*KJDX*   We remove the phone from the acoustic coupler producing a spurious display.

Although it is not evident to the user, the computer has stored the current contents of the active workspace in workspace *CONTINUE*. To see this we reestablish connection and sign on:

```
)2555411:SHIRLEY
146) 15.19.07 05/24/75 EAHARMS

  APL*PLUS SERVICE

SAVED 15.18.26 05/24/75
```

After sign-on the computer automatically loads a copy of the *CONTINUE* workspace into the active workspace. The last line of the sign-on dialogue specifies the date and time at which the connection was broken.

COMMENTS

```
     )WSID               CONTINUE is in the active workspace.
CONTINUE
     )LIB                CONTINUE is back in the library.
APL
CONTINUE
THREE
TWO
     )FNS
CONVERT FIVE   MINUS    PLUS    THREE
```

The *CONTINUE* feature has saved the function *MINUS*. If it was our intention, prior to the disconnection, to modify workspace *THREE*, we can attempt it at this point.

```
     )SAVE THREE
NOT SAVED, THIS WS IS CONTINUE
```

Since *THREE* is already a workspace, the system refuses to execute the *SAVE*. This protects us from inadvertently destroying a workspace.

To save the active workspace, we must first change its name from *CONTINUE* to *THREE*. This can be done using a modified form of the *WSID* command.

```
      )WSID THREE
WAS CONTINUE
      )SAVE
   15.28.12 05/24/75 THREE
```

The commands for accessing public libraries differ slightly from those for private libraries in that in accessing a public library a library number must be used.

```
      )LIB 1
ADVANCEDEX
APLCOURSE
CLASS
FILEAID
FILES
FORMAT
NEWS
TYPEDRILL
WSFNS
```

The contents of some of these workspaces is suggested by their titles. To find out more detail about the contents, we load one into the active workspace.

```
      )LOAD 1 TYPEDRILL
SAVED 9.43.56 01/10/71
```

We can list its contents using the)FNS and)VARS commands. Before doing this we set the width of the typed page.

```
      )WIDTH 65
WAS 120
```

The)WIDTH command is another system command.

```
      )FNS
DESCRIBE          IN       INSTRUCTIONS    MATCH     PRT     QUERY
STATISTICS        TIME     TYPEDRILL
```

By convention if there is a function or variable in the workspace with the name DESCRIBE or HOW, executing this function will give descriptive information on the contents of the workspace.

```
      DESCRIBE
```

THE MAIN FUNCTION IN THIS WORKSPACE IS TYPEDRILL; ALL OTHERS ARE SUBFUNCTIONS. TO USE IT, SIMPLY ENTER

```
      TYPEDRILL
```

TYPEDRILL IS A TIMED TYPING EXERCISE.   THE SYSTEM RESPONDS WITH THE STATEMENT 'YOU ARE IN CONTROL STATE'. FOUR COMMANDS ARE AT YOUR DISPOSAL: ENTER, DRILL, STAT, AND STOP. ENTERING ONE OF THEM BRINGS YOU INTO THAT STATE:

*ENTER: YOU   MAY   ENTER   ONE-LINE SENTENCES   OR
EXPRESSIONS ON WHICH YOU WISH TO BE DRILLED. ENTERING
A BLANK LINE (CARRIAGE RETURN ONLY) RETURNS YOU TO THE
CONTROL STATE.*

*DRILL: ONE OF THE LINES ENTERED VIA THE ENTER STATE IS
SELECTED AT RANDOM AND PRINTED. YOU ARE THEN EXPECTED
TO ENTER THE SAME LINE.   IF IT IS CORRECT, THE TIME
TAKEN IS PRINTED (IN SECONDS), IF NOT YOU ARE ASKED TO
RETYPE IT. A BLANK LINE CAUSES RETURN TO THE CONTROL
STATE.*

*STAT: THE   ACCUMULATED STATISTICS ARE PRINTED. THE
HORIZONTAL AXIS SHOWS THE   TRIAL   NUMBERS AND   THE
VERTICAL SHOWS THE TIME IN SECONDS. A VERTICAL ARROW
INDICATES   THAT THE   TIME EXCEEDED THE LIMITS OF THE
GRAPH. THE RETURN TO THE CONTROL STATE IS AUTOMATIC.*

STOP: STOPS THE DRILL AND PRINTS THE STATISTICS.

A complete table of system commands is given in Appendix 2.

EXERCISES

1. Consider the following functions:

```
      ∇ F1                          ∇ F4 A
[1]     C←2×B←2+A             [1]     C←2×B←2+A
      ∇                             ∇


      ∇ C←F2                        ∇ C←F5 A
[1]     C←2×B←2+A             [1]     C←2×B←2+A
      ∇                             ∇


      ∇ C←F3;B                      ∇ C←F6 A;B
[1]     C←2×B←2+A             [1]     C←2×B←2+A
      ∇                             ∇
```

Fill in the following table:

Instruction	Anticipated Display	Display
a.)ERASE A B C		
A←3		
F1		
A		
B		
C		
b.)ERASE A B C		
A←3		
F2		
A		
B		
C		

	Instruction	Anticipated Display	Display

c.)ERASE A B C
    A←3
    F3
    A
    B
    C

d.)ERASE A B C
    A←3
    F4 2
    A
    B
    C

e.)ERASE A B C
    A←3
    F5 2
    A
    B
    C

f.)ERASE A B C
    A←3
    F6 2
    A
    B
    C

2. Consider the following headers:

a. Z←S C
b. A D B
c. R;T
d. D←L P R;A;B;C
e. K←TCM X
f. Z2←FL3

Fill in the following table:

Program or Function Name	Dyadic, Monadic, or Niladic	Returns Explicit Result (Yes or No)	List of Local Variables
a.			
b.			
c.			
d.			
e.			
f.			

3. Consider the following APL function Q.

```
     ∇ Z←P Q R;S
[1]    Z←P+T
[2]    S←P×R
[3]    U←Z*2
     ∇
```

a. What are the argument variables?
b. What variables are local to this function?
c. Assuming we have made the assignment $R← S←T←U←5$ prior to execution of the function, which of the following represent valid usage of the function. (All other variables are undefined.)

   i. 3 Q 2
  ii. Q 3 2
 iii. 1 Q 3 2
  iv. 3 2 Q 1
   v. 3 2 Q
  vi. P Q R
 vii. P Q $R;S$

d. Using the *first* valid execution from c., what will be the result returned by the function?

e. What will be the result of the following displays?

   Z S

   P T

   R U

4. Consider the function A

```
     ∇ Y←A X;Z
[1]    Y←2+X
[2]    Z←Y+3
[3]    Y←Y+W
     ∇
```

Give the displays generated by the following sequence of instructions.

```
W←X←Y←Z←10
A 5
W
X
Y
Z
```

5. Consider the two groups of functions:

Group 1	Group 2
∇ $Z \leftarrow A1 \ X$	∇ $Z \leftarrow A2 \ X$
[1] $Z \leftarrow X \times Y$	[1] $Z \leftarrow X \times Y$
∇	∇
∇ $Z \leftarrow B1 \ Y$	∇ $Z \leftarrow B2 \ W$
[1] $Z \leftarrow A1 \ Y$	[1] $Z \leftarrow A2 \ W$
∇	∇

Explain the results obtained from the following executions:

```
        Y←7                          Y←7
        B1 2                         B2 2
```

(Note that the only difference between the sets is the choice of function names and the variable name for the arguments in B1 and B2.)

6. a. Create a monadic function *COST* that takes as its argument a vector *SALES* containing the cost of items purchased and returns a result which is the total price of the objects purchased.

    b. Convert the function *COST* into a dyadic function that takes as its left argument the sales tax rate to be applied to the vector *SALES*. The result returned by the function should now be the total cost including sales tax.

7. Create a niladic function, *CONSTANT*, which returns as its result the square root of two.

8. a. Write a monadic function *WAGES* that takes as its right argument a vector of hours worked. The function should return the total wages paid assuming a pay rate of $6 per hour.

    b. Modify *WAGES* so that it takes a left argument *RATE*, which is the rate of pay to be paid. Test the execution for the values.

    ```
    8 WAGES 40 45 35 50
    ```

    and

    ```
    6 6 7 8 WAGES 40 45 35 50
    ```

    c. Modify *WAGES* so that overtime is paid at a rate of 1.5 times regular pay for all hours over a base time period. The base period is contained in the global variable *BASE*. Test this function with the same execution as in part b. for *BASE*←35 and *BASE*←35 35 35 40.

9. a. Write a niladic program *QUOTEFORTHEDAY* that displays your favorite (lengthy) quotation. Each line in the display should be a separate line in the program. Use at least six lines of 60 characters or so each.

b. Use the line editing capability to insert additional
   blanks into each line so that the right-hand margin is
   even.

10. Charges for a taxi ride are 50 cents for the first tenth
    of a mile or fraction thereof and 20 cents for each addi-
    tional tenth or fraction. Write a program that takes as
    its argument the distance traveled as a decimal number and
    displays the distance traveled in miles and tenths and the
    fare to be paid. For example, for a trip of 3.37 miles the
    program should display

         TOTAL DISTANCE=3 AND 4 TENTHS MILES
         TOTAL FARE=7.1

    To help organize your thoughts, draw a flowchart outlining
    the steps necessary to perform the desired calculations.

11. a. The following program takes as its arguments the two
       sides of a right triangle and calculates the length of
       the hypotenuse, the perimeter, and the area of the
       triangle. The program contains a number of errors.
       Enter the program as shown here and then debug it using
       as test data a 3, 4, 5 right triangle and a 12, 5, 13
       right triangle.

```
        ∇ A RTΔ B
   [1]    'HYPOTENEUSE= ':C←(A*2+B*2)*0.5
   [2]    'PERIMETER= ';P→+/A B C
   [3]    'AREA= ';0.5 A×B
```

    b. Modify RTΔ so that variables P and C are local to the
       program.

12. The following function evaluates the cosine of x (x a
    scalar) by summing the first six terms in the series

$$\cos x = 1 - \frac{x^2}{2!} + \frac{x^4}{4!} - \frac{x^6}{6!} + \cdots$$

```
        ∇COS[□]∇
      ∇ Z←COS X;N
   [1]    N← 0 1 2 3 4 5
   [2]    N←2×N
   [3]    Z←X*N
   [4]    Z←Z÷!N
   [5]    Z←-/Z
      ∇
```

    a. Trace the execution of steps 2 through 5 using the
       trace control. Use X values of 0, .5, 1, 2, and 10.
    b. Remove the trace. Set the stop control so that !N can
       be displayed prior to executing line [4]. Make the
       display using any X value for input.
    c. How could you use the stop control to sum the first 10
       terms in the series? Do this for X equal to 2.

13. Execute the commands indicated and fill in the table.
    (You may find that your workspace quota limits the number
    of workspaces you may save.)

Commands	Anticipated Display	Display

Sign on to your system.

)WSID
)FNS
)VARS
)LIB
)SAVE NEW
)WSID

Define some functions and assign values to some
variables.

)SAVE
)FNS
)VARS
)SAVE NEWER
)LIB
)WSID

Define more functions and variables.

)SAVE SEVEN
)LOAD NEW
)FNS
)VARS

Copy some functions and variables from workspace *SEVEN*.

)SAVE OLD
)LIB
)LOAD NEW
)FNS
)VARS

Drop the workspaces created in this exercise.

14. a. Make a search of some of the public libraries on your
       system. Display the documentation contained in the
       different workspaces. List the workspaces you find
       that fall into the following classifications. (Give
       both library number and workspace name.)

       i. Workspace containing programming aids.
      ii. Workspaces containing plotting or other data
          display functions.
     iii. Workspaces containing APL learning aids.
    b. What other kinds of workspaces do you find?
    c. Take the workspace of greatest interest to you, read
       the documentation carefully, and use some of the
       functions contained in the workspace.

d. Workspaces often contain various auxiliary functions to help the user in preparing data or in specifying available options. Find an example of where this is done and describe how the functions are used.

e. One of the best ways to improve your programming ability is to study well written programs. Find some functions of interest to you and display their contents. You will not be able to understand all of the code until you have read the later chapters in this book, but you should be able to find some of interest to you.

15. Locate a public library workspace on your computer system containing an APL drill on the arithmetic functions discussed in Chapter 3. Use this drill to practice these functions.

SUPPLEMENTARY EXERCISES

1. What happens if, while in the definition mode, you enter [N□] where N is greater than the last statement number? Answer the same question for [□N], [N□M].

2. Explain the results of the following steps entered while in the *execution mode*. (Z is the name of a program with seven lines.)

   a. ∇Z   g. ∇

   b. ∇Z[□]   h. ∇Z[5□]

   c. ∇Z∇   i. ∇Z[3□10]

   d. ∇Z[□]∇   j. ∇Z[8□]

   e. ∇Z[0.1]   k. ∇Z[□0]

   f. ∇Z[0□]   l. ∇Z[7□8]

3. Explain the results of the following steps entered while in the *definition mode*. The function being defined has six lines.

   a. [□]   f. [5]∇

   b. [3]   g. [8]

   c. [4□]   h. [0□10]

   d. [3□10]∇   i. [0.1]

   e. ∇   j. [□2]∇

4. What happens if apostrophes are used in the input to quote-quad?

5. How would you input a character vector with a quad input?

6. In what case should quad be used for input? Quote-quad?

7. Consider the function *PLUS*.

```
    ∇ Z←X PLUS Y
[1]Z←X+Y
    ∇
```

What will be the results of the following instructions?

a. *PLUS* 1

b. 3 *PLUS* ¯1 *PLUS* 7

c. *PLUS*

d. 1 *PLUS* '1'

e. *PLUS*←|¯1

f. 3 4 *PLUS* 8 9

g. 1 2 3 *PLUS* 4 5

8. Write a monadic function to compute the current I drawn when a resistance R is placed across a voltage of 120 volts ($I=120÷R$).

9. Write programs which will convert linear measures in the metric system (meters and centimeters only) to equivalent measures in the English system (feet and inches only). (1 in. = 2.54 cm) Write these programs in dyadic, monadic, and niladic form. For the dyadic form make the arguments the length in meters and the length in centimeters. For the monadic function put the meters and centimeters in a two element vector. For the niladic program obtain the data from the keyboard.

10. Write a dyadic function that will convert monetary measures in pounds, shillings, and pence to dollars. There are 12 pennies to the shilling, 20 shillings to a pound. (You can find the relationship between dollars and pounds in your newspaper, or get the information from a bank.) The arguments to the function should be the exchange rate of pounds to dollars and a three element vector containing the value in the British currency.

11. Write a dyadic function to calculate a baseball player's batting average. The average is given by 1000 × (number of hits ÷ number of times at bat.) Round results to the nearest integer.

12. Write a monadic function to calculate the quantity:

$$E = (1+\frac{1}{N})^N$$

using N as an argument and returning E as the result. Show
that as N gets large, E approaches the base of the natural
logarithms, e, which can be obtained from *1.

13. Write a monadic function to convert temperature in degrees
Fahrenheit to temperature in degrees Centigrade.

$$T(°C) = (5÷9)×(T(°F)-32)$$

14. Assume that water leaks out of a vessel according to the
following orifice relation:

$$Q = A×\sqrt{H}$$

where Q is the flowrate of the leaking water in cubic
feet per second, A is a given constant, and H is the
height of the water level above the leak in feet. Write
a dyadic function that accepts A and H as arguments and
returns the flowrate as its explicit result. Investigate
these questions:

a. What must H be, if Q is to exceed 12 cu ft per sec?
   Let A = 0.1.
b. If H = 1, 5, 10 ft, find Q for A = 0.5.

15. A couple figures tips at restaurants as follows. They
will never leave less than a quarter. Providing it comes
to more than 25 cents, their normal tip is determined by
taking 15 percent of the bill before taxes and rounding
upward to the next half dollar. They give this as a tip
unless it is more than 20 percent in which case they give
20 percent, dropping any fractional cents. Give an APL
program which takes as its right argument the total amount
of the bill, as its left argument the amount of tax included in the bill. The program should display the amount
of tip to be left and the total amount paid along with
appropriate explanatory messages.
      Break the computation up into several steps and insert
comments into the program to explain the calculations.
Prepare some sample examples by hand and use the trace and
stop controls to insure each step is operating correctly.
Be sure that the sample data sets used handle all different ways of calculating the bill.

16. An object is tossed upwards with an initial velocity V.
It is subject to a constant acceleration A. The position
S of the object at any time T is given by the formula
(normal notation):

$$S = (V×T)+\tfrac{1}{2}AT^2$$

a. Write a program to compute the position of an object
   at any time T given V and A. What alternatives are
   available for inputting the necessary information?
b. Let A be the gravitational acceleration (-9.8 m/sec^2)
   and let V assume values of 10, 20, and 30 m/sec.
   Determine S after 1, 2 and 3 sec. Output the results
   in a neatly labeled format.

c. A stone is dropped from a bridge. If it takes 2 sec for the stone to hit the water, how high is the bridge? ($A = 9.8$ m/sec^2)

17. a. The ABC Company produces toys. It costs $10,000 to run the plant independent of how many toys are produced. It costs $10 in labor and materials to produce each toy up to 2000 units. For all units over 2000 it costs $12 per unit. Write a function *COST* that takes as its argument the number of units produced and returns as its result the total cost to produce these units, including the fixed $10,000 cost. (Sample data-1000 units cost $20,000, 3000 units cost $42,000.)

   b. Write a second function *PROFIT* that takes as its left argument the number of units sold, as its right argument the price at which each unit is sold, and returns a result which is the total profit made on the sales. Total profit is defined here as sales revenues, number of units sold times their price, minus the cost of producing these units. The cost should be calculated using the function *COST* of a. (Sample data for sales of 5000 units and prices of $10, $12, and $15, the profit (or loss) is ‾16000 ‾6000 9000 dollars.)

   c. The following are sales projections for the toys manufactured by the ABC Company.

Price	Projected Sales (Units)
15	5000
16	4800
17	4500
18	4000
19	3500
20	3000
21	2500
22	2000

   Which price is optimum in the sense that it maximizes profits?

18. Write a conversational program that will determine the per mile cost of car ownership. Examples of information that should be requested are

   a. Cost of car, the number of miles to be driven before reselling the car, and the estimated resale value. The contribution to the per mile cost is obtained by taking the difference between the purchase price and the resale price and dividing by the number of miles.

   b. The cost of a tuneup and the number of miles driven between tuneups. The contribution to the cost per mile is the cost of a tuneup divided by the number of miles driven between tuneups. (Similar information is needed for other periodic maintenance costs.)

   c. The cost of a gallon of gas and the estimated number of miles per gallon.

   d. Yearly costs such as insurance or property taxes and the number of miles driven per year.

The information should be requested with the appropriate
prompting messages. A final report should be displayed
giving individual per mile costs and the total. Organize
your output neatly.

19. Consider the following program:

∇ $P;A;B;C;\ldots;X$

```
[1]     Input and calculations
 .          performed here.
 .
[ ]
[13]    'ADJUST THE PAPER AND PRESS RETURN'
[14]    X←⎕
[ ]
 .          Long display of results produced here.
 .
[ ]
    ∇
```

Input of data and calculations are performed in the first
part of the program. The last section produces an extended display of results. What is the purpose of lines [13]
and [14]? Why is line [14] included?

20. Obtain a copy of the federal income tax forms. Write a
program that determines a person's income tax according
to the rules contained in these forms. For simplicity,
assume standard deductions and use rates appropriate to a
single person. The program should prompt the user to
enter the necessary information and calculate the users
tax and then display a report containing the input information, all intermediate results (for example, adjusted
gross income), amount of tax owed, and any additional
payment due or refund to be given. It may help you to organize your thoughts if you draw a flowchart for the
program before actually writing it.

Chapter 5
Logical Data

Current versions of APL usually allow for three different
types of data. Thus far we have encountered two of these,
numerical data and character data. The third type, *logical
data*, can have only two possible values, one or zero. The
value one signifies yes or true, and the value zero signifies
no or false. Logical data can take any of the various shapes
assumed by the other types of data. Thus a logical scalar
will be a single logical value either one or zero. We will
frequently be interested in logical vectors. These vectors
are comprised entirely of ones and zeros.

In many ways the logical data behave the same as the
integers one and zero. For example, they can be added to other
numerical data. On the other hand, because these two integers
have an additional meaning as logical variables, they have
properties of their own that are not possessed by other numerical data. In this chapter we consider some of these properties.

5.1 RELATIONAL FUNCTIONS

We have seen that the maximum and minimum functions enable us
to pick the larger and smaller of two numbers. In many instances, rather than knowing the value of the larger of two
numbers, we wish to answer the question of whether one number
is larger than another, or whether or not two numbers are
equal. For example, we may want a yes or no answer to such
questions as whether an account is overdrawn, a balance is
overdue, an exam grade is passing, or an error is within some
tolerance. The result desired here is a logical value, true
or false, yes or no.

To answer such questions, APL has available certain
relational functions, $<$, $\leq$, $=$, $\geq$, $>$, $\neq$. These symbols are
upper shift 3 through 8 on the keyboard and form a convenient
mnemonic sequence. These functions return a logical result,
1 or 0, depending on whether the relationship expressed is
true or false.

COMMENTS

	2.0=1.5	It is false that 2.0 equals 1.5.
0		
	2.0≠5	It is true that 2.0 is not equal to 5.
1		
	2.0=2.000	2 equals 2.
1		
	2.0≤2.5	2 is less than or equal to 2.5.
1		
	2.0>2.5	2 is not greater than 2.5.
0		

The arguments of these functions can also be variables or vectors. When used with a scalar and a vector these functions behave the same way as the arithmetic functions, the scalar being compared with *each* element in the vector. In the case of two vectors the arguments must have the same length.

```
      A←2
      B←1 2 3
      B=A
0 1 0
      B≤A
1 1 0
      B>A
0 0 1

      1 2 3≥2 4
LENGTH ERROR
      1 2 3 ≥ 2 4
          ∧
```

The = and ≠ functions can also have characters or character vectors for their arguments.

```
      'A'='CAT'
0 1 0
      'CAT'='RAT'
0 1 1
      'CAT'≠'RAT'
1 0 0
```

The relational functions (<, ≤, ≥, >) are not defined on character data.

```
      'A'<'B'
DOMAIN ERROR
      'A'<'B'
        ∧
```

The following examples illustrate the use of relational functions.

The vector *AGES* contains the ages of a group of people.

```
      AGES←10 66 17 18 17 27 46 35 65
```

We use the relational functions to extract information about
this group.

COMMENTS

```
     AGES<18
1 0 1 0 1 0 0 0 0                   Positions with a 1 indicate minors.
     +/AGES<18                       There are 3 minors.
3
     +/AGES≥65                       2 senior citizens.
2
```

In the above examples ones and zeros had two different
meanings. In the first example (*AGES*<18) they were used as
logical values to represent true or false. In the other
examples their numerical value was used in determining their
sum (+/*AGES*<18).

Relational operations can also be used to manipulate and
analyze a character vector.

```
     SENTENCE←'TO BE OR NOT TO BE'
     SENTENCE=' '
0 0 1 0 0 1 0 0 1 0 0 0 1 0 0 1 0 0
```

The ones indicate the position of the blanks in the character
vector *TO BE OR NOT TO BE*.

COMMENTS

```
     +/SENTENCE=' '                 There are five blanks.
5
     +/'E'=SENTENCE                 There are two E's in the character
2                                      vector.
```

5.2 COMPRESSION

In the previous section, we learned that the relational
functions produce logical values as their results and determined ways in which this logical information could be used.
Another function that uses logical values to extract useful
information is compression.

The general form of the compression function is

$$L/A$$

The left argument *L* is a logical scalar or a logical vector.
The right argument *A* can be of any shape, a scalar, a vector,
or a matrix. Compression as it relates to matrices is discussed in Chapter 8. The compression function selects those
elements in *A* that correspond to ones in *L*. Its use is
illustrated in the following examples.

We first consider the case where *L* and *A* are vectors.

```
L←1 0 1 1 0
A←1 2 3 4 5
L/A
1 3 4
```

The compression function selects those elements in *A* corresponding to 1's in *L*, in this case the 1st, 3rd, and 4th
elements of *A*. *A* may also be a character vector.

```
A←'ABCDE'
L/A
ACD
L/'TRICK'
TIC
```

When *L* and *A* are vectors they must have the same length or else
a *LENGTH ERROR* appears.

```
L/'WXYZ'
LENGTH ERROR
L/'WXYZ'
∧
```

The left argument, *L* may be a logical scalar. If *L* is 1, the
result of the compression will be the entire right argument.

COMMENTS

```
TIME←7
TIME>6
1                                    7 is larger than 6.
(TIME>6)/'I AM LATE'
I AM LATE                            The entire character vector is
                                        displayed.
```

If *L* is zero, the compression yields a blank line.

COMMENTS

```
TIME<6                               7 is not less than 6.
0
(TIME<6)/'I AM EARLY'


                                     A blank line is returned as the
                                        computer skips a line.
```

If the right argument, *A*, is a scalar the result will be a
vector made up entirely of *A*'s. The number of elements in the
result will be equal to the number of 1's in the left
argument.

```
1 0 1 1/'A'
AAA
1 0 0 1/'⊛'
⊛⊛
```

The compression function enables us to select desired elements from a vector. As an illustration we extract additional information about the ages of the group of people discussed in the previous section.

```
      AGES
10 66 17 18 17 27 46 35 65
      (AGES<18)/AGES
10 17 17
```

The logical vector *AGES*<18 compresses the numerical vector *AGES* to give the ages of all minors.

In the previous section we used the relational functions to determine which elements of *AGES* corresponded to minors and to count the number of minors. Combining the relational and compression functions, we select from *AGES* the elements corresponding to minors. Several additional examples will help illustrate the power of combining the relational and compression functions to manipulate data.

Example: Analyzing Account Balances

Customer balances at a department store are contained in the vector *ACCOUNT*.

```
      ACCOUNT← ̄33.27 0  ̄165 17.25
      RECVBLE←ACCOUNT<0
      RECVBLE
1 0 1 0
```

RECVBLE is a logical vector pointing to all accounts with an outstanding balance.

	COMMENTS
`    +/RECVBLE`	There are 2 such accounts.
`2`	
`    RECVBLE/ACCOUNT`	The balance in these accounts.
` ̄33.27  ̄165`	
`    +/RECVBLE/ACCOUNT`	Total accounts receivable.
` ̄198.27`	
`    +/0=ACCOUNT`	One account has a zero balance.
`1`	

Note the difference between the compression function and reduction operation. Although the form of these expressions is similar, compression compares a logical quantity with another vector while the reduction operation inserts a function between the elements of the vector and evaluates the resulting expression.

Compression is also useful for manipulating character data. Here we use it to extract blanks from a character vector.

```
        STRING←'MADAM IM ADAM'
        L←' '≠STRING
        L
1 1 1 1 1 0 1 1 0 1 1 1 1
        L/STRING
MADAMIMADAM
```

Example: Producing Variable Displays

Compression is often used in a program to produce appropriate displays. The program *SIGN* displays a character message giving the sign (positive, zero, or negative) of a number.

```
        ∇SIGN[□]∇
    ∇ SIGN X
[1]    (X>0)/'POSITIVE';(X=0)/'ZERO';(X<0)/'NEGATIVE'
    ∇

        SIGN 10
POSITIVE
        SIGN 0
ZERO
        SIGN ¯1
NEGATIVE
```

It is useful to give a pictorial representation of the operation of the compression function. If L and V are vectors and

$$R←L/V$$

we can think of L and V as being placed one above the other.

```
L        [1]   [1]   [0]   [1]   [0]   . . .   [1]   [0]
/         /     /     /     /     /             /     /
V        [A]   [B]   [C]   [D]   [E]   . . .   [Y]   [Z]
          |     |
R        [A]   [B]   [D]   . . .   [Y]
```

We then select out of V only those elements that are beneath a 1 in L. It is clear, then, why the length of L should equal the length of V. On the other hand, the length of R is equal to the number of 1's in L, that is $+/L$.

5.3 LOGICAL FUNCTIONS

Let's return to the group of people whose ages are given by the vector *AGES*.

```
        AGES
10 66 17 18 17 27 46 35 65
```

Suppose we want to find all those people who are either minors
or senior citizens. This can be done with the APL function *or*
which is symbolized by ∨ (upper shift 9). This function is a
dyadic function defined only for logical data. It gives the
result 1, true, if either of its arguments or both of them
are 1.

```
      1∨1
1
      1∨0
1
      0∨1
1
      0∨0
0
```

Its arguments can be vectors as well as scalars, providing that
if they are both vectors, they have the same length.

```
      1 1 0 0∨1 0 1 0
1 1 1 0
```

   Minors or senior citizens in our group are located with the
expression

```
      L←(AGES<18)∨AGES≥65
      L
1 1 1 0 1 0 0 0 1
```

which gives 1 if the age is greater than or equal to 65 or
less than 18.

In more detail:

                              COMMENTS

```
      AGES≥65
0 1 1 0 0 0 0 0 1          1's point to senior citizens.
      AGES<18
1 0 0 0 1 0 0 0 0          1's point to minors.
      (AGES<18)∨AGES≥65
1 1 1 0 1 0 0 0 1          1's point to minors or senior
                                    citizens.
      L/AGES
10 66 17 17 65
```

   Alternatively, those people 18 or older and younger than
65 can be determined using the *and* function, ∧ (upper shift 0).
This function gives 1 if both its arguments are 1 but gives 0
otherwise.

```
      1 1 0 0∧1 0 1 0
1 0 0 0
```

People between 18 and 65 are then located from

```
      L←(AGES≥18)∧AGES<65
      L
0 0 0 1 0 1 1 1 0
      L/AGES
18 27 46 35
```

There is a monadic logical function called *not*, ~ (upper shift *T*), which changes true to false and false to true.

```
      ~1 0
0 1
```

As with the other logical functions, *not* is defined only for logical data.

```
      ~3
DOMAIN ERROR
      ~3
      ∧
```

Table 5.1   Logical Functions

Logical Variables		AND	OR	NAND	NOR	NOT
A	*B*	*A*∧*B*	*A*∨*B*	*A*⍲*B*	*A*⍱*B*	~*A*
1	1	1	1	0	0	0
1	0	0	1	1	0	0
0	1	0	1	1	0	1
0	0	0	0	1	1	1

The relational and logical functions can be used as arguments of the reduction operation. The two most useful applications are the and-reduction and the or-reduction. Applied to a logical vector the and-reduction gives 1 if all of the elements in the vector are 1.

```
      ∧/1 1 1 1 1
1
      ∧/1 0 1 1 1
0
```

The or-reduction gives a 1 if any of the elements in the vector are 1.

```
      ∨/0 0 1 0 0 1
1
      ∨/0 0 0 0 0 0
0
```

Example: Comparing Two Vectors of the Same Length

> Two character vectors having the same number of elements are identical if all of their characters are identical. This can be checked using the function *COMPARE*.

```
    ∇COMPARE[□]∇
  ∇ Z←C1 COMPARE C2
[1]   Z←C1=C2
[2]   Z←∧/Z
  ∇
```

> *COMPARE* is a dyadic function. Its arguments are compared in line [1]. Line [2] uses the and-reduction to check if they are identical. Let's trace the execution of *COMPARE*.

	COMMENTS
`T∆COMPARE←1`	Trace line [1].
`'TWO' COMPARE 'TOO'`	Test with nonidentical arguments.
`COMPARE[1] 1 0 1`	They differ in the second character.
`0`	They are not identical
`'TOO' COMPARE 'TOO'`	
`COMPARE[1] 1 1 1`	
`1`	These vectors are identical.

> The and-reduction in line [2] gives 1 if all the elements of *Z* are 1. Otherwise it gives 0. The output of *COMPARE* is 1 if the vectors are identical and 0 if they differ.

> A *LENGTH ERROR* occurs if the input vectors do not have the same length.

	COMMENTS
`T∆COMPARE←0`	Trace is removed.
`'TWO' COMPARE 'TO'`	
`LENGTH ERROR`	
`COMPARE[1] Z←C1=C2`	
`        ∧`	
`)SI`	
`COMPARE[1] *`	One suspended function.
`→`	Remove the suspension.

Example: Analyzing Data

> The following vectors contain information about the percent growth of expenditures by the United States government. The five elements in each vector give growth rates for the periods 1960 to 1965, 1965 to 1970, 1970 to 1972, 1972 to 1973, and 1973 to 1974 respectively.

COMMENTS

EXP	Percent growth in total
5 9.9 8.2 6.1 8.5	expenditures.
REC	Percent growth in receipts.
4.6 9.9 3.7 10.4 13.3	
DEF	Percent growth in defense spending.
1.5 9.6 ¯1.2 ¯3 4.6	
INC	Percent growth in income security
6.7 10.1 19.4 13.3 14.5	programs.
EDUC	Education, manpower and social
14.2 23.2 19.4 1.7 ¯2.5	services.
INT	Percent growth in interest on debt.
4.5 11 5.9 10.1 20.8	

We can make some studies of these data.

COMMENTS

REC>EXP	Receipts grew faster than expendi-
0 0 0 1 1	tures only in the last two years.
DEF<0	The defense budget decreased from
0 0 1 1 0	1970 to 1973.
INT>REC	Interest expenses grew faster than
0 1 1 0 1	receipts in three of the five
	periods.
(EDUC<INT)∨INC<INT	One's indicate periods in which the
0 1 0 1 1	growth in interest expenses
	exceeds the growth in education
	expenditures or in income
	security expenditures.
INC≥DEF⌈EDUC⌈INT	Growth in income security expendi-
0 0 1 1 0	tures equaled or exceeded that
	in all other areas from 1970 to
	1973.

5.4 EXPANSION

The *expansion* function is a reverse of the compression
function. The general form is

$$R \leftarrow L/V$$

where L is a logical vector and V is any numerical or character vector. Expansion applied to matrices is discussed in
Chapter 8.

The result R is a vector of the same length as L. It is
formed by replacing the 1's in L with corresponding elements
taken from V. The 0's in L are replaced by blanks if V is a
character vector or 0's if V is a numerical vector. The
examples below illustrate the behavior of the expansion
function.

COMMENTS

```
        1 0 1 0 1\1 2 3          Zeros are inserted into the right
1 0 2 0 3                        argument.

        1 0 1 0 1\'ABC'          Blanks are inserted into the
A B C                            right argument.
```

The number of elements in the right argument must equal the
number of 1's in the logical vector.

```
        1 0 1 0 1\'ABCD'
LENGTH ERROR
        1 0 1 0 1 \'ABCD'
                ∧
```

The only exception to this is if the right argument is a
scalar, in which case it is repeated for each 1 in the logical
vector.

```
        1 0 1 1 0 1\'□'
□ □□ □
```

Example: Underlining a Heading

The following program employs the expansion function to display
a character vector and to underline the nonblank characters.

```
        ∇UNDERLINE[□]∇
    ∇ UNDERLINE X
[1]     X
[2]     (' '≠X)\'¯'
    ∇
```

Line [1] displays the input character vector. Line [2]
locates all nonblank characters and uses the expansion
function to create a character vector of blanks and negative
signs with the negative signs located in the position of the
nonblank characters. When displayed this underlines X. Here
is a sample execution.

```
        UNDERLINE 'THIS IS A HEADING'
THIS IS A HEADING
```

EXERCISES

Before executing the instructions shown, fill in what you
anticipate the display will be. Add an explanation for any
error you make.

Instruction	Anticipated Display	Display
1. a. 1 = 3		
b. 1 = 1 2 3		

	Instruction	Anticipated Display	Display
c.	1 ≠ 1 2 3		
d.	1 2 = 2 3		
e.	1 2 = 1 2 3		
f.	1 2 ≠ 2 3		
g.	1.1 > 2 1 ‾1		
h.	1.1 < 2 1 0		
i.	1 < 1.0		
j.	1 ≤ 1.0 2.0		
k.	2 ≥ ‾2		
l.	*'R' = 'RARE'*		
m.	*'FAR' = 'FIR'*		

2. a. 0 1 1 0 1/2 3 4 5 6

   b. *L←'ONE FOR THE MONEY'*
      L = ' '
   c. *+/' ' = L*

   d. *(' ' ≠ L)/L*

   e. *('E' = L)/L*

   f. *+/'E' = L*

3. Assume *A←*1 1 0 0 and *B←*1 0 1 0.

	Instruction	Anticipated Display	Display
a.	1∧*A*		
b.	1∨*B*		
c.	~*A*		
d.	~*A*∨*B*		
e.	*A*∧~*B*		
f.	~*A*≠*B*		

4. Enter the instruction +/*X*=*X* where *X* is a vector. What does the result represent?

5. Let $U \leftarrow 1\ 1\ 0\ 0$ and $V \leftarrow 1\ 0\ 1\ 0$. Compare the following with the logical functions of Table 5.1.

   a. $U = V$

   b. $U \neq V$

   c. $U < V$

   d. $U \leq V$

   e. $U \geq V$

   f. $U > V$

   g. $U \times V$

   h. $U \lfloor V$

   i. $U \lceil V$

6. Give an expression to find the sum of all the negative elements in a vector.

7. Give an expression that will determine if all grades in the vector G are passing.

8. Give APL expressions that given a numerical vector will:

   a. Extract all even numbers.
   b. Extract all numbers within the range 0 to 100.
   c. Extract all numbers with absolute value greater than 3.
   d. Extract all integers.

   Combine all these instructions into a monadic program that prints the results obtained and appropriate explanatory messages.

9. Team up with a partner and play the following game. One person assigns a value between 1 and 25 to the variable A using the roll function, $A \leftarrow ?25$. The other player then tries to determine the value of A by using any of the relational operations to compare A to other numbers. After he finds the value for A, the roles are reversed. The winner is the player requiring the fewest comparisons to guess A.

10. Write a program that will take as an input a character vector and display the following outputs:

   THERE ARE _ BLANKS IN THIS VECTOR

   inserting the number of blanks in place of _ or,

   THERE IS 1 BLANK IN THIS VECTOR

if there is only 1 blank. (HINT: what display will you get from *'BLANK';L/'S'* if *L* is 1? If *L* is 0?)

11. a. Write a function similar to *UNDERLINE* (as shown in this chapter) to locate all letters *E* in a character vector and place a ↑ beneath the *E*'s.
     b. Modify the function of a. to take a single character as its left argument and place a ↑ beneath this character wherever it appears in the right argument.

12. Let *C* be a character vector. Give a monadic function that returns as its explicit result a logical vector with ones for all vowels in *C* and zeros for all other characters. Use this function to:

     a. Determine the total number of vowels in *C*.
     b. Display *C* with all vowels removed.

13. Write a program to display any price, for example $2.95, as

          2 *DOLLARS AND* 95 *CENTS*

     However, a price of $3.00 should be displayed only as

          3 *DOLLARS*

     and a price of $0.75 should be displayed only as

          75 *CENTS*.

14. Consider the following dialogues. Stars (*) indicate information typed by the user.

     *   *L*
     WHAT IS YOUR NAME?
     **TOM*
     WHAT IS YOUR NUMBER?
     □:
     *   732
     SORRY TOM YOU LOSE

     *   *L*
     WHAT IS YOUR NAME?
     **ANN*
     WHAT IS YOUR NUMBER?
     □:
     *   563
     ANN YOU'RE A WINNER!

     Write a program *L* that will perform this dialogue. The winning number is contained in the global variable *N*. All other variables used by *L* should be made local to *L*.

15. Information about delinquent accounts in a department store is stored in three vectors. Vector *BILL* contains the amounts due in each delinquent account. Vector *TIME* contains the time in months that the account is overdue, and vector *NUMBER* contains the account numbers.

Write expressions to accomplish the following:

a. Display all amounts overdue more than two months.
b. Display the total of all bills overdue at least two months.
c. List all account numbers of bills overdue more than three months.

SUPPLEMENTARY EXERCISES

1. The global variables *G*, *N*, and *S* contain the exam grade, name, and sex ('*M*' or '*F*') of a student. Give a program that will produce the following display

   THE STUDENT'S NAME IS _____

   HIS(HER) GRADE IS _____

   Choose *HIS* or *HER* depending on the sex of the student. Fill in the two blanks with the student's name and grade.

2. The following vectors of data might be contained in an information system.

   a. Marital status: 1 indicates married; 2 indicates single

      $M \leftarrow$1 2 2 1 2 2 2 1 2

   b. Sex: '*M*' indicates male, '*F*' indicates female

      $S \leftarrow$'*MFFFMFFMF*'

   c. Age: actual age in years

      $A \leftarrow$30 75 60 67 82 59 73 26 66

   d. Social Security: logical vector, 1, indicates those persons receiving social security

      $SS \leftarrow$1 1 0 1 0 0 1 0 0

   Give an expression to produce a logical vector that will point to all single women, over 65, who do not receive social security. What type of person would fall into this category? Who might want this information?

3. Write a monadic function that takes as its argument a
   vector of integers and returns as its result those
   integers that are perfect squares (i.e., whose square root
   is also an integer).

4. a. Create a dyadic function *FACT* that, when used in the
      form *A FACT B*, returns as its result all values in *B*
      that are factors of *A* (i.e., that divide *A* evenly).
   b. Change the function created in a. to a program. The
      display of the program should be

      THERE (IS,ARE) _____ *FACTOR(S)*

      (IT IS,THEY ARE): _____

   The appropriate display should be chosen from the
   parentheses, depending on whether only one factor is
   present or not. The blanks should be filled in
   respectively with the number of factors and the actual
   factors.

5. Write the monadic functions *ALL*, *SOME*, and *NONE* which,
   when acting upon logical vectors, behave as follows:

   a. *ALL* returns a one if all elements in its argument are
      one and a zero otherwise.
   b. *SOME* returns a one if any of the elements in its argu-
      ment are one and a zero if they are all zero.
   c. *NONE* returns a one if all the elements in its argument
      are zero and returns a zero otherwise.

6. Using any logical vector *L* verify that the following
   expression pairs are equivalent:

   a. ∧/L and ~∨/~L
   b. ≠/L and 2|+/L
   c. =/L and ~2/+/~L

7. A bus company will increase its fleet of buses. Planned
   purchases for the next five years are

      P←20 25 15 10 5

   The cost per bus for each of the next five years is
   expected to be

      C←20000 20000 22000 22000 24000

   a. Give an APL expression to determine the total amount
      paid for buses over the next five years. The ex-
      pression should work for any vectors *P* and *C*.
   b. Give an APL expression to determine the total amount
      paid for buses over the next five years if a discount
      of 20 percent is given on the price of each bus over 10
      purchased in any one year. The expression should work
      for any vectors *P* and *C*.

c. Give an expression to determine the total amount paid
   for buses over the next five years if a discount of 10
   percent is given on the price of all buses purchased
   in any year in which more than 10 buses are purchased.
   The expression should work for any vectors P and C.

8. The payroll clerk has just computed the weekly payroll
   for seven employees and stored the amounts in a vector
   PAYROLL. Write a program to determine the number of coins
   of each denomination needed to pay each employee in cash.
   (HINT: delete all dollar amounts, then using logical
   vectors determine the number of half dollars, quarters,
   dimes, nickels, and pennies needed.)

   PAYROLL←225.65 193.07 235.98 141.44 164.26 179.22 185.12

9. Verify the equivalence of

   $(L1 \land L2)/V$ and $(L1/L2)/L1/V$

   where $L1$ and $L2$ are logical vectors and V is any vector
   of the same length. Explain this equivalence in words.

10. Assume that L is a logical vector of the same length as
    the numerical vector V. What is the result of
    $(L \backslash L/V) + (\sim L) \backslash (\sim L)/V$?

11. Assume that L is a logical vector and A and B are two
    numerical vectors such that $(+/L)$ equals the number of
    elements in A and $(+/\sim L)$ equals the number of elements in
    B; that is, the number of ones in L equals the number of
    elements in A and the number of zeros in L equals the
    number of elements in B. What is the result of
    $(L \backslash A) + (\sim L) \backslash B$?

12. Let A and B be two numerical vectors of equal length and
    L be a logical vector of the same length. Give an APL
    expression that will create a vector C by replacing the
    ones in L with the corresponding elements from A and the
    zeros in L by the corresponding elements from B.

13. Assume S←'NOW IS THE TIME FOR ALL GOOD MEN'.

    a. Write a statement to count the number of words in S.
       (HINT: count blanks, ' '.)
    b. Write a statement to count the number of times E
       appears in S.
    c. Write a statement to count the number of letters in S.

Chapter 6
Additional APL Functions

One of the aspects of APL which makes it so versatile a language is its facility in handling vectors of data. The arithmetic or relational functions, for example, can have both scalar and vector arguments. Special features, such as reduction and compression, are designed specifically for handling arrays of data. A number of other functions are available. In this chapter we introduce some of these functions and begin to get a feel for the unique structure and power of the APL language.

The functions we have considered up to the present (arithmetical, relational, and logical) form a class of functions known as *scalar functions*. The operation of these functions is specified between scalars and then extended, using the rules we have learned, to work for other data shapes. The functions to be discussed in this chapter are called *mixed functions*. The rules governing the shapes of the arguments of these functions and the relationship between the shapes of the arguments and of the results are not the same as for the scalar functions. These rules will be discussed individually for each function.

6.1   THE SHAPE AND RESHAPE FUNCTIONS (ρ)

We have used the term shape to refer to the manner in which data is organized, as scalars, vectors, or matrices. The ρ (rho, upper case R) has two uses associated with creating and analyzing the different data shapes.

In its dyadic form, ρ is called the *reshape* function and can be used to create vectors and matrices. The expression $N\rho A$, where N is a positive integer and A is a vector or a scalar, creates a new vector of N elements from the elements of A. If A has more than N elements, it will take the first N elements of A. If the number of elements in A is less than N, it will repeat the elements of A.

COMMENTS

```
      5ρ1
1 1 1 1 1
```
                        Creates a vector of 5 ones.

COMMENTS

```
      5ρ1 ¯2
1 ¯2 1 ¯2 1
```
The number of elements in the right argument is less than 5 so the elements are repeated until 5 elements are obtained.

```
      6ρ'E'
EEEEEE
      4ρ'NO'
NONO
```

```
      7ρ'NO! '
NO! NO!
```

```
      3ρ'ADDS'
ADD
```
The number of elements in A is greater than 3 so only the first 3 elements are used.

```
      ¯1ρ3
DOMAIN ERROR
      ¯1ρ3
      ∧
```
The left argument must be a nonnegative integer.

As we discuss in detail in Chapter 8, the reshape function can also be used to build matrices. In this case the left argument is a two element vector giving the number of horizontal rows and vertical columns in the matrix.

```
      M←2 4ρ'YOURBOAT'
      M
YOUR
BOAT
      BOXES←5 9ρ'□▣▨'
      BOXES
□▣▨□▣▨□▣▨
□▣▨□▣▨□▣▨
□▣▨□▣▨□▣▨
□▣▨□▣▨□▣▨
□▣▨□▣▨□▣▨
```

To ascertain the shape of data we use the monadic form of ρ, called the *shape* function. Used in the form ρV where V is a vector, the shape function gives the length of the vector, that is the number of elements in the vector.

COMMENTS

```
      A←1 3 5 7
      ρA
4
```
There are 4 elements in A.

```
      ρ'YOUR BOAT'
9
```
There are 9 elements in this character vector.

```
      ρρ'YOUR BOAT'
1
```
The length of the vector is itself a vector of length 1.

COMMENTS

```
      ρρρ'YOUR BOAT'
1
      A←'DON''T TREAD ON ME'
      A
DON'T TREAD ON ME
      ρA                        There are 17 elements in A
17                                including 3 blanks and one
                                  apostrophe.
```

Applied to a scalar, shape gives a blank display.

COMMENTS

```
      ρ14                       No display but skips a line.
```

Applied to a matrix it gives the number of rows and columns.

COMMENTS

```
      BOXES
□ℬ∪□ℬ∪□ℬ∪
□ℬ∪□ℬ∪□ℬ∪
□ℬ∪□ℬ∪□ℬ∪
□ℬ∪□ℬ∪□ℬ∪
□ℬ∪□ℬ∪□ℬ∪
      ρBOXES                    There are 5 rows and 9 columns.
5 9
      ρρBOXES                   The shape of a matrix is a
2                                 vector of length two.
```

The shape function is used quite frequently in applications in which we do not know ahead of time how many individual data items need to be processed. For example, the following program can be used to determine the average of the numbers contained in a numerical vector.

```
      ∇AVERAGE[□]∇
    ∇ Z←AVERAGE V
[1]   Z←(+/V)÷ρV
    ∇
```

Here the plus reduction totals the elements in the vector and the shape function is used to divide this total by the number of elements present.

COMMENTS

```
      WEIGHTS←240 310 260 270   Weights of football players on
                                  defensive line.
      ρWEIGHTS                  A four-man line.
4
      AVERAGE WEIGHTS           The function is executed and the
270                               average weight of the
                                  defensive line is displayed.
```

Example: Comparing Two Vectors of Any Length

The shape and reshape functions are also useful in controlling and checking the lengths of data used in functions. For example, the function *COMPARE* introduced in Chapter 5 is used to check if two vectors of the same length are identical.

```
      ∇COMPARE[□]∇
    ∇ Z←C1 COMPARE C2
[1]   Z←C1=C2
[2]   Z←∧/Z
    ∇
```

As we saw, one difficulty with this function is that its arguments must be of equal length.

A much more useful version of this function can be produced with the shape and reshape functions.

```
      ∇NEWCOMPARE[□]∇
    ∇ L←C1 NEWCOMPARE C2;L1
[1]   ⍝COMPARE LENGTHS
[2]   L←(ρC1)=ρC2
[3]   ⍝EQUALIZE LENGTHS AND COMPARE ELEMENTS
[4]   L1←∧/C1=(ρC1)ρC2
[5]   ⍝IDENTICAL IF LENGTHS AND CONTENTS ARE EQUAL
[6]   L←L∧L1
    ∇
```

In line [4] the expression $(ρC1)ρC2$ produces a vector of length $ρC1$ from the elements in $C2$ and guarantees that $C1$ will be compared with a vector of the same length. The result of this comparison is stored in the temporary variable $L1$ which is localized to *NEWCOMPARE* by including it after the semicolon in the header. The new function can now handle arguments of different length, and can distinguish between input with the same content but unequal lengths.

		COMMENTS
0	`'TO' NEWCOMPARE 'TOO'`	The function is dyadic.
0	`'HAPPY' NEWCOMPARE 'HAPPY '`	Note the extra blank at the end of the right argument.

As a fine point we consider the difference between the result of the instruction

		COMMENTS
	`□←A1←1ρ'A'`	Assign $A1$ a value and display it using the quad function.
A		

and the instruction

	`□←A2←'A'`
A	

The displays are identical but there actually is a difference
between the two results. The difference shows up using the
shape function:

                              COMMENTS

      ρ*A*1   *A*1 has length 1.
1
      ρ*A*2   A blank display results.

We see that *A*1 is a vector of length 1 but *A*2 is a scalar.

    In many instances the difference between scalars and one
element vectors is unimportant. For example, using a vector of
length 1 with any of the scalar (arithmetic, relational, or
logical) functions is the same as using a scalar. Thus

      L←1ρ2
      L
2
      ρ*L*
1
      L+3 4 5
5 6 7

Here *L* is added to each element of the right argument. This is
a slight extension of our previous rules on how such functions
work. At this point you may wish to go back over those rules
and replace the term *scalar* by *scalar or array with one element*.

    As we shall see shortly, however, there are instances in
which the difference between scalars and one element vectors
is important.

6.2   DEALING WITH INDIVIDUAL ELEMENTS IN A VECTOR, THE INDEX FUNCTION ([])

We have seen examples of how APL allows operations on one
entire vector. It is also possible to deal only with certain
elements in a vector. The *index* of an element within a vector
is the position that the element occupies in the vector. For
example, the third element in '*NAME*' is *M*. We can think of
each of the boxes comprising a vector as being numbered.

      [*N*] [*A*] [*M*] [*E*]
       1   2   3   4

    To obtain a particular element from a vector, type the name
of the vector followed by a left bracket, the index of the
desired element, and then a right bracket.

                              COMMENTS

      A←'*MY NAME IS*'   The seventh element is *E*.
      A[7]
E
      B←'1359'   The third element is 5.
      B[3]
5

COMMENTS

```
    A[3]                        Blank is displayed.  Note that
                                    blanks count as characters.


    ODD←1 3 5 7 9
    ODD[2]
3
    ODD[3]
5
```

We can also use indexing to change the value of specific elements in a vector.

COMMENTS

```
    A←'NANE'
    A
NANE
    A[3]←'M'                    Assign 'M' to the third element
    A                               in A.
NAME                            The assignment has been made.
    B←1 3 5 6 9
    B
1 3 5 6 9
    B[4]←7                      Assign 7 to the fourth element of B.
    B
1 3 5 7 9
```

An index must be a positive integer and less than or equal to the length of the vector.

COMMENTS

```
    A←'MARION'
    A[7]                        There are only six elements in A.
INDEX ERROR
    A[7]
    ∧

    A[¯2]                       A negative index is not valid.
INDEX ERROR
    A[¯2]
    ∧

    A[1.5]                      The index must be an integer.
DOMAIN ERROR
    A[1.5]
    ∧
```

More than one element of a vector may be referred to at one time by using a numerical vector as the index.

COMMENTS

	A←'NOW IS THE TIME'	Specify *A*.
	A[1 2 3]	The first three elements of *A* are
NOW		displayed.
	A[3 2 1]	The same elements in reversed order.
WON		
	A[1 2 8 10]	The first, second, eight, and tenth
NOTE		elements of *A*.

```
      B←A[5 6]          Specify B.
      B                 Display B.
IS

      T←'SHIELA'        Specify T.
      T
SHIELA                  Oops.
      T[3 4]←'EI'       Respecify using a vector as the
      T                     index.
SHEILA                  Done!

      A
NOW IS THE TIME
      A[4 7 11]←'*'      A scalar is assigned to more than
      A                     one element of a vector.
NOW*IS*THE*TIME

      A[4 7 11]←'--'
LENGTH ERROR            The length error results since an
      A[4 7 11]←'--'        attempt is made to modify three
      ∧                     elements of vector A with only
                            two characters.
```

   Scalars and vectors of length one are distinct as far as indexing is concerned.

```
      (1ρ10)[1]
10
      10[1]
RANK ERROR
      10[1]
       ∧
```

The element in a scalar is not numbered and an error results. The term *RANK* will be discussed more fully in Chapter 8. However, the message essentially means that we have tried to index a scalar. This is not allowed.

6.3   THE INDEX GENERATOR (ι)

   The symbol ι (iota, upper shift *I*) followed by an integer *N* produces a vector whose elements are the integers from 1 to *N*.

COMMENTS

```
      ι5
1 2 3 4 5
      N←4
      ιN
1 2 3 4
      2×ι4
2 4 6 8
      ¯1+2×ι4
1 3 5 7
      10-ι10
9 8 7 6 5 4 3 2 1 0
```

Generate the integers from one to five.

The argument can also be a variable.

Generates even integers.

Generates odd integers.

The integers in descending order.

The name *index generator* is given to the monadic use of ι because it is frequently used to help index elements in a vector.

COMMENTS

```
      T←'ALFRED SMITH'
      T[ι6]
ALFRED
      T[2×ι3]
LRD
```

Indexing the first six elements of T.

Indexing elements 2, 4, and 6 in T.

In the last example note that the expressions inside the brackets are evaluated before taking the desired elements.

Negative or decimal arguments are not valid.

```
      ι¯2
DOMAIN ERROR
      ι¯2
      ∧

      ι2.1
DOMAIN ERROR
      ι2.1
      ∧
```

Example: An Infinite Product

The product

$$4 \cdot (1-\frac{1}{3^2})(1-\frac{1}{5^2})(1-\frac{1}{7^2})(1-\frac{1}{11^2}) \ldots$$

contains an infinite number of factors. The general form for the nth factor is

$$1 \; - \; \div \; (1+2×N)*2$$

This factor approaches the value 1 as N gets large and the entire infinite product has the value π = 3.14159... We can investigate this product using the APL function *PROD*

```
                    ∇PROD[□]∇
              ∇  Z←PROD N
        [1]      Z←1-÷(1+2×ιN)*2
        [2]      Z←4××/Z
              ∇
```

The use of ιN in the expression

```
        1-÷(1+2×ιN)*2
```

in line [1] calculates the first N factors of the product.
The times reduction then multiplies them together.

COMMENTS

`    PROD 1`	The first term in the product.
`3.555555556`	
`    PROD 10`	The product of 10 terms.
`3.21378494`	
`    PROD 100`	The product shows a slow progression
`3.149378473`	toward the correct value.
`    PROD 1000`	
`3.142377365`	
`    PROD 10000`	
`WS FULL`	
`PROD[1] Z←1-÷(1+2×ιN)*2`	The active workspace does not con-
`        ∧`	tain enough room to evaluate
	ten thousand terms of the
	product.

Example: Making Selective Changes in a Vector

A frequently used technique is to combine the index generator,
compression, and indexing to make selective changes in a
vector. For example, suppose we wish to underline all of the
E's in the phrase

```
        PHRASE←'THESE ARE THE TIMES'
```

This can be done by first locating the E's

```
        L←'E'=PHRASE
        L
0 0 1 0 1 0 0 0 1 0 0 0 1 0 0 0 0 1 0
```

and then determining their position in the vector

```
        I←L/ιρPHRASE
        I
3 5 9 13 18
```

These are the key steps in the process. We generate a
logical vector with 1's in the positions of interest. The
expression ιρPHRASE generates the indices of all elements in
the vector, 1 through ρPHRASE. The logical vector is then
used to compress out the desired indices. Once we have the
necessary indices, the desired replacement is made by

```
                    PHRASE[I]←'E'
                    PHRASE
          THESE ARE THE TIMES
```

The entire replacement procedure can be accomplished in one expression

```
                    PHRASE←'THESE ARE THE TIMES'
                    PHRASE[('E'=PHRASE)/ιρPHRASE]←'E'
                    PHRASE
          THESE ARE THE TIMES
```

6.4   THE EMPTY VECTOR

At this point, we have the tools necessary to discuss a point that has been glossed over in previous sections. The expression ιN produces a vector of N elements. Consider the following examples:

		COMMENTS
	ι3	A vector of 3 elements.
1 2 3		
	ι2	A vector of 2 elements.
1 2		
	ι1	A vector of 1 element.
1		
	ι0	???
		A blank line is displayed.

The last expression, ι0, doesn't produce an error but what is it? It is a vector of length zero, the *empty vector*.

		COMMENTS
	X←ι0	Assign X the empty vector.
	X	
		A blank line is displayed.
	ρX	X has a zero length.
0		

Note that while no typed display is generated when we return an empty vector, an extra line is skipped in the output.

Some other examples that result in the empty vector are:

		COMMENTS
	0/'ABC'	Compression with zero gives the empty vector.
	ρ(0/'ABC')	The length of the empty vector is 0.
0		
	ρ(0 0 0/1 2 3)	
0		
	ρ1	The shape of a scalar is the empty vector.

  COMMENTS

      ρρ1   The length of the empty vector is
0   zero.
      ''   Two successive apostrophes form the
                                                  empty vector.
      ρ''
0
      0ρ'*'   Using a left argument of zero in
                                                  the reshape function produces
      ρ0ρ'*'   the empty vector.
0

    If we use the arithmetic functions to combine an empty
vector with a scalar or one element vector, the result is an
empty vector:

    (1ρ5)÷ι0

    5÷ι0

    ρ5÷ι0
0

Combining an empty vector with vectors of other lengths gives
a *LENGTH ERROR*. (Do you see how this is consistent with the
rules for scalar functions?)

    3 4 5 6+ι0
LENGTH ERROR
    3 4 5 6 +ι0
               ∧

    Expansion of an empty vector gives 0 if the empty vector is
formed from numerical data

    0\ι0
0

and a blank if it is formed from character data.

                                              COMMENTS

    0\''
                                              A blank is displayed.
    ' '=0\''   Check that it is a blank.
1

Example: Determining the Data Type

    The following program can be used to determine whether a vector
contains character data or numerical data by using expansion to
distinguish between empty numerical and character vectors.

```
        ∇DATATYPE[□]∇
      ∇ DATATYPE X
[1]   ⍝CONVERT TO AN EMPTY VECTOR
[2]    X←0/X
[3]   ⍝CONVERT TO A BLANK OR A ZERO
[4]    X←0\X
[5]    (X=' ')/'CHARACTER';(X=0)/'NUMERICAL';' DATA'
      ∇
```

The conversions done on lines [2] and [4] could have been done
in one instruction, X←0\0/X.

COMMENTS

```
      F←'SALMON'
      DATATYPE F                      Execute the program with the
CHARACTER DATA                            character vector F.


      DATATYPE 7 8 9 10
NUMERICAL DATA


      DATATYPE ι0                     An empty numerical vector.
NUMERICAL DATA


      DATATYPE ''                     An empty character vector.
CHARACTER DATA
```

6.5   CATENATION AND RAVEL (,)

The catenation function provides for the joining of two or more
scalars or vectors to form a single vector. The catenation
symbol is the comma (,) and is used dyadically.

COMMENTS

```
      A←3,4,5                         The scalars 3, 4, and 5 are cate-
      A                                   nated to form the vector 3 4 5.
3 4 5
      A←1,758,237
      A
1 758 237

      A←ι4
      B←5 6 7                         Specify B.
      C←A,B                           Catenate A and B to form C.
      C
1 2 3 4 5 6 7
      ρC                              C has 7 elements.
7

      A←'TO '
      B←'BE'
      A,B
TO BE
      A,B,A,B                         A has a blank as its last character,
TO BETO BE                                while B does not.
      A,A,A,B
TO TO TO BE
```

The result of catenating two vectors is another vector whose
length is the sum of the lengths of the original vector.
(Scalars act the same as one element vectors.)

It is not possible to catenate numerical and character data
to one another.

```
      1,'A'
DOMAIN ERROR
      1,'A'
      ∧
```

Example: Entering Long Vectors of Data

A specific use of catenation is to enter long vectors at the
terminal.

```
      A←327 786 143
      A←A,209 876 543
      A←A,887 643 234
      A
327 786 143 209 876 543 887 643 234
```

An alternate procedure is to combine catenation and the quad
function.

```
      A←327 786 143,□
□:
      209 876 543,□
□:
      887 643 234
      A
327 786 143 209 876 543 887 643 234
```

How would you similarly enter long vectors of character data?

Example: Generating Integers Between Given Limits

The integers from A to B can be generated as follows:

```
      A←10
      B←20
      A,A+ιB-A
10 11 12 13 14 15 16 17 18 19 20
```

This will not work if A is greater than B.

```
      A←20
      B←10
      A,A+ιB-A
DOMAIN ERROR
      A,A+ιB-A
         ∧
```

The problem is that B-A is ¯10 and a negative number is an invalid argument for ι.

The function *TO* generates a sequence of integers ranging in value from its left argument to its right argument.

                                      COMMENTS

        ∇*TO*[⎕]∇   The absolute value of *B-A* is used
     ∇ Z←A *TO* B   to determine the number of inte-
[1]   Z←B-A   gers to be generated. The sign
[2]   Z←A,A+(×Z)×⍳|Z   of *B-A* determines whether they
     ∇   should be added to *A* or
                                      subtracted.

        20 *TO* 10
20 19 18 17 16 15 14 13 12 11 10

        10 *TO* 20
10 11 12 13 14 15 16 17 18 19 20
        6 *TO* 6
6

The monadic use of the comma is called *ravel*. This function changes its argument into a vector having the same elements.

                                      COMMENTS

        ρ12   The number 12 is a scalar. Its
                                      shape is the empty vector.
        ρ,12   Here 12 is a vector of length 1.
1

        ρ'ABC'
3
        ρ,'ABC'   Vectors are unaffected.
3

Matrices are also turned into vectors.

        BOXES
☐☒▽☐☒▽☐☒▽
☐☒▽☐☒▽☐☒▽
☐☒▽☐☒▽☐☒▽
☐☒▽☐☒▽☐☒▽
☐☒▽☐☒▽☐☒▽

        ρ*BOXES*
5 9
        ρ,*BOXES*
45
        ,*BOXES*
☐☒▽☐☒▽☐☒▽☐☒▽☐☒▽☐☒▽☐☒▽☐☒▽☐☒▽☐☒▽☐☒▽☐☒▽☐☒▽☐☒▽☐☒▽

Various uses for ravel will be encountered in later chapters. One major use, as indicated above, is to convert scalars to one element vectors. This is important in applications in which the functions used assume that the input data are vectors.

Example: Scalars and One-Element Vectors

The function

```
        ∇AVERAGE[□]∇
     ∇  Z←AVERAGE V
[1]     Z←(+/V)÷ρV
     ∇
```

uses the shape function to determine the number of elements in
the input vector. However, if the input is a scalar this
function doesn't operate correctly.

	COMMENTS
AVERAGE 150	A line is skipped but there is no other display.
ρ*AVERAGE* 150	The result is an empty vector.
0	

The problem is that the length of a scalar is the empty
vector and division of a scalar by an empty vector results in
an empty vector. However, it is a simple matter to use ravel
to fix this bug.

	COMMENTS
∇*AVERAGE*[1□10]	Display for line editing.
[1] Z←(+/V)÷ρV	
1	Insert a blank.
[1] Z←(+/V)÷ρ,V	The corrected line.
[2] ∇	

Now before obtaining the length, the argument is raveled so
that a scalar becomes a vector of one element. Vectors are,
of course, unaffected.

```
        AVERAGE 150
150
        ρAVERAGE 150
1
```

6.6   TAKE (↑) AND DROP (↓) FUNCTIONS

The take (drop) function in the form *N*↑*A* (*N*↓*A*), where *N* is an
integer and *A* is a vector, takes (drops) the first *N* elements
of *A* if *N* is positive or the last *N* elements of *A* if *N* is
negative.

	COMMENTS
A←ι5	
A	
1 2 3 4 5	
3↑A	Takes the first three elements of *A*.
1 2 3	

```
      ¯3↑A                    Takes the last three elements of A.
3 4 5

      3↓A                     Drops the first three elements of
4 5                              A.

      ¯3↓A                    Drops the last three elements of A.
1 2

      A←'TIME'
      2↑A                     Operation with character vectors is
TI                               identical.
      3↓A

E

      5↑1 2 3                 Zeros are added at the end.
1 2 3 0 0
      ¯5↑1 2 3                Zeros are added at the beginning.
0 0 1 2 3
```

In the last two examples, the magnitude of the left argument is greater than the length of the right argument. Zeros are added so that the length of the result is the same as the magnitude of the left argument. Similarly, blanks are added for character right arguments.

```
      A←6↑'CAR'
      A
CAR
      ' '=A                   The last three elements are blank.
0 0 0 1 1 1
      ρA
6
      A←¯6↑'CAR'
      A
   CAR                        Note the shifted output position.
      ' '=A                   The first three elements are blank.
1 1 1 0 0 0
      ρA
6
```

If we attempt to drop more elements than are contained in the right argument, the result is the empty vector.

```
      5↓'CAR

      ρ5↓'CAR'
0
```

Example: Average Velocity of a Projectile

A projectile is launched from the surface of the earth. Its
position is measured at various times after launch. The
height in feet and the time of measurement in seconds are
stored in the vectors *POS* and *TIME* respectively.

```
      POS
0 736 1344 2176 2400 2496 2304 2016
      TIME
0 2 4 8 10 12 16 18
```

These data tell us for example that eight seconds after launch,
the object is 2176 feet above the surface of the earth.

The average speed between each position measurement can be
determined by dividing the change in height between the
measurements by the elapsed time.

The drop function is used to determine the changes in position and height.

	COMMENTS
`1↓TIME` `2 4 8 10 12 16 18`	Dropping the first element shifts the values one position to the left.
`¯1↓TIME` `0 2 4 8 10 12 16`	Dropping the last element gives a vector of the same length as `1↓TIME`.
`(1↓TIME)-¯1↓TIME` `2 2 4 2 2 4 2`	Subtracting the vectors gives the length of time between successive measurements.

The function *RATE* incorporates this procedure to determine
the velocity.

```
      ∇RATE[□]∇
    ∇ Z←X RATE T
[1]   ∩COMPUTE THE CHANGES IN X
[2]   X←(1↓X)-¯1↓X
[3]   ∩COMPUTE THE CHANGES IN T
[4]   T←(1↓T)-¯1↓T
[5]   ∩COMPUTE THE RATES
[6]   Z←X÷T
    ∇

      VEL←POS RATE TIME
      VEL
368 304 208 112 48 ¯48 ¯144
```

Negative velocities mean the object is moving downwards.

Example: Runs of Heads and Tails

A character vector representing successive flips of a coin can
be generated as follows:

```
FLIPS←'HT'[?20ρ2]
FLIPS
TTTTTHTHTTTHHTHTTTHH
```

The expression in brackets generates 20 random values equal to
either 1 or 2.   These values are used as indices to select
either *H* for head or *T* for tail.   We would like to find the
longest run of heads or tails.

```
END←FLIPS≠1↓FLIPS,' '
END
0 0 0 0 1 1 1 1 0 0 1 0 1 1 1 0 0 1 0 1
```

The logical vector *END* has a 1 at the end of each sequence
of flips.   It is calculated by shifting *FLIPS* one space to the
left and locating those elements which are not the same as in
the original vector *FLIPS*.   Catenating the blank to the end of
the shifted vector gives it the same length as *FLIPS* and guarantees that a 1 will appear in the last position.

	COMMENTS

`END←END/ιρEND`
`END`
`5 6 7 8 11 13 14 15 18 20`
	Determine the location of each 1
	which also gives the location of
	the end of each sequence.

`LTH←END-¯1↓0,END`
`LTH`
`5 1 1 1 3 2 1 1 3 2`
	Determine the length of each
	sequence by finding the differ-
	ence between successive end
	points.

`⌈/LTH` `5`	The longest sequence.

Can you give expressions that will determine whether the longest run is heads or tails and where it begins?

6.7   ROTATE AND REVERSAL FUNCTIONS (φ)

The dyadic use of the symbol φ (o, upper shift *O*, backspace |)
is called *rotate*.   In the form *N*φ*A*, *N* an integer *A* a vector,
this function moves the first *N* elements from the front of *A*
to the end of *A* if *N* is positive.   If *N* is negative, *N*φ*A* moves
the last |*N* elements to the front.

	COMMENTS

`A←'GROUP'`
`3φA`
`UPGRO`
	The first three elements of *'GROUP'*
	are placed at the end.

COMMENTS

```
        ¯3φA                          The last three elements are placed
OUPGR                                 first.
        2φA
OUPGR
        (ρA)φA
GROUP
```

The result of rotation always has the same shape as the right argument. In its monadic form, this symbol reverses the order of the elements in a vector and is called *reversal*.

COMMENTS

```
        φι4                           The integers in decreasing order.
4 3 2 1
        φ'LOOP'
POOL
        φ'POTS'
STOP
```

Example: Palindromes

A palindrome is a word that reads the same forward or backward, for example, *OTTO* or *MADAM*. The following program determines whether a character vector is a palindrome and illustrates the use of some of the functions introduced in this chapter.

```
        ∇PALINDROME[□]∇
      ∇ PALINDROME X;L
[1]     ⍝COMPARE THE ORIGINAL AND REVERSED INPUT
[2]     L←∧/X=φX
[3]     ⍝L IS 1 IF X IS A PALINDROME
[4]     X,' IS ',((~L)/'NOT '),'A PALINDROME'
      ∇
```

The local variable *L* stores the result of the test on line [2]. Note that the display in line [4] is formed by catenating character vectors together rather than using semicolons.

Executing the program gives

```
    PALINDROME 'MADAM'
MADAM IS A PALINDROME

    PALINDROME 'SHEILA'
SHEILA IS NOT A PALINDROME
```

6.8   GRADE UP (⍋) AND GRADE DOWN (⍒) FUNCTIONS

The *grade up* and *grade down* functions (⍋ or ∇ backspace |) are quite important, since data processing frequently requires sorting of data.

___

If A is a numerical vector, $\triangle A$ ($\triangledown A$) gives the indices of the elements in A in order of ascending (descending) value.

```
      A←17 51 11 35 27
      ∆A
3 1 5 4 2
```

The smallest number in A is 11. The display shows that the smallest element is in the third position of A. The next smallest, 17, has index 1 and so on to the largest, 51, which is the second element in A. The result of grade up tells us the order in which we would have to select the elements in A to have them in ascending order.

```
      ∇A
2 4 5 1 3
```

The result of $\triangledown A$ is the location in A of its elements in descending order. Thus, to put A into descending order we would take the second element, then the fourth, then the fifth, and so on. This can be done using the results of $\triangledown A$ to index A.

COMMENTS

```
      A[∆A]
11 17 27 35 51
      A[∇A]
51 35 27 17 11
```

The results of $\triangle A$ and $\triangledown A$ are used as indices to sort A.

The elements of A have been rearranged in order of ascending and descending value.

```
      CHAR←'TOBYERICMARIONSHEILAMIKEBRYAN'
      ∆CHAR
DOMAIN ERROR
      ∆CHAR
      ∧
```

The grade up function does not work for character vectors.

Example: Bowling Handicaps

Bowling handicaps in a league are determined from the average of the six highest scores of a bowler's last 10 games. The following program computes the average according to the league's rules.

```
      ∇BOWLING[□]∇
    ∇ BOWLING SCORES
[1]   ⍝SELECT THE LAST TEN SCORES
[2]    SCORES←¯10↑SCORES
[3]   ⍝REARRANGE IN DESCENDING ORDER
[4]    SCORES←SCORES[∇SCORES]
[5]   ⍝SELECT THE SIX HIGHEST SCORES
[6]    'SCORES ';SCORES←6↑SCORES
[7]   ⍝COMPUTE THE AVERAGE
[8]    'AVERAGE ';⌊(+/SCORES)÷6
    ∇
```

The program *BOWLING* takes a vector of scores as an argument
and calculates the desired average. The most recent scores
are located at the *end* of the input vector. (NOTE: this
program will not operate properly if the number of games
bowled is fewer than 6. Refer to the exercises at the end
of the chapter.)

```
      S←152 169 102 149 175
      S←S,195 183 205 173 153
      S←S,161 135

      S
152 169 102 149 175 195 183 205 173 153 161 135

      BOWLING S
SCORES 205 195 183 175 173 161
AVERAGE 182
```

6.9   INDEX OF (⍳)

The ⍳ symbol can also be used dyadically and is then called
index of. Used in the form *A*⍳*B*, the left argument must be a
vector while the right argument can have any shape. The result
of this function is obtained by replacing each element in the
right argument with the index of its *first* occurrence in the
left argument. If an element in the right argument does not
appear in the left argument, it is replaced by 1+⍴A in the
result, that is, one more than the length of *A*.

COMMENTS

```
      A←2×⍳4
      A
2 4 6 8
      A⍳2                    2 is the first element in A.
1
      A⍳6                    6 is the third element in A.
3
      A⍳6 2                  The right argument may be a vector.
3 1

      A←'ABCDEFGHIJKL'       Specify A.
      A⍳'DIG'               D, I, and G are the fourth, ninth,
4 9 7                        and seventh characters in A.
      'TOT'⍳'T'             The first occurrence of T is
1                            indicated.
      A⍳'XYZ'               X, Y, and Z are not in A.  The
13 13 13                     result is 1+⍴A.
      1+⍴A
13
```

In the last example the characters *XYZ* are not contained in *A*.
The result is 1+⍴A, one greater than the length of the vector
A.

Example: Sorting Character Data

In most APL systems the ⍋ and ⍒ functions are limited to
numerical sorting. Sorting of character data can be performed
with the aid of the index of function. The following function
sorts an alphabetic character vector.

```
      ∇ASORT[□]∇
    ∇ Z←ASORT X;A
[1]   A←'ABCDEFGHIJKLMNOPQRSTUVWXYZ'
[2]   ⍝FIND THE LOCATION IN THE ALPHABET OF THE LETTERS IN X
[3]   X←A⍳X
[4]   ⍝SORT THE INDICES
[5]   X←X[⍋X]
[6]   ⍝CONVERT TO A CHARACTER VECTOR
[7]   Z←A[X]
    ∇
```

The ⍳ function associates the letters in X with numbers, so
that A becomes one, B becomes two, and so on. We then sort the
numerical values and finally reconvert X to a character vector.
Note that ASORT is a monadic function which takes as its input
the character vector to be sorted and outputs the sorted
vector. The alphabet is stored in the local variable A.

```
    CHAR
TOBYERICMARIONSHEILAMIKEBRYAN

    ASORT CHAR
AAABBCEEEHIIIIKLMMNNOORRRSTYY
```

To follow the execution of the program ASORT, we will trace
steps [3] and [5].

	COMMENTS
T∆ASORT←3 5	Set the trace.
ASORT 'BEAD' ASORT[3] 2 5 1 4 ASORT[5] 1 2 4 5 ABDE	B is the second letter of the alphabet, E the fifth, etc. Sort the indices. The sorted result.
T∆ASORT←0	Trace is removed.
ASORT 'STEAM' AEMST	

6.10   MEMBERSHIP FUNCTION (ε)

The membership function in the form A∈B determines whether the
elements of A are contained in B. The result is a vector of
ones and zeros having the same length as A. A one occurs for
any element of A that is contained in B and a zero occurs
otherwise.

COMMENTS

	$1\ 2\ 3\epsilon 2\ 4\ 6\ 7$	Only the 2 in $1\ 2\ 3$ is contained in
0 1 0		$2\ 4\ 6\ 8$.
	$'CAT'\epsilon 'ABCDE'$	C and A are contained in $ABCDE$ but
1 1 0		not T.

Example: Intersection of Two Sets

The intersection of two sets of numbers is given by those numbers that are in both sets. The following function calculates the intersection of two sets.

COMMENTS

```
      ∇INTERSECT[□]∇
   ∇  Z←S1 INTERSECT S2
[1]   Z←(S1∈S2)/S1
   ∇
```
The two sets are arguments and the intersection is the result.

```
      S1←2 4 6 8 10
      S2←1 2 3 4 5 6 7
```
Assign the sets.

```
      S1 INTERSECT S2
2 4 6
```
Display the intersection.

```
      S2 INTERSECT S1
2 4 6
```
The result does not depend on the order of the arguments.

6.11 DEAL FUNCTION (?)

In the dyadic use of the symbol $?$, $M?N$ the function is called *deal* and generates M *distinct* random numbers between 1 and N.

```
      3?6
4 3 1
      6?6
6 5 2 1 4 3
      5?52
49 30 16 21 4
```

Note the distinction between the result of $?3\rho 6$ and $3?6$.

```
      ?3ρ6
4 5 6
      ?3ρ6
3 2 6
      ?3ρ6
5 5 4
```

The instruction $?3\rho 6$ may produce duplicate values while the instruction $3?6$ will not. The example $5?52$ shown above can be thought of as choosing, or dealing, five cards from a deck of 52 different cards without replacing the cards in the deck as they are dealt.

The arguments must be integers

```
      3.1?5
DOMAIN ERROR
      3.1?5
        ∧
```

and the left argument must be less than or equal to the right.

```
      7?6
DOMAIN ERROR
      7?6
      ∧
```

The arguments must be scalars.

```
      4?8 9
RANK ERROR
      4? 8 9
          ∧
```

6.12   FORMATTING OUTPUT (▼)

One weakness we have encountered so far in APL is our inability to control the way in which output is displayed. For example, suppose we store a monetary amount:

```
DOLLARS←370.10 285.00 160.75 62.20
```

In the display of these data

```
DOLLARS
370.1 285 160.75 62.2
```

trailing zeros are deleted.

Other problems are that results will often contain considerably more digits than we would like:

```
DOLLARS÷3
123.2666667 95 53.58333333 20.73333333
```

The number of digits displayed can be controlled using the system command)DIGITS.

```
      )DIGITS
IS 10
```

Normally the system displays a maximum of 10 digits. The maximum number of digits to be displayed can be changed by using the digits command in the form)DIGITS N, where N is the new maximum.

_____

                              COMMENTS

)*DIGITS* 5   Change *DIGITS* setting to display 5
WAS 10   figures.
        DOLLARS÷3   Only 5 digits are shown.
123.37 95 53.583 20.733
)*DIGITS* 4   Display 4 digits.
WAS 5
        DOLLARS÷3
123.4 95 53.58 20.73
)*DIGITS* 10   Reset *DIGITS* to 10.
WAS 4

Clearly this will not solve all problems and a more versatile
control over output is desirable. We would like to be able to
control the display of numbers specifying the number of digits
after the decimal point as well as the total space allocated for
each number. This is especially useful in producing tabular
displays.

We refer to the manner in which data are displayed as the
format. Most APL systems will provide some capability for
formatting numerical output. In older systems this is usually
done using a formatting function written in APL and stored in
one of the public libraries. This function can be copied into
the user's workspace.

Newer systems use the APL *format* function ⍕ (⊤, upper shift
N, backspace, ∘, upper shift *J*). We will assume the availability of the format function in what follows. The format
functions available on older systems will generally behave in
a similar manner.

Used monadically the format function returns a character
vector which exactly duplicates the display that would normally
be obtained.

        DOLLARS
370.1 285 160.75 62.2
        ρ*DOLLARS*
4
        A←⍕*DOLLARS*
        A
370.1 285 160.75 62.2
        ρ*A*
21

The result is a character vector of 21 (count them) characters.

        ⍕*DOLLARS*÷3
123.2666667 95 53.58333333 20.73333333
        ρ⍕*DOLLARS*÷3
38

The result depends on the)DIGITS setting

```
      )DIGITS 5
WAS 10
      ⍕DOLLARS÷3
123.37 95 53.583 20.733
      ρ⍕DOLLARS÷3
23
```

The format primitive provides an alternative to the semicolon
for producing single line displays of character and numerical
data. Format is used to convert the numerical data to character data which is then catenated to the other character data
and displayed. The programs FORMAT and SEMICOLON compare the
two techniques.

```
      ∇FORMAT[⎕]∇
    ∇ C FORMAT N
[1]   'DISPLAY NUMBERS ',(⍕N),' AND LETTERS ',C
    ∇
```

```
      ∇SEMICOLON[⎕]∇
    ∇ C SEMICOLON N
[1]   'DISPLAY NUMBERS ';N;' AND LETTERS ';C
    ∇
```

```
      'BFD' FORMAT 1 2 3
DISPLAY NUMBERS 1 2 3 AND LETTERS BFD
```

```
      'BFD' SEMICOLON 1 2 3
DISPLAY NUMBERS 1 2 3 AND LETTERS BFD
```

In its dyadic form the format function provides the user
with control over the spacing of the output and over the number
of decimal digits to be displayed. In general, the form of the
output is controlled by two numbers. The first controls the
spacing by specifying the number of characters to be used in
displaying each numerical value. The second number gives the
number of digits to be displayed after the decimal point. For
example:

```
      10 3⍕DOLLARS
   370.100    285.000    160.750     62.200
      ρ10 3⍕DOLLARS
40
      ρDOLLARS
4
```

Each value in DOLLARS is displayed in a *field* 10 spaces in
width. The values are displayed with three digits after the
decimal point, *including* trailing zeros. They are positioned
with the last digit as far to the right as possible (right-
justified).

The following examples illustrate the effect of varying the
format parameters

```
      10 2▼DOLLARS÷3
123.37      95.00      53.58       20.73

     8 2▼DOLLARS÷3
123.37    95.00    53.58    20.73

    12 1▼DOLLARS÷3
   123.4           95.0           53.6          20.7

    6 0▼ DOLLARS÷3
 123     95     54      21
```

The values can be displayed using different formats by providing a pair of integers for each value to be formatted.

```
    10 2 8 2 12 1 6 0▼DOLLARS÷3
  123.37     95.00          53.6        21
```

In this case the number of elements in the left argument must
be two times the number of elements in the right argument.

```
    10 2 10 2 10 2▼DOLLARS÷3
LENGTH ERROR
    10 2 10 2 10 2 ▼DOLLARS÷3
                  ∧
```

The mixed functions discussed in this chapter are summarized
in Table 6.1. A complete list is given in Appendix 3.

Example: A Sales Report

The format function is used most frequently to organize data
for output displays. Consider a car agency with three salesmen. The agency sells 2 car models, A and B. The sales of
each model, separated by salesman, are given by

```
    ASALES←15 11 8
    BSALES←6 9 13
```

Commissions on the sale of model **A** are $100 for the first 10
cars sold and $125 for subsequent sales. On model B the
commissions are $167.75 for each sale.

	COMMENTS
`ACOM←100×10⌊ASALES`	Calculate commissions on first 10 or lower sales.
`ACOM←ACOM+125×0⌈ASALES-10`	Add commissions on additional sales.

```
    ACOM
1625 1125 800

    BCOM←167.75×BSALES
    BCOM
1006.5 1509.75 2180.75
```

The following function can be used to display a report of this
data.

```
        ∇REPORT[□]∇
    ∇ REPORT;HEAD
[1]     HEAD←(¯10↑'BRYAN'),(¯10↑'ERIC'),¯10↑'MIKE'
[2]     UNDERLINE(15ρ' '),HEAD
[3]     (15↑'MODEL A SALES:'), 10 0 ▼ASALES
[4]     (15↑'COMMISSIONS:'), 10 2 ▼ACOM
[5]     (15↑'MODEL B SALES:'), 10 0 ▼BSALES
[6]     (15↑'COMMISSIONS:'), 10 2 ▼BCOM
[7]     (15ρ' '),30ρ' ',8ρ'='
[8]     (15↑'TOTAL SALES:'), 10 0 ▼ASALES+BSALES
[9]     (15↑'COMMISSIONS:'), 10 2 ▼ACOM+BCOM
    ∇
```

The first two lines create a heading. The names of the salesmen are right-justified in a field of 10 elements. The heading
is shifted 15 spaces to the right and then displayed and underlined using the program *UNDERLINE* of Chapter 5.

```
        ∇UNDERLINE[□]∇
    ∇ UNDERLINE X
[1]     X
[2]     (' '≠X)\'¯'
    ∇
```

The sales and commissions of each salesman are then displayed.
Line [7] in the program underlines the columns, while [8] and
[9] display the totals.

A display from the program is given below. We enter the
program name and advance the paper two lines before hitting
RETURN.

```
        REPORT

                        BRYAN     ERIC     MIKE

MODEL A SALES:             15       11        8
COMMISSIONS:         1625.00  1125.00   800.00
MODEL B SALES:             6        9       13
COMMISSIONS:         1006.50  1509.75  2180.75
                     =======  =======  =======
TOTAL SALES:              21       20       21
COMMISSIONS:         2631.50  2634.75  2980.75
```

Table 6.1 Mixed Functions

In the following, N and M stand for integers, V for vectors, and A and B for objects of any shape. Definitions are given for vector arguments. See Appendix 3 and Chapter 8 for extensions to matrices.

Function	Result	Name of Function
ρA	Gives the length of the vector A.	shape (length)
$N\rho A$	Makes a vector of length N from the elements in A.	reshape
ιN	Vector of integers from 1 to N.	index generator
$V\iota B$	Gives first position in V held by elements in B, otherwise $1+\rho V$.	index of
$\blacktriangle V$	Gives the indices of the elements in V in order of ascending value.	grade up
$\blacktriangledown V$	Gives the indices of the elements in V in order of descending value.	grade down
ϕA	Reverses the order of the elements in A.	reversal
$N\phi A$	Changes the first N elements of A from first to last if N is positive, puts last $\|N\|$ elements first if N is negative.	rotate
$A\epsilon B$	Gives a logical array with a one corresponding to each element in A that is present somewhere in B and a zero corresponding to each element in A that is not present in B.	membership
$,A$	Creates a vector from the elements in A.	ravel
A,B	Joins A and B to form one vector composed of the elements in A followed by the elements in B.	catenation
$N\uparrow A$	Takes the first N elements of A if N is positive; the last $\|N\|$ elements if N is negative.	take
$N\downarrow A$	Drops the first N elements of A if N is positive; the last $\|N\|$ elements if N is negative.	drop
$N?M$	Produces N different random integers from 1 to M.	deal

Table 6.1 Mixed Functions (continued)

Function	Result	Name of Function
⍕A	Produces a character vector displaying A.	format
V⍕A	Produces a character display of A as determined by V.	format

EXERCISES

Before executing the instructions, fill in the anticipated display column and then check against the computer result. When you make a mistake, jot down a short explanation of the mistake.

	Instruction	Anticipated Display	Display
1.	a. ρ1,3,5,9		
	A←'JOHN'		
	b. ρA		
	c. ιρA		
	d. A[ρA]		
	e. A[ιρA]		
2.	a. 5ρ2		
	b. 5ρ'2'		
	c. 6ρ'R'		
	d. 5ρ3,6		
	e. 6ρ'ABC'		
	f. 3ρ2×ι4		
	g. ((ρA)ρ1 0)/A		
3.	A←'ABCDEF'		
	a. A[1]		
	b. A[4]		
	c. A[2,5,4]		
	d. A[5 4 3]		
	e. A[9]		
	A[1]←'Z'		

	Instruction	Anticipated Display	Display
f.	A		
	$A[2,3] \leftarrow A[3,2]$		
g.	A		
h.	$A[2] \leftarrow 2$		
	$A[2] \leftarrow '2'$		
i.	A		
4.	$N \leftarrow 5$		
a.	ιN		
b.	$(2 \times \iota 10) - 1$		
c.	$2 \times \iota 10 - 1$		
	$T \leftarrow 'YOU\ TOO'$		
d.	$T[\iota 3]$		
e.	$T[4 + \iota 3]$		
	$I \leftarrow 2 \times \iota 3$		
f.	$T[I]$		
5. a.	$(1\ 2), (3\ 4)$		
	$A \leftarrow 'BALL'$		
	$B \leftarrow 'FOUR'$		
b.	A, B		
c.	$B, 'TH'$		
d.	$A, '\ ', B$		
e.	$\rho A, B$		
f.	$\rho 10$		
g.	$\rho, 10$		
6. a.	$X \leftarrow \iota 10$		
	$3 \downarrow X$		
b.	$^-5 \downarrow X$		
c.	$4 \uparrow X$		

Instruction	Anticipated Display	Display

d. $^{-}2\uparrow X$

e. $6\uparrow 5\downarrow X$

f. $^{-}7\uparrow 3\downarrow^{-}4\downarrow X$

7. a. $A\leftarrow 'ABCDEFG'$

   $3\phi A$

  b. $^{-}2\phi A$

  c. $11\phi A$

  d. $1\ 2\phi A$

  e. ϕA

  f. $\phi 4\phi\phi A$

  g. $R\leftarrow 'MISSISSIPPI'$

   $(R=1\phi R)/R$

8. $V\leftarrow 7\ 3\ 6\ 1\ 4$

  a. $\pmb{\Lambda} V$

  b. $\pmb{\Psi} V$

  c. $V[\pmb{\Lambda} V]$

  d. $V[\pmb{\Psi} V]$

  e. $\pmb{\Lambda\Lambda} V$

9. a. $'TOM'\ \iota\ 'M'$

  b. $'TOM'\iota'TM'$

  c. $'TOM'\ \iota\ 'R'$

   $L\leftarrow 'ABCDEF'$

  d. $L\iota'CAB'$

  e. $L\iota'BED'$

  f. $'RARE'\iota'R'$

  g. $(2\times\iota 8)\iota\ 6$

  h. $2\times(\iota 8)\iota\ 6$

  i. $L\leftarrow 'APPEARANCE'$

   $((L\iota L)=\iota\rho L)/L$

	Instruction	Anticipated Display	Display

10. a. `'FEET∈'ABCDE'`

    b. `7 8 9 ∈2×ι5`

    c. `1 ∈ 'E'='MOTHER'`

    d. `+/'STEAM'∈'DREAM'`

    e. `('STEAM'∈'DREAM')/'STEAM'`

11. a. `Y←7.5 2.8 3.14 2.713`

    `⍕Y`

    b. `ρ⍕Y`

    c. `6 0⍕Y`

    d. `ρ6 0⍕Y`

    e. `ρ□←10 2 ⍕ Y`

    f. `ρ□←10 0 9 1 8 2 7 3 ⍕ Y`

12. Assume that `G←80 70 75 90 40 85 30 90` is a vector of exam grades received by a student during a semester.

    a. Write a statement using the reduction process to add all these grades.
    b. Write a statement using in addition the ρ operation to average these grades.
    c. Write a statement to arrange the grades in order of increasing grade.
    d. Use in addition the drop operation to delete the two lowest grades.
    e. Write a program to compute and display a student's semester average. The grades are to be requested by the program and entered from the keyboard. The average is computed *after* dropping the two lowest grades.

13. You want to convince a friend that this is a friendly computer. Write a program that will ask for your friend's name (*first and last*). The computer should then skip a line and respond

    ```
    HELLO_____.
    MY NAME IS APL.
    BUT YOU CAN CALL ME APE!
    ```

    filling in your friend's *first* name in the blanks.

14. a. Modify program *BOWLING* to compute a bowler's handicap.
        Let the handicap be 80 percent of the difference be-
        tween his average and 200, or zero if his average is
        above 200.
     b. Modify the program of a. to handle the case when the
        number of games bowled is lower than 10. If the number
        of games bowled is 6, 7, 8, or 9 use the six highest
        scores. If the number of games bowled is fewer than 6,
        use their average to compute the handicap.

15. a. What happens in the function *ASORT* if the input con-
        tains characters other than letters?
     b. Modify *ASORT* to remove all characters from the input
        vector that are not letters and sort the rest of the
        characters.
     c. Modify *ASORT* to remove all characters that are not
        letters, sort the rest of the characters, and then
        attach the nonliteral characters to the end in the same
        order in which they appeared originally.

16. a. An imperfect palindrome is a statement that reads the
        same forward or backward after all nonalphabetic char-
        acters have been removed. Write a program to test
        whether a character vector is an imperfect palindrome.
        Test the program on

              MADAM I'M ADAM

              EGAD A BASE TONE DENOTES A BAD AGE

     b. Modify the program of a. to determine whether a
        character vector is a perfect palindrome, an imperfect
        palindrome, or not a palindrome. The output should be
        of the form *XXX IS ___* where *XXX* is the character
        vector at question and *___* should be replaced by *A
        PALINDROME*, or *AN IMPERFECT PALINDROME*, or *NOT A
        PALINDROME*. Test the program for the three cases; an
        example of a perfect palindrome is *ABLE WAS I ERE I SAW
        ELBA*.

17. Let *C* be a character vector. Give APL expressions to do
     the following (show how it works on two examples of your
     own choosing).

     a. Determine the number of vowels in *C*.
     b. Determine the number of different vowels in *C*.
     c. Determine which vowels are contained in *C*.
     d. Underline all vowels in *C* (i.e., *E* would be replaced
        by *E*).

18. a. Assume that *L* is a logical vector and *A* and *B* are two
        character vectors such that $(+/L)=\rho A$ and $(+/\sim L)=\rho B$,
        that is, the number of ones in *L* equals the number of
        elements in *A* and the number of zeros in *L* equals the
        number of elements in *B*. Give a series of APL express-
        ions that will produce a vector of the same length as *L*

formed by replacing successive ones in L with elements taken in order from A and by replacing zeros in L with elements drawn in order from B.

b. Let A and B be two character vectors of equal length and L be a logical vector of the same length. Give APL expressions that will create a character vector C by replacing the ones in L with the corresponding elements from A and the zeros in L by the corresponding elements from B.

19. A manufacturer makes toys. A marketing survey indicates that he can sell 10,000 toys if the price per toy is one dollar. For each one cent decrease in price, the number of toys sold will increase by 400. Similarly a raise in price by one cent causes sales to decrease by 400 units. It costs 60 cents to manufacture and sell each toy.

Write a program that uses a vector of trial selling prices, $PRICE$, to calculate the following vectors:

a. $SALES$: the number of toys sold at each price.
b. $REVENUE$: the sales revenue to be gained from the sale of the number of toys indicated by $SALES$ at the price indicated by $PRICE$.
c. $COSTS$: the manufacturing and selling costs associated with selling the number of units in $SALES$.
d. $PROFIT$: the total profit to be expected for each assumed selling price.

The program should print a report showing each of these vectors on a separate line. Use the formatting capabilities of your system to produce a neat, readable report.

SUPPLEMENTARY EXERCISES

1. a. Generate all even integers from 0 to 50.
   b. Generate all integers between 7 and 17 inclusive.
   c. Generate all fractions 1/3, 1/4, 1/5,...1/10.

2. Add up the squares of the odd integers from 101 to 299.

3. Compute the sum of the first 12 positive even integers.

4. Determine all 2, 3, and 4 digit numbers such that if the final digit is deleted, then the original number is divisible by the new.

5. Give an APL expression that will determine all of the integer factors of a positive integer N.

6. Assuming M and N are positive integers, what is the result of the following series of expressions?

$$F \leftarrow \iota M \lfloor N$$
$$\lfloor /((0=1 \mid M \div F) \wedge 0=1 \mid N \div F)/F$$

7. Let M and N be two positive integers. Give a dyadic APL function that calculates the smallest common multiple of these two integers; that is, find the smallest positive integer such that both M and N divide it evenly. (HINT: the value $M \times N$ is a common multiple. Can you calculate the M multiple of N less than or equal to this value?)

8. Give APL functions that take as an argument N and return as a result the sum or product of the first N terms in each of the following series. Investigate the sum or product of the terms in each series as the number of terms becomes large to see the value to which they converge.

   a. $\dfrac{1}{1 \times (1+2)} + \dfrac{1}{2 \times (2+2)} + \dfrac{1}{3 \times (3+2)} + \cdots$

   b. $2 \times (\dfrac{2}{1} \times \dfrac{2}{3} \times \dfrac{4}{3} \times \dfrac{4}{5} \times \dfrac{6}{5} \times \dfrac{6}{7} \cdots)$

   c. $\dfrac{1^3}{1^4+4} - \dfrac{3^3}{3^4+4} + \dfrac{5^3}{5^4+4} - \cdots$

   d. $\dfrac{4}{1 \times 2 \times 4 \times 5} + \dfrac{4}{3 \times 4 \times 6 \times 7} + \dfrac{4}{5 \times 6 \times 8 \times 9} + \cdots$

9. Write a function $GMEAN$ that, when given a vector of numbers, computes its geometric mean. The geometric mean of N numbers is the Nth root of their product.

10. Write a program to compute and display the mean and median of a vector of numbers.

11. What is the effect of

        $N \uparrow A$

    when

    a. N is positive and $< \rho A$.
    b. N is negative and the magnitude of N is $< \rho A$.
    c. N is positive and $> \rho A$.
    d. N is negative and the magnitude of N is $> \rho A$.

12. Under what conditions will the expression $(N \downarrow X), Y$ and $N \downarrow X, Y$ be identical? Consider all possible positive and negative N values.

13. What different techniques are available for selecting elements from a vector?

14. Do each of the following three ways by using indexing, take and drop, and compression.

    a. Select the seventh, eighth, and ninth elements from a vector. Assume the length of the vector is greater than nine.

b. Form a vector from the first three and the last five elements in another vector. Assume more than eight elements are present.

15. a. The same as a. of the previous problem, except do not assume any restriction on the vector length. Only those elements actually present should be selected.

b. The same as b. of the previous problem, except assume no restrictions on the length of the original vector. No duplications should arise.

16. Write a dyadic function *CENTER* that takes as its right argument a character vector and as its left argument the width of a page and returns a character vector equal in length to the width of the page, with the right argument centered in the resultant character vector.

17. The balances in a checking account at the end of each of the first six months of the year were

   $BAL \leftarrow 230\ 450\ 610\ 610\ 380\ 420$

If the balance on December 31 was $START \leftarrow 710$, give an APL function which takes *START* as its left argument, *BAL* as its right argument and returns a vector giving the net amounts deposited or withdrawn during each of the six months.

18. What is the effect of $X \leftarrow (X \in FILTER)/X$?

19. Suppose the variable *WORD* is a character vector containing only letters. Write an APL expression to determine the number of letters in *WORD* that are also in '*STAR*'.

a. If duplicate letters are counted separately.
b. If duplicates are only counted once.
c. Generalize this problem by creating functions that will solve a. and b. by determining the number of times the elements in the left arguments of the function appear in the right argument. Assume the left argument contains no duplicates.

20. Give APL functions to remove a. leading, and b. trailing blanks from a character vector, returning the new character vectors as their results.

21. For those with experience in set theory.

Let *A* be a character vector containing the alphabet. This will be our universe. The character vectors *S* and $\underline{S}$ contain only alphabetic characters. Regarding *S* and $\underline{S}$ as sets, create APL functions to evaluate the following:

a. The union of *S* and $\underline{S}$.
b. The intersection of *S* and $\underline{S}$.
c. The complement of *S*.
d. Those elements in *S* or $\underline{S}$ but not in the intersection of *S* and $\underline{S}$.

22. Let I be a vector of integers. Give APL expressions to determine:

    a. All integers equal in value to the integers on their right.
    b. The length of all sequences of identical integers.
    c. The length of the longest such sequence.

23. Using the results of the previous problem, construct a monadic APL function that returns the longest sequence of identical elements in a vector. If two sequences have equal length, the first should be returned.

24. Give APL expressions to

    a. Locate all blanks in a character vector.
    b. Find the length of all words in a character vector (assuming only single blanks or alphabetic characters are present).

25. Use the results of the previous problem to create a monadic function that will return as its result the longest word in its argument.

26. Assume A is a numerical vector. Give APL expressions to determine whether

    a. All elements are equal.
    b. The elements are in increasing order.
    c. The elements are in nonincreasing order.
    d. Any of the elements appear as duplicates.

    (The result of your expression should be 1 or 0.)

27. Repeat the previous problem except now assume A is a character vector.

28. a. Let V be a numerical vector. Give an expression that will produce a character vector that contains the symbol '+' in the same position as the positive values in V, the symbol '-' in the same positions as the negative elements, and '0' in the same positions as zero elements.
    b. The same as the previous problem except separate the characters by single spaces.

29. Give an APL expression that will sort a numerical vector V in increasing order of absolute value (i.e., neglecting signs). Do the same for decreasing order of absolute value.

30. Create an APL function that takes as its arguments a scalar S and a numerical vector V, and rearranges the vector V in order of increasing distance from S.

31. Write a function that when given the original cost C and lifetime L of an item, computes the yearly depreciation for this item using the method of the sum-of-the-year's digits. In this method the depreciation will be some fraction of the original cost. The denominator of this fraction is the sum of the integers from 1 to L (e.g., 1 + 2 + 3 + 4 + 5 for a five-year lifetime). For the first year the numerator will be L, for the second year it will be $L-1$, for the third year $L-2$, and so on until year L in which it is 1. The result returned by the function should be a vector of L elements giving the depreciation in each year.

32. Write a function that, given the original cost C and lifetime L of an item, computes the yearly depreciation for this item using the straight-line depreciation method. In this method the depreciation per year is a constant equal to the original cost divided by the lifetime. The result returned by the function should be a vector of L elements containing the depreciation for each year.

33. Write a function that when given the original cost C of an item and its lifetime L, computes the yearly depreciation using the double declining balance method. In this method the value of the item decreases by a constant percentage each year (hence, the depreciation in dollars will vary) equal to $2 \div L$. The depreciation is obtained by multiplying this fraction times the current value of the item. Your function should return a result that is a vector of L elements containing the depreciation for each year. Note that in the last year the depreciation should be shown so that the value becomes zero.

34. Using a zero to specify the field size with the format function, ⍕, causes the system to automatically choose the correct size for the field width. Investigate the behavior of this option using the vector $A \leftarrow 1.78\ 106.3\ 8790.32$ and the formats

    a. 0 3

    b. 0 0

    c. 0 3 0 3 0 3

    d. 0 0 0 0 0 0

    e. 0 1 0 2 0 3

35. Use the formatting capabilities available on your system to produce a program that prints a table of the second, third, fourth, and fifth roots of the integers from 2 through 10. The first line in the table should give the integers, the second, the square roots, the third, the cube roots, and so on. Print a title to the left of each line.

---

36. a. How do the following three expressions differ?

$$0 \qquad 1\rho0 \qquad 0\rho0$$

b. Is it possible to distinguish between $0\rho1$ and $0\rho5$?

c. Suppose A is a vector of numbers. What is the result of $0\uparrow A$ and $0\downarrow A$?

37. Modify the program *PALINDROME* of this chapter so that L will be 1 if X is not a palindrome. This simplifies the display on line [4], but you must modify the test on line [2].

38. Write a program to verify the following "magic trick".

Take any three digit number and subtract from it the number obtained by reversing the order of its digits. The resulting difference has the properties that the second digit is always a nine and the sum of the first and third digits is also nine. Then, adding this difference to the number obtained by reversing the order of its digits will always result in the number 1089. The only exception occurs when the first and last digits of the original number are the same. In that case all results are zero.

For example: original number = 846
                        846 - 648 = 198
                        198 + 891 = 1089

39. An old legend has it that a wise man, when offered any reward he desired, requested that the squares of a checkerboard be filled with kernels of wheat. One kernel was to be placed on the first square, two on the second, four on the third, eight on the fourth, and so on. How many kernels of wheat would be required to fill the checkerboard?

Chapter 7
Transfer Statements and Branching

The normal sequence of executing statements in a program is by increasing statement number. Statement [1] is executed first, statement [2] second, and so on until all statements are completed, at which time execution of the program ceases. In this chapter techniques are presented that allow programs to deviate from the normal sequence of execution. This process is called *branching* and is made possible by *transfer statements*. As a result, considerable versatility is added to computer programs since they can proceed through different sequences of instructions depending on conditions encountered during execution. For example, a sequence of instructions can be executed repeatedly, a process called *looping*.

7.1 TRANSFER STATEMENTS

We direct a program to execute a specific instruction by entering a right arrow (→) followed by the number of the instruction to be executed. We have previously encountered the right arrow in Chapter 4. At that point it was used to indicate the line at which execution of a suspended function was to resume. In this chapter we discuss how the right arrow may be incorporated into computer programs to direct the flow of execution.

Transfer statements may assume various forms. The simplest form of a transfer statement is a right arrow followed by a line number.

<table>
<tr><td></td><td></td><td>COMMENTS</td></tr>
<tr><td></td><td>.
.
.</td><td></td></tr>
<tr><td>[7]</td><td>→11</td><td>Upon reading line [7], the program will then next execute line [11] then [12], [13], etc.</td></tr>
<tr><td></td><td>.
.
.</td><td></td></tr>
<tr><td>[11]</td><td>$A \leftarrow B \times C$</td><td></td></tr>
<tr><td>[12]</td><td>....</td><td></td></tr>
<tr><td></td><td>.
.
.</td><td></td></tr>
</table>

If the expression to the right of the right arrow is a
numerical vector, the branch is made to the line indicated by
the first element of the vector.

COMMENTS

.
.
.

[6]   →10 11 12   Branch to the first element of the
                                vector, i.e., line [10].

.
.

[10]   P←2×B+H

.
.
.

An important special case is branching to an empty vector.
Since there are no line numbers available for branching no
transfer is made and execution proceeds with the next line in
sequence.

COMMENTS

.
.
.

[11]   →ι0   Execution continues with line [12]
[12]   .   i.e., in the usual order.
       .
       .

If the number following the right arrow is not an existing
line number in the program, an attempt to transfer to that line
will cause an exit from the program. Branching to zero (→0)
will always take us out of a program since [0] is never a line
number.

COMMENTS

.
.
.

[17]   →0   Causes an exit from the program.
       .
       .
       .

A plain right arrow will stop execution completely.

COMMENTS

.
.
.

[25]   →   Stops execution of the program and
                                any program that called its
                                execution.
.
.

The difference between →0 and → is illustrated in the following two functions.

COMMENTS

```
        ∇TEST1[□]∇
    ∇  Z←TEST1
[1]     Z←1
[2]     →0
    ∇
```

The two functions are identical except *TEST1* exits through →0 while *TEST2* stops execution with →.

```
        ∇TEST2[□]∇
    ∇  Z←TEST2
[1]     Z←1
[2]     →
    ∇
```

When *TEST1* is executed and line [2] reached, the result is exactly the same as if we had come to the end of the function.

```
    TEST1
1
```

Thus the last value assigned to *Z* is displayed. On the other hand, when line [2] is reached in *TEST2*, execution stops completely and no result is displayed.

```
    TEST2
```

The line number in the transfer statement may also be obtained as the result of a calculation.

COMMENTS

```
        .
        .
        .
[5]     →6+B
        .
        .
        .
```

Transfer is made to the line number specified by the expression $6+B$; for example, if $B=5$ transfer is made to line [11].

Transfer statements consisting of expressions provide considerable flexibility. They are called *conditional transfers*. The order of execution is controlled by conditions encountered within the expression of the branch statement.

Example: Producing Variable Displays

The following program determines whether a number is positive, negative, or zero and then displays the answer.

```
        ∇SIGN[☐]∇
     ∇ SIGN Z
[1]    →4+2××Z
[2]    'NEGATIVE'
[3]    →0
[4]    'ZERO'
[5]    →0
[6]    'POSITIVE'
     ∇
```

In line [1] the signum function is used to extract the sign of Z. Line [1] produces a transfer to line [2], [4], or [6] depending on whether Z is negative, zero, or positive. The branches to zero in lines [3] and [5] are necessary to insure that only one result is displayed. Note that in Chapter 5 we presented a program SIGN that accomplishes the same result as the program SIGN but uses compression rather than branching. We now execute the program.

```
     SIGN 7
POSITIVE
     SIGN 0
ZERO
     SIGN ⁻4
NEGATIVE
```

A convenient way to produce conditional transfers is to use the compression function. A transfer statement written in this manner has the form

$$→(TEST)/LINENO$$

Here TEST is an expression that will produce a logical result, either a 1 or a 0. Possible forms of the TEST expression are $(N≤100)$ or $(R<0)$. If the result of TEST is 1, the compression function then returns LINENO as its result, causing a branch to the associated line. If the result of TEST is 0, the compression produces an empty vector and execution proceeds to the next line in sequence.

COMMENTS

```
       .
       .
       .
[5]    A←B÷C
       .
       .
       .
```
```
[17]   →(N≤100)/5        If N is less than or equal to 100,
[18]   A←A*2                line [5] is executed next,
       .                    otherwise we execute line [18].
       .
       .
```
```
[6]    →(R<0)/0          If R is negative stop execution,
[7]    D←2×R                otherwise go to line [7].
       .
       .
       .
```

In all cases, if the condition inside the parentheses is
satisfied, the next line to be executed is given by the number
following the slash. If the condition is not satisfied, the
program proceeds to the line directly after the conditional
transfer since the result of the compression then yields an
empty vector.

In a flowchart these conditional transfers would appear as
shown in Figure 7.1 (line numbers are also shown).

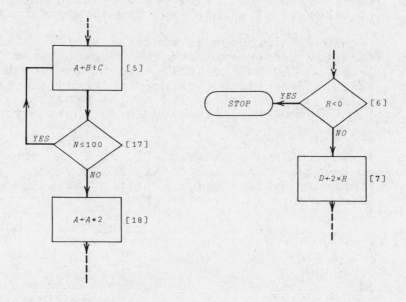

Figure 7.1   Flowcharts of conditional transfers.

The conditional branch marks a decision point in the program. The decision is enclosed in a decision box flowchart
symbol. Two ways of leaving the decision box are possible.
The exit path marked *YES* is taken if the indicated decision is
true, that is, if the result is 1. If the relationship is
false, the exit labeled *NO* is taken.

7.2   LABELS

A difficulty exists with the method of branching discussed so
far. In the above examples if the program is edited and instructions are added or deleted, subsequent line numbers will
change and as a result the numbers within transfer instructions
have to be changed accordingly. This is a tedious and error-
prone process. It can be avoided by assigning *labels* to lines
referenced within transfer statements. Use of labels modifies
the above example as follows:

```
[5]   LOOP:A←B÷C
      .
      .
      .
[17]   →(N≤100)/LOOP
[18]   A←A*2
      .
      .
```

The label is separated from the instruction by a colon. Labeled lines are displayed beginning one position to the left of other lines. This improves the readability of the program.

When the program is executed the label is treated as a variable and is assigned the line number of the instruction it labels. Labels are local variables. In the above example *LOOP* takes on the value 5, since it labels the instruction $A←B÷C$, which appears in line [5] of the program. The value of the label cannot be reassigned in an instruction, nor may the name appear in a header.

The following program will take the age of a person as an argument and will decide if the person is legally an adult or a child. A flowchart of the program with the corresponding line numbers is shown in Figure 7.2.

COMMENTS

```
       ∇AGE[□]∇
    ∇ AGE A
[1]    →(A≥18)/ADULT          If the argument A is greater than
[2]    'CHILD'                or equal to 18, a transfer occurs
[3]    →0                     to line [4] containing the label
[4]  ADULT:'ADULT'            ADULT.
    ∇
```

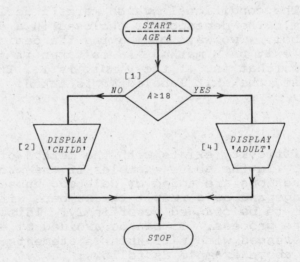

Figure 7.2 Flowchart for the program *AGE*.

The variable *A* in program *AGE* is entered as an argument. To indicate this the program header appears within the *START* terminal box of the flowchart.

```
      A←5
      AGE A
CHILD
      A←18
      AGE A
ADULT
      AGE 63
ADULT
```

The program first executes line [1]. If *A*≥18, it transfers to line [4] labeled *ADULT*, which prints out '*ADULT*', and then stops execution. If *A*<18, it continues with line [2], printing '*CHILD*', then stops execution upon reading line [3].

To further investigate how labeling works, we put a *STOP* on line [1] in *AGE*.

```
                                    COMMENTS

      SΔAGE←1                       Set the STOP control.
      AGE 7                         Execute AGE.

AGE[1]                              Execution interrupts at line [1].
      ADULT                         ADULT is a variable with the value
4                                       of the line it labels.
      →1                            Continue execution.
CHILD

      ADULT                         ADULT is local to the program AGE
VALUE ERROR                             and is undefined after execution.
      ADULT
      ∧
```

Example: Multiple Decisions

Suppose you are about to decide on your day's activity. If the outside temperature is less than 0°F you will stay home, if the outside temperature is higher than 40°F you will go to school, and otherwise you will go skiing. In this example a decision is to be made among more than two alternatives. These alternatives are displayed in Figure 7.3.

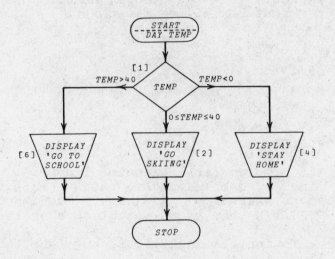

Figure 7.3   Flowchart illustrating a three-way decision.

The program *DAY* follows the flowchart.

```
        ∇DAY[☐]∇
     ∇ DAY TEMP
[1]     →((TEMP<0),TEMP>40)/HOME,SCHOOL
[2]     'GO SKIING'
[3]     →0
[4]     HOME:'STAY HOME'
[5]     →0
[6]     SCHOOL:'GO TO SCHOOL'
     ∇
```

In line [1] we again use the compression function to produce the desired branch. The multiple decision is generated
by using a logical vector as the left argument. This vector
will contain a one in the first or second element depending on
whether the temperature is less than 0 or greater than 40. It
will then select the desired line label for branching. If
neither condition is satisfied, an empty vector will result and
execution will continue at line [2].

Execution of program *DAY* for the three cases gives

```
        DAY ‾23
STAY HOME
        DAY 13
GO SKIING
        DAY 52
GO TO SCHOOL
```

7.3 LOOPING

One of the major advantages of computers lies in their ability to perform repetitive tasks rapidly and accurately. The steps that are repeated within a program form a *loop*. In general, a loop consists of four parts in which we initialize, process, increment, and test. The flowchart for a typical loop structure is shown in Figure 7.4.

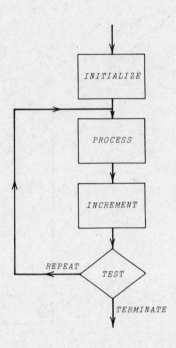

Figure 7.4   The four parts of a loop.

In the initialization stage, we assign starting values to the variables. For example, a counter may be initialized to 1. In the process section, the calculations are performed. The counter is then incremented and a test is performed to check whether the loop should be repeated or terminated.

A loop can, for example, be used to average the grades of a class of 25 students. In such a process a counter is initialized to 1. Here the counter designates the student being processed. In the process part the grades are read in and the average calculated. Then the counter is incremented by 1 and tested to check whether it exceeds 25, the number of students in the class. If it is less than or equal to 25, the loop is repeated so that the next student's average grade may be calculated. After 25 iterations the counter equals 26 and since it exceeds 25 the loop is terminated.

The order in which the process, increment, and test components appear in a loop is interchangeable. For example, we may place the test before the process and increment sections as in Figure 7.5. This arrangement, which is referred to as *leading decisions*, has the advantage of indicating at the beginning of the loop the range of values for which the loop will be executed. It also immediately detects those cases in which the process need not be evaluated at all.

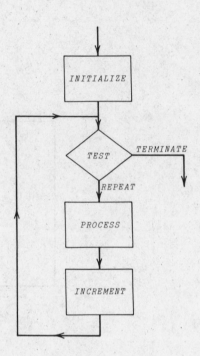

Figure 7.5   An alternative loop structure.

It is also possible to have loops that omit some of these four parts. For example, a counter is not always necessary as changes in the data itself may be used to terminate a loop.

Example: An Infinite Loop

The loop structure of Figure 7.6 is illustrated by the program *FOREVER*.

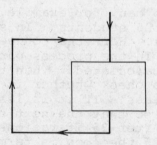

Figure 7.6   An infinite loop.

```
                    ∇FOREVER[⎕]∇
              ∇ FOREVER;X
       [1]      X←⍞
       [2]      →1
              ∇
```

The program contains an *infinite loop*.

COMMENTS

```
         FOREVER
1 2 3+5
7
STOP
PLEASE
NOW
→
→→
⍞
```

The program continues to branch to line [1], releasing the keyboard for a quote-quad input. The input has no effect.

To escape from the loop, type *O* backspace *U* backspace *T*, which terminates execution of a quote-quad.

Example: A Data Entry Function

A useful function for entering vectors of data is shown below.

COMMENTS

```
          ∇DATA[⎕]∇
        ∇ Z←DATA;STOP;Y
[1]      Z←⍳0
[2]      STOP←2*31
[3]  LP:Y←⎕
[4]      →(STOP=1↑Y)/0
[5]      Z←Z,Y
[6]      →LP
       ∇
```

Initialize Z to an empty vector.
Assign $STOP$ a large value.
Input Y.
If $STOP$ equals Y, stop execution.
Otherwise catenate Y onto Z.

The result variable Z is initialized as the empty vector. This provides a point to begin the accumulation of data without introducing any extraneous values. The data is read in and stored in the variable Y. If the response input through the quad was $STOP$, line [4] causes an exit from the function. The variable $STOP$ is assigned the value $2*31$ in line [2]. We assume that the large value will not be valid input data. The advantage of using the variable $STOP$ is that it provides an easily remembered exit from the loop. (See the execution below.)

If the first element in Y is not $STOP$, the data contained in Y is catenated to the end of Z and the input process is repeated.

COMMENTS

☐:   *NOS←DATA*   The function is executed. After
                                 execution the values will be
        3.2 4.56 .23 5.6   stored in *NOS*.

☐:

        6.3 4.5 6.8

☐:

        2.1 3.2

☐:

        STOP   The variable *STOP* is entered
                                 causing execution to terminate.

All data values are now stored in the variable *NOS* in the order
entered.

     NOS
3.2 4.56 0.23 5.6 6.3 4.5 6.8 2.1 3.2

Example: Tracing a Loop

To study the looping process more closely we consider the process of calculating the growth of assets earning interest at a
rate of 10 percent. A flowchart depicting how this may be done
with a loop is shown in Figure 7.7.

The flowchart has the general loop structure that we have
described. The initialization is performed in boxes [2] and
[3]. The first box obtains the starting assets while the second
box initializes the counter, *YEAR*, to 1. Processing takes
place in boxes [4], [5], and [6]. The first step is to add the
interest earned to the assets. The sum is then displayed along
with the value of *YEAR*. In box [6] the counter is incremented
by 1. The test controlling the loop is contained in box [7],
which is designed to repeat the loop for five years.

We now display the program *BALANCE* that follows the flowchart. The line numbers in the program correspond to the
numbers appearing in brackets in the flowchart. The loop includes lines [4] through [7].

```
      ∇BALANCE[☐]∇
    ∇ BALANCE;ASSETS;YEAR
[1]    'ENTER INITIAL DEPOSIT'
[2]    ASSETS←☐
[3]    YEAR←1
[4]  LOOP:ASSETS←ASSETS+0.1×ASSETS
[5]    'ASSETS AFTER YEAR ';YEAR;' EQUAL ';ASSETS
[6]    YEAR←YEAR+1
[7]    →(5≥YEAR)/LOOP
    ∇
```

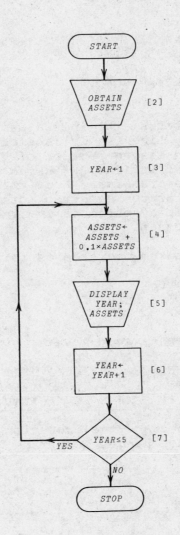

Figure 7.7 Calculation of compound interest.

The display of the program *BALANCE* is repeated for convenient reference during the following discussion.

```
        ∇BALANCE[□]∇
     ∇ BALANCE;ASSETS;YEAR
[1]    'ENTER INITIAL DEPOSIT'
[2]    ASSETS←□
[3]    YEAR←1
[4]  LOOP:ASSETS←ASSETS+0.1×ASSETS
[5]    'ASSETS AFTER YEAR ';YEAR;' EQUAL ';ASSETS
[6]    YEAR←YEAR+1
[7]    →(5≥YEAR)/LOOP
     ∇
```

In this program the initial assets are input with the quad in line [2]. Line [4] is labeled by *LOOP* and marks the beginning of the processing section of the loop. The decision box is implemented in line [7] using the compression function to create the transfer. Note that in this program, *YEAR* is used as a counter to keep track of the number of sweeps made as well as for display purposes in line [5]. *YEAR* and *ASSETS* are local to the program.

   The program operates as follows:

```
      BALANCE
ENTER INITIAL DEPOSIT
□:
      1000
ASSETS AFTER YEAR 1 EQUAL 1100
ASSETS AFTER YEAR 2 EQUAL 1210
ASSETS AFTER YEAR 3 EQUAL 1331
ASSETS AFTER YEAR 4 EQUAL 1464.1
ASSETS AFTER YEAR 5 EQUAL 1610.51
```

Now let us trace the execution of *BALANCE*, to take a closer look at the changes occurring within the loop. We set the trace for all lines:

```
      T∆BALANCE←ι7
      BALANCE
BALANCE[1] ENTER INITIAL DEPOSIT
□:
      1000
BALANCE[2] 1000
BALANCE[3] 1

BALANCE[4] 1100
BALANCE[5] ASSETS AFTER YEAR 1 EQUAL 1100        Iteration 1
BALANCE[6] 2
BALANCE[7] →4

BALANCE[4] 1210
BALANCE[5] ASSETS AFTER YEAR 3 EQUAL 1210        Iteration 2
BALANCE[6] 3
BALANCE[7] →4
```

```
BALANCE[4] 1331
BALANCE[5] ASSETS AFTER YEAR 3 EQUAL 1331        Iteration 3
BALANCE[6] 4
BALANCE[7] →4


BALANCE[4] 1464.1
BALANCE[5] ASSETS AFTER YEAR 4 EQUAL 1464.1      Iteration 4
BALANCE[6] 5
BALANCE[7] →4


BALANCE[4] 1610.51
BALANCE[5] ASSETS AFTER YEAR 5 EQUAL 1610.51     Iteration 5
BALANCE[6] 6
BALANCE[7]
```

In the actual execution the trace output would be single
spaced. We skipped lines to separate the five iterations.

   The trace clearly shows that lines [4] through [7] form a
loop and are executed repeatedly. Lines [4] and [5] calculate
and display the new assets. The trace of line [6] shows the
changing value of YEAR as it is incremented from its initial
value of 1 to a final value of 6. The trace of line [7] displays the line to which transfer is made at the end of each
iteration. As long as the value of the counter YEAR does not
exceed 5, transfer is made to the start of the loop, namely
line [4]. In the last iteration the counter equals 6 and execution exits out of the loop. Since line [7] is the last line
in the program, execution then stops.

   Another, more direct, program to do the same calculation is:

```
     ∇NOLOOPBAL[□]∇
 ∇   NOLOOPBAL;ASSETS
[1]    'ENTER INITIAL DEPOSIT'
[2]    ASSETS←□
[3]    'ASSETS AFTER YEAR 1 EQUAL ';ASSETS←ASSETS+0.1×ASSETS
[4]    'ASSETS AFTER YEAR 2 EQUAL ';ASSETS←ASSETS+0.1×ASSETS
[5]    'ASSETS AFTER YEAR 3 EQUAL ';ASSETS←ASSETS+0.1×ASSETS
[6]    'ASSETS AFTER YEAR 4 EQUAL ';ASSETS←ASSETS+0.1×ASSETS
[7]    'ASSETS AFTER YEAR 5 EQUAL ';ASSETS←ASSETS+0.1×ASSETS
 ∇
```

   This program contains the same number of lines as the looping version. However, if we were to do the calculation 10
times instead of 5, the loop process would be heavily favored,
since only the 5 in line [7] of BALANCE would need to be
changed. As we shall see, looping has additional versatility
that the direct approach does not possess.

   Lines [6] and [7] in program BALANCE were written in the
manner shown to keep separate the steps in the looping process.
A single statement that would serve the same purpose is

```
[6]    →(5≥YEAR←YEAR+1)/LOOP
```

The current value of *YEAR* is increased by 1 and transfer is
made to line [4] if the new value of *YEAR* does not exceed 5.

7.4   DEBUGGING LOOPS

Previous chapters have introduced various errors that occur
when writing APL programs. In this section we continue this
discussion by considering errors that are commonly made in programs containing loops.

The flowchart in Figure 7.8 illustrates a procedure for
computing the sum and average of the integers from 1 to *MAX*.
The procedure employs looping.

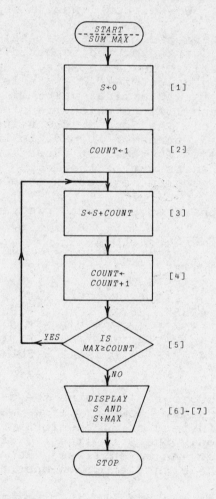

Figure 7.8   Computing the sum and average of integers.

The program *SUM* follows the flowchart of Figure 7.8, but contains a number of errors.

```
      ∇SUM[□]∇
    ∇ SUM MAX;COUNT;S
[1]    S←0
[2]    LOOP:COUNT←1
[3]    S←S+COUNT
[4]    COUNT←COUNT+1
[5]    →(MAX>COUNT)/LOOP
[6]    'THE SUM OF THE INTEGERS FROM 1 TO ';MAX;' IS ';S
[7]    'THE AVERAGE OF THE INTEGERS IS ';S÷MAX
    ∇
```

The local variable *COUNT* is used as the counter. The cumulative sum of the integers is stored in *S*. This variable is initialized to zero in line [1].

We now execute the program *SUM*.

COMMENTS

```
    SUM 3
↓
INTERRUPT
SUM[4] COUNT←COUNT+1
           ∧
    S
1096
    COUNT
1
```

Execute *SUM*. No response is obtained.

Interrupt execution by striking the ATTENTION (or BREAK) key.

Display the variable *S* and *COUNT*.

Something very unusual occurs when the instruction *SUM* 3 is entered. The computer gives no response and seems to be hung up, unable to terminate the computation. We then interrupt the execution by striking the ATTENTION key and display the current values of *S* and *COUNT*. We observe that the counter *COUNT* still has its initial value of 1 while the sum *S* has progressed to the sizable value 1096. We conclude that during the execution the computer was caught in an infinite loop with the counter *COUNT* unable to reach the upper limit *MAX*. Comparing the flowchart and the program, we note that line [3] should be labeled as loop rather than line [2]. As we had it, the program branches back to line [2] and reinitializes the counter to 1 each and every time. The necessary correction is readily made.

COMMENTS

```
      ∇SUM[2□6]
[2]    LOOP:COUNT←1
       /////
[2]    COUNT←1
[3]    [3□7]
[3]    S←S+COUNT
       5
[3]    LOOP:S←S+COUNT
[4]    ∇
SI DAMAGE

→
```

Display line [2] for line editing.

Remove the label from line [2].
The remainder is displayed.
Display line [3] for editing.
Insert the label in line [3].

Suspension information is destroyed if line labels are changed.
Remove the suspension.

We try to execute the program again.

```
      SUM 3
THE SUM OF THE INTEGERS FROM 1 TO 3 IS 3
THE AVERAGE OF THE INTEGERS IS 1

      SUM 4
THE SUM OF THE INTEGERS FROM 1 TO 4 IS 6
THE AVERAGE OF THE INTEGERS IS 1.5
```

It runs but checking these answers by hand, we note another problem. The sum of the integers from 1 to 3 is 6 and not 3 and similarly the sum of the first four integers is 10 and not 6. But 3 happens to be the sum of the first two integers and 6 is the sum of the first three. The computer program apparently excludes the last integer, *MAX*, from the sum. The test condition in line [5] is at fault.

```
        ∇SUM[5□10]
[5]     →(MAX>COUNT)/LOOP
          /1
[5]     →(MAX≥COUNT)/LOOP
[6]     ∇
```

Using > in the loop test causes the program to stop before adding *MAX* to *S*.

The two errors present in the original program are examples of mistakes that frequently occur in programs containing loops. Other examples of such errors will be covered in the chapter exercises.

We now successfully execute *SUM*.

```
      SUM 3
THE SUM OF THE INTEGERS FROM 1 TO 3 IS 6
THE AVERAGE OF THE INTEGERS IS 2
      SUM 4
THE SUM OF THE INTEGERS FROM 1 TO 4 IS 10
THE AVERAGE OF THE INTEGERS IS 2.5
      SUM 100
THE SUM OF THE INTEGERS FROM 1 TO 100 IS 5050
THE AVERAGE OF THE INTEGERS IS 50.5
```

Lines [4] and [5] of this program may be condensed into one instruction

```
[4]     →(MAX≥COUNT←COUNT+1)/LOOP
```

As you have probably realized, the full power of APL allows us to greatly simplify the program *SUM*. The following program, *NEWSUM* replaces program *SUM*.

```
       ∇NEWSUM[☐]∇
     ∇ NEWSUM MAX;S
[1]    S←+/ιMAX
[2]    'THE SUM OF THE INTEGERS FROM 1 TO ';MAX;' IS ';S
[3]    'THE AVERAGE IS ';S÷MAX
     ∇


     NEWSUM 100
THE SUM OF THE INTEGERS FROM 1 TO 100 IS 5050
THE AVERAGE IS 50.5
```

This program operates without any loops and runs more rapidly than program *SUM*, which used loops. You may verify this by executing both programs for a reasonably large value of *MAX*. The great versatility of APL will often allow us to write a single statement for an operation that in other languages would require a loop. This approach is often preferable, since it results in a program that is more easily understood and a saving in computer execution time. However, it is important to remember that complex one-line instructions are undesirable and a compromise must be made between clarity and brevity.

Example: Checking Account Update

Banks update customer checking accounts daily. Updating involves the posting of deposits and withdrawals to each account. The flowchart of Figure 7.9 illustrates a program that, given an account balance at the beginning of the day and a record of transactions for that day, updates the customer's account. The program must check for insufficient funds before allowing a withdrawal. If the balance is insufficient to cover a withdrawal, it displays a message showing the present account balance, and the size of the withdrawal. The program outputs the account balance at the end of the day.

The actual program, *UPDATE*, is displayed below.

```
       ∇UPDATE[☐]∇
     ∇ DEP UPDATE WDRAW;I
[1]    ⍝ADD DEPOSITS TO STARTING BALANCE
[2]    BAL←BAL++/DEP
[3]    ⍝INSURE THAT WDRAW IS A VECTOR
[4]    WDRAW←,WDRAW
[5]    I←0
[6]    LOOP:→((ρWDRAW)<I←I+1)/FINAL
[7]    ⍝CHECK FOR INSUFFICIENT FUNDS
[8]    →(BAL<WDRAW[I])/INSUF
[9]    ⍝DEBIT BALANCE IF THERE ARE SUFFICIENT FUNDS
[10]   BAL←BAL-WDRAW[I]
[11]   →LOOP
[12] INSUF:'INSUFFICIENT FUNDS ';WDRAW[I]
[13]   →LOOP
[14] FINAL:'FINAL BALANCE ';BAL
     ∇
```

The day's starting balance is contained in the global variable *BAL*. The two argument vectors *DEP* and *WDRAW* contain the deposits and withdrawals made during the day for this account.

The computer program requires a number of decision statements and a loop. We first update the balance by adding to it all deposits made during the day. A counter is then set up to process withdrawals. The current balance is compared with each withdrawal transaction to be sure there are sufficient funds in the account. This procedure is repeated in a loop until all withdrawals have been processed. All excessive withdrawals are identified by displaying *INSUFFICIENT FUNDS* and the amount of this attempted withdrawal. The final day's balance is displayed at the end of the program.

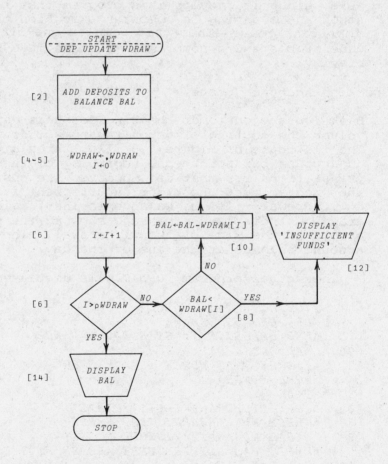

Figure 7.9   Updating a checking account.

A sample execution, illustrating the case of insufficient funds, uses the following data:

```
    BAL←1000
    DEP←225 35.75
    WDRAW←500.50 77 730.10 245.15

    DEP UPDATE WDRAW
INSUFFICIENT FUNDS 730.1
FINAL BALANCE 438.1
```

After withdrawing $500.50 and $77, the balance is less than $730.10 and the message insufficient funds is displayed. The final balance includes all deposits and withdrawals except the $730.10 transaction.

Example: Frequency Counts

As another example of looping, we give a program to determine the frequency of occurrence of the elements of one vector within another vector. A flowchart for this program is shown in Figure 7.10.

The program will, for example, determine the number of times certain vowels or letters appear in a text. It can also be used to ascertain the frequency distribution in a vector of random numbers. The program FREQUENCY is shown below, along with several sample executions.

```
        ∇FREQUENCY[□]∇
      ∇ CHAR FREQUENCY TEXT;I
[1]   ⍝THIS PROGRAM DISPLAYS THE NUMBER OF TIMES
[2]   ⍝      THE ELEMENTS OF THE LEFT ARGUMENT
[3]   ⍝      APPEAR IN THE RIGHT ARGUMENT.
[4]   ⍝TEST FOR EMPTY VECTOR IN LEFT ARGUMENT
[5]   →(0=ρCHAR←,CHAR)/0
[6]   'FREQUENCIES'
[7]   ''
[8]   I←1
[9]   ⍝COUNT AND DISPLAY THE FREQUENCY OF CHAR[I] IN TEXT
[10] LOOP:CHAR[I];' : ';+/CHAR[I]=TEST
[11]  →((ρCHAR)≥I←I+1)/LOOP
      ∇
```

We apply the program to the following text taken from the preface of "A Programming Language" by K. E. Iverson.

```
    INTRO
APPLIED MATHEMATICS IS LARGELY CONCERNED WITH THE DESIGN AND AN
ALYSIS OF EXPLICIT PROCEDURES FOR CALCULATING THE EXACT OR APPR
OXIMATE VALUES OF VARIOUS FUNCTIONS.  SUCH EXPLICIT PROCEDURES
ARE CALLED ALGORITHMS OR PROGRAMS.  BECAUSE AN EFFECTIVE NOTATI
ON FOR THE DESCRIPTION OF PROGRAMS EXHIBITS CONSIDERABLE STRUCT
URE, IT IS CALLED A PROGRAMMING LANGUAGE.
```

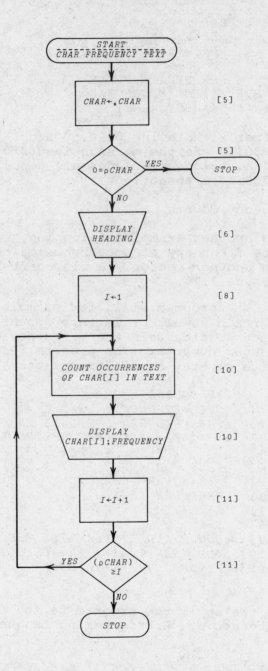

Figure 7.10   Determining frequencies of occurrence.

COMMENTS

```
        ALPH
ABCDEFGHIJKLMNOPQRSTUVWXYZ
        ALPH FREQUENCY INTRO
FREQUENCIES
```

Tabulate the occurrences of the alphabet in this text.

```
A : 23
B : 3
C : 19
D : 10
E : 31
F : 8
G : 5
H : 8
I : 24
J : 0
K : 0
L : 15
M : 5
N : 13
O : 19
P : 10
Q : 0
R : 20
S : 19
T : 21
U : 10
V : 3
W : 1
X : 5
Y : 2
Z : 0
```

```
        'AEIOU' FREQUENCY INTRO
```

Tabulate the underlined vowels. These are distinct from vowels without underlining.

```
FREQUENCIES

A : 5
E : 1
I : 1
O : 2
U : 1
```

The program also works with numerical input.

COMMENTS

```
    VEC←?200ρ6
```

Generate 200 random integers from 1 to 6.

```
    (ι6) FREQUENCY VEC
FREQUENCIES
```

```
1 : 31
2 : 33
3 : 36
4 : 29
5 : 35
6 : 36
```

The frequency of occurrence of each integer is fairly constant.

Example: Iterative Calculations

We illustrate a frequently used iterative technique by solving the equation

$$X^3 - 20X^2 + 60X - 48 = 0$$

The first step is to rewrite the equation as

$$X = 20 - \frac{60}{X} + \frac{48}{X^2}$$

which is obtained by moving the last three terms to the right side of the equation and dividing by X^2. The function F evaluates the right hand side of this equation.

```
     ∇F[□]∇
  ∇  Z←F X
[1]    Z←20+(⁻60÷X)+48÷X×X
  ∇
```

To start the iteration process we pick an initial guess for X, evaluate the right hand side of the equation using the function F, and then use the result as a new trial solution.

                                        COMMENTS

```
     F 3                     Evaluate F for X=3.
5.333333333                  The result.
     F 5.333333333           Use the newly calculated X as a new
10.4375                          trial.
     F 10.4375               Continue the iterative process.
14.69210083
```

The function $SOLVE$ automatically performs the iteration process for us.

                                        COMMENTS

```
     ∇SOLVE[□]∇
  ∇  Z←SOLVE X              X contains the first guess.
[1]   LP:Z←F X              Compute a new guess, Z.
[2]    →(0.001≥|(Z-X)÷Z)ρ0  Stop if X and Z differ by less than
[3]    X←Z                     0.1 percent.  Otherwise use Z as
[4]    →LP                     the new guess and repeat the
  ∇                            process.
```

To follow the process, we trace the execution of line [1] and display each successive X value.

COMMENTS

        $T\Delta SOLVE \leftarrow 1$ The trace is set to line [1].

        $RES \leftarrow SOLVE\ 3$ Execute using an initial guess of 3.
$SOLVE$[1] 5.333333333   The first three iterations reproduce
$SOLVE$[1] 10.4375   our previous results.
$SOLVE$[1] 14.69210083
$SOLVE$[1] 16.13854145
$SOLVE$[1] 16.46648654   The calculations are converging to
                                          a value near 16.5.

$SOLVE$[1] 16.53326238
$SOLVE$[1] 16.54655201   The last two values differ by less
                                          than 0.1 percent.

        RES The result returned is the last
16.54655201   value calculated for X.

EXERCISES

1. Give APL instructions that will perform the following:

   a. Stop execution if the absolute value of the variable Δ
      is less than the variable $EPSILON$.
   b. Branch to NEG if the value of X is negative; otherwise,
      execute the next line.
   c. Store input from a quad in the variable N and stop exe-
      cution if the value is the same as that of the variable
      $STOP$. Assume that the variable $STOP$ has already been
      assigned a value.
   d. Store input from a quote-quad in the variable Y and
      branch to HLP if the first four characters of the input
      are $'HELP'$.
   e. Branch to $LP1$ if the length of the vector Y is less than
      N.
   f. Increase a counter I by the value INC and transfer to
      $LOOP$ if I is less than or equal to MAX.
   g. Transfer to lines $YES1$, $NO1$, or $IN1$ depending on whether
      the first character of the input from a quote-quad is
      $'Y'$, $'N'$, or something else.
   h. Accept input through a quote-quad ($\square$), storing this in
      the variable X, and stopping execution if $STOP$ has been
      input. What would be the purpose of such a statement?

2. What value of A will be displayed in the following
   programs:

                          Anticipated Result   Actual Result
   a.

        $\nabla\ TEST1$
   [1] $A \leftarrow 2$
   [2] $B \leftarrow 6$
   [3] $A \leftarrow A + B$
   [4] $B \leftarrow B - 1$
   [5] $\rightarrow (B > 1)/3$
   [6] $A \leftarrow A + 6$
   [7] A
        ∇

During execution of the program how many times will the
computer execute:

line [2] _____
line [4] _____
line [6] _____

Check your answers using the trace control.

Anticipated Result   Actual Result

b.

```
     ∇ TEST 2
[1]    A←0
[2]    B←10
[3]    A←A*B
[4]    B←B-2
[5]    →(B≥0)/3
[6]    A←A+4
[7]    A
     ∇
```

During execution of the program how many times will the
computer execute:

line [2] _____
line [3] _____
line [5] _____
line [6] _____

3. Upon execution of program VECTOR, what will be the values
   of the elements of vector V?

Anticipated V   Actual V

```
     ∇ VECTOR
[1]    V←11ρ2
[2]    J←1
[3]    V[J]←J-1
[4]    J←J+2
[5]    →(J<10)/3
[6]    V
     ∇
```

How many times is line [5] read by the computer?_____
Check using the trace control.

4. Consider the following program.

```
    ∇ X←INPUT N;STOP
[1]    STOP←2*30
[2]  L1:X←,□
[3]    →(~STOP∈X)/L2
[4]    →
[5]  L2:→(N=ρX)/0
[6]    'INVALID INPUT, ENTER ';N;' NUMBERS.'
[7]    →L1
    ∇
```

Assuming that it is used with its right argument equal to
3, what will happen if the input typed by the user in
response to the □ in line [2] is

a. *STOP*
b. 1,*STOP*
c. 13
d. 6 7 8
e. *A*, where *A* was previously given the value 10 20 30
f. *C*, where *C* was previously given the value '*ABC*'
g. →

5. a. Program the following instructions using a loop.

      i. Initialize a counter to zero and an empty vector.
     ii. Input a value for X.
    iii. Store the value X.
     iv. Increment counter.
      v. Is counter less than 10? If yes, repeat ii. through
         v. If no, continue at vi.
     vi. Output all values of X and their sum.

    b. In a. we outlined a loop. The four sections of the loop
       were given in the following order: INITIALIZE, PROCESS,
       INCREMENT, and TEST.

       Rewrite your program for which the order of the TEST and
       INCREMENT sections is interchanged.

6. The following program was written to display a table of
    squares and cubes for *X*=1, 1.2, 1.4, ...3.

```
    ∇TABLE[□]∇
    ∇ TABLE
[1]    X←0
[2]    X* 1 2 3
[3]    X←X+0.2
[4]    →(X<3)/1
    ∇
```

    a. Find and correct all looping errors in this program.
    b. Diagram with a flowchart the loop structure of the
       correct version of the program.

7.   Modify program *BALANCE* of this chapter so that *ASSETS*
     could be computed and displayed annually for *M* years
     where *M* is a variable to be specified prior to execution
     of *BALANCE*.

8.   Modify program *UPDATE* of this chapter to include a $2
     service charge when the balance drops below $100.

9.   a. Draw a flowchart for a program similar to program *SUM*
        of this chapter that will compute the product of the
        integers from 1 to *M*. (HINT: in *SUM* the sum was ini-
        tially set to 0. Here the product should initially be
        set to 1.)
     b. Code this program in APL and check its operation.
     c. How can the full power of APL be used to shorten this
        program?

10. A vector *DATA* contains N elements. Each of the first N
     elements, except the first and Nth, is to be replaced by

     $DATA[I]=(DATA[I-1]+DATA[I]+DATA[I+1])\div3$

     Each new element is to be used in the following computa-
     tions. This is an example of data smoothing by averaging.
     Use the following vector *DATA*

     DATA←65 64.5 63.1 63.9 61.9 62 60.9 60.1 58.2 59.6
         58.2 56.9

11. a. Draw a flowchart and write a program *GRADES* that will
        obtain a grade *G* by means of keyboard response and will
        print the message '*PASS*' if *G*≥60 or '*FAIL*' if *G*<60.
     b. Generalize program *GRADES* of a. to input a vector of
        grades. Use a loop to display each grade and the
        words *PASS* or *FAIL* on separate lines. Include a flow-
        chart for this program.

12. Write an APL function that takes a numerical vector as its
     argument. If there are elements in the vector with values
     outside the range 0 to 100, the function should display
     these values along with the message *INVALID DATA*. The
     result returned by the function should be the average of
     the valid elements or the empty vector if there are no
     valid elements.

13. Write a program to generate the first 10 integers, compute
     their square roots, and print out the numbers and their
     square roots.

14. Consider the following function to calculate $5\times N$ by
     adding 5's in a loop.

```
      ∇ S←FIVES N
[1]     S←5
[2]   . I←1
[3]     LP:I←I+1
[4]     S←S+5
[5]     →(I=N)/0
[6]     →LP
      ∇
```

Execute the function four separate times with N assuming
the values 4, 2, 1, and zero. Explain the resulting
behavior. Design a loop that works correctly for these
four cases.

15. Enter the following functions $OUT1$, $OUT2$, $IN1$, and $IN2$.
Execute $OUT1$ and $OUT2$ using the values $M=1$ and $N=1$, $M=1$
and $N=2$, $M=5$ and $N=3$, and $M=5$ and $N=5$. Can you explain
the difference in the results?

```
      ∇ N OUT1 M                       ∇ IN1 N
[1]     I←1                      [1]     I←1
[2]     LP:→(I>M)/0              [2]     LP1:→(I>N)/0
[3]     I                        [3]     I←I+1
[4]     IN1 N                    [4]     →LP1
[5]     I←I+1                         ∇
[6]     →LP
      ∇
```

```
      ∇ N OUT2 M                       ∇ IN2 N;I
[1]     I←1                      [1]     I←1
[2]     LP:→(I>M)/0              [2]     LP1:→(I>N)/0
[3]     I                        [3]     I←I+1
[4]     IN2 N                    [4]     →LP1
[5]     I←I+1                         ∇
[6]     →LP
      ∇
```

16. For each of the following loops draw a flowchart depicting
the structure. For each structure also determine

a. The first I value used.
b. The last I value used.
c. The number of times the entire loop is executed.
d. The final value of S.

```
      ∇ L1                             ∇ L2
[1]     S←0                      [1]     S←0
[2]     I←1                      [2]     I←1
[3]     LP:S←S+2                 [3]     LP:→(I>10)/0
[4]     I←I+1                    [4]     S←S+2
[5]     →(I≤10)/LP               [5]     I←I+1
      ∇                          [6]     →LP
                                      ∇
```

```
      ∇ L3                          ∇ L4
[1]     S←2                   [1]     S←0
[2]     I←1                   [2]     I←0
[3]   LP:I←I+1                [3]   LP:S←S+2
[4]     →(10≤I)/0             [4]     →(10=I)/0
[5]     S←S+2                 [5]     I←I+1
[6]     →LP                   [6]     →LP
      ∇                             ∇
```

17. Mr. Smith is offered employment by the XYZ Company, and is given the opportunity to select from one of two different methods of payment. He can receive a monthly wage of $500 and a $5 raise each month, or he can receive a monthly wage of $500 with a yearly raise of $80. Write a program which will determine the monthly wages for the next eight years in each case. Determine the cumulative wages after each month, and from the information, determine which is the better method of payment over the next eight years.

18. Write a program that will keep track of the scores during a bowling match. Some features you might like to build into your program would be:

   a. Display the frame number before each ball.
   b. Display *FIRST* or *SECOND BALL*.
   c. Accept numerical input for the number of pins knocked down as well as *STRIKE* or *SPARE*.

19. Write a program to simulate craps. The rules are as follows. The player throws two dice. If on the first throw, the dice total 7 or 11 the player wins. If they total 2, 3, or 12 the player loses. Otherwise the total thrown becomes the player's point. The player then continues to throw the dice until either they show the same total value as the point, in which case the player wins, or until they show a total value of 7, which is a loss. You may want to include various outputs to indicate the progress of the game or allow for bets.

20. A new taxi company plans to purchase its fleet over the next five years. The number of cars to be bought each year is given by $P←20\ 20\ 15\ 10\ 10$.

   Maintenance on each car averages out to be $100 during its first year, $200 during its second year, $300 during its third year, and $500 during each of its fourth and fifth years of use. Assuming that the cars are bought at the beginning of each year, give an APL function that takes P as its right argument and the vector of maintenance costs as its left argument, and returns a vector giving the amount spent on maintenance during each of the years in which taxis were purchased.

21. a. Modify the function *SOLVE* of this chapter so that it takes a left argument which is the accuracy desired in the solution. Thus the new function used in the form

0.0001 *SOLVE* 7

would use an initial guess of 7 and solve to an accuracy of 0.01 percent.

b. Use this function to solve the equation

$$X^3 - 10X^2 + 10X + 5 = 0$$

The solution is (accurate to 10 figures)

1E$^-$12 *SOLVE* 3

8.798914063

22. A method that can be used to approximate the square root of a positive real number Z is given by the formula

$$X_{i+1} = \frac{1}{2} \left(X_i + \frac{Z}{X_i} \right)$$

where Xi + 1 is a new approximation to the square root of Z and Xi is the old or previous approximation. To start the approximation procedure, we specify a positive initial approximation X_1 and with it compute X_2 using the relation

$$X_2 = \frac{1}{2} \left(X_1 + \frac{Z}{X_1} \right)$$

Subsequently we compute the approximation X_3 from

$$X_3 = \frac{1}{2} \left(X_2 + \frac{Z}{X_2} \right)$$

and so on. This process continues until an approximation is computed which is satisfactory for our needs.

a. Draw a flowchart and write a program to implement this procedure. Test the program for Z = $\sqrt{5}$ using X_1 = 2. Limit the number of approximations to 10.
b. Trace the execution of your program to observe how your approximations converge to the actual value.
c. This procedure for determining the square root can also be terminated by introducing a test to see if the approximations have converged sufficiently close to the answer. A frequently used convergence criterion stops the process when the fractional change in X in any iteration is less than some tolerance E. That is, we stop when

$$\left| \frac{X_{i+1} - X_i}{X_i} \right| < E$$

Modify the program of a. to include this text. Use the value 0.001 (0.1 percent) for E.

SUPPLEMENTARY EXERCISES

1. Given two numbers A and B, perform a divisibility check, that is, check whether the ratio A÷B is an integer. If A÷B is an integer, display *DIVISIBLE*, otherwise display *NOT DIVISIBLE*. The program is to repeat the process for new values of A and B M times, where M is a variable included in the input. Check for division by zero.

2. Write a program using a loop to insert or delete blanks from a text so that two blanks appear after every period that appears in a text unless the period is the last character.

3. Write a program using a loop to insert the characters of one character vector between those of another. (Example: *CAT* and *DOG* becomes *CDAOTG*.)

4. Find all three-digit integers that are equal to the sum of the cubes of their digits.

5. Write a program to play the following game: The computer tries to guess a number you have in mind from 1 to 100. First it guesses a number and you tell it if the number is too high or too low or correct. On the basis of the information you give, the computer guesses again. This continues until the computer guesses right.

6. List N, $N!$, and $1/N$ in three columns for the first 10 integers. Also include appropriate column headings.

7. Write a program to take a text in the form of a character vector and display it using no more than 60 characters per line. If the 60th character is in the middle of a word, that word should start the next line.

8. Write a program to determine the solutions of a quadratic equation:

$$AX^2 + BX + C = 0$$

9. Draw flowcharts and write APL expressions for the following conditions:

   a. If A is larger than 5 stop execution, otherwise continue in normal sequence of line execution.
   b. If A is larger than B let C = A - B, otherwise stop execution.
   c. If A is positive and B is negative stop execution, otherwise display the message '*CONTINUE*'.
   d. If A is less than or equal to B transfer to line [2], otherwise check if A is positive. If A is positive stop execution, otherwise let $A \leftarrow -A$.

10. Modify program *UPDATE* of this chapter to accept input of all transactions in a single vector *TRANS* with withdrawals as negative numbers and deposits as positive numbers.

11. Demonstrate the divergence of the sum

$$1+\frac{1}{2}+\frac{1}{3}+\ldots\frac{1}{N}.$$

Compare the sum for several values of N. How many terms of the series

$$1+\frac{1}{2}+\frac{1}{3}+\frac{1}{4}+\ldots$$

must be added so that the sum will be greater than or equal to 4?

12. A sequence of numbers in which each number (after the first two) is the sum of the two previous ones is called a Fibonacci sequence.

   a. Write a program *FIBONACCI* to verify that the next term in the given Fibonacci sequence is 21. (1 1 2,3,5,8, 13,...).
   b. Modify program *FIBONACCI* to find the first value of the sequence larger than 100. Display its value and its position (element number) in the sequence.
   c. Modify program *FIBONACCI* to list the ratio R of all successive numbers in the sequence. Also compute $(2R-1)^2$ for each ratio R.

13. Write a program that will read 50 grades and then get a count of the number of grades in each of the given ranges 0 to 10, 11 to 20, 21 to 30, ... 91 to 100.

14. Write a program to find a moving average of length three. For example, with the following data 4, 5, 6, 9, 18, etc. we would first find the average of 4, 5, and 6, then find the average of 5, 6, and 9, and then find the average of 6, 9, and 18, etc.

15. Mr. Smith lives on a street where the house numbers are 1, 2, 3,... It is interesting to note that the sum of the house numbers less than Mr. Smith's house number is equal to the sum of the house numbers greater than his. His house number contains 3 digits. What is his house number and how many houses are there on the street?

16. A city has 1000 residents and is agriculturally self-sufficient; it produces enough food to feed itself. In fact, it produces enough food for 100,000 residents. However, every 10 years the population doubles and in that time enough food can be produced to feed 4000 more people than in the previous 10 years. Output a table of data in the following format:

After Year	Population	Food Supply for:
0	1000	100,000
10	2000	104,000
etc.	etc.	etc.

Stop the table when the population outgrows the food supply.

17. Print all different ways a dollar bill can be broken into change.

18. Consider a dart board that awards 40 points for a central hit and 39, 24, 23, 17, and 16 points for hits in circular areas progressively remote from the center. Write a program to determine how many darts you must throw to score exactly 100 points.

19. Change integers to Roman numerals.

Chapter 8
Matrices

Previous chapters have dealt primarily with data stored as vectors or scalars. This chapter discusses another frequently used data arrangement, the *matrix*. We will see that there are many situations for which the natural way to organize data is in a matrix. Multiplication tables, financial reports, graphs, and diagrams are examples. This chapter also discusses how the APL functions introduced in preceding chapters behave with matrix arguments.

8.1 CONSTRUCTION OF A MATRIX

A matrix is a rectangular array of numbers or characters. The elements in a matrix are arranged in rows and columns. Consider the problem of storing the ages of students in a classroom. The classroom has three rows of chairs with each row containing five seats. A matrix containing the desired information is shown below.

Row	Column				
	1	2	3	4	5
1	17	18	20	18	27
2	16	19	20	19	18
3	21	20	19	19	17

The storage of the information in a matrix follows the organization of the room. The matrix has three horizontal *rows* corresponding to the three rows of seats in the classroom. It has five vertical *columns* corresponding to the seats in each row. This matrix shows immediately that the student in the fifth seat (column) of row two is 18 years old.

We can build this matrix by using the reshape function (the dyadic ρ). The left argument is a two element vector containing the number of rows and the number of columns in the matrix. The right argument is a numerical vector or character vector containing the data to be used in the matrix.

The matrix of students' ages is constructed as follows:

```
      G←3 5ρ17 18 20 18 27 16 19 20 19 18 21 20 19 19 17
      G
17 18 20 18 27
16 19 20 19 18
21 20 19 19 17
```

The matrix consists of three rows and five columns and has a total of 15 elements. It is filled *row by row* going from left to right. The following examples further illustrate the procedure for constructing matrices.

	COMMENTS

`      M← 2 3ρι6`
`      M`
`1 2 3`
`4 5 6`
	Construct a matrix of two rows and three columns using the integers one to six. Elements are taken from the right argument filling the matrix row by row.

`      N←3 2ρι6`
`      N`
`1 2`
`3 4`
`5 6`
	A matrix with three rows and two columns using the same data.

`      CMAT←2 3ρ'FORBID'`
`      CMAT`
`FOR`
`BID`
	The elements of a matrix may be characters.

`      2 3ρ'ABCD'`
`ABC`
`DAB`
	If the elements of the right argument are exhausted, the first elements are used again.

As discussed in Chapter 6, the ravel function (monadic ,) converts a matrix into a vector. The vector has the same number of elements as the matrix and is formed by catenating together successive rows of the matrix.

	COMMENTS

`      N`
`1 2`
`3 4`
`5 6`	

`      ,N` `1 2 3 4 5 6`	The ravel of the matrix is a vector.
`      ,CMAT` `FORBID`	

In each of the examples displayed here, the data contained in the matrices could also have been stored in a vector. Instead of using the matrix *G* to store student ages,

```
      G
17 18 20 18 27
16 19 20 19 18
21 20 19 19 17
```

we could have used the vector from which *G* was created

```
,G
17 18 20 18 27 16 19 20 19 18 21 20 19 19 17
```

The matrix form is more appropriate, since it corresponds more closely to the organization of the data in the classroom.

Example: Building a Table of Population Data

Population data for the years

```
YEARS
1960 1965 1970 1972 1973 1974
```

for various sections of the United States are contained in the vectors

```
NORTHEAST
44.8 47.5 49.2 49.7 49.5 49.4
       NORTHCENTRAL
51.7 54.2 56.7 57.4 57.5 57.5
       SOUTH
55.2 59.6 63 65.1 66.2 67.2
       WEST
28.3 32.2 34.9 36 36.7 37.2
```

We can create a table of these population data as follows:

```
TABLE←5 6ρYEARS,NORTHEAST,NORTHCENTRAL,SOUTH,WEST
TABLE
1960      1965      1970      1972      1973      1974
   44.8      47.5      49.2      49.7      49.5      49.4
   51.7      54.2      56.7      57.4      57.5      57.5
   55.2      59.6      63        65.1      66.2      67.2
   28.3      32.2      34.9      36        36.7      37.2
```

The dates and population data are catenated into a vector and then reshaped into a matrix. The matrix has five rows, one for the date and each of the four regions, and six columns, one for each year of data.

8.2 SHAPE OF A MATRIX

A matrix should be pictured as a rectangular arrangement of data. The *shape* of a matrix is obtained using the monadic ρ and is a two element vector containing, in order, the number of rows and the number of columns in the matrix. Referring to the matrices specified in the previous section, we have

COMMENTS

```
ρG
3 5
```
Matrix *G* has three rows and five columns. Its shape is the vector 3 5.

                                        COMMENTS

          $(\rho G)[1]$ The first element of the shape
3   gives the number of rows in the
                                       matrix.
          $(\rho G)[2]$ The second element of the shape
5   gives the number of columns in
                                       the matrix.
          $\times/\rho G$ The times reduction of the shape
15   gives the number of elements in
                                       the matrix.
          ρ,G The number of elements in the ravel
15   of the matrix is also 15.

          ρM The shapes of the other matrices
2 3   created above.
          ρN
3 2
          $\rho CMAT$
2 3

The two elements in the shape vector give the size of the
matrix in the vertical and horizontal directions, respectively.
The first element specifies the number of rows contained in the
matrix and also the length of each of the columns. The second
element specifies the number of columns and, hence, the length
of each row.

8.3   CALCULATIONS WITH MATRICES

The arithmetic, relational, and logical functions are used with
matrices in much the same way that they are used with vectors.
If a dyadic function is used between a scalar and a matrix, the
indicated operation is performed between the scalar and each of
the elements of the matrix. If a dyadic function is used between two matrices, the matrices must have the same shape. The
function is then applied pairwise to the corresponding elements
in the matrices. A monadic function operates on every element
in the matrix. In all cases the result is a matrix with the
same shape as the input matrix.

                                        COMMENTS

       $NUM \leftarrow 2\ 3\rho 1\ ^-5\ 4\ ^-2$
       NUM
  1 $^-5$ 4
 $^-2$ 1 $^-5$

       $3+NUM$ Three is added to every element in
  4 $^-2$ 7 NUM.
  1 4 $^-2$

       $^-5=NUM$
 0 1 0   A 1 appears where a $^-5$ occurs in
 0 0 1 NUM.

COMMENTS

$$
\begin{array}{ccc}
 & -NUM & \\
^-1 & 5 & ^-4 \\
2 & ^-1 & 5
\end{array}
$$

The negative of each element in NUM.

$$
\begin{array}{ccc}
 & M & \\
1 & 2 & 3 \\
4 & 5 & 6
\end{array}
$$

Display the matrix M.

$$
\begin{array}{ccc}
 & NUM+M & \\
2 & ^-3 & 7 \\
2 & 6 & 1
\end{array}
$$

The corresponding elements in NUM and M are added.

$$
\begin{array}{ccc}
 & NUM\lfloor M & \\
1 & ^-5 & 3 \\
^-2 & 1 & ^-5
\end{array}
$$

The smaller value is taken from corresponding elements in NUM and M.

$$
\begin{array}{ccccc}
 & & G & & \\
17 & 18 & 20 & 18 & 27 \\
16 & 19 & 20 & 19 & 18 \\
21 & 20 & 19 & 19 & 17
\end{array}
$$

Matrix of students' ages.

$$
\begin{array}{ccccc}
 & & G<17 & & \\
0 & 0 & 0 & 0 & 0 \\
1 & 0 & 0 & 0 & 0 \\
0 & 0 & 0 & 0 & 0
\end{array}
$$

One student is less than 17 years old.

$$
\begin{array}{ccccc}
 & & G>20 & & \\
0 & 0 & 0 & 0 & 1 \\
0 & 0 & 0 & 0 & 0 \\
1 & 0 & 0 & 0 & 0
\end{array}
$$

Two students are older than 20.

$$
\begin{array}{ccccc}
 & (G<17) & \vee G & >20 & \\
0 & 0 & 0 & 0 & 1 \\
1 & 0 & 0 & 0 & 0 \\
1 & 0 & 0 & 0 & 0
\end{array}
$$

Three students are less than 17 or more than 20 years old.

8.4   INDEXING A MATRIX

Individual elements in a vector V are specified using the index function in the form $V[I]$, where I gives the location of the element we want. To specify an element in a matrix, we must indicate both the row and column position of the element. The indexing takes the form $M[I;J]$ where I and J indicate the rows and columns desired. If I is omitted, the columns designated by J are obtained. If J is omitted, the rows designated by I are obtained. Either I or J or both may be vectors. All elements of I and J must be positive integers.

COMMENTS

$$
\begin{array}{ccccc}
 & & G & & \\
17 & 18 & 20 & 18 & 27 \\
16 & 19 & 20 & 19 & 18 \\
21 & 20 & 19 & 19 & 17
\end{array}
$$

The matrix of students' ages.

COMMENTS

`G[2;1]`	Display the element from the second row, first column.
16	
`G[1;2]`	First row, second column.
18	
`G[3;5]`	Third row, fifth column.
17	
`G[4;1]`	Matrix *G* does not have a fourth row. This element does not exist.
INDEX ERROR	
`G[4;1]`	
∧	

`G[2 3;1 5]`	Select the second and third rows from columns 1 and 5.
16 18	Row 2, column 1 is 16; row 2, column 5 is 18.
21 17	Row 3, column 1 is 21; row 3, column 5 is 17.

`ρG[2 3;1 5]`	The result is a matrix of two rows and two columns.
2 2	

`G[1;]`	Row 1 is displayed. Missing column index implies all elements in row 1 should be displayed.
17 18 20 18 27	

`G[;2]`	Column 2 is displayed. Missing row index implies all elements in column 2 should be displayed.
18 19 20	
`ρG[;2]`	Column 2 is a vector of length 3.
3	

`G[1 3;]`	Rows 1 and 3 are displayed.
17 18 20 18 27	
21 20 19 19 17	
`ρG[1 3;]`	The result is a matrix with two rows and five columns.
2 5	

The following character matrix further illustrates indexing.

```
M←5 5ρ'FIRSTIRATERACERSTEAMTERMS'
M
FIRST
IRATE
RACER
STEAM
TERMS
```

COMMENTS

`M[3;]`	Row 3 is displayed.
RACER	
`M[;4]`	Column 4 is displayed.
STEAM	
`M[2;1+ι4]`	Columns 2, 3, 4, and 5 from row 2 are displayed.
RATE	

COMMENTS

	$X \leftarrow 2\ 3\ 4$	A variable can be used as an index.
	$\underline{M}[X;X]$	Columns 2, 3, and 4 from rows 2, 3,
RAT		and 4 are displayed.
ACE		
TEA		
	$\rho\underline{M}[X;X]$	The result is a matrix with 3 rows
3 3		and 3 columns.

	$\underline{M}[1\ 5;]\leftarrow'*'$	Indexing can be used to selectively
	$\underline{M}[;1\ 5]\leftarrow'*'$	replace data in a matrix. Be
	$\underline{M}[1\ 5;1\ 5]\leftarrow'\square'$	sure to distinguish between the
	$\underline{M}$	effects of the indexing used in
$\square***\square$		the first two replacements and
$*RAT*$		that used in the third. The
$*ACE*$		former replace the first and
$*TEA*$		fifth rows and columns with '*'.
$\square***\square$		The latter puts '$\square$' in the
		corners.

Example: Computer Pictures

The function *PICTURE* can be used to draw a picture using the computer.

```
      ∇PICTURE[□]∇
    ∇ PICT←PICTURE POINTS;I
[1]   PICT← 40 60 ρ' '
[2]   I←1
[3]   LOOP:PICT[POINTS[I;1];POINTS[I;2]]←'*'
[4]    →((ρPOINTS) [1]≥I←I+1)/LOOP
    ∇
```

Line [1] creates a blank matrix *PICT*. The picture is drawn in *PICT* by inserting the characters '*' in selected elements. The location of these elements is specified by the input matrix *POINTS*. This matrix has two columns. The elements in row *I*, *POINTS*[*I*;1] and *POINTS*[*I*;2] give the row and column indices of an element in *PICT* that is to contain a '*'. The loop in lines [2] through [4] is used to read each row in *POINTS* and to insert a star in the position in *PICT* indicated by the data in the row read. The number of elements in *PICT* that are to be replaced is equal to the number of rows in *POINTS*, (ρ*POINTS*)[1].

An example of the execution of *PICTURE* is shown in Figure 8.1 with the matrix *PTS* containing the input information.

Example: Selecting Randomly Located Data

If the data we wish to select from a matrix is located in a single column or row of the matrix, or if it forms a submatrix within the original matrix, the APL index function can be used to select these data directly. Frequently we encounter situations in which the data we want from a matrix is scattered throughout the matrix.

PTS[;1]
3 3 3 3 3 4 4 5 5 6 6 7 7 8 8 9 9 10 10 11 11 12 12 13 14
      14 15 15 16 16 17 17 18 18 18 18 18 19 19 19 19 20
      20 20 20 21 21 21 21 21 22 22 22 22 22 23 23 23 23
      23 24 24 24 24 25 25 25 26 26 26 27 27 27 27 27 28
      29 30

PTS[;2]
30 31 32 33 34 29 35 28 36 28 24 28 34 28 33 28 32 28 31
      28 30 28 29 28 26 28 24 28 22 28 20 28 19 27 28 30
      32 18 24 28 35 17 23 28 26 17 23 28 30 37 17 24 28
      31 37 18 25 28 31 37 19 27 29 36 20 28 35 22 28 34
      24 26 28 30 32 28 28 28

PICTURE PTS

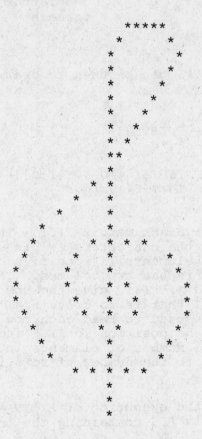

Figure 8.1 Execution of the function *PICTURE*

The matrix

```
    COSTMAT
2.01   2.61   3.56   6.04
2.82   3.98   6.22   7.43
2.63   2.99   4.12   4.82
```

gives the unit costs of items in a lumberyard. Each row of
the matrix corresponds to a type of building product, for
example plywood. Each column corresponds to the grade of
lumber involved.

A contractor wants prices for the items

```
    ITEMS
1 2
2 4
3 1
3 3
```

That is grade two of product one, grade four of product two,
and grades one and three of product three. The cost figures
desired are scattered irregularly throughout the matrix. We
could select the prices using a looping procedure as we did in
the picture drawing function. An alternative procedure is
illustrated by the function *INDEX*.

```
      ∇INDEX[☐]∇
    ∇ Z←MAT INDEX I;COLS
[1]   ⍝DETERMINE THE NUMBER OF COLUMNS
[2]    COLS←(ρMAT)[2]
[3]   ⍝CREATE A VECTOR FROM MAT
[4]    MAT←,MAT
[5]   ⍝DETERMINE THE LOCATIONS IN THE VECTOR
[6]    I←I[;2]+COLS×I[;1]-1
[7]   ⍝SELECT THE DESIRED ELEMENTS FROM THE VECTOR
[8]    Z←MAT[I]
    ∇
```

We trace the execution of *INDEX* so that we may see how it
works.

```
      T∆INDEX←2 4 6

      COSTMAT INDEX ITEMS
INDEX[2] 4
INDEX[4] 2.01 2.61 3.56 6.04 2.82 3.98 6.22 7.43 2.63 2.99
4.12 4.82
INDEX[6] 2 8 9 11
2.61 7.43 2.63 4.82
```

Line [2] stores the number of columns in the input matrix.
The desired elements are obtained by first raveling the matrix
in line [4] and then, in line [6], calculating the position of
the desired elements in the resulting vector.

For example, the third price requested comes from row three, column one. In the ravel of the matrix, this element is preceded by all elements from the first two rows. The desired element is then the next one. The general computation is shown in line [6]. Finally in line [8] the computed locations are used to select the desired costs.

It is interesting to note that the procedure in this function can be given as a single expression.

```
      (,COSTMAT) [ITEMS[;2]+(ρCOSTMAT)[2]×ITEMS[;1]-1]
2.61 7.43 2.63 4.82
```

8.5 PANK OF AN ARRAY

The term *array* is used as a general name for the forms that can be used to store data. Scalars, vectors, and matrices are particular examples of arrays. The *rank* of an array is defined as the number of dimensions in the array. This is the same as the number of indices needed to specify an element in the array.

A scalar has rank zero since it has a single value and no indices are needed to get this value. A vector on the other hand requires one index to access its elements and is therefore of rank 1. Matrices are of rank 2.

The rank of any array A is given by the expression $\rho\rho A$.

	COMMENTS
M	M is a matrix.
1 2 3	
4 5 6	
ρM	It has two rows and three columns.
2 3	
$\rho\rho M$	Matrices are of rank 2.
2	
V	V is a character vector.
ABCDE	
ρV	It has five elements.
5	
$\rho\rho V$	Vectors are of rank 1.
1	
10	A scalar.
10	
$\rho 10$	The shape of a scalar is the empty vector.
$\rho\rho 10$	Scalars have rank 0.
0	

Example: Describing the Rank and Shape of an Array

The following program describes its argument as either a scalar, vector, or a matrix.

```
        ∇ARRAYTYPE[□]∇
      ∇ ARRAYTYPE A;SHAPE;RANK
[1]     SHAPE←ρA
[2]     RANK←ρρA
[3]     →(RANK= 1 2)/VEC,MAT
[4]     'SCALAR'
[5]     →0
[6]   VEC:'VECTOR OF LENGTH ';SHAPE
[7]     →0
[8]   MAT:'MATRIX WITH ';SHAPE[1];' ROWS AND ';SHAPE[2];' COLS'
      ∇
```

The decision in line [3] uses the rank of the argument to
determine whether it is a matrix, vector, or scalar. Transfer
is made to the appropriate output line. Here is an example of
its execution.

```
        ARRAYTYPE M
MATRIX WITH 2 ROWS AND 3 COLUMNS
        ARRAYTYPE ι10
VECTOR OF LENGTH 10
        ARRAYTYPE '*'
SCALAR
```

8.6 REDUCTION APPLIED TO MATRICES

In Chapter 3 we introduced the reduction operation as a convenient method for combining the elements in a vector. Thus
for a vector V containing four elements, $V←7\ 3\ 8\ 1$, the plus
reduction of V

```
        +/V
19
```

is equivalent to the lengthier and less general expression

```
        V[1]+V[2]+V[3]+V[4]
19
```

If we try to extend the concept of reduction to matrices,
we run into a problem of interpretation. The difficulty is
that a vector has only one *coordinate direction*, which is
directed along the vector. A matrix has two coordinate
directions, one vertical and one horizontal. The first index
of a matrix, the row index, specifies the position along the
first or vertical coordinate. The second index of a matrix,
the column index, specifies the position along the second or
horizontal coordinate. The reduction operation can be applied
to matrices along either of the coordinate directions.

Consider a matrix of three rows and four columns.

```
      A←3 4ρι12
      A
 1  2  3  4
 5  6  7  8
 9 10 11 12
```

One way of combining the elements in A is to combine all of
the rows with one another. This is referred to as reduction
along the first coordinate and is denoted by

```
      +/[1]A
15 18 21 24
```

This has the same form as reduction for vectors except for the
[1] after the slash indicating the coordinate along which the
reduction is to be performed. The plus reduction along the
first coordinate is equivalent to the sum

```
      A[1;]+A[2;]+A[3;]
15 18 21 24
```

Remember that indicating an index for a row but leaving out the
column index causes the entire row to be used. A shorthand
notation for the reduction along the first coordinate is

```
      +/A
15 18 21 24
```

where /[1] is replaced by $\neq$, / backspace -.

Another way of combining the elements in A is to combine by
columns. This is referred to as reduction along the second
coordinate. A plus reduction along the second coordinate is
given by the sum

```
      A[;1]+A[;2]+A[;3]+A[;4]
10 26 42
```

This is specified by

```
      +/[2]A
10 26 42
```

where the 2 in brackets indicates that it is the second
coordinate. A short form for reducing along the last coordinate is

```
      +/A
10 26 42
```

Given the pictorial representation of the matrix A,

```
      [ 1] [ 2] [ 3] [ 4]
      [ 5] [ 6] [ 7] [ 8]
      [ 9] [10] [11] [12]
```

the reduction along the first coordinate is illustrated by

```
      [ 1] [ 2] [ 3] [ 4]
             +
      [ 5] [ 6] [ 7] [ 8]
             +
      [ 9] [10] [11] [12]
             ↓
      [15] [18] [21] [24]
```

The reduction yields the vector 15 18 21 24. In reducing along the first coordinate, the reduction is performed in the vertical direction, from the bottom to the top, due to the right-to-left rule.

Similarly, reduction along the second coordinate takes the form

```
[10]      [ 1]     [ 2]     [ 3]     [ 4]
[26]  ←   [ 5]  +  [ 6]  +  [ 7]  +  [ 8]
[42]      [ 9]     [10]     [11]     [12]
```

where the reduction is performed from right-to-left along the second, or horizontal, coordinate. The reduction yields the vector 10 26 42.

As with vectors any of the arithmetic, relational, and logical functions can be used in conjunction with the reduction operation for matrices. The general form for the reduction of a matrix M along coordinate K is

    function/[K]matrix

Here function stands for any of the dyadic arithmetic, relational, or logical functions. Alternatively, reduction along the first coordinate can be indicated by $\neq$ (/ backspace -) rather than /[1]. Reduction along the *last* coordinate can be indicated by a single slash.

	COMMENTS
M	Display the matrix M.
1 2 3	
4 5 6	
×/[2]M	The products of the elements in each row.
6 120	
÷/[1]M	The ratios of the elements in each column.
0.25 0.4 0.5	
⌊/M	The smallest element in each row.
1 4	
⌈/M	The largest element in each column.
4 5 6	
⌈/⌈/M	The largest element in the matrix.
6	
⌊/,M	The smallest element in the matrix.
1	

COMMENTS

```
    FLIPS←? 2 8ρ2          Create a 2 by 8 matrix.
    FLIPS
2 1 2 1 1 1 1 2
2 2 2 2 2 2 1 2


    FLOPS←?2 8ρ2           Create another 2 by 8 matrix.
    FLOPS
1 1 2 1 2 2 2 2
1 2 1 1 1 2 2 2


    FLIPS=FLOPS           Compare corresponding elements in
0 1 1 1 0 0 0 1              the two matrices.
0 1 0 0 0 1 0 1


   ∧≠FLIPS=FLOPS          Identical columns in the two
0 1 0 0 0 0 0 1              matrices are represented by a 1.


   ∧/FLIPS=FLOPS          The two matrices have no identical
0 0                          rows.
```

Example: Department Store Sales

The manager of a department store is concerned about the daily
sales in four of the store's departments. He would like to
analyze the departments' daily sales to assess their success
in promoting their merchandise. The sales of the individual
departments during one week are

```
    DEP1
1838.98 1839.63 2168.82 801.07 1020.07
    DEP2
1764.24 1790.25 2094.83 734.71 952.75
    DEP3
2097.83 737.71 960.75 1774.24 1791.25
    DEP4
1631.73 1644.84 1926.94 700.54 898.57
```

A matrix SALES is constructed with four rows representing the
sales of each department.

```
    SALES←4 5ρDEP1,DEP2,DEP3,DEP4
    SALES
 1838.98   1839.63   2168.82    801.07   1020.07
 1764.24   1790.25   2094.83    734.71    952.75
 2097.83    737.71    960.75   1774.24   1791.25
 1631.73   1644.84   1926.94    700.54    898.57
```

The manager can now extract important information about the
pattern of sales in his store by performing several reduction
operations.

Total weekly sales for each department:

```
    +/SALES
7668.57 7336.78 7361.78 6802.62
```

Total sales for each day:

        +/SALES
7332.78 6012.43 7151.34 4010.56 4662.64

The best day of sales for each department:

        ⌈/SALES
2168.82 2094.83 2097.83 1926.94

The largest gross for each day of the week:

        ⌈/SALES
2097.83 1839.63 2168.82 1774.24 1791.25

The worst day of sales for each department:

        ⌊/SALES
801.07 734.71 737.71 700.54

The smallest gross for each day of the week:

        ⌊/SALES
1631.73 737.71 960.75 700.54 898.57

The largest departmental total sales for the week:

        ⌈/+/SALES
7668.57

The best day of sales for the four departments combined:

        ⌈/+/SALES
7332.78

   The data stored in matrix *SALES* was originally contained in
the vectors *DEP*1, *DEP*2, *DEP*3, and *DEP*4. To perform the above
calculations we reorganized the data into the matrix. The advantage of storing the sales data in a matrix over storing it
in several vectors is quite significant. We are able to
extract useful information much more simply using the matrix
SALES than dealing independently with different vectors. The
reader may wish to try out the above calculations using the
vectors.

8.7   MATRICES APPLIED TO FORMATTING

   In Chapter 6 we discussed the use of the format function, ⍕, to
control the display of numerical results. This function
extends in a natural way to handle matrix right arguments.
Thus consider the matrix *RATIOS*

        RATIOS
1   0.5   0.25   0.125
1   0.25   0.0625   0.015625
1   0.2   0.04   0.008
1   0.125   0.015625   0.001953125
1   0.1   0.01   0.001

```
      ρRATIOS
5 4
```

RATIOS is a matrix with five rows and four columns formed by raising the integers 2, 4, 5, 8 and 10 to the 0, ⁻1, ⁻2 and ⁻3 powers.

Applying ▼ monadically we get a character matrix identical in appearance to the above display.

```
      ▼RATIOS
1              0.5            0.25          0.125
1              0.25          0.0625        0.015625
1              0.2           0.04          0.008
1              0.125         0.015625      0.001953125
1              0.1           0.01          0.001

      ρ▼RATIOS
5 64
```

Note the number of columns in this output, indicating that it is, in fact, a character matrix.

The dyadic form of ▼ may be used to control the number of decimal places displayed.

```
      6 3▼RATIOS
1.000   .500   .250   .125
1.000   .250   .063   .016
1.000   .200   .040   .008
1.000   .125   .016   .002
1.000   .100   .010   .001
```

The values are right justified in a field six characters wide. The last digit displayed is rounded if necessary.

```
      ρ6 3▼RATIOS
5 24
```

The result is a character matrix of five rows, one for each row in *RATIOS*, and 24 columns, six for each column in *RATIOS*.

The output format of each *column* is individually controlled by using a left argument containing one pair of integers for each column in the matrix.

```
      2 0 6 3 6 3 8 4▼RATIOS
1   .500   .250   .1250
1   .250   .063   .0156
1   .200   .040   .0080
1   .125   .016   .0020
1   .100   .010   .0010
```

Notice that the resulting spacing and the number of displayed decimal places may vary for each column but are applied uniformly along each column. The resulting character matrix has five rows and 22 columns.

          ρ2 0 6 3 6 3 8 4⍴*RATIOS*
5 22

Can you account for the 22 columns?

8.8   CATENATION

As described in Chapter 6, catenation allows us to join two
vectors to form a single vector. Catenation can also be used
to join matrices. Since matrices have two dimensions, the
direction in which catenation takes place must be specified.
We will use the following matrices as examples.

```
        LET    |       ST     |      BX    |        CR
     ABCDE     |    *****      |    □□      |      OOOOO
     FGHIJ     |    *****      |    □□      |      OOOOO
     KLMNO     |    *****      |    □□      |
     PQRST     |    *****      |    □□      |
               |    *****      |            |
        ρLET   |       ρST     |      ρBX   |        ρCR
   4 5         |     5 5       |    4 2     |      2 5
```

Catenation onto the second coordinate serves to increase the
the number of columns and leaves the number of rows constant.
Catenation onto the first coordinate increases the number of
rows and leaves the number of columns unchanged.

COMMENTS

          LET,[2]*BX*   *LET* and *BX* are joined. The number
     ABCDE□□   of columns in the resulting
     FGHIJ□□   matrix is the sum of the number
     KLMNO□□   of columns in *LET* and *BX* .
     PQRST□□

          BX,*LET*   Here the [2] has been omitted.
     □□*ABCDE*   Joining on the last coordinate
     □□*FGHIJ*   is understood. Note the way the
     □□*KLMNO*   resulting matrix is formed in
     □□*PQRST*   this example as compared with
                                     the previous one in which the
                                     order of *BX* and *LET* was reversed.

          ST,[2]*BX*   To catenate two matrices parallel to
LENGTH ERROR   the second coordinate, the number
          ST,[2] *BX*   of rows must be the same in each.
          ∧   Here *ST* has 5 rows and *BX* has 4.
          ρ*ST*
5 5
          ρ*BX*
4 2
          ST,[1]*CR*   *ST* and *CR* are joined in the vertical
     *****   direction, along the first co-
     *****   ordinate. The number of columns
     *****   in *CR* and *ST* are equal.
     *****
     *****
     *****
     OOOOO
     OOOOO

COMMENTS

```
      CR,[1]ST
OOOOO
OOOOO
*****
*****
*****
*****
*****
```

Note how the order of the arguments of catenation changes the result from the previous example. The number of rows is the sum of the number of rows in *CR* and the number of rows in *ST*.

It is also possible to catenate vectors to matrices. Catenation onto the second coordinate uses the vector to form an additional column. Catenation onto the first coordinate adds a new row. Of course, the vector must have the same length as the other columns or rows in the matrix.

COMMENTS

```
      BX,[2]'← ← '
□□←
□□
□□←
□□

   '  → →',BX

   □□
→□□
   □□
→□□
```

The vectors have four elements, equal to the number of rows in *B*. They are used to form additional columns. Note that [2] can be omitted when catenating along the last coordinate. Whether the vector comes before or after the matrix in these expressions determines whether the column added will be the first or last.

```
   '↓ ↓ ↓',[1]CR,[1]'↑ ↑ ↑'
↓ ↓ ↓
OOOOO
OOOOO
↑ ↑ ↑
```

Catenations onto the first coordinate add additional rows.

Example: Adding a Border to a Character Matrix

Scalars can be catenated to matrices. This produces a new row or column made from duplicates of the scalar. Consider the following function:

```
      ∇BOX[□]∇
    ∇ Z←CHAR BOX MAT
[1]   Z←(CHAR,CHAR,[1] MAT,CHAR),[1] CHAR
    ∇
```

The right argument to this function is a matrix. The left is a scalar. The behavior of the function is illustrated in the following example.

```
        'o' BOX LET
○ ○ ○ ○ ○ ○ ○
○ABCDE○
○FGHIJ○
○KLMNO○
○PQRST○
○ ○ ○ ○ ○ ○ ○
```

The function creates a border around the matrix *LET*.

You should check for yourself to see what happens if the parentheses in line [1] of *BOX* are removed.

```
        CENTER←1 1ρ'□'
        ρCENTER
1 1
        'o' BOX 'O' BOX '*' BOX '□' BOX CENTER
○ ○ ○ ○ ○ ○ ○ ○ ○
○ O O O O O O O ○
○ O * * * * O ○
○ O * □ □ □ * O ○
○ O * □ □ □ * O ○
○ O * □ □ □ * O ○
○ O * * * * O ○
○ O O O O O O O ○
○ ○ ○ ○ ○ ○ ○ ○ ○
```

Note that *CENTER* was defined to be a matrix, albeit with only one element. As usual, the right-to-left rule applies to the evaluation of this expression.

Example: Department Store Sales Report

In a previous example we constructed the matrix *SALES* containing the weekly departmental sales data of a store.

```
        SALES
   1838.98   1839.62   2168.82    801.07   1020.07
   1764.24   1790.25   2094.83    734.71    952.75
   2097.83    737.71    960.75   1774.24   1791.25
   1631.73   1644.83   1926.94    700.54    898.57
```

The function *SALESREPORT* uses the catenation and the format functions to produce a character matrix containing a report that presents these data.

```
              ∇SALESREPORT[□]∇
          ∇ REPORT←SALESREPORT SALES;DEPT;DAILY;TOTAL;H
[1]     ⍝TOTAL WEEKLY SALES FOR EACH DEPARTMENT
[2]      DEPT←+/SALES
[3]     ⍝TOTAL SALES FOR EACH DAY
[4]      DAILY←+⌿SALES
[5]     ⍝TOTAL SALES FOR THE WEEK
[6]      TOTAL←+/DAILY
[7]     ⍝FORMAT DAILY AND WEEKLY SALES BY DEPARTMENT
[8]      REPORT← 9 2⍕SALES,DEPT
[9]     ⍝CATENATE ON DEPARTMENT LABELS
[10]     REPORT←(4 5 ρ'DEPT.'),(2 0 ⍕ 4 1 ρι4),REPORT
[11]    ⍝FORM A HEADING OF THE PROPER LENGTH
[12]     H←'MON     TUES     WED     THURS     FRI     TOTAL
[13]     H←(-(ρREPORT)[2])↑H
[14]    ⍝CATENATE AN UNDERLINED HEADING TO THE REPORT
[15]     REPORT←H,[1]((' '≠H)\'‾'),[1] REPORT
[16]    ⍝UNDERLINE COLUMNS
[17]     REPORT←REPORT,[1](-(ρREPORT)[2])↑54ρ'       ',7ρ'='
[18]    ⍝DISPLAY DAILY TOTALS AND GRAND TOTAL
[19]     REPORT←REPORT,[1] 'TOTAL  ', 9 2 ⍕DAILY,TOTAL
        ∇
```

An execution of this function is shown below.

```
    RP←SALESREPORT SALES
    RP
```

```
              MON        TUES        WED        THURS        FRI        TOTAL

DEPT. 1     1838.98     1839.63     2168.82      801.07     1020.07     7668.57
DEPT. 2     1764.24     1790.25     2094.83      734.71      952.75     7336.78
DEPT. 3     2097.83      737.71      960.75     1774.24     1791.25     7361.78
DEPT. 4     1631.73     1644.84     1926.94      700.54      898.57     6802.62
            =======     =======     =======     =======     =======     =======
TOTAL       7332.78     6012.43     7151.34     4010.56     4662.64    29169.75
```

```
    ρRP
8 61
```

Lines [1] through [6] compute summary totals to be included in the report. In line [8] the weekly totals for each department are catenated to the end of the sales matrix as a new column, and a character matrix is produced from the resulting data using the format function. Each column will be printed with two decimal places in a field of nine characters. Line [10] attaches to each row in the report the appropriate department label. This is done by successive catenations of character matrices.

Lines [12] through [15] attach an underlined heading to the top of the report. Line [13] assures that the heading produced in line [12] is the correct length for adding to the REPORT matrix. Line [15] first attaches to the report a vector of underscores in the positions of the nonblank characters in the heading and catenates the heading to the report. Similar techniques are used in lines [17] and [19] to underline the columns and print column totals.

8.9 MEMBERSHIP AND INDEX OF

Two functions for which the extension from vector to matrix arguments is particularly direct are membership and index of. *Membership* (ϵ) replaces each element in its left argument by a one if it is contained in its right argument or by a zero if it is not. The arguments of membership can have any combination of shapes. The shape of the result is the same as the shape of the left argument. To illustrate the behavior of ϵ, we use the character matrix *NAMES*.

	COMMENTS

```   NAMES```
```JONES```
```SMITH```
```BROWN```
```THOMAS```
```GREY```
	Display the matrix *NAMES*.

```   NAMESε'AEIOU'```
``` 0 1 0 1 0 0```
``` 0 0 1 0 0 0```
``` 0 0 1 0 0 0```
``` 0 0 1 0 1 0```
``` 0 0 1 0 0 0```
	Ones locate vowels in the matrix.

```   ρNAMES```
```5 6```
```   ρNAMESε'AEIOU'```
```5 6```
	The shape of the left hand argument is the same as the shape of the result.

```   +/NAMESε'AEIOU'```
```2 1 1 2 1```
```   'AEIOU'εNAMES```
```1 1 1 1 0```
	Determine the number of vowels in each name.
	A matrix can be used as the right argument as well.

``` ('AEIOU'εNAMES)/'AEIOU'``` ```AEIO```	Displays which vowels are present in the matrix.

For the *index of* function (dyadic ι) the left argument must be a vector. Each element in the right argument is replaced by its position in the left argument if it is contained in the left argument or one more than the length of the left argument if it is not. The result has the shape of the right argument.

	COMMENTS
``` ALPH``` ```ABCDEFGHIJKLMNOPQRSTUVWXYZ```	Display the vector *ALPH* which contains the letters of the alphabet.

```   ALPHιNAMES```
```10 15 14 5 19 27```
```19 13 9 20 8 27```
``` 2 18 15 23 14 27```
```20 8 15 13 1 19```
``` 7 18 5 25 27 27```
	Each letter in matrix *NAMES* is replaced by its position in the alphabet. The blanks in the matrix are replaced by 27, one more than the length of *ALPH*.

COMMENTS

```
         (ALPH,'*')[ALPHιNAMES]
JONES*
SMITH*
BROWN*
THOMAS
GREY**
```

Replaces the blanks in the matrix by stars. The result of the previous example is used to index from the vector *ALPH,**. This vector has the letters of the alphabet as its first 26 elements and the star as element 27. Note that using a matrix of an index produces a matrix result.

8.10   COMPRESSION AND EXPANSION

The *compression* and *expansion* functions both can take matrices for their right arguments. The compression function allows us to use a logical vector to select certain rows (compression along the first coordinate) or columns (compression along the second coordinate). The following examples illustrate the use of compression with matrices.

COMMENTS

```
         LET
ABCDE
FGHIJ
KLMNO
PQRST
```

Display the character matrix *LET*.

```
         L←1 0 1 0 1

         L/[2]LET
ACE
FHJ
KMO
PRT
```

L has five elements, the same as the number of columns in *LET*. Compression selects from *LET* those columns corresponding to 1's in *L*.

```
         L/LET
ACE
FHJ
KMO
PRT
```

As in reduction, the index two can be omitted.

```
         L/[1]LET
LENGTH ERROR
         L/[1]LET
         ∧
```

The number of elements in *L* must correspond to the numbers of rows (or columns) in the right argument.

```
         1 0 1 1/[1]LET
ABCDE
KLMNO
PQRST
```

Rows in *LET* corresponding to 1's in the left argument are selected.

```
         1 0 1 1/LET
ABCDE
KLMNO
PQRST
```

As in reduction, the symbol ≠ is synonomous with /[1].

Example: Analyzing Stock Data

The matrix *COMP* contains the names of four corporations for which the matrix *PRICE* specifies last year's and this year's stock prices.

COMMENTS

```
      COMP,10 2⍕PRICE
ABC        18.30      24.60
INTCO      16.40      42.90
MFGCO      32.80      22.20
XYZ        41.50      50.80
```

Use the format function and catenation to create a tabular display of company names and stock prices.

```
      (25≥PRICE[;2])/COMP
ABC
MFGCO
```

Use compression to display companies whose stocks are selling for less than $25 this year.

```
      (</PRICE)/COMP
ABC
INTCO
XYZ
```

Determine the companies whose stocks have increased in price.

```
      </PRICE
1 1 0 1
```

The less-than reduction along the second coordinate indicates rows in which the first element is less than the second element.

Companies whose stock is valued at less than $25 and whose stock has increased by more than 25 percent are obtained from

```
      ((25≥PRICE[;2])∧PRICE[;2]≥1.25×PRICE[;1])/COMP
ABC
```

In using compression with matrices, we may visualize the process as follows. For compression on the first coordinate, the logical vector is placed vertically alongside the matrix. Rows in the matrix corresponding to 1's in the logical vector are selected.

```
[A] [B] [C] [D]    [1]     [A] [B] [C] [D]
[I] [J] [K] [L] ←  [0]     [E] [F] [G] [H]
[M] [N] [O] [P]    [1]  /  [I] [J] [K] [L]
                   [1]     [M] [N] [O] [P]
                   [0]     [Q] [R] [S] [T]
```

For compression along the second coordinate, the logical vector is placed horizontally above the matrix. Columns corresponding to 1's in the vector are chosen.

```
            [1] [0] [0] [1]
                     /
[A] [D]     [A] [B] [C] [D]
[E] [H]     [E] [F] [G] [H]
[I] [L] ←   [I] [J] [K] [L]
[M] [P]     [M] [N] [O] [P]
[Q] [T]     [Q] [R] [S] [T]
```

The extension of expansion to matrices should now be clear.
We can either expand along the first or second coordinate,
thereby inserting rows or columns of blanks (or zeros if the
matrix contains numerical data).

Example: Displaying Zero Values as Blanks

The matrix *PARTS* contains prices charged by three suppliers
for five different parts.

```
      10 2▼PARTS
      1.50          .00       2.90          .00       2.90
       .80         3.80        .00         2.90        .00
       .00          .00        .00          .00       1.70
```

A zero entry means that a part is not available from the suppliers. It is frequently desirable to display a matrix containing many zeros so that the zeros are printed as blanks, making
nonzero data more apparent. The function *BPRTZ* (for Blank
PRint of Zero) will do this.

```
        ∇BPRTZ[☐]∇
     ∇  Z←FMT BPRTZ X;R;L
[1]    ⍝DETERMINE THE SHAPE OF X
[2]     R←ρX
[3]    ⍝SELECT NONZERO ELEMENTS FROM X
[4]     X←,X
[5]     L←X≠0
[6]     X←L/X
[7]    ⍝CREATE CHARACTER MATRIX, ONE ELEMENT OF X PER ROW
[8]     FMT←2↑FMT
[9]     Z←((ρX),FMT[1])ρFMT▼X
[10]   ⍝INSERT BLANK ROWS WHERE ZERO ELEMENTS WERE
[11]    Z←L\Z
[12]   ⍝GIVE OUTPUT THE CORRECT SHAPE
[13]    Z←((¯1↓R),FMT[1]×¯1↑1,R)ρZ
     ∇
```

The left argument of this function is a two element vector
giving the format code for the function ▼. The right argument
is the array of numbers to be displayed.

The shape of X is stored in line [2]. Since the zero elements may be located at any points in X and do not necessarily
form a simple pattern, they are compressed out of the ravel of
array X in lines [4] through [6]. After creating a character
matrix containing the nonzero values printed one per row,
expansion is used to insert blank rows where zero elements
were originally located. Line [13] reshapes the data into the
appropriate shape for display, essentially by multiplying the
last coordinate by the field display width, *FMT*[1].

Executing the function *BPRTZ* we now find all zero elements
of the matrix *PARTS* replaced by blanks.

```
          10 2 BPRTZ PARTS
       1.50                    2.90                        2.90
        .80         3.80                    2.90
                                                          1.70
```

   The expression used in line [13] is actually quite general, allowing this function to be used with vector arguments

```
          10 2 BPRTZ 3.4 7.2 0 1.5
       3.40         7.20                    1.50
```

and scalar arguments.

	COMMENTS
`     10 2 BPRTZ 4`	A nonzero value is displayed.
`  4.00`	
`     ρ□←10 2 BPRTZ 0`	A zero value produces a blank
`  10`	vector of 10 elements.

8.11 TAKE AND DROP

   When using ↑ and ↓ with matrices, the left argument is a two element vector giving the number of rows and columns to be taken or dropped.

	COMMENTS
`      LET`	
`ABCDE`	
`FGHIJ`	
`KLMNO`	
`PQRST`	
`     2 3↑LET`	The first two rows of the first
`ABC`	three columns are selected.
`FGH`	
`    ¯2 ¯2↓LET`	Drops off the last two rows and the
`ABC`	last two columns.
`FGH`	
`    ¯2 3↑LET`	Selects the last two rows of the
`KLM`	first three columns.
`PQR`	
`     0 2↓LET`	Drops the first two columns. Rows
`CDE`	are unaffected.
`HIJ`	
`MNO`	
`RST    N`	
`  1 2 3`	
`  4 5 6`	
`       3 5↑N`	
`  1 2 3 0 0`	Zeros (or blanks for character
`  4 5 6 0 0`	matrices) are added if the number
`  0 0 0 0 0`	of rows or columns to be taken
	exceeds the number of rows or
	columns in the matrix.

8.12   REVERSAL AND TRANSPOSE

To see how reversal is applied to matrices, consider the
following matrix:

```
     Q
11 12 13 14
21 22 23 24
31 32 33 34
```

The elements in Q are two-digit integers. The first digit
gives the number of the row in which the element is located,
the second gives the column. By using this matrix it is easy
to keep track of the changes in position of the elements.

Applying the *reversal function* (ϕ) to Q, we find

```
     φQ
14 13 12 11
24 23 22 21
34 33 32 31
```

The row indices have been unaffected but the column indices
have been reversed. This is reversal along the second coordinate.

```
     φ[2]Q
14 13 12 11
24 23 22 21
34 33 32 31
```

Reversal along the first coordinate behaves analogously.

```
     φ[1]Q
31 32 33 34
21 22 23 24
11 12 13 14
```

A special symbol $\ominus$ (o, upshift O, backspace -) is available for
reversal along the first coordinate.

```
     ⊖Q
31 32 33 34
21 22 23 24
11 12 13 14
```

Another useful function for changing the arrangement of data
in a matrix is *transpose* ϕ (o backspace \). The function
changes rows into columns and columns into rows.

COMMENTS

```
     ⍉Q
11 21 31
12 22 32
13 23 33
14 24 34
```

The first column is now the first
row. The second row is the
second column and so on.

COMMENTS

```
        ρQ
3  4
        ρ⍉Q                        The number of rows and columns are
4  3                                  interchanged.
```

The table of population data

```
        TABLE
   1960      1965      1970      1972      1973      1974
    44.8      47.5      49.2      49.7      49.5      49.4
    51.7      54.2      56.7      57.4      57.5      57.5
    55.2      59.6      63        65.1      66.2      67.2
    28.3      32.2      34.9      36        36.7      37.2
```

can be displayed with the years listed by rows through use of the transpose function.

```
        ⍉TABLE
   1960   44.8   51.7   55.2   28.3
   1965   47.5   54.2   59.6   32.2
   1970   49.2   56.7   63     34.9
   1972   49.7   57.4   65.1   36
   1973   49.5   57.5   66.2   36.7
   1974   49.4   57.5   67.2   37.2
```

The symbols for reversal and transpose provide useful mnemonics for their behavior with matrices. Thus in reversing along the second coordinate, ⌽, we can imagine rotating the matrix about a vertical line passing through the center of the matrix.

```
                   |
    [ ] [ ] [|] [ ] [ ]
    [ ] [ ] [|] [ ] [ ]
    [ ] [ ] [|] [ ] [ ]
    [ ] [ ] [|] [ ] [ ]
    [ ] [ ] [|] [ ] [ ]
                   |
```

Reversal along the first coordinate, ⊖, corresponds to rotation about a horizontal line.

```
    [ ] [ ] [ ] [ ] [ ]
    [ ] [ ] [ ] [ ] [ ]
    E-]-E-]-E-]-E-]-E-]
    [ ] [ ] [ ] [ ] [ ]
    [ ] [ ] [ ] [ ] [ ]
```

Transpose, ⍉, then corresponds to rotation about a diagonal line.

```
    [ ] [ ] [ ] [ ] [ ]
    [ ] [ ] [ ] [ ] [ ]
    [ ] [ ] [ ] [ ] [ ]
    [ ] [ ] [ ] [ ] [ ]
    [ ] [ ] [ ] [ ] [ ]
```

Example: Testing a Matrix for Symmetry

The character matrix _M_ is symmetric about the diagonal.

COMMENTS

```
      M
FIRST
IRATE
RACER
STEAM
TERMS
```

_M_ reads the same horizontally as vertically.

```
     M=⍉M
 1 1 1 1 1
 1 1 1 1 1
 1 1 1 1 1
 1 1 1 1 1
   ∧/,M=⍉M
 1
```

The elements in _M_ are identical to the elements in the transpose of _M_.

Example: Producing a Multiplication Table

We use the transpose function to produce a multiplication table.

COMMENTS

```
      ⎕←NOS←6 6⍴⍳6
 1 2 3 4 5 6
 1 2 3 4 5 6
 1 2 3 4 5 6
 1 2 3 4 5 6
 1 2 3 4 5 6
 1 2 3 4 5 6
```

Create a matrix with the elements 1 through 6 in each of six rows.

```
      NOS×⍉NOS
 1  2  3  4  5  6
 2  4  6  8 10 12
 3  6  9 12 15 18
 4  8 12 16 20 24
 5 10 15 20 25 30
 6 12 18 24 30 36
```

The desired table is obtained by multiplying the matrix _NOS_ by its transpose, a matrix which has 1 through 6 in each column.

```
      (⍳6)∘.×⍳6
 1  2  3  4  5  6
 2  4  6  8 10 12
 3  6  9 12 15 18
 4  8 12 16 20 24
 5 10 15 20 25 30
 6 12 18 24 30 36
```

This table can also be obtained using the _outer product_ operation. See Appendix 3.

8.13 ROTATE

The *rotate* function (dyadic φ) is extended to matrices with
two modifications. First, we may rotate elements along the
first or second coordinate using the appropriate index in
brackets or the symbols φ and ⊖. Secondly, each individual
column or row can be rotated a different amount by using a
vector for the left hand argument.

	COMMENTS

`Q`
`11 12 13 14`
`21 22 23 24`
`31 32 33 34`
	We illustrate rotation using the matrix `Q`.

`1φQ`
`12 13 14 11`
`22 23 24 21`
`32 33 34 31`
	The first element in each row is moved to the end. Only column indices are affected.

`1φ[2]Q`
`12 13 14 11`
`22 23 24 21`
`32 33 34 31`
	The coordinate along which the rotation is made can be explicit.

`Q[;1φ1 2 3 4]`
`12 13 14 11`
`22 23 24 21`
`32 33 34 31`
	The result is the same as doing a rotation on the column indices.

`2⊖Q`
`31 32 33 34`
`11 12 13 14`
`21 22 23 24`
	Rotation along the first coordinate.

`(ι3)φQ`
`12 13 14 11`
`23 24 21 22`
`34 31 32 33`
	Each row can be rotated by a different amount by using a vector left argument. The first row is rotated one position, the second two positions and the third three positions.

`(ι4)φQ`
LENGTH ERROR
`(ι4)φQ`
`∧`
	The length of the left argument must equal the number of rows.

`0 ¯1 ¯2φQ`
`11 12 13 14`
`24 21 22 23`
`33 34 31 32`
	Negative rotations move elements from the end of the rows to the front.

`0 1 2 3⊖Q`
`11 22 33 14`
`21 32 13 24`
`31 12 23 34`
	Rotations along the first coordinate change the positions of the elements in each column.

Example: Magic Squares

Consider the following matrix.

```
      SQUARE
 23   6  19   2 15
  4  12  25   8 16
 10  18   1  14 22
 11  24   7  20  3
 17   5  13  21  9
```

The matrix is a magic square, having the property that the sum of the numbers along each row, column, and diagonal is the same.

COMMENTS

```
      +/SQUARE
65 65 65 65 65
```
Sum the rows. All give 65.

```
      +/SQUARE
65 65 65 65 65
```
Sum the columns.

```
      P←0 1 2 3 4ΦSQUARE
      P
23   6  19   2 15
12  25   8  16  4
 1  14  22  10 18
20   3  11  24  7
 9  17   5  13 21
```
To evaluate the sums along the left-to-right diagonals, we first perform a rotation on the rows and then reduction. The diagonals now lie along the columns.

```
      +/P
65 65 65 65 65
```
The sum of each diagonal is 65.

```
      P←0 ¯1 ¯2 ¯2 ¯3ΦSQUARE
      P
23   6  19   2 15
16   4  12  25  8
14  22  10  18  1
 7  20   3  11 24
 5  13  21   9 17
```
The right-to-left diagonals are evaluated in a similar manner.

```
      +/P
65 65 65 65 65
```

Example: Analyzing Voting Results

The matrix NAMES contains the names of five candidates who ran for the same office in a town consisting of five election districts. The matrix VOTES contains the votes obtained by each candidate in each district. These data are displayed in the following table:

```
(¯7 6↑NAMES),(6 0▼ι(ρVOTES)[2]),[1]' ',[1]6 0▼VOTES
```

(The display is shown on next page.)

	1	2	3	4	5
JONES	1480	1362	1636	2774	2305
SMITH	1301	2362	1772	1776	2000
BROWN	1296	2175	2692	2181	2911
THOMAS	2113	1297	2967	1818	1284
GREY	2130	1505	1978	1929	2923

COMMENTS

```
    TOTAL←+/VOTES
    TOTAL
9557 9212 11255 9479 10465
```
Compute the total number of votes obtained by each candidate.

```
    (TOTAL=⌈/TOTAL)/[1]NAMES
BROWN
```
The winner!

```
    WVD←⌈⌿VOTES
    WVD
2130 2362 2967 2774 2923
```
The winning number of votes in each district.

```
    DW←VOTES=(ρVOTES)ρWVD
    DW
0 0 0 1 0
0 1 0 0 0
0 0 0 0 0
0 0 1 0 0
1 0 0 0 1
```
Displays the winner of each district.

```
    +/DW
1 1 0 1 2
```
The number of districts won by each candidate.

Finally the name of the winner in each district is given by

```
    NAMES[(,⍉DW)/,(ρVOTES)ρ⍳(ρVOTES)[1];]
GREY
SMITH
THOMAS
JONES
GREY
```

EXERCISES

1. Enter a matrix *M* consisting of 4 rows and 6 columns and the elements in ⍳24. Before executing the indicated instructions, be sure to write down the anticipated display.

a. *M*	g. 10⌈*M*	m. *M*[5;5]	s. ⌈⌿*M*
b. ρ*M*	h. 15≤*M*	n. *M*[1 2;3 4]	t. ⌊/[2]*M*
c. ρρ*M*	i. *M*[2;1 2]	o. ρ*M*[1 2;2]	u. ×/[1]*M*
d. *M*+2	j. *M*[1 2;2]	p. ρ*M*[1 2;3 4]	v. ρ+/[2]*M*
e. *M*÷2	k. *M*[2;]	q. (ρ*M*)ρ1	w. ρ×/[1]*M*
f. -*M*	l. *M*[;2]	r. +/*M*	x. +/*M*[4;]

2. Using the matrix $M \leftarrow 4 \ 6\rho$'$ABCDEFGHIJKLMNOPQRSTUVWX$' and the
    vectors $L1 \leftarrow 1 \ 1 \ 0 \ 1$ and $L2 \leftarrow 1 \ 1 \ 0 \ 1 \ 1 \ 0$ determine the results
    of the following expressions.

    a. $,M$ g. $L1/[1]M$ m. $\lozenge M$ s. $4 \ 6 \downarrow M$

    b. ρ,M h. $L1/M$ n. ϕM t. $\rho 4 \ 6 \downarrow M$

    c. $M\epsilon$'$AEIOU$'   i. $L2/[2]M$ o. $\ominus M$ u. $^{-}1 \ 3 \uparrow M$

    d. $M\iota$'$AEIOU$'   j. $L2\backslash M$ p. $(\iota 4)\phi M$ v. $4 \ 5 \downarrow M$

    e. $M\epsilon,M$ k. $\rho L1 \neq M$ q. $(\iota 4)\phi[1]M$ w. $\rho 4 \ 5 \downarrow M$

    f. $(,M)\iota M$ l. $L1\backslash M$ r. $L1 \ominus M$ x. $^{-}6 \ ^{-}8 \uparrow M$

3. Construct the matrices M and N where

    M is 5 7 8   and N is   1   3   5
            3 9 2   7   9 11
            4 2 1   13 15 17

    Before executing the indicated instructions, be sure to
    write down the anticipated display.

    a. $M+N$ e. $N-M$ i. $M|N$

    b. $M=N$ f. $N\times M$ j. $M\epsilon N$

    c. $N<M$ g. $(M\leq 7)\wedge N>10$ k. $(M\epsilon N)\vee\sim M>N$

    d. $N\lceil M$ h. $(M>8)\vee N<3$ l. $(,M)\iota N$

4. For each of the following dyadic functions, indicate the
    allowed shapes of the right and left arguments (scalar,
    vector, or matrix), any restrictions on the type of data
    allowed (numerical, character, integer, logical), and how
    the shape of the result is related to the shape of the
    arguments.

    a. $+$ d. ι g. $?$

    b. $\leq$ e. ϵ h. $/$

    c. $\wedge$ f. ϕ i. $,$

5. Write a monadic program that describes its argument as one
    of the following:

    CHARACTER SCALAR, *CHARACTER VECTOR*, *CHARACTER MATRIX*,

    NUMERICAL SCALAR, *NUMERICAL VECTOR*, or *NUMERICAL MATRIX*.

6. The following is a table of students and exam grades.

	G1	G2	G3	G4	G5
S1	80	85	80	90	85
S2	75	70	60	80	75
S3	90	95	90	85	100
S4	75	80	90	80	80

Write APL expressions to do the following (the expressions, except for the first, should work for any matrix of grades):

a. Enter this table into a matrix E.
b. From E find the number of students.
c. From E find the number of exams.
d. Average the exams for each student.
e. Average the grades for each exam.
f. Change the grade of student 3 on the fourth exam to 90.
g. Find the highest exam grade for the semester.
h. Find the number of 90 grades during the semester.

7. Store matrix G containing the ages of students in a class as given in this chapter. Write APL expressions to determine:

a. The average age of all students.
b. The row containing students of the highest average age.
c. The ages of the youngest and oldest students.
d. The seating positions of the youngest and oldest students (give row and column). Assume there is only one person with the youngest age and one with the oldest.

8. Let S be a vector of N scores and W a vector of N weights. The weighted average of the scores in S is given by

$$AV \leftarrow ((S[1] \times W[1]) + (S[2] \times W[2]) + \ldots (S[N] \times W[N])) \div (W[1] + \ldots + W[N])$$

a. Derive a concise APL expression for evaluating this average.
b. Assume M is a matrix of scores containing N columns and an unspecified number of rows. If each row in M is a set of scores, give an APL expression to compute the weighted average of each row.
c. The same as b. but assume the role of columns and rows is interchanged.

9. The following contains the weekly car sales of three salesmen over a period of one month.

	1	2	3	4
ERIC	43,775	46,472	30,064	55,135
MIKE	37,055	27,371	52,899	32,388
BRYAN	66,035	43,829	34,100	52,120

Give APL expressions to:

a. Determine what percentage of the total sales for the
   month is represented by each element of the matrix.
b. Determine what percentage of each salesman's monthly
   sales is given by his sales each week.
c. Determine what percent of the dealer's weekly sales
   was made by each salesman.

10. Let M be a matrix and U be a matrix of the same shape but
    comprised solely of zeros and ones.

    a. Give a dyadic function that will create a vector V made
       up of those elements in M that correspond to ones in U.
       The elements should be stored in row order; elements
       from row one come first, those from row two second, and
       so on.
    b. Give a function that will reverse the process by taking
       the vector of elements found in a. and the matrix U and
       create a matrix that has the same shape as U with the
       elements in V in the positions of the ones in U.

11. a. Write a program to read the row and column of two rooks
       on a chessboard, and determine whether they can capture
       each other.
    b. Do the same for two bishops.

12. The following is a table giving the mileage between four
    different cities.

	C1	C2	C3	C4
C1	0	840	637	378
C2	840	0	279	478
C3	637	279	0	311
C4	378	478	311	0

    a. Enter this in a matrix M.
    b. A trip can be described by a vector of numbers giving
       the cities visited. For example, 1 4 2 is a trip
       starting in City 1 and going to City 2 by way of City
       4. Give an APL expression or sets of expressions that
       compute the distance traveled in any such trip.
       Assume the trip is stored in a vector T.

13. a. Write a dyadic function MATINDEX that takes a matrix as
       its left argument and a scalar as its right argument.
       The result returned should be a two element vector
       giving the row and column index of the first (in the
       sense of row order) appearance of the scalar in the
       matrix.

b. Generalize the function of a. to take a vector right
   argument and return a two column matrix where the rows
   in the result give the position in the input matrix of
   each element in the vector.

14. The matrix *BASKETS* gives the scores made by a basketball
    team in one game. Each row in the matrix corresponds to
    a different player. The columns in the matrix have the
    following meaning:

    Column 1 = Field goals converted
    Column 2 = Field goals attempted
    Column 3 = Foul shots converted
    Column 4 = Foul shots attempted

    Give APL expressions to determine the following:

    a. Total points scored in the game by the team.
    b. The team's highest scorer.
    c. The player with the best overall shooting percentage.
    d. The player with the highest field goal percentage.
    e. The overall field goal percentage for the team.

    Be careful of division by zero. Test your expression on
    the following matrix.

        BASKETS
       7 11   8 10
       3   4   2   3
       6   7   0   2
      12 18   7   9
      15 20 11 11
       1   3   0   0
       0   0   2   3

15. The following 4x4 matrix is from a calendar month

       7   8   9 10
      14 15 16 17
      21 22 23 24
      28 29 30 31

    Write APL expressions to:

    a. Sum the numbers along each diagonal.
    b. Sum the four corner numbers.

    Extract any 3x3 matrix from the 4x4 matrix and evaluate

    c. The sum of the middle row.
    d. The sum of the middle column.
    e. The total of either diagonal.
    f. Confirm that one third of each of the sums found in
       c., d., and e. equals the number in the center of the
       3x3 matrix.

16. Enter the following poem in the form of a matrix, each
    line corresponding to a row of characters in the matrix.
    The longest line has 37 characters including blanks
    between words. When entering the rows of the matrix add
    stars (*) at the end of each line to make each row 37
    characters in length.

> *THE SUN THE WIND THE SOUND OF THE SEA*
> *THE GREAT HILLS ROLL ON ETERNALLY*****
> *THERE ARE NO TIES LIFE IS SO FREE*****
> *ALL THE WORLD WAS MADE FOR ME*********

Write APL expressions to determine

a. How many words there are in each line.
b. How many words there are in the poem.
c. The least number of letters in one line.
d. Which line has the least number of letters.
e. Which line has the most *E*'s.
f. Which letters of the alphabet do not appear in the
   poem.
g. How many letters there are in the poem.
h. Replace all vowels in the poem by underlined vowels.

Can you think of ways to do the above if the stars are
replaced by blanks?

17. Rewrite the function *BOX* of this chapter so that only one
    column or row is added to the matrix on any one line in
    the function. Trace the execution of the function.

18. a. Write a monadic function *ENCLOSE* that takes a character
       matrix as its argument and creates a box around the
       matrix by attaching rows of dashes to the top and
       bottom of the matrix and columns of vertical bars to
       the front and back. You can handle the corners in any
       way that you wish.
    b. Write a monadic function *FRAME* that, given a character
       vector, surrounds the vector with blank characters
       (creating a matrix of three rows) and then uses
       ENCLOSE to put a box around the matrix.

19. Use the matrices $A \leftarrow 8\ 3\rho'\uparrow'; B \leftarrow 2\ 5\rho'\square'; C \leftarrow 4\ 3\rho'o';$
    $D \leftarrow 2\ 3\rho'.'; E \leftarrow 6\ 2\rho'\epsilon'$
    to create the following display

```
↑↑↑□□□□□
↑↑↑□□□□□
↑↑↑...ϵϵ
↑↑↑...ϵϵ
↑↑↑oooϵϵ
↑↑↑oooϵϵ
↑↑↑oooϵϵ
↑↑↑oooϵϵ
```

20.   Store a picture of the American flag in a matrix.

21.   Write a function to build a matrix containing a checker-
        board of arbitrary size. The size (the number of rows
        and columns in the matrix) should be its argument. Use
        any symbols you wish (including blanks) to differentiate
        the dark from light squares. What procedures are avail-
        able for handling sizes that are not multiples of eight?
        (HINT: what would the raveled form of the matrix look
        like?)

22.   Give a function that will take a character matrix and
        remove from it any rows or columns that are completely
        blank.

23.   a. Give a dyadic function that takes a numerical matrix
           as its right argument and a single number as its left
           argument and removes all columns and rows in the matrix
           that contain the left argument.
        b. The same as a. except remove all rows and columns
           which, when the sum of the absolute value of their
           elements is taken, total to less than the left argu-
           ment.

24.   Given the matrix *STAR*

                ρ□←*STAR*

        X....
        XX...
        XXX..
        XXXX.
        XXXXX
        5 5

        Give APL expressions using the rotation, reversal, and
        transpose functions to transform *STAR* into the following
        forms:

        a. *XXXXX*
           XXXX.
           XXX..
           XX...
           X....

        b. *XXXXX*
           .XXXX
           ..XXX
           ...XX
          X

        c. *....X*
           ...XX
           ..XXX
           .XXXX
           XXXXX

```
d.  .....
    .....
    XXXXX
    XXXXX
    XXXXX
```

How could you convert it into

```
e.  ....X....
    ...X.X...
    ..X.X.X..
    .X.X.X.X.
    X.X.X.X.X
```

25. a. Let M be a character matrix. Give an expression using
        the take function that will surround M with a double
        layer of blanks. That is, two columns of blanks
        should be added to the front and back of M and two rows
        of blanks should be added to the top and bottom.
     b. Do the same as a. except use the expansion function.

SUPPLEMENTARY EXERCISES

1. Construct a matrix with rows consisting of the names of
    the members in your family.

2. Let C be a vector of course numbers and N be the number
    of students in each course. What is the result of the
    expression

    $$(2,(\rho C))\rho C,N$$

3. The identity matrix is a matrix with ones along the
    diagonal (for instance, $M[1;1]$, $M[2;2]$, etc.) equal to one
    and zeros everywhere else. Write an APL expression that
    will create an identity matrix with N rows and N columns.

4. Write programs that will show the allowable moves of the
    different chess pieces on the board. (For example, the
    program $KNIGHT$ will take as its input the initial posi-
    tion of the piece on the board and will display all
    possible final positions of the knight.)

5. Create matrices A through Z that hold the alphabet as
    block letters.

    Example: C CCCCCCC
                              CCCCCCC
                              CC
                              CC
                              CC
                              CCCCCCC
                              CCCCCCC

6. Draw a picture by creating a large blank character matrix
    and inserting characters at various positions.

7. Draw a random design by filling in a character matrix at points selected with the ? function.

8. Draw a geometric picture using a mathematical expression to choose the locations in a character matrix in which characters are to be inserted.

9. Write a program *TICTACTOE* to display a blank *TIC-TAC-TOE* board.

10. If *M* is a matrix, what are the results of the following:

    a. $(\rho M)\rho,M$
    b. $(\rho M)\rho M$
    c. $(\rho M)\rho'E'$
    d. $M=M$

11. Construct a matrix of words that rhyme for example,

    MAD
    PAD
    DAD
    GLAD
    .
    .
    .

    Write a program that uses the random number generator to select some of these words and combine them into a phrase.

12. Using words that rhyme (as in the previous problem) and others that don't, write a program to compose random limericks.

13. Write a program to create a triangular matrix with ones below and on the diagonal and zeros above.

14. Write a program to create a matrix containing the following daily temperature readings taken at 1 A. M., 7 A. M., 1 P. M., and 7 P. M.

Temperature (°F) at

	1 AM	7 AM	1 PM	7 PM
Monday	33	26	30	27
Tuesday	20	33	42	38
Wednesday	39	38	58	49
Thursday	39	35	52	46
Friday	40	43	64	51
Saturday	36	32	66	42
Sunday	33	34	52	48

a. Compute the daily degree days (DD) based on the average of the 4 daily temperatures (DD are the larger of zero and 65 minus the average day's temperature.

b. Compute the daily DD based on the daily high and low
   temperatures. (DD = 65 - 0.5 x high+low temperatures).
c. Compute the total degree days for the week in a. and b.
   and compare the results.

15. Different arrangements of the elements in a matrix can be
    formed from successive applications of ⏀, ⊖, and ⍉.

    a. Find a combination that will be equivalent to a rota-
       tion about the diagonal from the lower left hand corner
       to the upper right hand corner.
    b. Find all of the distinct arrangements that can be
       formed by successive applications of these functions.

16. Which pairs of the functions ⏀, ⊖, ⍉ commute? For
    example, we would say that ⏀ and ⊖ commute if ⏀⊖A is the
    same as ⊖⏀A for any matrix A.

17. The game of JOTTO is played by two players in the follow-
    ing way. Player A picks a five letter word in which all
    five letters are different. Player B guesses five letter
    words (some letters may be duplicated) and A responds by
    indicating how many letters in A's word are contained in
    B's. If a letter in A's word appears as a double letter
    in B's, it is only counted once. The game ends when B
    guesses A's word.

    a. Give an APL expression to indicate how many letters in
       A's word are contained in B's. (Put A's word in a
       character vector A and B's in a character vector B.)
    b. Write a computer program to play the part of player A
       in this game. (HINT: create a matrix of five-letter
       words from which A can choose a word at random. Each
       time B responds check that B's word has five letters,
       determine whether or not it is identical with A's, and
       calculate the number of letters in the word chosen by
       the program which are contained in B's word.)

18. Generate matrix *RATIOS*, which is used in this chapter.

19. Suppose A is a vector and V is a numerical vector of 2
    elements. Under what conditions is A the same as ,$V\rho A$?

20. The following matrix contains the responses of 5 persons
    (P1, P2, ... P5) to a 7 question (Q1, Q2, ... Q7) multiple
    choice questionnaire. The responses range from strong
    agreement by the respondent to strong disagreement and
    these choices correspond to the numerical values 1 through
    6 respectively.

	Q1	Q2	Q3	Q4	Q5	Q6	Q7
P1	1	2	5	5	4	2	4
P2	6	4	1	6	2	3	6
P3	3	2	2	5	6	5	3
P4	5	6	5	1	3	5	6
P5	3	5	4	3	4	3	1

a. Determine the sum of the responses by each person.
b. Determine the most favorable person (smallest sum in a).
c. Determine the most unfavorable person.
d. Suppose a national norm has been established with the following responses to the seven questions

    $NORM \leftarrow 2\ 4\ 3\ 5\ 3\ 2\ 4$

Determine the person who is most compatible with the national norm. Assume the index of compatability to be defined as the sum of the absolute values of the differences of the responses when compared with the national norm.

21. Write an APL expression to generate a table of powers. The first row of this matrix is to contain the first, second, third, fourth, and fifth power of 2, the second row is to contain the powers of 3 and so on up to the tenth row.

Part II
Case Studies

Chapter 9
Sorting Data

All data processing whether it be done by hand or by the latest electronic methods consists of three basic steps. In the first step, the data must be recorded in some format that allows them to be entered into the system. This process usually involves the transcribing of facts and figures on a data record. For the second step the recorded data are arranged in some desired order of sequence. This arrangement of data can be a time consuming task since data volumes are usually large. In the final step the data is processed to create the desired information and output.

The second step, putting the records into some particular order, is called *sorting*. This process involves rearranging the data numerically or alphabetically according to some criterion. An example of this would be the sorting and reporting of employee records. Such a report can be produced according to employee names listed alphabetically, or according to employee social security numbers listed in ascending numerical order.

Sorting is so frequently used in data processing that a number of techniques have been developed. In this case study we present by way of introduction two basic algorithms: comparator and bubble sorting. The APL functions grade up and grade down can be used to sort APL vectors. The purpose of this section is to give the student insight into the inner workings of grade up and grade down and to present material useful in data processing. In the case of ⍋, the algorithm is coded in machine language and is not visible to the user.

9.1 FINDING THE SMALLEST ELEMENT IN A VECTOR

The *comparator sort* technique orders the elements in a numerical vector in ascending order by first locating the smallest element in the vector, then the second smallest and so on, using the elements so obtained to build the sorted vector. The discussion of this sorting procedure is separated into two parts.

This section describes the program *SMALLEST* which uses a looping procedure to locate the smallest element of the vector. The next section develops the program *ASCEND* which incorporates the program *SMALLEST* to sort the entire vector by means of the comparator sort technique. A flowchart for the program *SMALLEST* is shown in Figure 9.1.

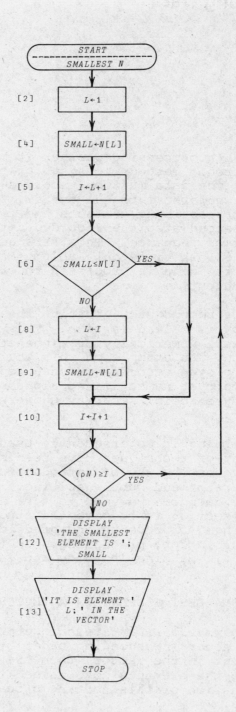

Figure 9.1 Locating the smallest element in a vector.

The smallest element of vector N is found by assuming that the
first element of the vector $N[1]$ is the smallest element. The
value of $N[1]$ is stored in a temporary variable $SMALL$. This
variable will eventually contain the value of the smallest element in the vector. The variable L will be assigned the position of the smallest element of the vector and is initially set
to 1.

Variable $SMALL$ is compared to subsequent elements of N,
$N[2]$, $N[3]$, and so on. Whenever an element of N is encountered
that is less than $SMALL$, variable $SMALL$ is assigned this
smaller value. The position in N of this element is stored in
L. The new value of $SMALL$ is then compared to subsequent elements of N. After all the elements have been compared, $SMALL$
will contain the smallest element of N, and L will contain its
position in the vector.

The program $SMALLEST$ is written according to the flowchart
of Figure 9.1 with corresponding line numbers appearing in the
flowchart.

```
      ∇SMALLEST[⎕]∇
    ∇ SMALLEST N;SMALL;L;I
[1]    ⍝L IS INDEX OF SMALLEST ELEMENT, INITIALIZED TO 1
[2]    L←1
[3]    ⍝SMALL IS VALUE OF SMALLEST ELEMENT, INITIALIZED TO N[1]
[4]    SMALL←N[L]
[5]    I←L+1
[6]  LPI:→(SMALL≤N[I])/ENDI
[7]    ⍝N[I]<SMALL. RESET L AND SMALL
[8]    L←I
[9]    SMALL←N[L]
[10] ENDI:I←I+1
[11]   →((⍴N)≥I)/LPI
[12]   'THE SMALLEST ELEMENT IS ';SMALL
[13]   'IT IS ELEMENT ';L;' IN THE VECTOR'
    ∇
```

A sample execution of the program follows.

```
    X
8 7 8 9 6 6 3 7 9 5 963 0 65 78 8 4 7 5 34 8


    SMALLEST X
THE SMALLEST ELEMENT IS 0
IT IS ELEMENT 12 IN THE VECTOR
```

The program not only displays the smallest element in the
vector, but also locates its position.

To gain further insight into how the program $SMALLEST$ works,
the trace control is set to observe the changes that variables
L and $SMALL$ undergo. Displayed lines would normally appear one
after the other, but they are separated below to indicate the
groups of assignments to L and $SMALL$. In each group the L
value appears first, giving the location of the smallest element in the vector that has been encountered so far. The value
of $SMALL$ appears second and gives the value of the element $N[L]$.

COMMENTS

        $T\Delta SMALLEST \leftarrow 2\ 4\ 8\ 9$ Set the trace to observe changes
                                    in L and $SMALL$.

        $SMALLEST\ 4\ 9\ 2\ 3\ ^-1\ 2$
$SMALLEST[2]\ 1$ Lines [2] and [4] initialize L
$SMALLEST[4]\ 4$ and $SMALL$.

$SMALLEST[8]\ 3$ The third element is smaller
$SMALLEST[9]\ 2$ than the current value of
                                    $SMALL$. L and $SMALL$ are re-
                                    assigned.
$SMALLEST[8]\ 5$ The fifth element is smaller
$SMALLEST[9]\ ^-1$ still. It's value is assigned
                                    to $SMALL$.

$THE\ SMALLEST\ ELEMENT\ IS\ ^-1$
$IT\ IS\ ELEMENT\ 5\ IN\ THE\ VECTOR$

        $T\Delta SMALLEST \leftarrow 0$ Remove the trace.

The function $SMALL$ uses the full power of APL and achieves the same results as $SMALLEST$

```
     ∇SMALL[☐]∇
  ∇ SMALL N;S
[1]    'THE SMALLEST ELEMENT IS ';S←⌊/N
[2]    'IT IS ELEMENT ';N⍳S;' IN THE VECTOR'
  ∇
```

        $SMALL\ 4\ 9\ 2\ 3\ ^-1\ 2$
$THE\ SMALLEST\ ELEMENT\ IS\ ^-1$
$IT\ IS\ ELEMENT\ 5\ IN\ THE\ VECTOR$

9.2   COMPARATOR SORT

The program $SMALLEST$ locates the smallest element in the vector N. The next step is to rearrange the entire array in ascending order. A flowchart for doing this is given in Figure 9.2. We first place the smallest element of the vector in the first position by interchanging the smallest element and the first element. We then locate the next smallest element in N by comparing the second element with the third, and all the following elements until the smallest among these elements is found. Similarly the next larger values are placed in the third, fourth, fifth, and so on positions, until finally all the elements of N have been arranged in ascending order.

The flowchart for the program $ASCEND$ is an extension of the flowchart for $SMALLEST$. An *outer loop* using the variable J as a counter specifies the element which is to be determined in the sorted array. The procedures of the program $SMALLEST$ are contained within this loop. Several steps in $SMALLEST$ have been combined to create a more compact program. For example, lines [8] and [9] of $SMALLEST$ are combined into a single expression $SMALL\leftarrow N[L\leftarrow I]$ which appears as line [9] in $ASCEND$. Similarly line [10] in $ASCEND$ is a combination of lines [10] and [11] in $SMALLEST$.

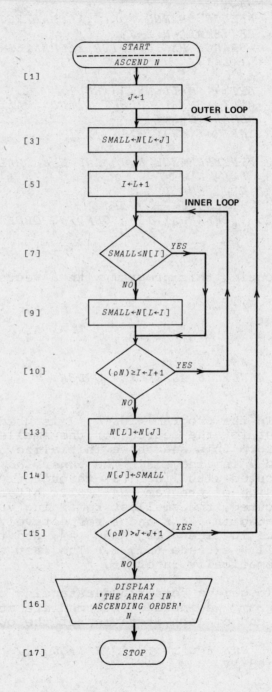

Figure 9.2 The comparator sort algorithm

```
              ∇ASCEND[☐]∇
          ∇ ASCEND N;I;J;L;SMALL
[1]     J←1
[2]     ⍝BEGIN SEARCH FOR JTH SMALLEST ELEMENT
[3]     LPJ:SMALL←N[L←J]
[4]     ⍝SEARCH BEGINS WITH ELEMENT L+1
[5]     I←L+1
[6]     ⍝
[7]     LPI:→(SMALL≤N[I])/ENDI
[8]     ⍝N[I]<SMALL. RESET L AND SMALL
[9]       SMALL←N[L←I]
[10]    ENDI:→((ρN)≥I←I+1)/LPI
[11]    ⍝
[12]    ⍝INTERCHANGE N[J] AND THE SMALLEST ELEMENT
[13]    N[L]←N[J]
[14]    N[J]←SMALL
[15]    →((ρN)>J←J+1)/LPJ
[16]    'THE ARRAY IN ASCENDING ORDER'
[17]    N
          ∇
```

Executing this program with a vector of integers gives

```
      X←10?10
      X
5 1 3 9 8 6 4 7 2 10

      ASCEND X
THE ARRAY IN ASCENDING ORDER
1 2 3 4 5 6 7 8 9 10
```

In the program *ASCEND*, *J* is used to locate the starting point for the search for the smallest remaining element. To perform this search we initialize *SMALL* to the value *N[J]* and *L* to *J* in line [3]. The *inner loop* (see flowchart) is then executed with lines [3] through [10] representing a compact version of program *SMALLEST*. After this inner loop has been executed, the smallest remaining value and its position are located in *SMALL* and *L* respectively. The interchange takes place in lines [13] and [14], and the *outer loop* is repeated until *J* exceeds (ρ*N*)-1. The last element of the vector is automatically in order.

To gain a better understanding of the operation of the program, we include intermediate steps to display the array at the end of each iteration of the outer loop.

```
      ∇ASCEND[14.1]'ITERATION ';J
[14.2] N∇
```

To emphasize the interchanges taking place in the sorting
process, elements that have been interchanged are shaded in
the execution below.

                              COMMENTS

```
     X
5 1 3 9 8 6 4 7 2 10
     ASCEND X
ITERATION 1                      The smallest element of X, 1, is
1 5 3 9 8 6 4 7 2 10                interchanged with the first
ITERATION 2                         element.
1 2 3 9 8 6 4 7 5 10
ITERATION 3
1 2 3 9 8 6 4 7 5 10
ITERATION 4                      The interchanged elements are
1 2 3 4 8 6 9 7 5 10                shaded.
ITERATION 5
1 2 3 4 5 6 9 7 8 10
ITERATION 6
1 2 3 4 5 6 9 7 8 10             The 6 is the sixth smallest element;
ITERATION 7                         it happens to be already in
1 2 3 4 5 6 7 9 8 10                position 6 and is consequently
ITERATION 8                         interchanged with itself.
1 2 3 4 5 6 7 8 9 10
ITERATION 9                      Nine iterations are required since
1 2 3 4 5 6 7 8 9 10                ρX is 10.
THE ARRAY IS ASCENDING ORDER
1 2 3 4 5 6 7 8 9 10

       ∇ASCEND[15□]             Remove the lines that were added to
[15]   'ITERATION ';J              display intermediate steps of the
[15]                               sorting process.
       ∨
[16]
       ∨
[17]   ∇
```

The comparator sort algorithm requires as much effort to
sort an array that is completely scrambled as one with only
one element out of place. The next algorithm to be discussed,
the bubble sort, is considerably more efficient in arranging
an array that is almost in order.

9.3   BUBBLE SORT

The *bubble sort* algorithm is designed to be particularly efficient for sorting an array of numbers which is almost in order.
In the algorithm, Figure 9.3, the array is searched until an
element is located that is smaller than the previous element.
The smaller element is out of order. We then move it back up
the vector making successive comparisons until its proper position is located. When an element of the array is out of order,
the sort process bubbles it to its proper position in a manner
similar to an air bubble rising in water.

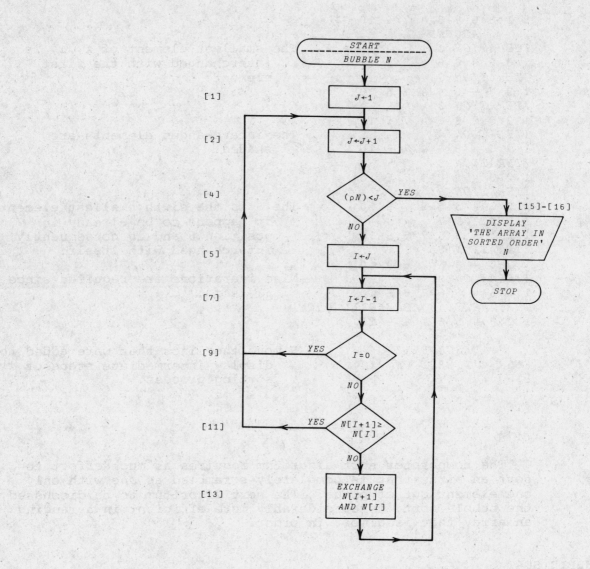

Figure 9.3 A bubble sort algorithm

```
       ∇BUBBLE[□]∇
     ∇ BUBBLE N;I;J
[1]    J←1
[2]   LPJ:J←J+1
[3]   ⍝TEST FOR END OF THE VECTOR
[4]    →((ρN)<J)/OUT
[5]    I←J
[6]   ⍝SEARCH BACKWARDS TO FIND PROPER LOCATION
[7]   LPI:I←I-1
[8]   ⍝CHECK FOR BEGINNING OF THE VECTOR
[9]    →(I=0)/LPJ
[10]  ⍝CHECK FOR PROPER POSITION
[11]   →(N[I+1]≥N[I])/LPJ
[12]  ⍝INTERCHANGE N[I+1] AND N[I]
[13]   N[I+ 0 1]←N[I+ 1 0]
[14]   →LPI
[15] OUT:'THE ARRAY IN SORTED ORDER'
[16]   N
     ∇
```

The counter J indicates the element whose proper position is
currently being located. This is done by searching backwards
from position J, using the variable I as a counter. Line [9]
tests whether the element has bubbled to the first position.
If so, no more interchanges are possible. Line [11] checks
if the element is in its correct position. This occurs if the
preceding element is smaller in value.

The program *BUBBLE* is executed in the same way as *ASCEND*.

```
      X
5 1 3 9 8 6 4 7 2 10
      BUBBLE X
THE ARRAY IN SORTED ORDER
1 2 3 4 5 6 7 8 9 10
```

An intermediate step is now inserted into the program to
demonstrate the sorting process. The element which is bubbling
up is shaded.

	COMMENTS
∇*BUBBLE*[13.1]N∇	A line is inserted into the program to display the array as any element out of order bubbles up.
X←21 25 33 23 37	In this vector, only the 23 is out of place.
BUBBLE X	Execute *BUBBLE*.
21 25 23 33 37	The 23 and 33 are interchanged.
21 23 25 33 37	Now the 23 and 25 are interchanged.
THE ARRAY IN SORTED ORDER	The 23 has bubbled into place. A
21 23 25 33 37	total of two switches were necessary.

COMMENTS

```
        X←21 25 26 33 23 37
        BUBBLE X
21 25 26 23 33 37                      Only the 23 is out of order.
21 25 23 26 33 37                      Second switch.
21 23 25 26 33 37                      Third switch.
THE ARRAY IN SORTED ORDER              Three switches were necessary
21 23 25 26 33 37                         to bubble the 23 into
                                          place.


        X←21 25 26 33 23 37 15 31
        BUBBLE X
21 25 26 23 33 37 15 31                The 23 moves up.
21 25 23 26 33 37 15 31                The element that is bubbling
21 23 25 26 33 37 15 31                   is shaded.
21 23 25 26 33 15 37 31
21 23 25 26 15 33 37 31                The 15 is out of order and
21 23 25 15 26 33 37 31                   bubbles to the first
21 23 15 25 26 33 37 31                   position.
21 15 23 25 26 33 37 31
15 21 23 25 26 33 37 31
15 21 23 25 26 33 31 37                Finally 31 bubbles up.
15 21 23 25 26 31 33 37
THE ARRAY IN SORTED ORDER
15 21 23 25 26 31 33 37


        ∇BUBBLE[14□]                   Line [14], the intermediate
[14]    N                                 step added to display the
[14]                                      sorting process, is
        ∇                                 removed by striking
                                          ATTENTION.
[15]    ∇
```

In APL it is also possible to perform a sort with the primitive functions grade up (⍋) and grade down (⍒). Using the ⍋ function, the program to rearrange a numerical vector N into ascending order now becomes

```
        ∇GRADEUPSORT[□]∇
     ∇ GRADEUPSORT N
[1]     'THE SORTED ARRAY'
[2]     N[⍋N]
     ∇Z
```

The program GRADEUPSORT emphasizes the great power of the APL language. It is an extremely efficient language and requires very little detail.

9.4   COMPARISON AMONG THE ALGORITHMS

At this point it might be interesting to compare the speeds of execution for the three sort programs that have been presented. The *time of execution* of an APL program may be obtained through the function ⍳21 (⍳ beam 21, upshift N backspace upshift B). This function gives the CPU time used since sign-on in 60ths of a second. (Some systems use the system variable, $□AI$. See Appendix 3.)

COMMENTS

⍳21	The CPU time used since sign-on is
1731	1731 sixtieths of a second.
A←0.1×⍳1000	A is a vector of 1000 elements.
⍳21	It took 4 sixtieths of a second to
1735	create A.
B←A×A	1000 multiplications are done in 3
⍳21	sixtieths of a second.
1738	
T←⍳21	
T	Time elapsed for the assignment is
1738	less than 1 sixtieth of a second.
C←A⋆2	
(⍳21)-T	It took 8 sixtieths of a second to
8	square vector A.

To estimate the CPU time elapsed during execution of a program,
or any section of a program, we initialize a variable to ⍳21
and on completion of the calculation subtract the stored value
of ⍳21 from the current value of ⍳21.

COMMENTS

A←⌽⍳1000	Assign A.
T←⍳21	T stores the initial value of ⍳21.
B←A[⍋A]	Sort A.
(⍳21)-T	It took 17 sixtieths of a second
17	to sort A into ascending order.

The following program displays the execution times in
seconds for sorting a given vector using programs *GRADEUPSORT*,
ASCEND, and *BUBBLE*.

```
      ∇COMPARESORT[□]∇
    ∇ COMPARESORT X;T
[1]   T←⍳21
[2]   GRADEUPSORT X
[3]   '***GRADEUPSORT CPU=';((⊤21)-T)÷60
[4]   T←⍳21
[5]   ASCEND X
[6]   '***ASCEND SORT CPU=';((⍳21)-T)÷60
[7]   T←⍳21
[8]   BUBBLE X
[9]   '***BUBBLE SORT CPU=';((⍳21)-T)÷60
    ∇
```

We are now ready to investigate the speed of execution for
the sorting programs with several vectors. We create a vector
of 23 elements, three of which are out of order.

```
      X←20?100
      X←X[⍋X]
      X←X,13 54 89
      X
1 4 5 6 9 16 19 23 33 34 38 40 46 51 54 55 57 91 94 98 13 54 89
```

```
        COMPARESORT X
THE SORTED ARRAY
1  4  5  6  9  13  16  19  23  33  34  38  40  46  51  54  54  55  57  89  91  94  98
***GRADEUPSORT CPU=0.01666666667
THE ARRAY IN ASCENDING ORDER
1  4  5  6  9  13  16  19  23  33  34  38  40  46  51  54  54  55  57  89  91  94  98
***ASCEND SORT CPU=1.516666667
THE ARRAY IN SORTED ORDER
1  4  5  6  9  13  16  19  23  33  34  38  40  46  51  54  54  55  57  89  91  94  98
***BUBBLE SORT CPU=0.45
```

The grade up function took 1/60 of a second to order the vector. Programs *ASCEND* and *BUBBLE* took 1.5167 and 0.45 seconds respectively. As we shall see, the grade up will always be the fastest method for any vector *X*. The reason for this is that the sort procedure associated with the function ⍋ is stored in the computer in machine language and is automatically executed when the interpreter recognizes the function ⍋ in the program. Programs *ASCEND* and *BUBBLE*, on the other hand, contain loops that are repeated a large number of times with each instruction interpreted during every iteration. In the case of *ASCEND* vs. *BUBBLE*, we note in the above example that *BUBBLE* is considerably faster. This is because only the last three elements of the original vector *X* are out of sequence. For arrays which have more elements out of sequence, this is not so. Note in the examples below that the comparator sort technique requires about the same amount of time independent of the data used.

```
        X←20?100
        X
42  96  14  31  36  47  25  6  76  84  85  18  56  72  4  63  90  70  19  92


        COMPARESORT X
THE SORTED ARRAY
4  6  14  18  19  25  31  36  42  47  56  63  70  72  76  84  85  90  92  96
***GRADEUPSORT CPU=0.01666666667
THE ARRAY IN ASCENDING ORDER
4  6  14  18  19  25  31  36  42  47  56  63  70  72  76  84  85  90  92  96
***ASCEND SORT CPU=1.3
THE ARRAY IN SORTED ORDER
4  6  14  18  19  25  31  36  42  47  56  63  70  72  76  84  85  90  92  96
***BUBBLE SORT CPU=1.066666667
```

If the vector to be sorted is extremely out of sequence the bubble method is the slowest:

```
        X←⌽⍳20
        X
20  19  18  17  16  15  14  13  12  11  10  9  8  7  6  5  4  3  2  1


        COMPARESORT X
THE SORTED ARRAY
1  2  3  4  5  6  7  8  9  10  11  12  13  14  15  16  17  18  19  20
***GRADEUPSORT CPU=0.01666666667
THE ARRAY IN ASCENDING ORDER
1  2  3  4  5  6  7  8  9  10  11  12  13  14  15  16  17  18  19  20
***ASCEND SORT CPU=1.383333333
THE ARRAY IN SORTED ORDER
1  2  3  4  5  6  7  8  9  10  11  12  13  14  15  16  17  18  19  20
***BUBBLE SORT CPU=2.15
```

In summary it should be noted that CPU time is not the sole criterion by which one would select a method of sorting. Another important consideration is the ease by which the method is programmed. In addition, it is important to take into account how sensitive the method is to the order of the initial data, and how dependent the scheme is on the number of items to be sorted. In large scale applications the amount of extra storage needed to carry out the sort may also play an important role.

EXERCISES

1. Modify the following programs to sort a vector in descending order.

    a. *GRADEUPSORT*
    b. *ASCEND*
    c. *BUBBLE*

2. Write programs similar to *ASCEND* and *BUBBLE* which will sort a character vector alphabetically.

3. You are given the employees' social security numbers and hourly wages in two vectors *SOC* and *WAGE*. The personnel office would like all the employees' social security numbers listed in ascending order along with the respective hourly wages. Modify the programs

    a. *GRADEUPSORT*
    b. *ASCEND*
    c. *BUBBLE*

    to accomplish this.

4. Let X be a vector containing, in ascending order, all the integers from 1 to 99 excluding the integers 3, 50, and 98. Use program *COMPARESORT* along with *GRADEUPSORT*, *ASCEND*, and *BUBBLE* to investigate the execution times for the vectors

    a. X,3
    b. X,50
    c. X,98
    d. 3,X
    e. 50,X
    f. 98,X

    Explain your results.

5. One possible variation of the bubble method is to compare the first element with the second and if necessary make an interchange. Then compare the second with the third and again if need be make a change. Subsequently compare the third and fourth elements, fourth and fifth, and so on. Finally, when the first pass is complete, the largest element will be in the last position. This process continues until no interchanges are required during a pass. Write a program for this technique.

6. Modify the programs *ASCEND* and *BUBBLE* so that they return an explicit result which is equivalent to the function ⍋.

7. The following program determines the average amount of CPU time to execute a loop N times.

```
     ∇TIME[□]∇
   ∇ Z←TIME N;I
[1]    Z←⍳21
[2]    I←1
[3] LP:→(N≥I←I+1)/LP
[4]    Z←((⍳21)-Z)÷N
   ∇
```

a. Execute this function several times for N=500. How consistent are the results?

Write similar functions which in addition to a loop contain the following calculations:

b. Add 100 numbers.
c. Multiply 100 numbers.
d. Create a vector of 100 random numbers.
e. Take the square root of 100 numbers.

By executing these programs for large N and correcting for the time needed to perform the loop, determine the average amount of time needed to do each of these calculations. At the rates charged by your computer center, how much do each of these cost?

8. Using timing programs, compare the relative execution times of the following pairs of equivalent expressions. (*A* is a vector of 100 numbers, *S* is a numerical scalar.)

a. $A×A$ and $A*2$
b. $∨/S=A$ and $S∈A$
c. $⌈/A$ and $(A[⍋A])[⍴A]$
d. $+/A÷⍴A$ and $(+/A)÷⍴A$
e. $3+⍳197$ and $3↓⍳200$

Chapter 10
Searching Data

A very important aspect of data processing is information
retrieval. A request is entered from a terminal device and
the computer then executes an algorithm to search a file for
the data in question. The airline reservation system, which
controls the inventory of available seats is an example of such
a process. It accepts input from many terminals, all operating
simultaneously. Inquiries may be answered by access to
up-to-the-minute records. In seconds a customer may request
and receive information about flights and available seats.
Other examples in which searching is important are systems designed to keep track of the availability of motel rooms, or for
searching the library catalog data file for a certain volume.

Searching for information is a frequent task in data processing and, as with sorting, there exist several techniques
for searching data. Two search algorithms are presented in
this case study: the linear and binary techniques. We will
see that if the vector to be searched is in sorted form, the
binary method is preferable. The index of function provided
by APL is also used for comparison purposes. Its algorithm is
stored in the computer in machine language and is not visible
to the user.

10.1 LINEAR SEARCH

Linear search, also called *sequential search*, is the simplest
of all search algorithms. Given a numerical vector A, we wish
to determine the position of a number B in the vector. The
basic idea of a linear search algorithm is to compare B in
succession with each element in A, using a counter to keep
track of where we are in A. The search stops either when a
match is found or when the value of the counter exceeds the
length of the vector A, that is when its value is $1+\rho A$. In
that case we conclude that the number B does not occur in
vector A.

A procedure for performing this search is shown in the
flowchart of Figure 10.1. The corresponding function, *LINSRCH*,
is displayed below.

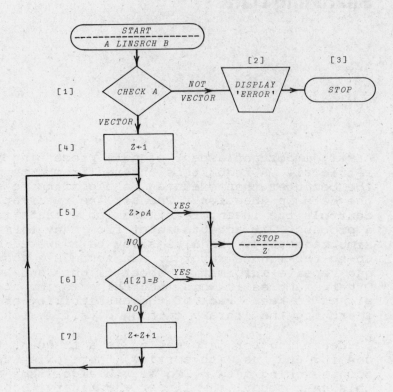

Figure 10.1   Linear Search Algorithm

```
      ∇LINSRCH[□]∇
    ∇ Z←A LINSRCH B
[1]    →(1=ρρA)/OK
[2]    'LEFT ARGUMENT OF LINSRCH MUST BE A VECTOR'
[3]    →0
[4]   OK:Z←1
[5]   LP:→(Z>ρA)/0
[6]    →(A[Z]=B)/0
[7]    Z←Z+1
[8]    →LP
    ∇
```

The linear search function, *LINSRCH*, returns the value *Z*.
For this reason the terminal box in the flowchart includes *Z*.
The result *Z* is the location of *B* within the vector *A*. If *B*
appears more than once, the location of the first occurrence
will be returned. The line numbers in the function correspond
to the numbers in the flowchart. Lines [1] through [3] check
that the left argument of *LINSRCH* is a vector. Line [4] initializes the counter *Z*. The actual search is contained in
lines [5] through [8].

The first decision in line [5] checks that Z does not exceed
the length of A. If Z is greater than ρA, the entire vector
has been searched without finding B. In this case the transfer
statement causes a branch out of the function, and the current
value of Z, $1+\rho A$, is returned.

If Z is less than the length of A, the loop proceeds to line
[6] where a test is performed to see if the element $A[Z]$ is the
desired element. If so, the function stops execution and
returns the current value of Z, the desired location in the
vector A. Otherwise, the counter is incremented in line [7]
followed by a transfer to the beginning of the loop, line [5].

Additional insight into the function is gained from a trace
of line [7], which shows that B is compared with each element
of A until a match is found.

	COMMENTS
$X \leftarrow 10 + \iota 10$	Specify vector X.
X	
11 12 13 14 15 16 17 18 19 20	
$T \Delta LINSRCH \leftarrow 7$	Set a trace on line [7].
$X\ LINSRCH\ 14$	Where in X is 14?
$LINSRCH[7]\ 2$	The counter Z is now 2.
$LINSRCH[7]\ 3$	The counter is 3.
$LINSRCH[7]\ 4$	The counter is 4.
4	14 is in the fourth position of X.
$X\ LINSRCH\ 21$	Where in X is 21?
$LINSRCH[7]\ 2$	
$LINSRCH[7]\ 3$	The trace of line [7] displays
$LINSRCH[7]\ 4$	the value of the counter as
$LINSRCH[7]\ 5$	the entire vector is searched
$LINSRCH[7]\ 6$	for the value 21.
$LINSRCH[7]\ 7$	
$LINSRCH[7]\ 8$	
$LINSRCH[7]\ 9$	
$LINSRCH[7]\ 10$	
$LINSRCH[7]\ 11$	
11	21 is not contained in X. $1+\rho X$ is displayed.

In the last example the function $LINSRCH$ returned 11, one
more than ρX. This is the same result the index of function
(dyadic ι) would return in this case.

10.2 INDEX OF SEARCH

The index of function presents a convenient way of searching
a vector. The actual instructions associated with this
function are stored in the computer in machine language and are
not visible to the user. However, it should be clear from the
previous section that the algorithm is essentially that of a
linear search and differs from the $LINSRCH$ function only in
that the right argument of the dyadic ι can have any shape.
Use of the index of function for search simplifies matters
greatly.

COMMENTS

```
    ∇INDEXOF[□]∇
  ∇ Z←A INDEXOF B
[1]   Z←AιB                          Where in A is B?
  ∇


    X←2×ι5
    X
2 4 6 8 10
    X INDEXOF 8
4                                    8 is element 4 in X.
    X INDEXOF 5
6                                    5 is not an element of X.
```

10.3 BINARY SEARCH

The linear search method will work for all vectors of data.
Frequently, however, we will have some information about the
data being searched, and this information can be used to
improve the efficiency of the search process. In particular,
if the data being searched is sorted, arranged in ascending or
descending order, the powerful *binary search* technique can be
applied.

In this method the vector to be searched is divided into
two parts. By comparing the value of the element at the midpoint of the vector with the value being searched for, we
determine which of the two portions contain the desired number.
The search is then confined to that portion, which is subsequently divided into two more parts. This process continues
until we locate the desired value or until it is determined
that the value is not present.

A flowchart showing this procedure in more detail is shown
in Figure 10.2. The function *BINSRCH* following this flowchart
is shown below.

```
     ∇BINSRCH[□]∇
   ∇ Z←A BINSRCH B;HIGH;LOW
[1]    →(1=ρρA)/OK
[2]    'LEFT ARGUMENT TO BINSRCH MUST BE A VECTOR'
[3]    →0
[4]   ⍝INITIALIZE HIGH AND LOW
[5]   OK:LOW←1
[6]    HIGH←ρA
[7]   ⍝B IS NOT PRESENT IN A IF LOW>HIGH
[8]   LP:→(LOW>HIGH)/OUT
[9]   ⍝CALCULATE THE MIDPOINT OF THE CURRENT INTERVAL
[10]   Z←⌊0.5×LOW+HIGH
[11]  ⍝TEST FOR THE DESIRED VALUE
[12]   →(A[Z]=B)/0
[13]   →(A[Z]<B)/LW
[14]  ⍝IF A[Z]>B, RESPECIFY HIGH
[15]   HIGH←Z-1
[16]   →LP
[17]  ⍝IF A[Z]<B, RESPECIFY LOW
[18]  LW:LOW←Z+1
[19]   →LP
[20]  ⍝ASSIGN Z IF B IS NOT IN A
[21]  OUT:Z←1+ρA
     ∇
```

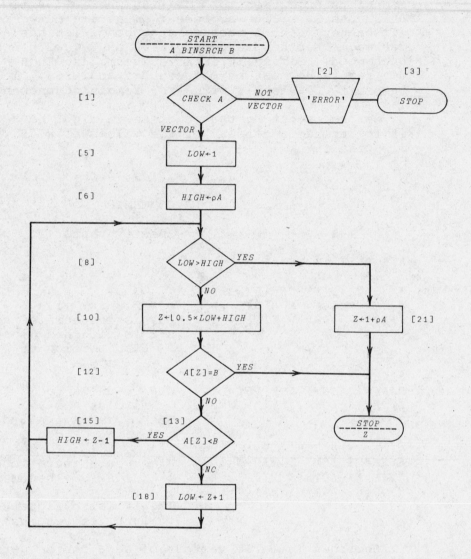

Figure 10.2 Binary search algorithm

The function uses two variables LOW and $HIGH$ to mark the end points of the interval being searched. These are initialized to 1 and ρA respectively in lines [5] and [6]. If the value B is not present in vector A, the value of LOW will eventually exceed that of $HIGH$. This condition is checked in line [8].

The midpoint of the interval being searched is determined in line [10] and stored in the variable Z. Line [12] checks to see if the desired element is at the midpoint of A. If so, $A[Z]=B$, and execution stops. The value of Z, the desired location, is returned. It is important to note that Z, $HIGH$, and LOW are not elements of the vector A. They are indices. If

the value at the midpoint exceeds the desired value, line [13]
transfers execution to line [15] where *HIGH* is respecified. In
this case *B*, if it is present, must lie between *LOW* and *Z*-1.
(It cannot be at *Z* because that condition has already been
tested.) We then respecify *HIGH* as *Z*-1 with *LOW* remaining
unchanged. Similarly if *A*[*Z*] is smaller than *B*, then the
desired value must be between *Z*+1 and *HIGH*. In line [18] we
respecify *LOW* as *Z*+1 with *HIGH* remaining unchanged.

Before executing the function it might be helpful to edit
it to include a display of the values of *HIGH*, *LOW* and the
midpoint *Z*.

$\quad$ ∇*BINSRCH*[10.1]'*HIGH*= ';*HIGH*;' *LOW*= ';*LOW*;' *MIDPT*= ';*Z*∇

COMMENTS

```
    X←3×ι7                      Specify vector X.
    X
3 6 9 12 15 18 21


    X BINSRCH 18
HIGH= 7 LOW= 1 MIDPT= 4          MIDPT=0.5×(7+1)=4.
HIGH= 7 LOW= 5 MIDPT= 6          LOW is respecified as 4+1=5.
6                                A 6 is returned since 18 is in the
                                    6th position of X.

    X BINSRCH 9
HIGH= 7 LOW= 1 MIDPT= 4
HIGH= 3 LOW= 1 MIDPT= 2          LOW is unchanged; HIGH is respeci-
HIGH= 3 LOW= 3 MIDPT= 3              fied as 4-1=3.
3                                The 15 is in the 3rd element of X.


    X BINSRCH 14
HIGH= 7 LOW= 1 MIDPT= 4          After each iteration the interval
HIGH= 7 LOW= 5 MIDPT= 6             (HIGH-LOW) becomes smaller.
HIGH= 5 LOW= 5 MIDPT= 5
8                                The 14 is not located in X; the
                                    function returns 1+ρX which is 8.
```

Searches in large vectors of data can be performed effi-
ciently with the binary search technique.

```
    X←ι1000
    X BINSRCH 576
HIGH= 1000 LOW=1 MIDPT=500
HIGH= 1000 LOW=501 MIDPT=750
HIGH= 749 LOW= 501 MIDPT= 625
HIGH= 624 LOW= 501 MIDPT= 562
HIGH= 624 LOW= 563 MIDPT= 593
HIGH= 592 LOW= 563 MIDPT= 577
HIGH= 576 LOW= 563 MIDPT= 569
HIGH= 576 LOW= 570 MIDPT= 573
HIGH= 576 LOW= 574 MIDPT= 575
HIGH= 576 LOW= 576 MIDPT= 576
576
```

The *BINSRCH* algorithm works rapidly. The number 576 was located during the tenth sweep through the loop. In contrast, the linear search method would have required 576 iterations to locate this value.

We remove the inserted display line from *BINSRCH*.

```
      ∇BINSRCH[11□]
[11]  'HIGH= ';HIGH;' LOW= ';LOW;' MIDPT= ';Z
[11]
      ∇
[12]  ∇
```

10.4 A COMPARISON AMONG THE ALGORITHMS

The following program compares the execution times among the index of, linear, and binary algorithms.

```
      ∇COMPARESRCH[□]∇
    ∇ A COMPARESRCH B;T
[1]   T←ɪ21
[2]   'LOCATION ';A INDEXOF B
[3]   '***INDEXOF SEARCH ';((ɪ21)-T)÷60
[4]   T←ɪ21
[5]   'LOCATION ';A LINSRCH B
[6]   '***LINEAR SEARCH ';((ɪ21)-T)÷60
[7]   T←ɪ21
[8]   'LOCATION ';A BINSRCH B
[9]   '***BINARY SEARCH ';((ɪ21)-T)÷60
    ∇
```

The technique used for determining execution times is identical to that introduced in Chapter 9. A sample execution is shown below.

	COMMENTS
`A←ɪ3000`	
`A COMPARESRCH 50`	
`LOCATION 50`	Index of requires less than one
`***INDEXOF SEARCH 0`	sixtieth of a second.
`LOCATION 50`	
`***LINEAR SEARCH 0.316666667`	Linear search requires 0.31667
`LOCATION 50`	sec.
`***BINARY SEARCH 0.15`	Binary search requires 0.15 sec.

Program *COMPARESRCH* is now used to compare the CPU times for the algorithms. Table 10.1 summarizes the results obtained in these calculations for several values of B and $A←ɪ3000$.

Table 10.1 Comparison of CPU Times

B	ι Search	Linear Search	Binary Search
1	0	0.017	0.167
10	0	0.067	0.15
50	0	0.317	0.15
100	0	0.55	0.15
500	0	2.783	0.117
1000	0	5.133	0.133
2000	0	10.733	0.133

Some interesting conclusions can be drawn from this example.

1. Using the index of function, the CPU time to locate B in vector A is negligible for all B.

2. For the linear search, as B increases so does the CPU time.

3. For the binary search, the CPU times are fairly constant regardless of B as it takes approximately the same number of iterations to locate B.

4. For low values of B the binary search times exceed the linear search times. There is a crossover somewhere between $B=10$ and $B=50$ with the linear search taking more time thereafter. Can you explain this trend? (See Exercises.)

The CPU times using the index of function are all zero since only time intervals of sixtieth of a second are displayed. The actual times are less than 1/60 of a second for all the values searched. On an APL system the index of function will generally be the fastest search method for any vector A. The reason for this is that the search procedure associated with the index of function is stored in the computer in machine language and is automatically executed when the interpreter recognizes the dyadic ι in the program. Functions $LINSRCH$ and $BINSRCH$ on the other hand contain loops that are repeated a large number of times with each instruction interpreted during every iteration. This argument does not apply, however, if the data being searched is not completely contained in the workspace but resides in the files available with many systems.

EXERCISES

1. Modify the binary search function to handle a vector sorted in descending order.

2. Write a program to insert a given number in its proper place within a sorted array.

3. Convert the functions $BINSRCH$ and $LINSRCH$ to act like ϵ; that is, return a one if $B \epsilon A$ and a zero otherwise.

4. Modify *LINSRCH* and *BINSRCH* to return all the locations where *B* occurs in *A*.

5. For $A \leftarrow \iota 3000$ use program *COMPARESRCH* to determine the value of *B* for which *LINSRCH* and *BINSRCH* take the same CPU time. Explain why the CPU times differ for these functions.

6. Execute program *COMPARESRCH* with *A* a character vector and *B* a search character. Can you rectify the difficulties?

7. Modify the functions *LINSRCH* and *BINSRCH* to take vectors as their right arguments.

8. Modify the functions *LINSRCH* and *BINSRCH* to find the element in *A* which is closest in value to *B*. Also give a solution to this problem that does not require a loop. Compare times of execution.

Chapter 11
Computer Generated Random Numbers

One of the most interesting and most rapidly expanding uses of
computers is the simulation of the real world. Some true-to-
life situations are strictly causal, showing a smooth connection between cause and effect. Others, however, display a
randomness in their nature which only on the average leads to
a predictable pattern.

Waves lap against a boat in a random pattern. Climate,
though fairly constant over long time periods, shows marked,
seemingly random, fluctuations from day to day or year to year.
The distribution of political beliefs throughout the community
possesses its random aspects. To simulate on the computer such
systems and others that behave in a random or semi-random manner
requires the ability to reproduce this randomness in our computer programs. This case study considers the most frequently
used method for doing this, producing random numbers.

At first thought this may seem to be a contradictory statement since great pains have been taken to design computers so
that their behavior is totally reliable and free from randomness. Thus any computer program given the same starting information should perform in the same way every time. Random
numbers generated by the computer are therefore more correctly
referred to as pseudorandom numbers. While they are generated
by means of a well-defined algorithm and hence are not truly
random, they appear to be random both to the casual observer
and when carefully tested statistically.

11.1 USING RANDOM NUMBERS

As indicated in previous chapters, APL has two random number
generating functions, both symbolized by $?$. In the monadic
form $?N$, the function is called roll and generates a random
integer between 1 and N inclusive.

		COMMENTS
	$?6$	Generate a random integer from 1 to
5		6. This time a 5 is returned by the function.
	$?6$	Generate a second random integer.
1		This time a 1 is returned.
	$?6\ 6\ 6$	Generate three random values each
1 4 2		in the range 1 to 6.
	$?3\rho6$	Generate three more.
3 6 3		

The last two examples illustrate a convenient procedure for drawing a set of random integers from the same range. Note that the values returned can have duplicates.

In the dyadic form $M?N$, the function is called *deal* and generates M distinct random numbers between 1 and N.

                              COMMENTS

```
      3?6                 Generate three distinct integers
6 2 3                         from 1 to 6.
      6?6                 Randomly rearrange the integers
5 3 2 1 6 4                   from 1 to 6.

      5?52                Select five integers from 1 to 52.
26 48 32 35 27
```

Note the distinction between $?3\rho6$ and $3?6$. The former may produce duplicate values while the latter will not.

Random numbers are used in a wide variety of applications, some serious and some mainly for fun. For example, your system libraries probably contain several game programs that make use of random numbers to simulate drawing cards or rolling dice. Random numbers can be used to select persons at random for interviewing in a demographic study or to simulate the random fluctuation of the environment in a computer model.

In this section we consider some techniques for using random numbers. Others will be presented in the Exercises. As an illustrative example of the use of random numbers, consider the following program to simulate the throw of a die N times and to determine the fraction of the throws in which a four is obtained.

```
      ∇PROB[□]∇
    ∇ Z←PROB N
[1]   Z←(+/4=?Nρ6)÷N
    ∇
```

The calculation in parentheses generates N random numbers from one to six and determines the number of fours present. Dividing by the number of throws gives the desired fraction. Here is an example of the execution of this program.

```
      PROB 1
0
      PROB 10
0.3
      PROB 100
0.19
      PROB 1000
0.173
      PROB 1000
0.167
```

We anticipate that on the average 1/6 or .1666... of all throws will result in a four. However, as expected from real life, the computer simulations do not always produce this expected value. The actual number of fours obtained differs from execution to execution. For example, the two runs with N=1000 produce different numbers of fours in each run. For large numbers of throws we approach the expected average.

In the previous example each of the values 1 through 6 had an equal probability of turning up. In other situations some of the possible outcomes may be more probable than others. As a standard example, suppose we had a bag of marbles in which half the marbles were red, a quarter were blue and the other quarter were green. How would we represent the choosing of one marble at random from the bag? The chance of picking a red marble must be twice that of picking a blue or a green one. We simulate this behavior by generating a random number from 1 to 4. If the number is one or two, we say that a red marble has been picked. Three will represent a blue marble and four a green one. The program $MARBLE$ will do this for us.

```
        ∇MARBLE[□]∇
     ∇ MARBLE;X
[1]    X←?4
[2]    ((X∈ 1 2)/'RED'),((X=3)/'BLUE'),(X=4)/'GREEN'
     ∇
```

Line [1] chooses a random value for X. Line [2] displays the color of the marble using the compression and catenation functions. Note the use of parentheses here. The program $MARBLE$ executes as follows:

                                        COMMENTS

```
     TΔMARBLE←1                Trace the execution of the first
                                 line.
     MARBLE                   The value of X is displayed.
MARBLE[1] 4                   The associated color is displayed.
GREEN


     MARBLE
MARBLE[1] 1
RED
```

11.2   COMPUTER SIMULATION OF A CARD GAME

The rules of a simple, one-person card game are as follows. A deck of 52 cards is shuffled thoroughly and placed face down. The player turns over the top card and at the same time calls out "ace of clubs." The player then turns over the second card and calls out "two of clubs" and continues in this manner turning over cards and calling out card names in succession. The order of card names called is ace through king of clubs, ace through king of diamonds and so on for hearts and spades.

The game is *lost* if at any time the card that is turned over
is the same as that called out. It is won if the player goes
through the entire deck without making a match between a turned
card and a called card.

The question we try to answer in this simulation is what is
the probability of winning the card game. Later we will use
the laws of probability to compute the odds. Now we try to
determine experimentally the probability of winning.

One way of doing this would be to play the game over and
over, keeping track of the number of games we play and the
number of times we win. This gives us an *experimental estimate*
of the probability as

probability = (numer of games won) ÷ (number of games played)

We should realize that this is only an estimate. For
example, if we were to toss a coin six times and keep track of
the number of heads obtained, it could happen that all six
tosses would produce tails. In this case our experimental estimate of the probability of getting a head would be zero. Of
course this does not mean that the probability is actually
zero, but merely that our experimental estimate is not very
good. If we were to toss the coin many times, 500 or 1000
times for example, we would expect our experimental estimate
of the probability to be very close to the correct value of 0.5.
We saw a similar behavior with the function *PROB* that simulated
the throwing of a die.

To use the experimental procedure with our card game, we
would follow the steps outlined in the flowchart in Figure 11.1.
This procedure would be followed whether we were to play the
games ourselves or were to let the computer play them for us.
Let's interpret the flowchart as though we were going to play
the games ourselves. We would first decide on the number of
games to play (box [1] of the flowchart). On a scratch pad we
would set up two columns, one for games played and the other
for games won (box [2]).

For each game we would shuffle the cards (box [3]) and
compare the shuffled deck with the natural order (box [4]) by
turning over the cards one by one and calling out the cards in
the ordered deck. If we made it through the deck without a
match, we would add one to the win column (box [5]) and, win or
lose, we would add one to the games played column (box [6]).
This would be repeated until the desired number of games were
played. We would then divide the number of games won by the
number played to get our probability estimate (box [8]).

Since many games must be played to get a reliable estimate
for the probability of winning, it would be necessary to spend
a considerable amount of time turning over cards to play the
games ourselves. (Try the game once and time yourself. How
long would it take for 100 games?)

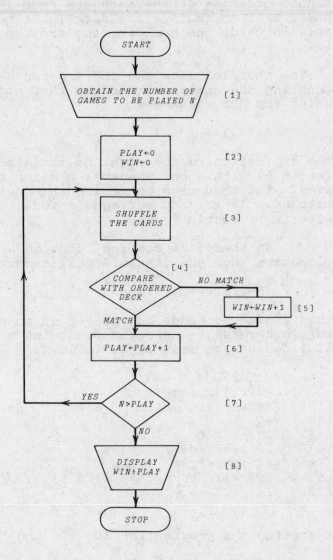

Figure 11.1   Experimenting with a card game

The advantage of solving this problem by computer simulation is that the great speed of the computer allows us to play many games in a short period of time. However, in order to follow the procedure of the flowchart, we must convert boxes [3] and [4] to computer recognizable statements. Computers cannot shuffle a deck of cards.

A deck of cards can be represented by the integers 1 through 52. The ace of clubs corresponds to 1, the deuce of clubs to 2 and so on to 52 which stands for the king of spades. The shuffling of the deck of cards in box [3] of the flowchart

can then be performed by the APL statement 52?52 which gives a
random ordering of the integers from 1 to 52. (Why don't we
use ?52ρ52 to shuffle the deck?) Using the above correspondence
between cards and numbers, the ordered deck is given in APL by
ι52.

The shuffled deck and the ordered deck can be compared by
counting the number of matches that occur. This may be done
using the APL statement

$$+/(\iota 52)=(52?52)$$

The expression to the right of the slash produces a vector of
length 52 with a one whenever a match occurs and a zero otherwise. The reduction operation then determines the number of
matches. If this number equals zero, the game is won. Otherwise it is lost.

We can therefore combine boxes [3], [4], and [5] of the
flowchart into the single APL statement

$$WIN \leftarrow WIN+0=+/(\iota 52)=(52?52)$$

This expression adds one to WIN if no matches occur, and adds
zero otherwise. A program following the flowchart in Figure
11.1 can now be written as follows:

```
        ∇CARDS[□]∇
      ∇ CARDS;N;PLAY;WIN
[1]     'ENTER THE NUMBER OF GAMES TO BE PLAYED'
[2]     N←□
[3]     PLAY←WIN←0
[4]   LP:WIN←WIN+0=+/(ι52)=52?52
[5]     →(N>PLAY←PLAY+1)/LP
[6]     'ESTIMATE OF PROBABILITY OF WINNING'
[7]     WIN÷PLAY
      ∇
```

Executing the program for 10, 50, and 500 games we obtain:

```
      CARDS
ENTER THE NUMBER OF GAMES TO BE PLAYED
□:
      10
ESTIMATE OF PROBABILITY OF WINNING
0.6

      CARDS
ENTER THE NUMBER OF GAMES TO BE PLAYED
□:
      50
ESTIMATE OF PROBABILITY OF WINNING
0.3

      CARDS
ENTER THE NUMBER OF GAMES TO BE PLAYED
□:
      500
ESTIMATE OF PROBABILITY OF WINNING
0.358
```

Experimentally we find that the probability of winning this game is about 0.35. The actual chance of winning the game can be determined from the laws of probability. The game is won by making 52 consecutive *non*-matches. Probability theory tells us that the probability of the occurrence of a sequence of events is equal to the *product* of the probabilities of the individual events. The probability of not making a match is 51/52. (Out of 52 cards, there are 51 that will not match the card we have called out.) Thus

probability of winning = (51÷52)*52=.364

The experimental estimate was very close and could have been improved by playing additional games.

11.3   GENERATION OF RANDOM NUMBERS

The procedure most frequently used for generating random numbers on the computer is to perform a series of arithmetical operations, the results of which will be randomly scattered in value. A possible sequence of operations to generate random integers is shown in the function *RANDOM*.

```
        ∇RANDOM[□]∇
     ∇  Z←RANDOM MAX
   [1]    ST←ADD+MULT×ST
   [2]    ST←BASE|ST
   [3]    Z←ST÷BASE
   [4]    Z←1+⌊MAX×Z
     ∇
```

This procedure requires some explanation. Before executing the function we must specify a starting number, which is stored in the global variable *ST*. This number is frequently referred to as the random number *seed* or *link*. The variable *MAX*, the argument of *RANDOM*, gives the range of integers from which the random number is to be drawn.

In addition to these input values, three other integer quantities need to be specified, a multiplier *MULT*, an addend *ADD*, and a base *BASE*. These global variables are used in the calculations and along with *ST* determine the sequence of the random numbers generated.

The calculations in *RANDOM* proceed as follows:

Line [1]: We multiply the current value of *ST* by the multiplier and add the result to the addend. The result is retained in *ST*.

Line [2]: By using the residue function, *ST* is redefined as the remainder left after dividing *BASE* into the value calculated in step 1. After this step, *ST* is an integer between 0 and *BASE*-1.

Line [3]:   The variable Z is defined as the ratio of ST to $BASE$.
             Since as calculated in step 2, ST is between 0 and
             $BASE$-1, Z will have a value between 0 and
             ($BASE$-1)÷$BASE$. If the value of $BASE$ is much larger
             than 1, this upper limit will be very close to 1.
             With a good choice of ADD, $BASE$, and $MULT$, Z will
             be randomly located in this interval.

Line [4]:   This step uses the random number Z to produce a
             random integer in the desired range, 1 to MAX.
             Multiplying MAX by Z gives a number which is greater
             than or equal to 0 and less than MAX. The applica-
             tion of the floor function turns this into an
             integer in the range 0 to MAX-1. Adding 1 gives the
             desired result.

After the execution of these four steps, the desired random
number is stored in Z, and the starting value ST has been
redefined. If, as is usually the case, more than one random
number is desired, this *new* value of ST should be used as the
starting value. Since ST is a global variable, this will automatically occur as long as we do not explicitly redefine ST.

To use $RANDOM$ we must choose values for ADD, $BASE$, and $MULT$.
As a simple choice (not a good one) we set:

        ADD←10
        $BASE$←17
        $MULT$←5

and specify a starting value

        ST←11

We now generate several random values.

	COMMENTS
$T\Delta RANDOM$←ι4	We trace the function execution.
$RANDOM$ 10	Generate an integer between 1 and 10.
$RANDOM$[1] 65	10+5×11
$RANDOM$[2] 14	The new ST value.
$RANDOM$[3] 0.82353	Line [3] gives a result between 0 and 1.
$RANDOM$[4] 9	
9	The generated random number.
ST	The global value of ST is that
14	generated in line [2].
$RANDOM$ 10	Generate a second integer from 1 to to 10.
$RANDOM$[1] 80	10+5×14
$RANDOM$[2] 12	The new value of ST.
$RANDOM$[3] 0.70588	The result of line [3] is always a decimal between 0 and 1.
$RANDOM$[4] 8	
8	The random value generated.
ST	
12	

COMMENTS

```
      T∆RANDOM←ι0                    Remove the trace.
      RANDOM 10
2
      ST
2
      RANDOM 10
2
      ST
3
```

The reader is invited to verify these results in desk calculator mode to get a feel for the way each step in the function behaves.

The APL function roll (monadic ?) behaves in a manner similar to *RANDOM*.

```
      ?10
9
      ?10
1
      ?10
8
```

One difference between roll and *RANDOM* is that roll can generate a sequence of random numbers by using a vector argument.

```
      ?10 10 10
1 10 10
      ?10 10 10
6 7 5
```

A defined function *ROLL* for generating random numbers in a manner similar to the primitive roll is shown below.

```
      ∇ROLL[□]∇
    ∇ Z←ROLL V;I
[1]   V←,V
[2]   Z←ιI←0
[3]   LP:→((ρV)<I←I+1)/0
[4]   Z←Z,RANDOM V[I]
[5]   →LP
    ∇
```

Line [1] insures that the input *V* is a vector so that it can be indexed. In line [2] a counter is initialized to zero, and the result variable *Z* is initialized to the empty vector. The final result is built by catenating random numbers one at a time onto *Z*. This initialization gives a starting point, onto which to attach the first element. Line [3] controls the loop. The counter is compared to the length of *V* to determine when the loop is finished. The essential step in the function is performed in line [4], where *RANDOM* generates a random integer that is catenated to *Z* as element *I*. The integer generated is in the range 1 to *V[I]*.

	COMMENTS
$ST \leftarrow 11$	Reset the starting value.
$ROLL$ 10 10 10 10	
9 8 2 2	The results are the same as when
ST	we previously executed $RANDOM$.
3	

The random number generating procedure in APL follows that used in $RANDOM$. The values used for ADD, $MULT$, and $BASE$ may differ from system to system; however, a common choice is to use an addend of zero, a multiplier of $7*31$, and a base of $\bar{}1+2*31$.

The analogue of the starting value, ST, in $RANDOM$ is called the *random link*. The value of the Random Link can be ascertained using the system variable $\Box RL$, (see Appendix 3) available on newer systems or the function $SETLINK$ contained in the workspace $WSFNS$ in Library 1 in older systems.

	COMMENTS
$X \leftarrow \Box RL$	Obtain the current value of the
X	random link.
949468869	
$\Box RL \leftarrow 7*5$	Respecify the random link.
$\Box RL$	Display the new value.
16807	

In a clear workspace, the value of the random link is $7*5$, the same as the multiplier.

After a random number has been generated, the value of the random link is changed and is used to generate the next random number.

	COMMENTS
$?10$	Generate a random integer.
2	
$\Box RL$	The random link has changed.
282475249	
$?10$	Generate another random number.
8	
$\Box RL$	The new link is displayed.
1622650073	
$?10$ 10 10 10	
5 6 3 1	
$\Box RL$	
101027544	

We can duplicate the behavior of the APL random number generator by choosing the appropriate values for the constants in *RANDOM*.

	COMMENTS
$ADD \leftarrow 0$ $BASE \leftarrow {}^-1 + 2 * 31$ $MULT \leftarrow 7 * 5$	Choose the values for the addend, base, and multiplier appropriate to the APL random number generator.
$ST \leftarrow 7 * 5$	Set the starting value to the initial value used for $\Box RL$ in the above examples.
RANDOM 10 2 *ST* 282475249 *RANDOM* 10 8	The random numbers generated with the defined function *RANDOM* are identical to those generated with *?*. The succeeding values of *ST* are the same as the values taken by the APL random link.
ST 1622650073 *ROLL* 10 10 10 10 5 6 3 1 *ST* 101027544	

If we continue to generate random numbers, the link will assume all possible values from 1 to $^-2 + 2 * 31$, roughly two billion values. The sequence of random numbers will not repeat itself until after that many random numbers have been generated.

If we want to generate a sequence of random numbers more than once, for example, to run two different programs with the same random numbers or to check the calculations while debugging a function, we can do this by resetting the random link.

	COMMENTS
$\Box RL \leftarrow 11546$	Set the value of the link.
?8 8 8 1 6 2	Generate three random numbers.
$\Box RL$ 470406430	Display the link.
?8 8 8 5 3 1	
$\Box RL \leftarrow 11546$	Reset the link to the original value.
?6ρ8 1 6 2 5 3 1	The numbers generated are the same as above.

EXERCISES

1. We want to test the randomness of the results of the roll
   (?) function. Write a program that will generate and store
   a vector of *N* random integers from 1 to 20. The function
   should then calculate and display the following properties
   of the stored numbers.

   a. The average of the random numbers.
   b. The number of values less than or equal to 10.
   c. The number of odd integers.
   d. The number of times a value appears twice in succession.

   Compare the results obtained from several executions of the
   function with the results you would expect on the average.

2. Give APL expressions that can be used to simulate the
   following operations:

   a. Rolling 6 dice.
   b. Finding the total of a roll of 3 dice.
   c. Rolling 6 dice and finding the total of the three
      highest.
   d. Shuffling a deck of 52 cards.
   e. Choosing 5 cards from a deck of 52, replacing each card
      after it is drawn.
   f. Choosing 13 cards from a deck of 52 without replacing
      the cards after they are drawn.
   g. Spinning a roulette wheel.
   h. The birthdates of N people.
   i. Repeat d. through f. assuming that the suit of the card
      drawn can be neglected.

3. There are numerous possible variations of the card game
   given in this case study. Modify the program *CARDS* to
   handle the case in which the rules are that a game is won
   if you have no more than one match, that is, a single match
   between the shuffled deck and ordered decks also counts as
   a win. Get experimental estimates of the probability of
   winning. (The theoretical probability is 0.736.)

4. As another variation of this game, when calling out the
   cards we could call out only the face value and not the
   suit. This game is much more difficult to win since now
   the chance of making a match is 1 in 13 rather than 1 in
   52.

   a. Using the laws of probability, what is the chance of
      winning this game?
   b. How many times would you expect to have to play the game
      in order to win once? In order to win 100 times?
   c. Since the chance of winning this game is so small, we
      would have to play many games to get a reasonable esti-
      mate for the probability of winning. Make the game
      easier to win by calling out only the face value of the
      card but allowing three matches before losing the game,
      that is, four matches and you're out. Modify the pro-
      gram *CARDS* in order to play this game. (HINT: since we

are interested in the face value only, there are now only 13 *different* cards although there are still 52 cards in all. We can therefore represent the cards by the integers 1 through 13.)

d. Experimentally determine the probability of winning this game. (The theoretical probability is 0.426.)

5. Suppose the APL random number generator was not really random so that, for example, when reordering the 52 numbers by 52?52 the even numbers in this vector tended to turn up as elements with an even index and the odd numbers to turn up as elements with an odd index. Would this influence the accuracy of the simulation of the card game? Would the program win too often or too infrequently? Can you think of some way to test your answer?

6. a. Give a function *UNIFORM* that when used in the form *UNIFORM N* returns a vector of *N* random numbers with values between 0 and 1. The number of different possible values should be large with a small, uniform spacing between the values. (HINT: what is the result of $(?X) \div X$ where *X* is a very large number?)

   b. How could you use this function to generate random numbers in the interval *A* to *B*?

7. Write an expression that will generate 100 random numbers equal to either 1 or ¯1 with equal probability for each.

8. Use the random number generator to simulate the flipping of a coin. Flip the coin 10 times, 100 times, and 1000 times, each time determining the fraction of the throws that give heads. What do you conclude?

9. At a carnival game there are three shelves of prizes. Shelf one has the least valuable prizes and shelf three the most valuable. The game is played by picking a duck from a tank of water. The shelf you pick your prize from is written on the bottom of the duck. Of the 75 ducks in the tank, sixty have one on the bottom, thirteen have two, and the other two have three. Write a niladic program to simulate the drawing of a single duck. The program should display the message *SHELF X* where *X* is 1, 2, or 3.

10. A guessing game can be played as follows: Person *A* picks a number from 1 to 10 and gives another person, *B*, three tries to guess the number. After each of *B*'s three guesses, *A* tells him if he is too high, too low, or correct. If *B* guesses correctly he wins; if he doesn't guess the number in three tries he loses.

    Draw a flowchart for this game. Make the flowchart in a form that could be turned directly into an APL program. The first step in the program should be the specification of the number that is to be guessed. It should be chosen using the random number generator and stored in the variable *N*. The program should contain a *loop* to allow for three guesses, should allow for the entry of the

guesses from the keyboard and should check the guesses
indicating messages 'TOO HIGH', 'TOO LOW', or 'YOU WIN'
depending on the guess. If the number is not guessed
correctly in three guesses, the message 'YOU LOSE' should
be displayed.

Write the corresponding program and test its operation
with the trace control.

11. A dart board has 3 circles. The inner circle is worth 15
     points, the middle circle is worth 5 points, and the outer
     circle is worth 1 point. Two players, A and B, have the
     following probabilities for hitting each of the circles:

	A	B
1 point circle	10%	30%
5 point circle	50%	65%
15 point circle	40%	5%

a. Give an APL expression or series of expressions that
    simulate the throwing of 1 dart by A. The result
    should be the number of points A scores.
b. Give an APL expression or series of expressions that
    simulate the throwing of 2 darts by B. The result
    should be the *total* number of points obtained by B.
c. Using the results of a. and b., write an APL program
    to simulate the results of a dart game between A and
    B in which A throws 1 dart and B throws 2. The winner
    is the player with the largest total points. The pro-
    gram should display the message 'A WINS' or 'B WINS'
d. Write a program to play the game a large number of
    times, keeping track of who wins and the number of
    games played. Estimate A's chance of winning.

12. A game frequently found at carnivals is played as follows.
     A board contains 36 holes. Each hole has a number on it,
     the numbers ranging between 1 and 6. Six balls are rolled
     onto the board and settle in the holes. The total score
     is then obtained by adding together the numbers on the
     holes occupied by balls. This score is used to determine
     a prize. The numbers on the holes are distributed as
     follows:

Number	Number of holes with this number
1	3
2	6
3	9
4	9
5	6
6	3

Write a niladic function THROW that simulates this game.
The result returned by the function should be the total
points obtained on a roll of 6 balls.

13. Write a program to simulate the dealing of a bridge hand. Have the program list the hand by suit (clubs, diamonds, hearts, and spades) and rank. Use ace, king, queen, and jack for the picture cards.

14. Write a program to deal out a bridge hand and evaluate the point count.

15. Write a program to deal out 7 cards and determine the best 5 card poker hand in those cards.

16. A candy jar is filled with different flavored candies. Half of these are cherry, 30 percent are lemon, and the rest are grape. How would you represent the random drawing of 20 pieces of candy from the jar?

17. A large jar is filled with dimes and pennies. Twenty percent of the coins are dimes. Children are allowed to reach reach into the jar and pull out as many coins as they can hold. The number of coins drawn from the jar by children reaching into it is as follows:

Number of coins drawn	Percent of children drawing this number
8	1%
9	9%
10	15%
11	25%
12	25%
13	20%
14	5%

Write a program that imitates a child drawing coins from the jar. The result displayed should be the total value of the coins drawn. (HINT: there are two random quantities here, the number of coins drawn and the mix between dimes and pennies.)

18. The function *ROLL* converts its argument to a vector and returns a vector as a result. Modify the function to return a result having the same shape as its argument.

Chapter 12
A Financial Model

One area in which the use of APL is rapidly increasing is business applications. The adoption by the business community of a
language that was originally considered very scientific and
mathematical in nature attests to the simplicity and versatility
of APL. Indeed, many of the features of APL, notably its simplified handling of vectors and matrices of data, its ease of
programming, and the large number of primitive functions, make
it ideally suited for many business applications.

Previous chapters have illustrated these features of APL by
drawing in part upon examples from the business field. This
case study considers a more extended example, a model for marketing a new product, and presents techniques for storing,
displaying, and processing input data and results.

12.1   THE PROBLEM

The HITECH Corporation has developed a new, high capacity
widget. The demand for widgets is continuing to expand and the
company feels that it can capture a reasonable share of the
market. Initial investment costs and production costs are high.
Before a decision is made to go into production, the company's
financial planning division has been asked to prepare a model
that will portray the financial factors involved in marketing
the new widgets over the next five years.

The director of financial planning gives the assignment to
Mike Bryant, a recent MBA graduate from a prestigious business
school that requires all MBA candidates to acquire a working
knowledge of APL. Mike's first step is to go to the marketing
division to take a look at forecasts for sales of the new
widget.

During the later stages of the development of the new
widgets, the marketing division did an intensive study of the
widget market. This study, which relied heavily on computer
models to analyze past and expected future use of widgets in
various industries, indicates that the present level of widget
sales, 800,000 units per year, can be expected to rise at an
annual rate of 10 percent over the next five years.

Using computer models of different marketing strategies based on survey data and previous experience, the division has devised a marketing plan for the new widgets. The normal expenditure for marketing in the industry is 6 percent of sales revenue. In addition to this expenditure the plan would involve expenditures of $100,000 per year over the first two years and $50,000 during the third year on an intensive advertising and salesman training program. In subsequent years the marketing costs would drop to the industry norm of 6 percent of sales revenue.

Assuming a competitive price of $10 for each widget, this plan is expected to give the company 5 percent of the total market for widgets during the first year, 14 percent during the second year, and 18 percent during the third year. In subsequent years, the company's market share would level off at 20 percent.

Mike's next stop is at the manufacturing and production division. This division has undertaken a study of the manufacturing costs associated with the production of the new widgets. These involve both fixed costs associated with plant overhead, fixed salaries, and so on and variable per unit costs, reflecting raw material costs, variable labor costs, and other expenses that depend on the number of units made. The fixed costs are expected to run $25,000 per year over the five years. The anticipated variable costs are $6.00 for each widget manufactured.

In addition, since the technology for producing the widgets is relatively new and complicated, a high rate of defects is anticipated. In the first year the defect rate is expected to be 25 percent of the number actually sold. As experience with the manufacturing process accumulates, however, the rate should drop. The production division expects the defect rate to decrease by 5 percent a year over the next three years until it stabilizes at 10 percent.

After obtaining this information, Mike heads back to his office to collect his thoughts. Pulling together all the information he has obtained, he comes up with the summary of input information shown in Table 12.1.

Table 12.1   Input Information

Item	Value
Current Industry Sales	800,000 units
Industry Growth Rate	0.10
HITECH Market Share	0.05 0.14 0.18 0.20 0.20
Sales Price	$10
Normal Marketing Costs (fraction of sales revenue)	0.06
Special Marketing Costs	$100,000 100,000 50,000 0 0
Fixed Production Costs	$25,000
Variable Production Costs	$6 per unit
Defect Rate (fraction of units produced)	0.25 0.20 0.15 0.10 0.10

In the table vectors give values for each of the five years in the projection period.

12.2 STORING THE INPUT DATA

Mike's next problem is how to store the input information. One possibility is to store each piece of data in a separate variable. These variables can be given mnemonic names to indicate the meaning of their contents. However, the number of variables needed is likely to be large and handling them, in particular for reporting purposes, will be difficult. Mike decides on an alternative scheme.

The input data as well as the output data will be of two types. Some data, such as the market share or special marketing costs, will be vectors of five values, one for each year of the model. Other data, such as the sales price or production costs, will be a single value constant over the entire five-year period. A convenient way to store the vectors of data is in a matrix with five columns. Each row in the matrix corresponds to one vector of data. Each column is associated with one of the five years of the model. This matrix is called DS, for Data Series. The values of constant information items are stored in a vector. Each element in the vector corresponds to one data item. This vector is called P for Parameter.

Storing data in this manner makes it easy to handle but presents problems remembering what the rows in the matrix and elements in the vector mean. To solve this problem Mike creates two character matrices DSN (for Data Series Names) and PN (for Parameter Names) and stores in them a description of each row in DS and each element in P. He also writes a short program that will summarize the input data.

```
      ∇INPUTDATA[☐]∇
    ∇ INPUTDATA
[1]   '****DATA SERIES****'
[2]   (((ρDS)[1],3)ρ 3 0 ⍕⍳(ρDS)[1]),' ',DSN,8 2 ⍕DS
[3]   ' '
[4]   '****PARAMETERS****'
[5]   (((ρP),3)ρ 3 0 ⍕⍳ρP),' ',PN,((ρP),8)ρ 8 2 ⍕P
[6]   ' '
[7]   '     SALES VOLUMES AND COSTS SCALED BY 1000'
    ∇
```

The expressions within parentheses on lines [2] and [5] are used to put the numbers to the left of the data. So, for example

$$((ρP),3)ρ3\ 0⍕⍳ρP$$

creates a vector of integers, one for each parameter, formats them into a character vector, and reshapes the character vector into a matrix.

The program prints a convenient table to which he can refer. The execution below shows the values used in the model. Note that the data for special marketing costs, industry sales, and fixed production costs are given in thousands.

```
    INPUTDATA
****DATA SERIES****
  1 HITECH MARKET SHARE       .05      .14     .18    .20    .20
  2 SPEC MARKETING COSTS   100.00   100.00   50.00    .00    .00
  3 DEFECT RATE               .25      .20     .15    .10    .10

****PARAMETERS****
  1 INDUSTRY SALES         800.00
  2 INDUSTRY GROWTH RATE      .10
  3 SALES PRICE            10.00
  4 MARKETING COST RATIO      .06
  5 FIXED PROD. COSTS      25.00
  6 VAR. PROD. COSTS        6.00

    SALES VOLUMES AND COSTS SCALED BY 1000
```

12.3   OUTPUT REPORTS

To present a complete picture of the prospects for the new product, the input information needs to be supplemented with additional derived financial figures. Mike decides to present his boss with a report in the format shown in Table 12.2.

Table 12.2   Output Report Format

Item	Storage Location
SALES ANALYSIS	
INDUSTRY SALES	$L[1;]$
MARKET SHARE	$L[2;]$
SALES VOLUME	$L[3;]$
AVERAGE SALES	$R[1]$
SALES REVENUE	$L[4;]$
AVERAGE REVENUE	$R[2]$
PRODUCTION ANALYSIS	
DEFECT RATE	$L[5;]$
PRODUCTION VOLUME	$L[6;]$
PRODUCTION COSTS	$L[7;]$
PROFIT ANALYSIS	
SALES REVENUE	$L[4;]$
PRODUCTION COSTS	$L[7;]$
MARKETING COSTS	$L[8;]$
TOTAL COSTS	$L[9;]$
AVERAGE COSTS	$R[3]$
PROFIT	$L[10;]$
TOTAL PROFIT	$R[4]$
AVERAGE PROFIT	$R[5]$

As in the case of the input data, the output information can consist of vectors with five elements or single values. The vectors are stored as rows in the matrix L (for report Lines) and the single values are stored in the vector R (for Results). The rows in L or elements in R associated with each item of information are also shown in Table 12.2. Note that some items will appear more than once in the output report but are only stored once in L. In addition, two other matrices, LN (for Line Names) and RN (for Result Names), are created containing a description of the contents of L and R. Some of the output information duplicates the input information. However, the duplication is amply rewarded in decreased complexity when the reports are to be generated.

12.4 THE FINANCIAL MODEL

The next step is the creation of the model. The relationships between the input and output data are established. The program $MODEL$ that performs the necessary computations is shown in Figure 12.1 along with the function $AVERAGE$ which is used in some of the calculations.

The model is a series of steps, each of which calculate one or more of the output lines or results. The comments indicate which quantities are being calculated and which data are being used in the calculations. For example, line [14] in $MODEL$ stores the defect rate $DS[3;]$ in $L[5;]$. Line [16] adds 1 to the defect rate and multiplies the sum by the sales volume $L[3;]$, giving the required production volume $L[6;]$. Note that all five years are being handled at once in these calculations. The reader is encouraged to study the program carefully referring to Tables 12.1 and 12.2 to trace the computations.

To display the results of $MODEL$, Mike uses a report generating program.

```
        ∇REPORT[□]∇
     ∇ REPORT;WIDTH
[1]     'ADJUST PAPER AND PRESS RETURN'
[2]     WIDTH←□
[3]     WIDTH←70
[4]     WIDTH CENTER 'HITECH CORPORATION'
[5]     WIDTH CENTER 'WIDGET SALES ANALYSIS'
[6]     WIDTH CENTER 'FIVE YEAR STUDY'
[7]     ''
[8]     20 10 COLHEAD 5 6 ρ'YEAR 1YEAR 2YEAR 3YEAR 4YEAR 5'
[9]     UNDERLINE 'SALES ANALYSIS:'
[10]    10 2 PRINT 1 2 3 0 ¯1 0 4 0 ¯2 0
[11]    UNDERLINE 'PRODUCTION ANALYSIS:'
[12]    10 2 PRINT 5 6 7 0
[13]    UNDERLINE 'PROFIT ANALYSIS:'
[14]    10 2 PRINT 4 7 8 9 0 ¯3 0 10 0 ¯4 ¯5
     ∇
```

```
      ∇MODEL[□]∇
    ∇ MODEL
[1]   ⍝INDUSTRY SALES FROM CURRENT SALES AND GROWTH RATE
[2]    L[1;]←P[1]×(1+P[2])* 0 1 2 3 4
[3]   ⍝HITECH MARKET SHARE
[4]    L[2;]←DS[1;]
[5]   ⍝HITECH SALES FROM INDUSTRY SALES AND MARKET SHARE
[6]    L[3;]←L[1;]×L[2;]
[7]   ⍝AVERAGE SALES
[8]    R[1]←AVERAGE L[3;]
[9]   ⍝SALES REVENUE FROM SALES VOLUME AND PRICE
[10]   L[4;]←P[3]×L[3;]
[11]  ⍝AVERAGE SALES REVENUE
[12]   R[2]←AVERAGE L[4;]
[13]  ⍝DEFECT RATE
[14]   L[5;]←DS[3;]
[15]  ⍝PRODUCTION VOLUME FROM SALES VOLUME AND DEFECT RATE
[16]   L[6;]←L[3;]×1+L[5;]
[17]  ⍝PRODUCTION COSTS FROM VOLUME AND FIXED AND VARIABLE COSTS
[18]   L[7;]←P[5]+P[6]×L[6;]
[19]  ⍝MARKETING COSTS FROM NORMAL AND SPECIAL COSTS
[20]   L[8;]←DS[2;]+P[4]×L[4;]
[21]  ⍝TOTAL AND AVERAGE COSTS
[22]   L[9;]←L[7;]+L[8;]
[23]   R[3]←AVERAGE L[9;]
[24]  ⍝PROFIT FROM SALES REVENUE AND TOTAL COSTS
[25]   L[10;]←L[4;]-L[9;]
[26]  ⍝TOTAL AND AVERAGE PROFIT
[27]   R[4]←+/L[10;]
[28]   R[5]←AVERAGE L[10;]
    ∇


      ∇AVERAGE[□]∇
    ∇ Z←AVERAGE V
[1]    Z←(+/V)÷⍴,V
    ∇
```

Figure 12.1   The financial model

The program *REPORT* uses four other programs, *CENTER*, *COLHEAD*, *UNDERLINE*, and *PRINT*. The program *UNDERLINE*

```
      ∇UNDERLINE[□]∇
    ∇ UNDERLINE X
[1]    X
[2]    (' '≠X)\'‾'
    ∇
```

displays and underlines its right argument. The programs *CENTER* and *COLHEAD* are used to create the headings at the top of a report and the headings over each column.

```
        ∇CENTER[□]∇
    ∇ W CENTER X
[1]     ((⌊0.5×W-ρX)ρ' '),X
    ∇


        ∇COLHEAD[□]∇
    ∇ S COLHEAD M
[1]     S←(S[1]ρ' '),,((ρM)[1],-S[2])↑M
[2]     S
[3]     (ρS)ρ'‾'
    ∇
```

CENTER causes the character vector in its right argument to be centered in the page. The width of the page is given by its left argument. *COLHEAD* takes a character matrix as its right argument. Its left argument is a numerical vector S of two elements. The first element in S gives the number of spaces by which the headings should be indented from the left margin. The second element in S gives the width of the columns. Each column heading is formed by taking a row in the character matrix and placing it to the extreme right in a field of width $S[2]$. The entire heading is underlined.

The actual printing of the output lines is done by *PRINT*.

```
        ∇PRINT[□]∇
    ∇ FMT PRINT S;I;J
[1]     S←,S
[2]     I←0
[3]     LP:→((ρS)<I←I+1)/0
[4]      →(1 0 ‾1 =×J←S[I])/LPRT,SK,RPRT
[5]     LPRT:'   ',LN[J;],FMT▼L[J;]
[6]      →LP
[7]     SK:''
[8]     →LP
[9]     RPRT:J←|J
[10]    '           ',RN[J;],FMT▼R[J]
[11]     →LP
    ∇
```

The right argument of the program is an integer vector that controls the display of lines from L, a blank line, or results contained in R, depending on the sign of the elements in the vector. Thus a value 3 causes the display of $LN[3;]$ followed by the contents of $L[3;]$ formatted according to *FMT*. A value of ‾3 produces a display of $RN[3;]$ followed by $R[3]$ formatted according to *FMT*. A value of 0 produces a blank line. Thus statement [10] in *REPORT* causes the display of the first three rows in L, a blank line, $R[1]$, a blank line, $L[4;]$, a blank line, $R[2]$, and a final blank line. Each of the numerical displays is properly formatted and preceded by the descriptive character information in LN and RN.

Equipped with these tools, Mike is ready to run his model. Prior to executing *MODEL*, L and R must be created.

COMMENTS

$L \leftarrow 10\ 5 \rho 0$ Create L and R.
$R \leftarrow 5 \rho 0$

MODEL   Execute *MODEL*.

The execution of *MODEL* replaces the zeros in L and R with the desired numerical values.

The results can be displayed using *REPORT*.

REPORT
ADJUST PAPER AND PRESS RETURN

Inserting a piece of clean paper and pressing RETURN, Mike receives the report shown in Figure 12.2.

HITECH CORPORATION
WIDGET SALES ANALYSIS
FIVE YEAR STUDY

	YEAR 1	YEAR 2	YEAR 3	YEAR 4	YEAR 5
SALES ANALYSIS:					
INDUSTRY SALES	800.00	880.00	968.00	1064.80	1171.28
MARKET SHARE	.05	.14	.18	.20	.20
SALES VOLUME	40.00	123.20	174.24	212.96	234.26
AVERAGE SALES	156.93				
SALES REVENUE	400.00	1232.00	1742.40	2129.60	2342.56
AVERAGE REVENUE	1569.31				
PRODUCTION ANALYSIS:					
DEFECT RATE	.25	.20	.15	.10	.10
PRODUCTION VOLUME	50.00	147.84	200.38	234.26	257.68
PRODUCTION COSTS	325.00	912.04	1227.26	1430.54	1571.09
PROFIT ANALYSIS:					
SALES REVENUE	400.00	1232.00	1742.40	2129.60	2342.56
PRODUCTION COSTS	325.00	912.04	1227.26	1430.54	1571.09
MARKETING COSTS	124.00	173.92	154.54	127.78	140.55
TOTAL COSTS	449.00	1085.96	1381.80	1558.31	1711.64
AVERAGE COSTS	1237.34				
PROFIT	‾49.00	146.04	360.60	571.29	630.92
TOTAL PROFIT	1659.84				
AVERAGE PROFIT	331.97				

Figure 12.2 The final report

EXERCISES

The following problems involve the construction of functions that would be useful in creating models such as described in this case study.

1. Create a function *ENTER* that when used in the form

    CMAT←ENTER CMAT

    allows you to add additional rows to the character matrix *CMAT*. The character information should be input through a quote-quad (⍞). The function should add any necessary blanks and catenate the input to the bottom of *CMAT*. The process should continue until an end is signaled, for example when *STOP* or *END* is entered.

2. Create a function *CHANGE*, which when used in the form

    CMAT←CHANGE CMAT

    allows the user to change specific rows in the matrix *CMAT*. The function should ask for the row number, display the current contents of that row and allow for the input of the new contents. The process should loop until an end code is encountered.

3. Modify program *PRINT* so that it will automatically display the title such as '*SALES ANALYSIS*:'. The titles should be stored one per row in a character matrix *T*. To display a title a value of 1000+N should be entered in the new *PRINT* program. Here N is the row in *T* which is to be printed. Thus 1002 would cause title 2 to be printed and underlined.

4. Write a program *OUTPUTNAMES* that will display the contents of *LN* and *RN* under appropriate headings. Each row in *LN* and *RN* should be numbered in the display.

The following problems require modification of the *MODEL* presented in this case study. They may be incorporated one at a time or in any combination.

5. In addition to costs already included in the model, there will be administrative costs of $40,000 the first year, increasing by $5,000 every year thereafter. Modify the model to include these costs.

6. Modify *REPORT*, *R* and *RN* so that the sales price is displayed in the report immediately after the average sales.

7. The company in question in this model makes it a policy to maintain an inventory that is 10 percent of the sales volume. Modify the model to satisfy this condition. (Add an additional parameter giving the inventory level and an

additional line giving production for inventory. Note
that the production for inventory depends only on changes
in sales. If sales remain constant and the inventory
level is correct to start with, the only goods that must
be produced are those for sale.)

8. To finance this new venture, the company must borrow
    $800,000. This is to be paid back in 10 yearly payments
    of $80,000. In addition, interest at a rate of 10 percent
    must be paid on the outstanding balance of the loan at the
    beginning of each year. Modify the model to include these
    facts.

9. In any year in which the company loses money on the
    venture, funds must be borrowed to make up the deficit.
    These funds are borrowed at a rate of 11 percent and are
    to be paid back as rapidly as possible, for example, as
    soon as the model makes money. Modify the model to
    include these facts.

10. By changing the selling price of the widgets, the company
    can increase or decrease its market share over the next
    five years. It is estimated that the following relation-
    ships exist.

Selling Price	Market Share				
$8	0.7	0.16	0.20	0.22	0.23
$9	0.6	0.15	0.19	0.21	0.21
$11	0.4	0.13	0.16	0.17	0.17
$12	0.3	0.12	0.13	0.14	0.14
$13	0.3	0.08	0.10	0.11	0.11

    Store the data along with the data for the $10 selling
    price. Modify *MODEL* by adding a loop so that the entire
    model is executed six times. On each iteration a differ-
    ent selling price and market share should be selected and
    inserted into $P[4]$ and $DS[1;]$. Use *PRINT* to create a
    report at the end of each iteration. The report should
    display enough information to determine the optimum sell-
    ing price for the new widgets.

Chapter 13
Graphical Presentation of Data

Graphical presentation of both technical and nontechnical data is an efficient and effective means of conveying information. Business and professional groups, manufacturing personnel, engineers, and scientists all resort to graphs and charts in daily activities. Quite sophisticated drawing and plotting systems have been developed by government and industry. Such systems may provide the capability for creating three-dimensional drawings and multi-color or half-tone displays.

In this case study we present a method for using the computer to produce graphical displays. Similar programs may be found in the public libraries of your system.

13.1 PROGRAM TO PLOT A GRAPH

The program *GRAPH* shown in Figure 13.1 will plot a set of ordered pairs of numbers. The values to be plotted are specified by the vector *X*, the independent variable, and *Y*, the dependent variable. They are entered through the vector *DAT*, which equals *X*,*Y*. The other input vector is *LIM* whose four elements specify the limits of the graph. They are respectively the lower limit of the X axis, the upper limit of the X axis, the lower limit of the Y axis, and the upper limit of the Y axis.

The plot is contained in the character matrix *M*. To form the graph we divide the X and Y axes into increments. The limits of the axes are specified by *LIM*. The number of intervals along the X and Y axes equal respectively the number of columns and the number of rows in the matrix *M*. The plotting process involves locating the appropriate interval in which the point is to lie and inserting a plot character in the matrix at this site. A detailed explanation of the program follows:

```
     ∇ LIM GRAPH DAT;NX;NY;M;I;X;Y;XINC;YINC
[1]   ⍝INITIALIZE BLANK MATRIX
[2]    NX←60
[3]    NY←30
[4]    M←(NY,NX)ρ' '
[5]   ⍝CHECK VALIDITY OF INPUT DATA
[6]    →(0≠2|ρDAT)/ER
[7]    →(4≠ρLIM)/ER
[8]   ⍝SEPARATE INDEPENDENT AND DEPENDENT VARIABLES
[9]    I←(ρDAT)÷2
[10]   X←I↑DAT
[11]   Y←I↓DAT
[12]  ⍝COMPUTE X AND Y INCREMENTS
[13]   XINC←(LIM[2]-LIM[1])÷NX
[14]   YINC←(LIM[4]-LIM[3])÷NY
[15]  ⍝COMPUTE PLOT POSITIONS IN GRAPH
[16]   X←1⌈NX⌊⌈(X-LIM[1])÷XINC
[17]   Y←1⌈NY⌊⌈(LIM[4]-Y)÷YINC
[18]  ⍝SETUP HORIZONTAL AND VERTICAL AXES
[19]   M[1⌈NY⌊⌈LIM[4]÷YINC;]←'-'
[20]   M[;1⌈NX⌊⌈-LIM[1]÷XINC]←'|'
[21]  ⍝PLOT DATA POINTS
[22]   I←1
[23]  LOOP:M[Y[I];X[I]]←'*'
[24]   →((ρX)≥I←I+1)/LOOP
[25]  ⍝DISPLAY PLOT AND KEY
[26]   M
[27]   'LOWER X LIMIT ';LIM[1]
[28]   'UPPER X LIMIT ';LIM[2]
[29]   'X INCREMENT   ';XINC
[30]   'LOWER Y LIMIT ';LIM[3]
[31]   'UPPER Y LIMIT ';LIM[4]
[32]   'Y INCREMENT   ';YINC
[33]   →0
[34]  ⍝DISPLAY ERROR MESSAGE IF INPUT DATA IS INCORRECT
[35]  ER:'INCORRECT INPUT DATA'
     ∇
```

Figure 13.1 Program to plot a graph

Lines [2-4]:   *M* is initialized as a blank matrix with *NY* rows and *NX* columns.

Lines [6-7]:   A data validity check: if the number of elements in vector *DAT* is not even or if the number of elements in vector *LIM* does not equal 4, a branch to line [35] occurs and the message *INCORRECT INPUT DATA* is displayed.

Lines [9-11]:   The first half of the elements in *DAT* are assigned to vector *X*, the independent variable, and the second half to *Y*, the dependent variable.

Lines [13-14]:   The increments associated with each plot posi-
                  tion are calculated, *XINC* in the X direction
                  and *YINC* in the Y direction. *XINC* equals the
                  upper bound on X,*LIM*[2], minus the lower bound
                  on X,*LIM*[1], divided by the total number of
                  characters in the X direction, *NX*. Similarly
                  for *YINC* in line [14].

Lines [16-17]:   The plot positions in the horizontal and
                  vertical direction of the data points are
                  computed. Points that lie off the graph are
                  brought to the edge of the graph. A sample
                  execution of this process is shown below.

Lines [19-20]:   Set up the X and Y axes by inserting dashes
                  into the appropriate row and column of the
                  matrix *M*. If either X or Y equal to zero
                  does not appear on the graph, the correspond-
                  ing axis is plotted at the edge of the graph
                  closest to zero.

Lines [22-24]:   This loop places a special character, in this
                  case a star, in the appropriate elements of *M*
                  according to the vectors *X* and *Y*, which rep-
                  resent the data points to be graphed. The Y
                  axis is vertical and consequently the Y coor-
                  dinate of the points is placed into the matrix
                  rows. The X axis is horizontal and the vector
                  X is associated with column positions in the
                  matrix *M*. The stars are placed in the matrix
                  in place of the previously inserted blanks
                  and dashes.

Line [26]:   The graph is plotted by displaying matrix *M*.
                  The axes appear as dashes and the points as
                  stars.

Lines [27-32]:   A key giving the limits of the graph and the
                  spacing of points is printed below the graph.

   The calculations in lines [13-17] determine the position of
each plot character in the graph. The following example illustrates the process. We use the values

        NX←60
        LIM←200 800
        X←125.8 250 800 1412

                                    COMMENTS

        XINC←(*LIM*[2]-*LIM*[1])÷*NX*   Compute the increment in the X
        XINC   direction. Each plot posi-
10   tion in this direction
                                           corresponds to 10 units.

        Q←(*X*-*LIM*[1])÷*XINC*   *Q* gives the *X* positions in
        Q   multiples of *XINC* beyond the
¯7.42 5 60 121.2   lower limit *LIM*[1].

	COMMENTS
$\lceil Q$ $^-7$ 5 60 122	Values are rounded to the next largest integer, giving the column in the graph in which the value is to be plotted.
$NX \lfloor \lceil Q$ $^-7$ 5 60 60	Integer X positions exceeding NX are set equal to NX (60 in this case.)
$1 \lceil NX \lfloor \lceil Q$ 1 5 60 60	Integer positions less than 1 are set equal to 1. All points exceeding the range of the graph are plotted along the nearest edge of the graph.

Positions in the Y direction are computed similarly. However, the largest Y value corresponds to row one in the matrix. The positions of other Y values in the matrix are given as multiples of $YINC$ below the maximum value.

Program $GRAPH$ is now used to plot the cubic equation

$$Y = (X+25) \times (X+6) \times (X-28)$$

or

$$Y = X^3 + 3X^2 - 718X - 4200$$

To plot this equation we use X values from $^-30$ to 30 in increments of 2. The corresponding Y values are computed from the above equation. The limits of the graph are set at $^-30$ to 30 in the X direction and $^-11000$ to 4000 in the Y direction. The initializations and program execution are shown in Figure 13.2. The key displayed at the bottom of the graph indicates that each character position in the X direction corresponds to one unit while each position in the Y direction is worth 500 units. The points that lie on the X axis represent the zeros of the function. Knowing $XINC$ they can be read directly from the graph. The zeros occur at X = 28, $^-6$, $^-25$.

As a second example Figure 13.3 shows program $GRAPH$ used to plot the weekly New York Stock Exchange Composite Stock Index for the year 1973. The plot characters have been changed from stars to lines.

```
X←¯32+2×ι31
Y←(X+25)×(X+6)×X-28
LIM←¯30 30 ¯11000 4000

LIM GRAPH X,Y
```

```
LOWER X LIMIT  ¯30
UPPER X LIMIT   30
X INCREMENT      1
LOWER Y LIMIT  ¯11000
UPPER Y LIMIT  4000
Y INCREMENT     500
```

```
        STOCK
65.3 65 64.5 63.1 61.9 61.9 62 60.9 60.1 61 60.6
        58.2 59.6 58.2 58.7 59.6 56.9 58.8 57.4
        54.9 56.9 54.9 56.3 55.4 54.5 54.8 53.3
        55.1 57.1 58.3 56.8 55.8 54.5 54.2 55.6
        56.1 55.9 57.8 58.5 59.3 60.2 59.5 59.9
        57.7 56.6 55.5 53.1 51.2 51.3 49.6 49.6
        51.8

        X
1 2 3  4  5  6  7  8  9 10 11 12 13 14 15 16 17 18 19
        20 21 22 23 24 25 26 27 28 29 30 31 32 33
        34 35 36 37 38 39 40 41 42 43 44 45 46 47
        48 49 50 51 52

        LIM
‾1 59 40 70

        LIM GRAPH X,STOCK
```

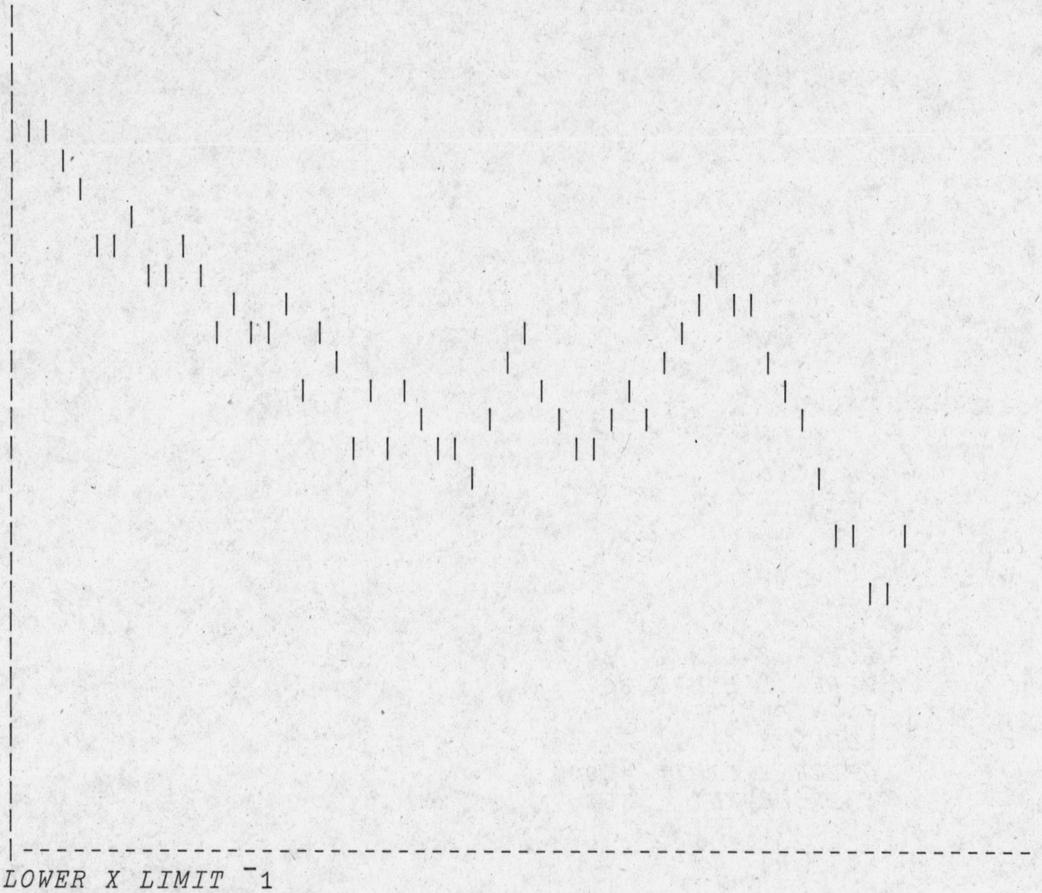

```
LOWER X LIMIT ‾1
UPPER X LIMIT 59
X INCREMENT    1
LOWER Y LIMIT 40
UPPER Y LIMIT 70
Y INCREMENT    1
```

Figure 13.3 Graph of 1973 Composite Stock Index

```
        LIM←¯1 59 50 65

        LIM HISTOGRAM X,STOCK
|□□□
|□□□
|□□□
|□□□□
|□□□□
|□□□□  □
|□□□□□□□
|□□□□□□□  □
|□□□□□□□□□□□
|□□□□□□□□□□□
|□□□□□□□□□□□□ □  □                              □□□
|□□□□□□□□□□□□ □  □                              □□□□
|□□□□□□□□□□□□ □ □□ □                            □□□□□
|□□□□□□□□□□□□□□ □        □                       □□□□□
|□□□□□□□□□□□□□□ □        □                      □□□□□□
|□□□□□□□□□□□□□□ □□      □□               □□□□□□□□
|□□□□□□□□□□□□□□□□ □     □□□              □□□□□□□□
|□□□□□□□□□□□□□□□ □ □    □□□        □ □□□□□□□□□
|□□□□□□□□□□□□□□□□□ □ □   □□□□      □□□□□□□□□□□□□
|□□□□□□□□□□□□□□□□□ □ □□  □□□□□     □□□□□□□□□□□□□
|□□□□□□□□□□□□□□□□□□□□□□  □□□□□□  □□□□□□□□□□□□□
|□□□□□□□□□□□□□□□□□□□□□□  □□□□□□□  □□□□□□□□□□□□□
|□□□□□□□□□□□□□□□□□□□□□□  □□□□□□□  □□□□□□□□□□□□□
|□□□□□□□□□□□□□□□□□□□□□□□□□□□□□□□□□□□□□□□□□□□□□□□
|□□□□□□□□□□□□□□□□□□□□□□□□□□□□□□□□□□□□□□□□□□□□□□□
|□□□□□□□□□□□□□□□□□□□□□□□□□□□□□□□□□□□□□□□□□□□□□□□
|□□□□□□□□□□□□□□□□□□□□□□□□□□□□□□□□□□□□□□□□□□□□□□□  □
|□□□□□□□□□□□□□□□□□□□□□□□□□□□□□□□□□□□□□□□□□□□□□□□□□ □
|□□□□□□□□□□□□□□□□□□□□□□□□□□□□□□□□□□□□□□□□□□□□□□□□□ □
|□□□□□□□□□□□□□□□□□□□□□□□□□□□□□□□□□□□□□□□□□□□□□□□□□□□-------
LOWER X LIMIT ¯1
UPPER X LIMIT 59
X INCREMENT   1
LOWER Y LIMIT 50
UPPER Y LIMIT 65
Y INCREMENT   0.5
```

Figure 13.4   Histogram of 1973 Composite Stock Index

13.2   PROGRAM TO PLOT A HISTOGRAM

A slight modification of program *GRAPH* results in a program to plot a *histogram*.

```
        ∇GRAPH[0□10]
[0]     LIM GRAPH DAT;NX;NY;M;I;X;Y;XINC;YINC
           /////9
[0]     LIM HISTOGRAM DAT;NX;NY;M;I;X;Y;XINC;YINC
[1]     [23]
[23]    LOOP:M[(Y[I]-1)↓ιNY;X[I]]←'□'
[24]    ∇
```

The name of the program is changed to *HISTOGRAM* in the first editing step. The second step replaces line [23] with a new instruction. In a histogram each data value is displayed as a vertical bar extending upwards from the X axis. The program creates the bar using the character □. The value of *Y* speci-fies the height of the bar and consequently the number of characters which make up the bar. Since the bars are printed upwards from the X axis and since the first row in the matrix *M* corresponds to the maximum Y value, it is necessary to place the □ character into all the column positions of matrix *M* except those located *above* the Y value. The new calculation on line [23] uses the drop function to insert □ into the appro-priate positions.

The Composite Stock Index example of the previous section is presented in histogram form in Figure 13.4. Note that the in-put data is identical to that used in Figure 13.3 but the range on *X* and *Y* has been altered for better resolution.

EXERCISES

1. Modify the program *GRAPH* so that the plot symbol is speci-fied by the global variable *PLOTVAR*.

2. Modify program *GRAPH* to delete data that is not in the range of the graph.

3. Modify the program *GRAPH* to allow for the input of *LIM* and the plot symbol from the keyboard. The plot variables *X* and *Y* should now be entered as the left and right argu-ments.

4. Modify the program *GRAPH* so that the data to be plotted is input in a matrix *DAT* containing two columns. The inde-pendent variable X and the dependent variable Y are stored in the first and second columns of the matrix. The plot symbol is specified by the global variable *PLOTVAR*.

5. Modify the program obtained in the previous exercise to plot any number of dependent variables against a single independent variable. The data to be plotted is stored in a matrix. The first column of the matrix contains the independent variable X and subsequent columns contain the dependent variables stored one per column. The plot symbols to be used for each dependent variable should be stored in the global vector *PLOTVAR*.

6. Modify the program *GRAPH* so that it will plot a histogram if the value of the global variable *PLOTTYPE* is 2 and will give a normal plot if the value of *PLOTTYPE* is 1.

7. Modify the program *GRAPH* to produce the plot without looping by storing the plot character in the appropriate positions within the ravel of the plot matrix *M*.

8. Modify program *GRAPH* to place tic marks on the *X* and *Y* axes at various intervals, for example at *X*=0, 5, 10, 15, etc.

9. The program *HISTOGRAM* presented in this chapter actually only works properly if the X axis appears at the bottom of the graph. Modify the program to work properly for all cases. The bar created should extend from the X axis to the data points.

10. Check the public libraries of your system for graphing programs. List their names as well as a brief description.

Chapter 14
Weekly Payroll

Computers are used in business for a variety of tasks. They
can save time or money in producing reports for management and
government, in writing invoices to customers, in keeping
records of accounts payable to suppliers, in preparing checks
and earning statements for employees, and numerous other business applications.

Payroll is part of the company's overall information flow
system. The payroll system is directly related to the personnel, manufacturing, and finance systems. The personnel system
provides information for the payroll system as it relates to
newly hired employees, promotions, and wage rate changes. The
manufacturing system along with the payroll system provides
valuable information regarding job cost. The hours worked and
corresponding payroll are compared with production volume to
assess the shop productivity. Finally, the payroll system
along with other data concerning company expenses and income
provides accounting and financial information.

The basic idea of the weekly payroll sounds deceptively
simple: given information on the employee hourly pay rates,
accumulated payroll totals, and time cards showing hours
worked, we compute wages, print checks, and update the totals.
This job is complicated by the many deductions to be made, the
requirement for continuous updating of employee data, and the
need to add and delete records due to turnover of personnel.

The approach we take in this case study is one of *structured
programming*. It is a manner of organizing and coding programs
that makes the programs easily understood and modified. The
payroll system consists of a number of *main programs*. Each of
the main programs performs a specific function and may call
several *subprograms*. The programs themselves are fairly short
and are accordingly easy to read and understand.

14.1 THE ORGANIZATION OF THE PAYROLL SYSTEM

The hourly payroll system may vary from company to company
depending on the nature of the employees' contracts, the pre-
vailing local tax structure, the fringe benefits, and so on.
In the following we present an hourly payroll system consisting
of three major sections.

1. Input: Employees' ID numbers along with the regular and
                overtime hours are entered. Some data validity
                check may be appropriate here.

2. Process: Compute employees' gross pay, net pay, and all
                deductions; compute the totals for all company
                employees; update employees' earnings, hours
                worked regular and overtime, and deductions with-
                held to date.

3. Output: Display a payroll report which includes the
                regular, overtime, gross, and net pay for each
                employee; a deduction report showing separately
                all deductions for each employee; a report show-
                ing the totals for each department within the
                company.

Having divided the payroll system into three sections it is
now possible to write individual programs for each of the tasks.
It is first necessary, however, to make some very basic decisions about the structure of the *data base*. A data base is an
integrated file containing all pertinent data in readily accessible storage. The data are stored in such a way that they can
be used as input without having to rearrange or reproduce them.
Since certain deductions depend on year-to-date data and since
we plan to display such data in the form of reports, we must
make provisions for storing this employee information. These
records can be stored in files in any one of the many available
auxiliary memory devices such as, for example, on disk.

In this case study we organize the employee data in a matrix
called *EMP*. Since our example deals just with a few employees,
this matrix is stored in the workspace. Each row of the matrix
corresponds to data belonging to one employee with each column
representing specific payroll information as shown in Table 14.1.

Table 14.1   Contents of Payroll Matrix

Column No.	Payroll Information
1.	Employee ID number; first digit refers to a department number.
2.	1 = single, 2 = married
3.	Number of dependents
4.	Hourly wage
5.	Hours to date
6.	Wages to date
7.	Overtime wages to date
8.	Income tax withheld to date
9.	Hours for this week
10.	Wages for this week
11.	Overtime for this week
12.	Income tax for this week
13.	FICA for week
14.	Unemployment tax for week

Columns one through four of the matrix contain descriptive
information about the employee. Columns five through eight
contain cumulative totals of hours worked, wages, and deductions. These totals are updated during each weekly payroll
run. Columns nine through fourteen contain information about
hours worked, wages, and deductions for the current week.

The organization of the payroll system is shown in Figure
14.1. The flow of information between the central data base
and the three activities input, process, and output is indicated by arrows. The activity boxes contain the names of the
main programs and subprograms to be described in the following
sections.

14.2 INPUT

Each week we must enter the number of regular and overtime
hours for each employee. We shall assume here that all hours
in excess of 35 hours per week are to be paid as overtime. We
consequently enter a single value for the hours along with the
employee's ID number. To be sure that the ID number entered
is a valid number we test to see if it is in storage. This
test is performed in line [5] of program *TIME*.

```
        ∇TIME[□]∇
      ∇ TIME;END;ID;IDNOS;LOC
[1]     END←-2*7
[2]     IDNOS←EMP[;1]
[3]   IN:'ENTER ID NO:'
[4]     →(END=ID←□)/0
[5]     →((ρEMP)[1]≥LOC←IDNOS⍳ID)/OK
[6]     'INVALID ID'
[7]     →IN
[8]   OK:'ENTER HOURS WORKED'
[9]     EMP[LOC;9]←□
[10]    →IN
      ∇
```

The ID numbers are stored in column 1 of matrix *EMP* and the
hours worked are stored in column 9. The program permits
entry of employee time card information in any sequence. Line
[5] locates the row *LOC* of matrix *EMP* corresponding to the ID
number. In line [9] the hours worked are then entered into
column 9 of that row. To exit the program the operator types
END as shown in the following sample input.

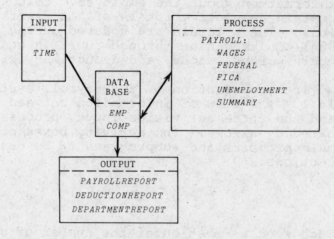

Figure 14.1 Organization of the payroll system

```
       TIME
ENTER ID NO.
□:
       3004
INVALID ID
ENTER ID NO.
□:
       300004
ENTER HOURS WORKED
□:
       45
ENTER ID
□:
       300006
ENTER HOURS WORKED
□:
       40
ENTER ID NO.
□:
       300007
ENTER HOURS WORKED
□:
       35
ENTER ID NO.
□:
       END
```

In the above example we did input one invalid ID number that was rejected. No provisions have been made in program *TIME* to check for invalid entries of the hours worked (see Exercises). This aspect of data processing is quite important. Generally all data should be checked and verified before processing.

For illustrative purposes let us assume the following employee data.

```
    10 0 10 0 10 0 10 2 ⍊ EMP[;⍳4]
100001            2            2            5.00
100003            2            3            4.50
100010            1            1            4.25
200002            2            4            5.25
200003            1            1            5.00
300001            2            4            7.30
300002            1            1            7.00
300004            2            5            6.90
300006            2            6            6.75
300007            2            5            6.75
```

In the above table we display respectively in the four columns the employees' ID numbers, their marital status, their number of dependents, and their hourly wages. The first digit of the ID number refers to the employee's department number. In this case we have ten employees associated with three different departments.

To illustrate the payroll program, *TIME* is used to enter the following hours for each employee.

ID Number	Hours Worked
100001	38
100002	35
100010	35
200002	39
200003	35
300001	45
300002	35
300004	45
300006	40
300007	35

14.3   PROCESS

Now that the hours worked by each employee have been entered and stored in the matrix *EMP*, we can proceed to compute the weekly payroll. In the process of determining the net pay we must compute the gross pay and the deductions. In this case study we will compute all overtime pay at time-and-a-half. Also, we will limit the deductions to federal income tax to be withheld from the employee, social security payments to be withheld from the employee and matched by the employer, and finally unemployment tax to be paid by the employer.

The approach we take is to write a main program *PAYROLL* which calls separately and successively short programs called subprograms, Figure 14.1. In these subprograms we compute the net wages (subprogram *WAGES*), the federal income tax (subprogram *FEDERAL*), the social security (subprogram *FICA*), and the unemployment tax (subprogram *UNEMPLOYMENT*). The last program referred to as subprogram *SUMMARY* computes the company totals.

The main program, *PAYROLL*, is displayed:

```
      ∇PAYROLL[□]∇
   ∇ PAYROLL
[1]    WAGES
[2]    FEDERAL
[3]    FICA
[4]    UNEMPLOYMENT
[5]    SUMMARY
   ∇
```

and when executed it will cause successive executions of the
five subprograms, first subprogram *WAGES*, then *FEDERAL*, and so
on. Having the payroll information in a matrix makes it convenient to maintain a top-down structure without looping and
repetitive executions of the subprograms. We process the payroll for all the employees at once. In larger applications
where all the necessary data may not fit into the workspace, a
modified scheme would have to be used.

   The first subprogram is *WAGES*:

```
      ∇WAGES[□]∇
   ∇ WAGES
[1]    ACALCULATE OVERTIME WAGES
[2]    EMP[;11]←1.5×EMP[;4]×0⌈EMP[;9]-35
[3]    ACALCULATE TOTAL PAY
[4]    EMP[;10]←EMP[;11]+EMP[;4]×35⌊EMP[;9]
[5]    AUPDATE CUMULATIVE TOTALS
[6]    EMP[; 5 6 7]←EMP[; 5 6 7]+EMP[; 9 10 11]
   ∇
```

In line [2] of *WAGES* we compute the overtime pay by multiplying all hours in excess of 35 by 1.5 times the hourly wages,
which are stored in *EMP[;4]*. Recall that the payroll data is
stored one row per employee in matrix *EMP*. Operating on an
entire column of the matrix thus includes all employees. The
overtime pay for the week for all employees is then stored in
EMP[;11]. In line [4] we add the overtime pay to the regular
pay; the total wages for the week are stored in *EMP[;10]*. In
line [6] we update hours worked to date, wages to date, and
overtime wages to date by adding the values for the current
week to the corresponding previous totals.

   The second subprogram is *FEDERAL*. In this subprogram we
compute the weekly federal income tax for each employee using
the percentage method as published by the Internal Revenue
Service, Employer's Tax Guide, shown in Figure 14.2.

TABLE 1. WEEKLY Payroll Period

(a) SINGLE person—including head of household:				(b) MARRIED person—			
If the amount of wages is:		*The amount of income tax to be withheld shall be:*		*If the amount of wages is:*		*The amount of income tax to be withheld shall be:*	
Not over $25 0				Not over $48 0			
Over—	But not over—		of excess over—	Over—	But not over—		of excess over—
$25	—$67	16%	—$25	$48	—$96	17%	—$48
$67	—$115	$6.72 plus 20%	—$67	$96	—$173	$8.16 plus 20%	—$96
$115	—$183	$16.32 plus 23%	—$115	$173	—$264	$23.56 plus 17%	—$173
$183	—$240	$31.96 plus 21%	—$183	$264	—$346	$39.03 plus 25%	—$264
$240	—$279	$43.93 plus 26%	—$240	$346	—$433	$59.53 plus 28%	—$346
$279	—$346	$54.07 plus 30%	—$279	$433	—$500	$83.89 plus 32%	—$433
$346		$74.17 plus 36%	—$346	$500		$105.33 plus 36%	—$500

Figure 14.2   Income tax withholding for weekly payroll

The wage limits of the above table, for example, over $25 but
not over $67, are stored in a 2 row matrix *LIMIT* (line [3],
subprogram *FEDERAL*). The first row contains the limits for
single persons and the second row stores the limits for a
married person. The appropriate percentages of the wages to
be withheld are stored in the two row matrix *PERCENT* (line [4]).
In this method we compute the taxable wages by subtracting from
the gross pay the product of the number of dependents and the
allowance. For a weekly payroll this allowance equals $14.40
(line [2]). Since we are dealing with a matrix containing the
payroll information for all employees, *WAGES* in line [8] is a
vector containing taxable wages for all the employees.

```
        ∇FEDERAL[□]∇
     ∇ FEDERAL;ALLOWANCE;LIMIT;PERCENT;ΔPER;TAX;WAGES
[1]     ⍝CONSTANTS AS PRESCRIBED BY TAX LAWS
[2]     ALLOWANCE←14.4
[3]     LIMIT← 2 7 ρ 25 67 115 183 240 279 346 48 96 173
        264 346 433 500
[4]     PERCENT← 2 7 ρ 0.16 0.2 0.23 0.21 0.26
        0.3 0.36 0.17 0.2 0.17 0.25 0.28 0.32
        0.36
[5]     ⍝CALCULATE INCREMENTAL PERCENTAGES
[6]     ΔPER←PERCENT- 0 ¯1 ↓0,PERCENT
[7]     ⍝CALCULATE TAXABLE WAGES
[8]     WAGES←EMP[;10]-EMP[;3]×ALLOWANCE
[9]     ⍝DETERMINE TAX
[10]    TAX←0
[11]    I←1
[12] LP:TAX←TAX+ΔPER[EMP[;2];I]×0⌈WAGES-LIMIT[EMP[;2];I]
[13]    →((ρLIMIT)[2]≥I←I+1)/LP
[14]  ⍝STORE CALCULATED TAX AND UPDATE CUMULATIVE TOTALS
[15]    EMP[;8]←EMP[;8]+EMP[;12]←TAX
     ∇
```

In line [6] we specify a matrix containing the difference in
the withholding percentages for successive income intervals.
In lines [10] through [13] we compute the income tax for the
week for each employee (vector *TAX*) by adding the taxes to be
withheld according to successive wage intervals up to the appropriate interval. The income tax withheld to date from each
employee is updated in line [15].

Social security deductions are computed in subprogram *FICA*. We assume a rate of 5.85 percent and a maximum taxable income of $14,100.

```
     ∇FICA[□]∇
   ∇ FICA;RATE;MAX
[1]   ⍝FICA RATE
[2]    RATE←0.0585
[3]   ⍝MAXIMUM TAXABLE INCOME
[4]    MAX←14100
[5]   ⍝CALCULATE EMPLOYEE FICA PAYMENTS
[6]    EMP[;13]←RATE×0⌈EMP[;10]-0⌈EMP[;6]-MAX
   ∇
```

The actual computations are performed in line [6]. From right to left we first subtract $14,100 from gross wages to date. Note that *EMP*[;6] already includes wages for the current week as computed in subprogram *WAGES* and may exceed the maximum of $14,100. That excess is subtracted from this week's wages and multiplied by 5.85 percent to yield the FICA for the week. If, on the other hand, the total wages to date are less than *MAX*, the wages for the week, *EMP*[;10], are multiplied by *RATE* to give the FICA deductions for the employees. Again, since we are dealing with matrices containing payroll information for all employees, we compute in one line of code the FICA deductions for all the employees.

Unemployment tax is computed based on a maximum taxable income of $6000 and a tax rate of 3 percent. This tax is imposed on the employer and is not deducted from the employee's wages. The calculations are performed in line [5] and closely parallel those in line [6] of subprogram *FICA*.

```
     ∇UNEMPLOYMENT[□]∇
   ∇ UNEMPLOYMENT;RATE;MAX
[1]   ⍝UNEMPLOYMENT TAX RATE
[2]    RATE←0.03
[3]   ⍝MAXIMUM TAXABLE INCOME
[4]    MAX←6000
[5]    EMP[;14]←RATE×0⌈EMP[;10]-0⌈EMP[;6]-MAX
   ∇
```

SUMMARY is the final subprogram called by the main program *PAYROLL*. The purpose of this subprogram is to compute for all employees the totals for the week and the totals to date. Such data may be of interest to management, particularly as they relate to data concerning other expenses, budgets, and income.

To store the summary information an additional vector *COMP* is introduced. The arrangement of data in *COMP* is shown in Table 14.2.

Table 14.2   Contents of Summary Vector *COMP*

<u>Element</u>   <u>Payroll Information</u>

1   Total hours to date
2   Total wages to date
3   Total overtime to date
4   Total income tax to date
5   Total FICA to date (=2×employee withholding)
6   Total unemployment to date
7   Total hours for week
8   Total wages for week
9   Total overtime for week
10   Total income tax for week
11   Total FICA for week
12   Total unemployment for week

Let us assume that prior to this week's payroll computations, the following data is stored in the first six elements of vector *COMP*:

```
      10 2▼COMP[ι6]
   5899.00   35670.63    2798.63    4137.66    4173.46    1070.12
```

In subprogram *SUMMARY* summations are performed by combining the rows with one another. In line [2] FICA for the week is taken as twice *COMP*[11] since the company matches the employee's contributions. In line [3] totals to date are computed.

```
      ∇SUMMARY[□]∇
    ∇ SUMMARY
[1]   COMP[6+ι6]←+/EMP[;8+ι6]
[2]   COMP[11]←2×COMP[11]
[3]   COMP[ι6]←COMP[ι6]+COMP[6+ι6]
    ∇
```

14.4   OUTPUT

In this section we present three typical reports: a payroll report, a deduction report, and a departmental report. In the program *PAYROLLREPORT* each employee is identified by his ID number. Along with his ID number and pay rate, the program displays the hours worked for the week, as well as the employees' weekly pay broken down according to his regular pay, overtime pay, gross, and net pay. The totals for each of these columns are also computed and displayed.

```
        ∇PAYROLLREPORT[□]∇
      ∇  PAYROLLREPORT;FMT;T
[1]    '    ID NO.       RATE     HOURS     REGULAR        O.T.   GROSS
           PAY     NETPAY'
[2]    FMT←10 0 10 2 10 0 ,8ρ 10 2
[3]    FMT▼EMP[; 1 4 9],(-/EMP[; 10 11]),EMP[, 11 10],EMP[;10]
       -+/EMP[; 12 13]
[4]    ' '
[5]    T←(+/FMT[1 3])↑'       TOTALS'
[6]    T,(4↓FMT)▼COMP[7],(-/COMP[8 9]),COMP[9 8],COMP[8]
                    -+/ 1 0.5 ×COMP[10 11]
      ∇
```

In lines [1] and [2] we specify the column headings and the
format for the report. In line [3] we print the appropriate
weekly payroll information for all employees. Note that regular
pay for the week is computed by subtracting the overtime pay
(O.T.) from the gross pay. Similarly we compute the net pay
by subtracting the employee's FICA contribution and the federal
income tax from the gross pay. Column totals are displayed in
line [6] according to the format set in line [5]. Using the
sample input presented earlier we now generate the following
payroll report.

```
    PAYROLL REPORT
ID NO.        RATE        HOURS     REGULAR        O.T.   GROSSPAY        NETPAY
100001        5.00          38      175.00       22.50      197.50       163.25
100003        4.50          35      157.50        0.00      157.50       136.47
100010        4.25          35      148.75        0.00      148.75       119.28
200002        5.25          39      183.75       31.50      215.15       182.17
200003        5.00          35      175.00        0.00      175.00       137.95
300001        7.30          45      255.50      109.50      365.00       293.77
300002        7.00          35      245.00        0.00      245.00      1 8.71
300004        6.90          45      241.50      103.50      345.00       283.54
300006        6.75          40      236.25       50.63      286.88       241.86
300007        6.75          35      236.25        0.00      236.25       200.62

    TOTALS                 382     2054.50      317.63     2372.13      1947.61
```

It is important to note that all calculations in this case
study are performed without roundoff to cents. Not until the
final figures are displayed in form of the report do we round
off with the aid of the format function. Although this approach
is in variance with the real-life situation, we have assumed it
in an attempt to keep the programs and subprograms somewhat
simplified.

In the next report, DEDUCTIONREPORT, we itemize the deductions for each employee. This information is useful to the
company comptroller who must disperse the dedu tions made to
the various federal agencies. In the case of FICA the company
must match the employee's contribution. A distinction is therefore made between employee FICA and total FICA. The deduction
totals include employee and company FICA, federal tax, and
unemployment.

```
           ∇DEDUCTIONREPORT[☐]∇
        ∇ DEDUCTIONREPORT;FMT
[1]     '      ID NO.  EMP_FICA  TOT_FICA   FED_TAX    UNEMPL
           TOTAL
[2]     FMT← 10 0 ,10ρ 10 2
[3]     FMT▼EMP[; 1 13],(2×EMP[;13]),EMP[; 12 14],
           +/EMP[;13 13 14 12]
[4]     ''
[5]     '   TOTALS   ',(2↓FMT▼(COMP[11]÷2),COMP[11 10 12],
           +/COMP[10 11 12]
        ∇
```

In the following execution the totals may be off by several pennies due to rounding errors.

```
    DEDUCTIONREPORT
    ID NO.   EMP_FICA   TOT_FICA    FED_TAX    UNEMPL    TOTAL
    100001     11.55      23.11      22.70      5.93     51.73
    100003      9.21     118.43      11.82      4.73     34.97
    100010      8.70      17.40      20.77      4.46     42.64
    200002     12.59      25.18      20.49      6.46     52.13
    200003     10.24      20.48      26.81      5.25     52.53
    300001     21.35      42.71      49.88     10.95    103.54
    300002     14.33      28.67      41.96      7.35     77.97
    300004     20.18      40.37      41.28     10.35     92.00
    300006     16.78      33.56      28.23      8.61     70.40
    300007     13.82      27.64      21.81      7.09     56.54

  TOTALS      138.77     277.54     285.75     71.16    634.45
```

The final report we present in this case study may be of particular interest to management as it summarizes the weekly work load and gross pay on a departmental basis.

```
           ∇DEPARTMENTALREPORT[☐]∇
        ∇ DEPARTMENTALREPORT;DEPTS;N;FMT;I;T
[1]     DEPTS← 3 10 ρ'OFFICE    SHIPPING   PRODUCTION'
[2]     N←⌊EMP[;1]÷100000
[3]     'DEPARTMENT      HOURS    REGULAR      O.T.   GROSSPAY'
[4]     ''
[5]     FMT← 10 0 ,6ρ 10 2
[6]     I←1
[7]   LP:T←+/(N=I)⌿EMP[; 9 10 11]
[8]     DEPTS[I;],FMT▼T[1],(-/T[2 3]),T[3 2]
[9]     →(3≥I←I+1)/LP
[10]    ''
[11]    '   TOTALS   ⁺ FMT▼COMP[7],(-/COMP[8 9]),COMP[9 8]
        ∇
```

The first digit in the employee ID number refers to the department in which the employee works. This digit is isolated for all employees in line [2] of program DEPARTMENTALREPORT and stored in vector N. The departmental totals are computed and displayed in the loop of lines [7]-[9]. In our example we have three departments, namely OFFICE, SHIPPING, and PRODUCTION. These are specified in line [1] of program DEPARTMENTALREPORT.

```
           DEPARTMENTALREPORT
DEPARTMENT        HOURS    REGULAR      O.T.    GROSSPAY

OFFICE            108      481.25       22.50     503.75
SHIPPING           74      358.75       31.50     390.25
PRODUCTION        200     1214.50      263.83    1478.13

   TOTALS         382     2054.50      317.63    2372.13
```

In this case study we have presented a sample payroll sub-system. It is a subsystem because the weekly payroll is only a small portion of the entire payroll system. The organization and contents represent but one approach that might be taken and is by no means offered as the only format for a payroll program that a company might use. The following exercises point to areas in which the scope of this case study may be broadened.

EXERCISES

1. Modify program TIME to include a validity check for hours worked data. Try to think of errors that are most likely to occur. Provide a check for these errors and an opportunity for reentry. Once all the data are entered have it displayed followed by the inquiry, ARE THE DATA CORRECT AS ENTERED? This will give the operator a chance to make final changes.

2. Modify programs TIME and PAYROLL to insure that PAYROLL will not perform its calculations unless the hours worked for the week have been entered for every employee since its previous execution. (HINT: use a global logical vector with one element per employee. Once the hours are entered for a certain employee, change the appropriate element of the vector from zero to one.)

3. Can you devise an algorithm to compute the federal income tax withholdings without using incremental percentages (variable ΔPER)? Modify program FEDERAL accordingly.

4. Is it necessary to keep a record of FICA withholdings to date? Explain.

5. Write a program TOTALSTODATEREPORT, which displays totals to date for each employee. Payroll information should include regular wages, overtime wages, income tax and FICA withholdings, unemployment tax, and net pay.

6. Modify programs WAGES, FEDERAL, FICA, and UNEMPLOYMENT to include

   a. truncation of all computed values to cents
   b. round off of all computed values to cents; 0.005 and above is to be rounded up and values less than 0.005 are to be rounded down.

   Investigate the effects of a. and b. on the payroll results of the example presented in this case study.

7. How would you add a new employee to the payroll? What changes are necessary?

8. Suppose an employee is on an extended leave without pay. How would you handle this case given the programs of this case study? Any suggestions for improvement?

9. Suppose an employee leaves the company. What changes (if any) would you make to the programs?

10. The president of the company is quite cost conscious and would like the following information for the company as a whole printed weekly in report form.

    a. The average total hourly wages including overtime. (*TOTAL GROSSPAY÷TOTAL HOURS WORKED*).
    b. The ratio of overtime hours to regular hours worked by all the employees.
    c. The ratio of overtime pay to regular pay earned by all employees.
    d. Repeat a. and b. for totals to date.

11. Assume that for every hour that an employee works he earns for the company a certain percentage of his gross pay according to the following schedule:

Department	Percentage
Office	20%
Shipping	30%
Production	45%

    Write a program, *EARNINGSREPORT*, which displays each employee's contribution to the company's earnings. In addition, compute the company total weekly earnings and earnings to date.

Chapter 15
Computer Assisted Instruction

CAI is an abbreviation for Computer Aided Instruction or Computer Assisted Instruction, and refers to a wide range of educational techniques that rely on a computer to assist in the presentation of learning material. CAI can be quite extensive in capability, with a powerful computer time-shared between many students, each one having his own display terminal. The computer may have an extensive library of programs and information stored within, providing the capability of reference to a variety of subject matters. On the other hand CAI is also suitable for use with minicomputers. These computers are currently in use in many public schools where their primary function is for classroom implementation of curricula.

CAI supplements rather than replaces the teacher. A CAI segment offers only limited types of presentation and cannot answer all of the student's questions. A typical segment presents material, drills the student on what has just been learned, and periodically tests his or her progress. During periods of drill, the computer usually helps the student and occasionally offers answers to missed questions. During a test, problems are presented in the same way but no help is offered.

In evaluating the student's progress, the computer can record all information including the student's answers to those problems that he missed, as well as a final count of the number of incorrect answers. From this information, the computer can be programmed to give reports to the teacher.

15.1   CAI IN ALGEBRA

Let us now consider the following 9th grade classroom situation with Johnny meeting his Algebra I teacher, Miss Smith, after class:

Johnny: "Miss Smith, I am not sure I understand today's work on solving open sentences. I need extra help."

Miss Smith: (Well aware of Johnny's general difficulty in comprehending new material, replies with a smile) "I think a computer drill will give you some practice. Go to the terminal room and use the program *ALGEBRA* in workspace *DRILL*, which is in Library 1. Do several practice problems, and be sure to follow the instructions. When you are done bring the output back to me so that we can look over your progress together."

Johnny: "O. K., I'll stop in after 7th period."

In workspace *DRILL*, Johnny finds the drill program *ALGEBRA* on solving open sentences of the form *AX+B=C*. A sample execution follows. Student responses are indicated by stars in the margin.

```
     ALGEBRA
THIS PROGRAM IS TO PRACTICE SOLVING EQUATIONS OF THE FORM
               A×X+B=C
HOW MANY PROBLEMS DO YOU WANT?
☐:
```
**
```
          2

PROBLEM NUMBER 1 IS      ¯45×X+25=¯605
THE ANSWER IS X=?
☐:
```
**
```
          ¯14
YOUR ANSWER IS INCORRECT; THE SOLUTION IS AS FOLLOWS


          ¯45×X+25=¯605
          ¯45×X+25+¯25=¯605+¯25
          ¯45×X=¯630
          ¯45×X÷¯45=¯630÷¯45
          X=14


PROBLEM NUMBER 2 IS     11×X+43=¯122
THE ANSWER IS X=?
☐:
```
**
```
          ¯15
YOUR ANSWER IS CORRECT

YOU DID 1 CORRECT OUT OF 2
YOUR GRADE IS 50


....... YOU DO NEED MORE PRACTICE .......

WANT TO DO MORE?
```
**
```
YES
HOW MANY PROBLEMS DO YOU WANT?
☐:
```
**
```
          1

PROBLEM NUMBER 1 IS     14×X+¯100=¯156
THE ANSWER IS X=?
☐:
```
**
```
          ¯4
```

YOUR ANSWER IS CORRECT

YOU DID 1 CORRECT OUT OF 1
YOUR GRADE IS 100

... VERY GOOD ... VERY GOOD ... VERY GOOD ...

WANT TO DO MORE?
**   *NO*

I ENJOYED WORKING WITH YOU

.... HAVE A GOOD DAY ....

In this sample execution Johnny first elected to try two problems and scored a 50. The computer then suggested he practice some more and asked Johnny: *WANT TO DO MORE?* Johnny responded *YES* and requested one additional problem. When Johnny answered that problem correctly he was complimented and since no additional problems were requested the computer bid him farewell.

Now that we have seen how this CAI program *ALGEBRA* operates from the user's point of view, you probably have a good idea how it is written. The flowchart in Figure 15.1 describes the approach taken in writing this particular drill. The flowchart is, however, general enough so that it can be adapted to drills on a variety of topics.

A program following the flowchart is shown below. Note the student does not display the program, but merely executes it.

```
        ∇ALGEBRA[□]∇
      ∇ ALGEBRA;A;ANS;B;C;CORR;I;N;X
[1]     'THIS PROGRAM IS TO PRACTICE SOLVING EQUATIONS OF THE FORM'
[2]     '                A×X+B=C'
[3]    NUMBER:'HOW MANY PROBLEMS DO YOU WANT?'
[4]     N←□
[5]     CORR←0
[6]     I←1
[7]    START:' '
[8]   ⍝A,B, AND X ARE RANDOMLY GENERATED INTEGERS IN THE RANGE
[9]   ⍝   ¯50 TO 50, ¯100 TO 100, AND ¯20 TO 20 RESPECTIVELY.
[10]  ⍝   THE CASE OF A=0 IS EXCLUDED.
[11]    A←(?50)× 1 ¯1[?2]
[12]    B←¯101+?201
[13]    X←¯21+?41
[14]  ⍝COMPUTE C FROM A,B, AND X TO INSURE AN INTEGRAL ANSWER
[15]    C←B+A×X
[16]    'PROBLEM NUMBER ';I;' IS     ';A;'×X+';B;'=';C
[17]    'THE ANSWER IS X=?'
[18]    ANS←□
[19]    →(ANS=X)/CORRECT
[20]    'YOUR ANSWER IS INCORRECT; THE SOLUTION IS AS FOLLOWS'
[21]    ' '
```

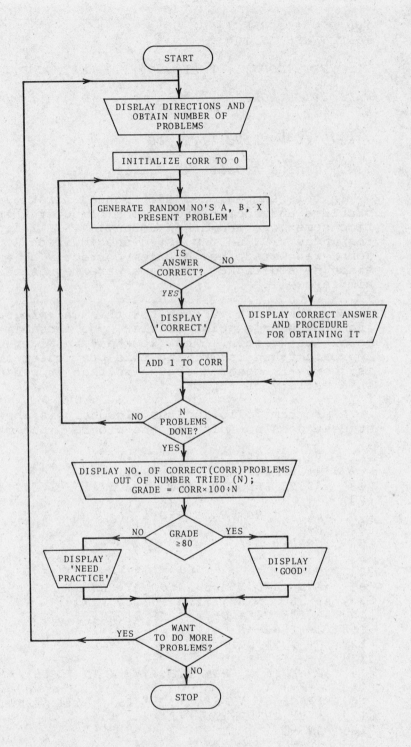

Figure 15.1 General algorithm for a CAI program

```
[22]  '              ';A;'×X+';B;'=';C
[23]  '              ';A;'×X+';B;'+';-B;'=';C;'+';-B
[24]  '            ';A;'×X=';C-B
[25]  '            ';A;'×X÷';A;'=';C-B;'÷';A
[26]  '          X=';X
[27]  →LOOP
[28]  CORRECT:'YOUR ANSWER IS CORRECT'
[29]  CORR←CORR+1
[30]  LOOP:→(N≥I←I+1)/START
[31]  ' '
[32]  'YOU DID ';CORR;' CORRECT OUT OF ';N
[33]  'YOUR GRADE IS ';⌈CORR×100÷N
[34]  ' '
[35]  →((CORR×100÷N)≥80)/COMPLIMENT
[36]  '...... YOU DO NEED MORE PRACTICE .......'
[37]  →MORE
[38]  COMPLIMENT:'... VERY GOOD ... VERY GOOD ... VERY GOOD ...'
[39]  MORE:' '
[40]  'WANT TO DO MORE?'
[41]  →('Y'=1↑⎕)/NUMBER
[42]  ' '
[43]  'I ENJOYED WORKING WITH YOU'
[44]  ' '
[45]  '....... HAVE A GOOD DAY .......'
      ∇
```

In the CAI program *ALGEBRA* we have presented an example of a drill with which the student may practice solving open sentences. The student enters the number of problems requested by the teacher. The computer generates the problems at random, evaluates the student's answer, and grades his or her performance. To minimize a student's frustration, the computer's response includes correct answers to missed problems as well as steps necessary to attain the correct answer. The program thus emphasizes the great power of conversational programming.

15.2 CAI IN ENGLISH GRAMMAR

A common first reaction is that CAI can only be used with subject matter related to mathematics. It is true that it is easier to tell the computer how to carry out a drill and practice program in mathematics particularly on the elementary level, than it is to have it teach English grammar. However, an examination of CAI literature developed at various institutions would reveal not only mathematical subject matter, but also a wide range of other subjects. Computer assisted instruction has indeed been attempted in every area of instruction.

The second example of computer assisted instruction focuses on the English language. In the program *GRAMMAR*, the student learns new material and is then drilled. This is in contrast to the drill program *ALGEBRA*, which is more useful as a followup to a classroom lecture since the program does not teach the student new material.

The program *GRAMMAR* is a complete lesson on pronouns used as predicate nominatives. In this CAI program the student is taught some relevant rules, given sample examples to read as an oral exercise, and asked to practice what he has just learned. The program thus combines several teaching methods: lecture, look and say, as well as drill.

```
        ∇GRAMMAR[□]∇
    ∇ GRAMMAR;NAME;NCORR;WAIT
[1]   'HI WHAT IS YOUR NAME?'
[2]   NAME←□
[3]   ' '
[4]   'NICE TO MEET YOU ',NAME
[5]   ' '
[6]   'TODAY I WOULD LIKE TO TEACH YOU THAT'
[7]   '.... A PREDICATE NOMINATIVE IS IN THE NOMINATIVE CASE ....'
[8]   ' '
[9]   ' '
[10]  '    A PRONOUN USED AS A PREDICATE NOMINATIVE MUST BE '
[11]  '        IN THE NOMINATIVE CASE: I, HE, SHE, WE, THEY. '
[12]  '    A PREDICATE NOMINATIVE, AS YOU LEARNED EARLIER,'
[13]  '        OCCURS AFTER A FORM OF THE VERB TO BE.  THE FORMS'
[14]  '        OF THE VERB TO BE ARE AM, IS, ARE, WAS, WERE,'
[15]  '        AND VERB PHRASES ENDING IN BE OR BEEN.'
[16]  '  '
[17]  '        EXAMPLES:'
[18]  '                1. MY BEST FRIENDS ARE YOU AND SHE.'
[19]  '                   (YOU AND SHE ARE PREDICATE'
[20]  '                   NOMINATIVES.)'
[21]  ' '
[22]  '                2. IT MUST HAVE BEEN THEY. (THEY IS A'
[23]  '                   PREDICATE NOMINATIVE.)'
[24]  '  '
[25]  'ORAL DRILL'
[26]  '            THE FOLLOWING SENTENCES CONTAIN PRONOUNS'
[27]  '        CORRECTLY USED AS A PREDICATE NOMINATIVE.  READ'
[28]  '        THE SENTENCES ALOUD, PAYING SPECIAL ATTENTION TO'
[29]  '        THE PRONOUNS IN THE NOMINATIVE CASE.'
[30]  '  '
[31]  '    1. THE UNKNOWN CALLER MAY BE HE.'
[32]  '    2. IT SHOULD BE THEY.'
[33]  '    3. THE BEST SPEAKERS ARE TOBY AND SHE.'
[34]  '    4. IT''S HE AT THE DOOR.'
[35]  '    5. WAS IT YOU AND THEY?'
[36]  '  '
[37]  'PRESS RETURN WHEN YOU ARE READY TO CONTINUE.'
[38]  WAIT←□
[39]  NAME,', I WOULD LIKE YOU TO TRY THE FOLLOWING MULTIPLE'
[40]  '       CHOICE EXERCISES. ENTER YOUR ANSWER AFTER THE '
[41]  '       SENTENCE IS DISPLAYED.'
[42]  '  '
[43]  NCORR←0
[44]  '1. COULD IT HAVE BEEN (THEM,THEY)?'
[45]  CHECK 'THEY'
[46]  '2. THE ACTRESS IS NOT (SHE,HER) BUT HER SISTER.'
[47]  CHECK 'SHE'
```

```
[48]   '3. THE BEST PITCHER IS EITHER ERIC OR (I,ME).'
[49]   CHECK 'I'
[50]   '4. IT COULD NOT HAVE BEEN (WE,US).'
[51]   CHECK 'WE'
[52]   '5. IT MIGHT HAVE BEEN (THEM,THEY) AFTER ALL.'
[53]   CHECK 'THEY'
[54]   ' '
[55]   'YOU DID ';NCORR;' OUT OF 5 CORRECTLY ',NAME
[56]   →(NCORR>3)/FINI
[57]   'I AM A LITTLE DISAPPOINTED IN YOUR SCORE'
[58] FINI:' '
[59]   '    TAKE CARE, ',NAME,', SEE YOU AROUND'
       ▽
```

GRAMMAR calls the subprogram CHECK which accepts and then compares the student's answer with the correct answer CANS. If the student's response is incorrect, the correct answer is displayed before the next question appears.

```
     ▽CHECK[□]▽
   ▽ CHECK CANS;ANS
[1]   ANS←,⍞
[2]   →(∧/ANS=(ρANS)↑CANS)/CORR
[3]   'SORRY THE CORRECT ANSWER IS ',CANS
[4]   →0
[5]  CORR:NCORR←NCORR+1
     ▽
```

A sample execution follows with student responses indicated by stars in the margin.

```
     GRAMMAR
HI WHAT IS YOUR NAME?
**   TOBY

NICE TO MEET YOU TOBY
TODAY I WOULD LIKE TO TEACH YOU THAT
.... A PREDICATE NOMINATIVE IS IN THE NOMINATIVE CASE ....

A PRONOUN USED AS A PREDICATE NOMINATIVE MUST BE
     IN THE NOMINATIVE CASE: I, HE, SHE, WE, THEY.
A PREDICATE NOMINATIVE, AS YOU LEARNED EARLIER,
     OCCURS AFTER A FORM OF THE VERB TO BE.  THE FORMS
     OF THE VERB TO BE ARE AM, IS, ARE, WAS, WERE,
     AND VERB PHRASES ENDING IN BE OR BEEN.

     EXAMPLES:
             1. MY BEST FRIENDS ARE YOU AND SHE.
                  (YOU AND SHE ARE PREDICATE
                  NOMINATIVES.)

             2. IT MUST HAVE BEEN THEY. (THEY IS A
                  PREDICATE NOMINATIVE.)

ORAL DRILL
        THE FOLLOWING SENTENCES CONTAIN PRONOUNS
     CORRECTLY USED AS A PREDICATE NOMINATIVE.  READ
     THE SENTENCES ALOUD, PAYING SPECIAL ATTENTION TO
     THE PRONOUNS IN THE NOMINATIVE CASE.
```

        1. *THE UNKNOWN CALLER MAY BE HE.*
        2. *IT SHOULD BE THEY.*
        3. *THE BEST SPEAKERS ARE TOBY AND SHE.*
        4. *IT'S HE AT THE DOOR.*
        5. *WAS IT YOU AND THEY?*

PRESS RETURN WHEN YOU ARE READY TO CONTINUE.
**

TOBY, I WOULD LIKE YOU TO TRY THE FOLLOWING MULTIPLE
     CHOICE EXERCISES. ENTER YOUR ANSWER AFTER THE
     SENTENCE IS DISPLAYED.

1. COULD IT HAVE BEEN (THEM,THEY)?
**   *THEM*
SORRY THE CORRECT ANSWER IS THEY
2. THE ACTRESS IS NOT (SHE,HER) BUT HER SISTER.
**   *SHE*
3. THE BEST PITCHER IS EITHER ERIC OR (I,ME).
**   *I*
4. IT COULD NOT HAVE BEEN (WE,US).
**   *WE*
5. IT MIGHT HAVE BEEN (THEM,THEY) AFTER ALL.
**   *THEY*

YOU DID 4 OUT OF 5 CORRECTLY TOBY

     TAKE CARE, TOBY, SEE YOU AROUND

EXERCISES

1. List five specific topics in different subject areas where
    a CAI program might be useful.

2. Modify program *ALGEBRA* to include provisions for the com-
    puter to recall all missed problems. These are to be
    printed in summary form at the end of the drill session
    along with the student's grade.

3. Execute program *GRAMMAR* and instead of responding *THEY* to
    question 1, enter *THE*. What happens? Modify the program
    so that it will accept *only* the correct answer. (This is
    not as easy as it seems. After you think you have a solu-
    tion see if a friend can make it accept a wrong answer or
    reject the right one.)

4. Modify *GRAMMAR* so that it asks the student how many ques-
    tions he would like to try and then selects them at random,
    without duplication, from 25 available examples. There are
    a number of ways to do this. The basic decisions you have
    to make are how the questions are to be stored and then
    how the order of asking the questions is to be controlled.
    Try to come up with a couple of solutions and then pick
    what you judge to be the best from the standpoint of pro-
    gramming ease and the ease with which questions can be
    added and changed.

5. Write a drill to practice multiplication of numbers between 50 and 100. Problems are to be generated randomly.

6. Write a CAI program to drill students on the APL functions presented in Chapters 3, 5, or 6.

7. Write a CAI program in an area of interest to you.

8. Write a program to quiz the student on the names of the capitals of five states (use multiple choice questions) and to assess the student's performance.

9. Write a program that will have a limited conversation with a user. The topic is up to you. The program should ask a few questions and be able to recognize a small variety of responses for each question. The order of execution of the program should depend, to a certain extent, on the answers received as input. You may decide upon any procedure you like for handling unrecognizable input.

10. Check the public libraries of your system for CAI programs. Execute those programs that are of interest to you.

Appendix 1
Error Messages

The following list summarizes the common APL error messages and system error messages including a brief description of their cause and corrective action. Some of these error messages may depend on the APL implementation.

Error Message	Cause (Corrective Action)
CHARACTER	Illegal overstrike.
DEPTH	Excessive use of defined functions within one another. (Clear state indicator.)
DEFN	Incorrect use of ∇ or ☐. ∇ is not in first position. Incorrect use of function name. ∇ used to open a pendant function. (Display state indicator and clear as required.) Improper request of line display or edit.
DOMAIN	Function undefined for the given argument, for example adding literals or dividing by zero.
IMPROPER LIBRARY REFERENCE	A *)SAVE*, *)DROP*, or *)LIB* command has been used with a private library number other than the one signed on.
INCORRECT COMMAND	Invalid form of system command used.
INCORRECT SIGN-ON	Sign-on procedure violated.
INDEX	Reference to a nonexistent element of an array. Index out of range.
LABEL	A previously defined function name used as a label or colon used incorrectly.
LENGTH	Arrays are of nonconformable shapes.

Error Message	Cause (Corrective Action)
MESSAGE LOST	Due to an interruption a message is lost before it is received.
NOT GROUPED, NAME IN USE	An attempt has been made to form a group under a name currently in use.
NOT ERASED: (NAMES)	Function is pendant or is being edited and cannot be erased.
NOT SAVED, WS QUOTA USED UP	Unsuccessful attempt to save; allotted number of library workspaces is exceeded.
NOT SAVED, THIS WS IS WSID	An attempt is made to save something other than an active workspace name.
NOT WITH OPEN DEFINITION	Certain system commands cannot be executed while in the definition mode.
NUMBER IN USE	Somebody else with the same ID number is already signed on.
NUMBER NOT IN SYSTEM	Number is either not on system, is locked, or wrong key is used.
OBJECT NOT FOUND	The referenced workspace does not contain the function or variable.
RANK	Attempt made to combine arrays of nonconformable rank.
RESEND	Problem is with transmission to computer. (Re-enter and repeat transmission.)
SI DAMAGE	Suspension information has been destroyed. (Clear the state indicator and execute again.)
SYMBOL TABLE FULL	Symbol table size exceeded in the workspace. Too many names used. (Erase some functions or variables, then save, clear, reset *)SYMBOLS*, and copy.)
SYNTAX	Incorrectly formed statement, invalid syntax; for example, operation sign missing or unmatched parentheses.
SYSTEM	Computer internal operation error. (Inform the system manager.)

Error Message	Cause (Corrective Action)
VALUE	Reference is made to a variable that has not been assigned a value. (Assign the variable a value.)
WS FULL	Workspace is filled; storage capacity is exceeded. (Clear state indicator, erase unused objects.)
WS LOCKED	No key or incorrect key used.
WS NOT FOUND	Library does not contain a workspace by that name.

Appendix 2
System Commands

I. SIGN-ON, SIGN-OFF COMMANDS

)XXXXXX:LOCK   Signs on with user number *XXXXXX*.
                                   LOCK is the sign-on lock and is
                                   necessary if the sign-on number has
                                   been locked.

)OFF   Signs off a user.

)OFF:LOCK   Signs off and locks workspace or
                                     changes user number lockword to *LOCK*.

)OFF HOLD[:LOCK]   Signs off without breaking dial-up con-
                                   nection. The next user need only
                                   enter the sign-on command to gain
                                   access to the system.

)CONTINUE[:LOCK]   Saves active workspace as the workspace
                                   CONTINUE in the user's library. At
                                   the next sign-on, the *CONTINUE* work-
                                   space is automatically loaded into
                                   the active workspace. This is useful
                                   for continuing work from one session
                                   to the next, but be careful of stor-
                                   ing information in *CONTINUE* as it can
                                   be destroyed by an unintentional
                                   interrupt.

)CONTINUE HOLD[:LOCK] Executes a *)CONTINUE* but holds the
                                   phone connection.

II. WORKSPACE MANAGEMENT COMMANDS

)CLEAR   Replaces the active workspace with a
                                   clear workspace.

)LOAD WSNAME[:LOCK]   Loads a copy of workspace *WSNAME* into
                                   the active workspace. *LOCK* must be
                                   included if the workspace was locked.

)COPY WSNAME[:LOCK]   Copies all global objects from a stored
                                   workspace into the active workspace.

`)COPY WSNAME[:LOCK]` `   NAME(S)`	Copies all objects in the list *NAMES* from the workspace *WSNAME* into the active workspace.
`)PCOPY WSNAME[:LOCK]`	Same as `)COPY` except protects and does not replace objects in the active workspace that have the same name as objects in *WSNAME*.
`)PCOPY WSNAME` `   [:LOCK]NAME(S)`	Like `)COPY NAME(S)` but protects the contents of the active workspace.
`)SAVE`	Stores a copy of the active workspace into the library workspace of the same name. Any lock currently active remains in effect.
`)SAVE WSNAME[:LOCK]`	Stores a copy of the active workspace under the name *WSNAME* and locks it if *LOCK* is present.
`)DROP WSNAME`	Deletes the stored workspace *WSNAME*. Users can only delete workspaces from their private libraries.
`)WSID`	Displays the name of the active workspace.
`)WSID NEW[:LOCK]`	Changes name of active workspace to *NEW*.
`)LIB`	Lists the names of stored workspaces in the user's private library.
`)LIB N`	Lists names of stored workspaces in public library number *N*.

III. FUNCTIONS AND VARIABLES IN THE ACTIVE WORKSPACE

`)FNS`	Lists alphabetically names of defined functions in active workspace.
`)FNS LETTER`	Starts function listing with designated letter.
`)VARS`	Lists alphabetically the names of the global variables in the active workspace.
`)VARS LETTER`	Starts the variable listing with the designated letter.
`)SI`	Lists the state indicator.
`)SIV`	Lists the state indicator and the associated local variables.

)ERASE NAME(S)	Deletes named global objects from active workspace.
)GROUP GNAME NAMES	Forms a group named GNAME from the objects in the list NAMES. This is convenient for applications which use more than one function or variable. A group name can be used in a)COPY command and causes all members of the group to be copied into the active workspace. If NAMES is absent, this command causes the group GNAME to disperse.
)GRP GNAME	Lists members of group GNAME in active workspace.
)GRPS	Lists alphabetically names of group in active workspace.
)GRPS LETTER	Starts listing with designated letter.

IV.   OTHER PARAMETERS IN THE ACTIVE WORKSPACE

)DIGITS N	Sets the number of significant digits in output to N ($1 \leq N \leq 16$).
)WIDTH N	Sets maximum width of an output line to N.
)SYMBOLS	Displays current size of the symbol table.
)SYMBOLS N	Sets the size of the symbol table to N. Can only be executed in a clear workspace.
)ORIGIN N	Sets the index origin to 0 or 1, depending on the value of N.

V.   COMMUNICATION COMMANDS

)MSG PORT TEXT	Sends message TEXT to designated port and locks keyboard to await reply.
)MSGN PORT TEXT	Sends message TEXT to designated port and unlocks keyboard.
)OPR TEXT	Sends message TEXT to operator and locks keyboard awaiting a reply.
)OPRN TEXT	Sends message TEXT to operator, and unlocks keyboard.
)PORTS	Displays port number and user code for all terminals signed on.
)PORT CODE	Displays port number(s) associated with specified user's code.

Appendix 3
APL Functions

The appendix is divided into the following sections:

I.   Primitive scalar monadic and scalar dyadic functions.

II. Primitive mixed functions.

III. Primitive operators.

IV. Additional APL symbols.

V.   System variables.

The following examples use the notation S for a scalar, V for a vector, M for a matrix, A and B for any of these. The symbol $\leftrightarrow$ used in these examples should be read as "is the same as."

I. PRIMITIVE SCALAR AND DYADIC FUNCTIONS

I.1 Monadic Arithmetic Functions

Computations are performed on each element of the argument. The result has the same shape as the argument.

Name	Usage	Description/Example
Identity	$+A$	$+A\leftrightarrow 0+A\leftrightarrow A$; $+3\leftrightarrow 3$
Negative	$-A$	Additive inverse; $-A\leftrightarrow 0-A\leftrightarrow ^-1\times A$; $-3\leftrightarrow ^-3$
Signum	$\times A$	Sign of A, result is 1, 0, or $^-1$ depending on whether A is positive, zero, or negative; $\times 3\leftrightarrow 1$; $\times ^-3\leftrightarrow ^-1$; $\times 0\leftrightarrow 0$
Reciprocal	$\div A$	The reciprocal of A ; $\div A\leftrightarrow 1\div A$; $\div 2\leftrightarrow 0.5$
Exponential	$*A$	The base of the natural logarithm, e, raised to the power A ; $*A\leftrightarrow (2.71828...)*A$; $*3\leftrightarrow e^3$
Ceiling	$\lceil A$	The smallest integer greater than or equal to A ; $\lceil 2.1\leftrightarrow 3$; $\lceil 2.9\leftrightarrow 3$; $\lceil ^-2.1\leftrightarrow ^-2$; $\lceil 2\leftrightarrow 2$

Name	Usage	Description/Example
Floor	$\lfloor A$	The largest integer less than or equal to A; $\lfloor 2.1 \leftrightarrow 2$; $\lfloor 2.9 \leftrightarrow 2$; $\lfloor {}^-2.1 \leftrightarrow {}^-3$; $\lfloor 2 \leftrightarrow 2$
Magnitude	$\|A$	The absolute value of A; $\|{}^-2 \leftrightarrow 2$; $\|2 \leftrightarrow 2$
Natural Logarithm	$\circledast A$	The natural logarithm of A; $\circledast 3 \leftrightarrow$ log of 3 to base e; $\circledast {\star} A \leftrightarrow A \leftrightarrow {\star} \circledast A$
Factorial	$!A$	The product of all integers from 1 to A $(1 \times 2 \times 3 \times \ldots \times A)$; $!3 \leftrightarrow 3 \times 2 \times 1 \leftrightarrow 6$; $!0 \leftrightarrow 1$. For $A \neq$ positive integer $!$ is given by the gamma function $!A \leftrightarrow \Gamma(A+1)$
Roll	$?A$	For integer A produces a random integer selected from the integers 1 to A.

I.2   Dyadic Arithmetic Functions

For dyadic functions the arguments A and B must have the same shape. The shape of the result is the same as the shape of the arguments. The only exception is when one of the arguments is an array containing only one element. In this case the other argument can have any shape.

Name	Usage	Description/Example
Plus	$A+B$	The sum of A and B; $2.5+2 \leftrightarrow 4.5$
Minus	$A-B$	The difference between A and B; $3-2 \leftrightarrow 1$; $3-{}^-2 \leftrightarrow 5$
Times	$A \times B$	The product of A and B; $3 \times 2 \leftrightarrow 6$
Divide	$A \div B$	The quotient of A divided by B; $3 \div 2 \leftrightarrow 1.5$
Power	$A {\star} B$	A raised to the power B; $3 {\star} 2 \leftrightarrow 9$
Maximum	$A \lceil B$	The larger of A and B; $2 \lceil 3 \leftrightarrow 3$; $3 \lceil 2 \leftrightarrow 3$; ${}^-2 \lceil {}^-3 \leftrightarrow {}^-2$
Minimum	$A \lfloor B$	The smaller of A and B; $2 \lfloor 3 \leftrightarrow 2$; $3 \lfloor 2 \leftrightarrow 2$; ${}^-2 \lfloor {}^-3 \leftrightarrow {}^-3$
Residue	$A \| B$	For A and B positive integers gives the remainder of B divided by A. In general for any A and B: $A\|B \leftrightarrow B$ if $A=0$; if $A \neq 0$ the result lies between A and zero and equals $B-N{\star}A$ for some integer N. $1\|3.14 \leftrightarrow 0.14$; ${}^-2\|3.14 \leftrightarrow {}^-0.86$
Logarithm	$A \circledast B$	The logarithm of B to the base A; $2 \circledast 8 \leftrightarrow \log_2 8 \leftrightarrow 3$

Name	Usage	Description/Example
Combination (Binomial Coefficients)	$A!B$	Number of combinations of B things taken A at a time. $A!B \leftrightarrow (!B) \div (!A) \times !B-A$; $0\ 1\ 2\ 3\ 4!4 \leftrightarrow 1\ 4\ 6\ 4\ 1$. For A and $B \neq$ positive integer $A!B \leftrightarrow$ complete beta function.

I.3 Relational Functions

These are dyadic functions that return logical results. The result is one if the relationship is true and zero if the relationship is false.

Name	Usage	Example
Less than	$A < B$	$5 < 4\ 5\ 6 \leftrightarrow 0\ 0\ 1$
Less than or equal	$A \leq B$	$5 \leq 4\ 5\ 6 \leftrightarrow 0\ 1\ 1$
Equal	$A = B$	$5 = 4\ 5\ 6 \leftrightarrow 0\ 1\ 0$
Greater than or equal	$A \geq B$	$5 \geq 4\ 5\ 6 \leftrightarrow 1\ 1\ 0$
Greater than	$A > B$	$5 > 4\ 5\ 6 \leftrightarrow 1\ 0\ 0$
Not equal	$A \neq B$	$5 \neq 4\ 5\ 6 \leftrightarrow 1\ 0\ 1$

I.4 Logical Functions

These functions take logical data as their arguments and return logical results. There is one monadic function $\sim A \leftrightarrow$ not A; $\sim 1\ 0 \leftrightarrow 0\ 1$ and there are four dyadic functions.

Name	Usage	Example
And	$A \wedge B$	$1\ 1\ 0\ 0 \wedge 1\ 0\ 1\ 0 \leftrightarrow 1\ 0\ 0\ 0$
Or	$A \vee B$	$1\ 1\ 0\ 0 \vee 1\ 0\ 1\ 0 \leftrightarrow 1\ 1\ 1\ 0$
Nand	$A \barwedge B$	$1\ 1\ 0\ 0 \barwedge 1\ 0\ 1\ 0 \leftrightarrow 0\ 1\ 1\ 1$
Nor	$A \barvee B$	$1\ 1\ 0\ 0 \barvee 1\ 0\ 1\ 0 \leftrightarrow 0\ 0\ 0\ 1$

I.5 Circular (Trigonometric) Functions

These functions provide the capability to perform standard trigonometric calculations. The circular functions are designated by the symbol $\circ$ (upper shift letter O). In its monadic form, this function is called pi times

$$\circ B \leftrightarrow \pi \times B \leftrightarrow (3.14159...) \times B$$

In the dyadic form $A \circ B$, the elements in A must be integers from $^-7$ to 7 inclusive. The calculations performed on the corresponding elements in B are given in the table below:

_A_	_A_○_B_	(-_A_)○_B_
0	(1-_B_*2)*.5	(1-_B_*2)*.5
1	sin _B_	arc sin _B_
2	cosine _B_	arc cos _B_
3	tangent _B_	arc tan _B_
4	(1+_B_*2)*.5	(‾1+_B_*2)*.5
5	sinh _B_	arc sinh _B_
6	cosh _B_	arc cosh _B_
7	tanh _B_	arc tanh _B_

II.   PRIMITIVE MIXED FUNCTIONS

The examples in the following table of mixed functions use _S_ for scalar, _V_ for vector, _M_ for matrix, _A_ or _B_ for any scalar, vector, or matrix or n-dimensional array. Except for the first argument for _S_ι_A_ or _S_[_A_], a scalar may be used instead of a vector. A one-element array may replace any scalar. The symbol ↔ should be read as "is the same as."

The variables _R_, _N_ and _C_ are used in the examples.

$$R ↔ 2\ 8\ 5 \qquad N ↔ \begin{matrix} 1 & 2 & 3 \\ 4 & 5 & 6 \end{matrix} \qquad C ↔ \begin{matrix} ABCD \\ EFGH \end{matrix}$$

The following notes are referenced within the table:

<1>   Function result depends on index origin.

<2>   Elimination of any index selects all along the coordinate.

<3>   The function is applied along the last coordinate; the symbols ⌿, ⍀, and ⊖ are equivalent to /, \, and ⌽ respectively, except that the function is applied along the first coordinate. If [_S_] appears after any of the symbols, the relevant coordinate is determined by the scalar _S_. The application of _S_ depends upon the index origin.

Name	Usage	Description/Example
Shape	ρ_A_	ρ_A_ is a vector representing the dimension of array _A_. ρ_R_↔3;ρ_N_↔2 3; ρρ_N_↔2;ρ7↔ι0
Reshape	_V_ρ_A_	Elements from _A_ are structured to form an array having the dimension _V_. 7ρ_R_↔2 8 5 2 8 5 2; 0ρ_R_↔ι0↔empty vector. (ι0)ρ_R_↔2;_N_↔2 3ρι6;6ρ_N_↔ι6
Ravel	,_A_	Make _A_ into the vector (×/ρ_A_)ρ_A_;_R_↔,_R_; ,_N_↔ι6;ρ,7↔1

Name	Usage	Description/Example

Catenate
<1 3>

A,B
$A,[I]B$

Join two arrays along a coordinate to form a new array. A and B must conform. Arrays of the same rank conform if $(I\neq\iota\rho\rho A)/\rho A\leftrightarrow(I\neq\iota\rho\rho B)/\rho B$, i.e., the length of all coordinates except that along which they are being joined must be the same. Thus two matrices can be catenated along their second coordinate if they have the same number of rows. Arrays differing in rank by one conform if the shape of the array with lower rank is identical to the shape of the other array with coordinate I deleted. A vector can be catenated as a new row on a matrix if the length of the vector equals the number of columns in the matrix. A scalar is reshaped to conform to the other arguments.

```
'T','HIS'↔'THIS';R,ι2↔2 8 5 1 2
C,[1]C↔ABCD    C,'*'↔ABCD*
         EFGH          EFGH*
         ABCD    R,[1]N↔2 8 5
         EFGH           1 2 3
                        4 5 6
```

Laminate
<1 3>

$A,[I.J]B$

Joins the two arrays A and B along a new axis. A and B must have the same shape and rank. The new axis is added between old axis I and $I+1$.
```
R,[0.5]R↔2 8 5   R,[1.5]R↔2 2
         2 8 5            8 8
                         5 5
```

Index
<1 2>

$V[A]$
$M[A;A]$

The index of an element (row or column) within a vector (matrix) is the position that the element (row or column) occupies in the vector (matrix).
```
R[2]↔8;NN[;1]↔1 4
N[2;]↔4 5 6;N[1 2;3 2]↔3 2
                       6 5
```

Index generator
<1>

ιS

Generates the first S integers in ascending order $\iota3\leftrightarrow1\ 2\ 3;\iota0\leftrightarrow$empty vector

Index of
<1>

$V\iota A$

Gives the index of the first occurrence of A in V, if A does not occur in V result is $1+\rho V$
```
RιN↔4 1 4;1+ρR↔4;
     4 3 4
```

5 6 5ι5↔1 (only the first 5 is indicated)

Name	Usage	Description/Example
Take	$V \uparrow A$	Take the $|V[I]$ first (if $V[I]>0$) or last (if $V[I]<0$) elements along the Ith coordinate of A. $3 \uparrow \iota 5 \leftrightarrow 1\ 2\ 3; 2\ 2 \uparrow C \leftrightarrow AB$ EF $^-5 \uparrow R \leftrightarrow 0\ 0\ 2\ 8\ 5$ (zeros are added)
Drop	$V \downarrow A$	Drop the $|V[I]$ first (if $V[I]>0$) or last (if $V[I]<0$) elements along the Ith coordinate of V. $^-3 \downarrow \iota 5 \leftrightarrow 1\ 2;\ 2 \downarrow 'THIS' \leftrightarrow 'IS'$ $6 \downarrow 'THIS' \leftrightarrow EMPTY\ VECTOR$ $^-1\ 2 \downarrow C \leftrightarrow CD$
Grade up <1>	ΛV	Gives the permutation which orders V such that $V[\Lambda V]$ is sorted in ascending order. $\Lambda R \leftrightarrow 1\ 3\ 2; R[\Lambda R] \leftrightarrow 2\ 5\ 8$
Grade down <1>	ΨV	Gives the permutation which orders V such that $V[\Lambda V]$ is sorted in descending order. $\Psi R \leftrightarrow 2\ 3\ 1; R[\Psi R] \leftrightarrow 8\ 5\ 2$
Compress <3>	V/A $V/[I]A$ $V \neq A$	Selects those elements in A that correspond to ones in V (V is a logical vector). $1\ 0\ 1/R \leftrightarrow 2\ 5;$ $0\ 1\ 0\ 1/C \leftrightarrow 0\ 1\ 0\ 1/[2]C \leftrightarrow BD$ FH
Expand <3>	$V \backslash A$ $V \backslash [I]A$ $V \backslash A$	Replaces the ones in V with corresponding elements taken from A, zeros in V are replaced by blanks if A is a character vector or zeros if A is a numerical vector (V is a logical vector). $1\ 0\ 1 \backslash \iota 2 \leftrightarrow 1\ 0\ 2;\ 1\ 0\ 1 \backslash 'AM' \leftrightarrow 'A\ M'$ $1\ 0\ 1 \backslash N \leftrightarrow 1\ 2\ 3$ $0\ 0\ 0$ $4\ 5\ 6$
Reverse <3>	ϕA $\phi[I]A$ ΘA	The order of elements in A is reversed along a coordinate. $\phi \iota 4 \leftrightarrow 4\ 3\ 2\ 1;$ $\phi C \leftrightarrow DCBA; \Theta C \leftrightarrow EFGH \leftrightarrow \Theta[1]C$ $HGFEABCD$

Name	Usage	Description/Example
Rotate <1 3>	$B\phi A$ $B\phi[I]A$ $B\Theta A$	Moves B elements along coordinate I of A from the front to the end if B is positive; if B is negative it moves the last B elements to the front. B must be a scalar or the shape of B must be the same as that obtained by deleting the Ith element from ρA. Thus a vector can be used to rotate a matrix along its second coordinate if the number of elements in the vector equals the number of rows in the matrix. $2\phi R \leftrightarrow {}^{-}1\phi R \leftrightarrow 5\ 2\ 8$ $1\ 0\ {}^{-}1\ 0\Theta C \leftrightarrow EBGD \leftrightarrow 1\ 0\ {}^{-}1\ 0\Theta[1]C$ $\qquad\qquad\qquad AFCH$
Transpose <1 3>	$V\lozenge A$	Coordinate I of A becomes coordinate $V[I]$ of result $2\ 1\lozenge N \leftrightarrow 1\ 4\ ;1\ 1\lozenge N \leftrightarrow 1\ 5$ $\qquad\qquad\quad 2\ 5$ $\qquad\qquad\quad 3\ 6$
	$\lozenge A$	Reverses the order of the axes of A $2\ 1\lozenge N \leftrightarrow \lozenge N$
Membership	$A\epsilon B$	Determines whether the elements of A are contained in B. Result is an array of ones and zeros having the same shape as A. Ones occur for any element of A that is contained in B, zeros occur otherwise $'CAT'\epsilon'ABCD' \leftrightarrow 1\ 1\ 0;$ $N\epsilon R \leftrightarrow 0\ 1\ 0$ $\qquad\qquad 0\ 1\ 0$
Deal <1>	$S?S$	$W?Y$ selects W values from ιY without repetitions. $2?6 \leftrightarrow 3\ 5$ for example $2?6 \leftrightarrow 1\ 2$ $52?52 \leftrightarrow$ card deck shuffle.
Decode	$B\perp A$	A is the array to be converted, B is a vector called the radix vector, whose elements are the factors needed to make the conversion from one unit to the next. A and B may be scalars, vectors, or matrices with either A or B a scalar, or $(\rho B)[2]$ equal to $(\rho A)[1]$, or $(\rho B)[2]$, or $(\rho A)[1]$ equal to one. The decode function acts across the first coordinate of the matrix. Convert 1 hour, 3 minutes, and 10 seconds to seconds: $0\ 60\ 60\perp 1\ 3\ 10 \leftrightarrow 3790$ since

Name	Usage	Description/Example

(1×60×60)+(3×60)+10=3790; note ρA=ρB
and B[1] can have any value, in this
case 0. Convert 4 2 7 to scalar 427:
10 10 10⊥4 2 7↔427↔10⊥4 2 7
A a scalar: 2⊥1 1 0 1↔13
B a scalar: 10 10 10 ⊥1↔111
10 10⊥N↔14 25 36

Encode B⊤A Converts from a value to some predeter-
mined representation; radix conversion
of A to base B. Encode function is
the opposite of the decode function.
10 10 10⊤427↔4 2 7
0 60 60⊤8790↔1 3 10

0 1⊤3.1415↔3 0.1415 (split integer and
fraction)

N↔10 10⊤14 25 36

Format ⍕A Converts numerical arrays to character
arrays. Used monadically the format
function returns a character array
which duplicates the display normally
produced by its argument.
⍕(2 3⍴⍳6)↔1 2 3 and ρ⍕(2 3⍴⍳6)↔2 6
4 5 6
⍕'ABC'↔ABC and ρ⍕'ABC'↔3

V⍕A A may only consist of numerical data. B
may be a single number, a pair of
numbers, or a vector of length
2×⁻1↑1,ρA. Generally a pair of numbers is used to control the result.
The first controls the spacing by
specifying the number of characters to
be used in displaying each numerical
value. The second number gives the
number of digits to be displayed after
the decimal point.

10 3⍕370.1 285↔   370.100   285.000

A pair of integers may be provided for
each value to be formatted:
7 1 8 2⍕123.366 95↔   123.4   95.00

A single control number is treated as
a number pair with a width indicator
of zero. A zero width indicator
yields at least one space between
adjacent numbers.

A↔1.24 ⁻10.123   2⍕A↔1.24 ⁻10.12
0   1.0   then   .00   1.00

Name	Usage	Description/Example
Execute (Unquote)	⍎A	Evaluates or executes the characters in A as an APL expression. Argument must be a character vector or scalar. +/⍎'5 1'↔6 For requesting input ⍎⎕↔⎕ ⍎'A' ,F[I],'B' where F←'+-×÷*⌈⌊' performs a variety of calculations depending on I. ⍎'I←+/W×',F,' X' where F is a function, gives flexibility as F may be taken as one of several defined functions, for example F←'SQUARE'.
Matrix divide	⌹A	Finds the inverse of matrix A. A must have the same number or more rows than columns. If A is nonsquare, the result is a left inverse; if A is square its determinant must be nonzero. 4 5 2 ‾5.5 1.5 5 ⌹2 5 4↔ 7 ‾2 ‾6 4 4 1 ‾6 2 5
	B⌹A	Dyadic matrix divide is equivalent to the inner product (primitive operators) B⌹A↔(⌹A)+.×B Must have: ⍴⍴A=2; ⍴⍴B=1 or 2; (⍴A)[1]≥(⍴A)[2];(⍴A)[1]=(⍴B)[2]; N⌹13↔1.3 1.7 2.1 The result is the solution, X of the linear equations AX=B where A is the matrix of coefficient and B the constant terms.

III. PRIMITIVE OPERATORS

Operators represent extensions of the primitive scalar functions to arrays. They are characterized by having functions for their arguments. Comments and arrays used are the same as in Section II.

Name	Usage	Description/Example
Reduction <3>	f/A f/[S]A f⌿A	Reduction along last coordinate of A where f may be any one of the primitive scalar dyadic functions: +-×÷*⍟⌈⌊|!○<≤=≥>≠∨∧⍱⍲ Result of process is to place the function between each pair of adjacent elements of A and then perform the resulting sequence of evaluations using the right-to-left rule. +/⍳3↔1+2+3↔6

Name	Usage	Description/Example

$N \leftrightarrow 1\ 2\ 3$
         $4\ 5\ 6$
$+/[1]N \leftrightarrow 5\ 7\ 9 \leftrightarrow +\!\!/N ; +/[2]N \leftrightarrow 6\ 15 \leftrightarrow +/N$

Scan $f\backslash A$ f is any primitive scalar dyadic func-
         $f\backslash[S]A$ tion. Scan does a series of partial
         $f\backslash A$ reductions. Shape of result is the
                 same as the shape of the argument.
                 When f is + a series of partial sums
                 are calculated; $+/\iota 3 \leftrightarrow 1\ 3\ 6$ last element
                 of results equals $+/\iota 3$
                 $+\backslash N \leftrightarrow 1\ 3\ 6 \leftrightarrow +\backslash[2]N ; +\backslash N \leftrightarrow 1\ 2\ 3 \leftrightarrow +\backslash[1]N$
                     $4\ 9\ 15$ $5\ 7\ 9$
                 For a vector $(f\backslash V)[I] \leftrightarrow f/I\uparrow V$, i.e.
                 element I of the f-scan of V is the
                 f-reduction of the first I elements
                 of V. Similar definitions apply to
                 matrices.

Inner $Af.gB$ f and g are any primitive scalar dyadic
product   functions; A and B are any arrays with
                 $(^{-}1\uparrow\rho A)=1\uparrow\rho B$. The dimensions of the
                 result (except for scalars) are
                 $(^{-}1\downarrow\rho A),1\downarrow\rho B$. $A+.\times B \leftrightarrow$ algebraic
                 matrix multiplication
                 $1\ 2+.\times 1\ 2\ 3 \leftrightarrow 9\ 12\ 15$
                 $3\ 4\quad 4\ 5\ 6\quad 19\ 26\ 33$
                 For matrices A and B
                 $(Af.gB)[I;J] \leftrightarrow f/A[I;]gB[;J]$
                 $'BF' \wedge .=ABCD \leftrightarrow 0\ 1\ 0\ 0$
                         $EFGH$

Outer $A\circ.fB$ f is an primitive scalar dyadic function.
product   Arguments can be arrays of any rank.
                 Rank of result is the sum of the ranks
                 of the arguments, and the dimensions
                 of the result the catenation of those
                 of the arguments. When f is +, the
                 result is an array whose components
                 are the sum of every element of A
                 added to every element of B.
                 $1\ 2\circ.+\iota 3\ \leftrightarrow 2\ 3\ 4$
                             $3\ 4\ 5$
                 $(\iota 3)\circ.=\iota 3 \leftrightarrow 1\ 0\ 0$ (identity matrix)
                             $0\ 1\ 0$
                             $0\ 0\ 1$
                 $(\iota 3)\circ.<\iota 3 \leftrightarrow 0\ 1\ 1$
                             $0\ 0\ 1$
                             $0\ 0\ 0$

                 If A and B are vectors, then
                 $(A\circ.fB)[I;J] \leftrightarrow A[I]fB[J]$.

IV.   ADDITIONAL APL SYMBOLS

Symbol	Name	Description/Example
→	Branch Arrow	→X branch to X where X may be a line number or a label; →3; →LOOP. → Terminate entire execution sequence of functions.
←	Specification Arrow	A variable is defined or assigned a value; A←4.
⎕	Quad	A←⎕ Request input to be assigned to A. ⎕←A Display A.
⍞	Quote-Quad	A←⍞ Request character data input; assign it to A. ⍞←A Bare output. No carriage return is sent.
∇	Del	Used to change from execution mode to definition mode and vice versa.
⍫	Function Protect	Locks a function when used to change from the definition mode to the execution mode. Prohibits future function editing.
[ ]	Brackets	Used to refer to the indexed items of an array. Indices are separated by a semicolon; A[1;2]. Also used to indicate function editing instructions.
( )	Parentheses	Operation within parentheses are executed first; overrides right-to-left rule.
:	Colon	Separates label from statement. [1] START:A←1
;	Semicolon	Used to separate character and numeric data in same output statement. [6] 'THE RESULT IS';A Also to indicate local variables in a function header and to separate indices within brackets.
'	Quote	Used to specify data as literals or character data.

Symbol	Name	Description/Example
⍝	Lamp	First character in comment statement; [1] ⍝*THIS FUNCTION*
∧	Caret	Used in error situations as pointers to the approximate location of the error.
T∆F←V	Trace	Set trace vector of statement numbers for function *F*; *T∆NAME*←3 5 7 will trace lines [3], [5], and [7] of function *NAME*. (Useful in debugging.)
S∆F←V	Stop	Set stop vector of statement numbers for function *F*. *S∆NAME*←3 5 will suspend execution of *NAME* at lines [3] and [5]. (Useful in debugging.)

V.   SYSTEM VARIABLES

Alternative procedures are available for displaying and modifying parameters and information about the state of the current workspace of the entire APL system. The primary notation used in this section is that of APLSV (APL Shared Variables) and VS APL.

Alternative facilities for achieving the same purpose are also shown. These are of three types, i-beam functions (⍳, ⊥ backspace ⊤), system commands (indicated by <1>), or executable functions contained in the workspace 1 *WSFNS* on most systems (indicated by <2>).

The first set of system variables represent parameters of the active workspace that can be displayed and modified by the user.

Variable	Description of Use	Alternative Facility
⎕*CT*	Comparison Tolerance: Used by <, ≤, =, ≥, >, ≠, ⌈ and ⌊ to adjust for the inaccuracy in computer representation of numbers. Thus values differing by less than the (relative) tolerance contained in ⎕*CT* are considered equal.	*SETFUZZ*<2>

Variable	Description of Use	Alternative Facility
$\Box IO$	Index Origin: Contains the current value of the Index Origin, 0 or 1. The value of $\Box IO$ affects both forms of ι and ?, all forms of indexing and dyadic transpose.	ORIGIN<1 2>
$\Box LX$	Latent Expression: When $\Box LX$ is assigned a character vector representing an executable APL expression, this expression will be executed whenever a work-space is loaded into the active workspace. This is useful for displaying messages to anyone using the workspace $\Box LX\leftarrow'''THE\ MESSAGE\ WILL\ BE\ DISPLAYED'''$ or causing a function to begin execution as soon as the workspace is loaded $\Box LX\leftarrow'INSTRUCTIONS'$ The function $INSTRUCTIONS$ will execute when the work-space is loaded.	None
$\Box PP$	Printing Precision: The value of $\Box PP$ gives the maximum number of significant fig-ures displayed in numerical output.	DIGITS<1 2>
$\Box PW$	Printing Width: Gives the maximum width of a printed line.	WIDTH<1 2>
$\Box RL$	Random Link: The current value of the random link. Used by ?.	SETLINK<2>

The value of the following system variables cannot be modified by the users.

Variable	Description of Use	Alternative Facility
$\Box AI$	Account Information: A four-element integer vector giving the user account number followed by the accumulated CPU connect and keying time for the current session. All times are in milli-seconds.	ɪ29 21 24 19 (Times from ɪ functions are in sixtieths of a second.)

Variable	Description of Use	Alternative Facility
□AV	Atomic Vector: A 256-element character vector containing the full set of characters recognized by the APL system. Some useful characters are: □AV[157]←→Carriage Return □AV[158]←→Idle □AV[159]←→Backspace □AV[160]←→Linefeed	Frequently scalar variables are provided containing characters that are not obtainable from the keyboard, or the analogue of □AV may be available.
□LC	Line Counter: An integer vector giving the line numbers of all functions in execution or suspended. The numbers appear in the same order as in)SI. Thus □LC[1] gives the number of the line currently being executed. If this function was used by another function, □LC[2] gives the line in which it is being used. If execution is suspended →□LC causes execution to resume at the point of suspension.	I27 The result of I26 is (I27)[1].
□TS	Time Stamp: A seven-element vector giving the time as year, month, day, hour, minute, second, milli-second.	I25 - A six digit integer, each pair of digits giving the month, day, and year. I20 - Elapsed time in sixtieths of a second since mid-night.
□TT	Terminal Type: An integer giving the type of terminal being used; 0 for 1050 terminals, 1 for Selectric, 2 for BCD, 5 for ASCII. (Not available in VS APL.)	I28
□UL	User Load: Number of users currently signed on to the system. (Not available in VS APL.)	I23
□WA	Working Area: The amount of unused storage space available in the active workspace. The result is in bytes.	I22

Bibliography

The texts and articles listed below provide additional readings on APL computer programming and computer applications. The bibliography serves as a starting point and is by no means complete. Texts and articles also pertaining to the case study chapters are identified.

I. TEXTS AND ARTICLES ON APL AND ITS APPLICATIONS

APL/360-OS and APL/360-DOS User's Manual, IBM Program Product GH 20-0906-1, 1973.

APL Congress 73, P. Gjerlov, H. J. Helms, and J. Nielsen, eds., American Elsevier Publishing Co., 1973.

APL Language, IBM Program Product GC-26-3847-1, 1976.

APL Quote-Quad, published quarterly.

Berry, P. C., *APL/1130 Primer*, IBM Program Product GC 20-20-1967, 1968.

   APL/360 Primer, IBM Program Product GH 20-0689-2, 1971.

Bork, A. M., APL as a Language for Interactive Computer Graphics, *Proceedings of the Sixth International APL Users' Conference*, Anaheim, May 1974, pp. 50-57, (Chapter 13).

Buckley, J. S., M. R. Nagaraj, D. L. Sharp, and J. W. Schenck, *Management Problem-Solving with APL*, Wiley/Melville, 1974.

Carlson, J. G. H., and R. Gilman, Management Information/Decision Systems Using APL, *Proceedings of the Sixth International APL Users' Conference*, Anaheim, May 1974, pp. 65-78.

Coffey, C. E., J. Eskinazi, F. H. Fraser, and D. J. Macero, A Program for Filing and Searching Literature References, *APL Quote-Quad*, Jan. 1973, pp. 28-32, (Chapters 9, 10).

Cronklin, R. F., Instant CAI, *Proceedings of the Sixth International APL Users' Conference*, Anaheim, May 1974, pp. 100-105, (Chapter 15).

Falkoff, A. D., and K. E. Iverson, *APL/360 User's Manual*,
    IBM Program Product GH-20-0683, 1973.

Gilman, L., and A. J. Rose, *APL-An Interactive Approach*, 2nd
    ed., Wiley, 1974.

Grey, L. D., *A Course in APL with Applications*, 2nd ed.,
    Addison-Wesley, 1976.

Greenberg, S. G., and C. I. Johnson, An Interactive APL
    Graphics System, *Proceedings of the Fourth International
    APL Users' Conference*, Atlanta, June 1972, pp. 37-44,
    (Chapter 13).

Halmstadt, D. G., APL/SOLID-A Life Insurance Management Game,
    APL Congress 73, North-Holland, 1973, pp. 179-184,
    (Chapter 12).

IBM 5100 APL Reference Manual, IBM Program Product SA 21-9213,
    1975.

Iversen, K. E., *A Programming Language*, Wiley, 1962.

    The Story of APL, *Computing Report in Science and
    Engineering*, Vol. 6, No. 3, 1970, pp. 14-18.

    Use of APL in Statistics, *Statistical Computations*,
    R. C. Milton and J. A. Nelder, eds., Academic Press, 1969,
    pp. 285-292.

Katzan, H., *APL Programming and Computer Techniques*, Van
    Nostrand-Reinhold, 1970.

Niehoff, W. H. and A. L. Jones, An APL Approach to Interactive
    Terminal Graphics, *Proceedings of the Fourth International
    APL Users' Conference*, Atlanta, June 1972, (Chapter 13).

Orgass, R. J., APL in the Teaching of Computational Complexity
    APL Congress 73, North-Holland, 1973, pp. 339-343.

Pakin, S., *APL/360 Reference Manual*, 2nd ed., Science Research
    Associates, 1971.

Pakin, S. and Staff of Computer Innovations, *APL: A Short
    Course*, Prentice-Hall, 1973.

Peele, H. A., Teaching Children Thinking via APL, *Proceedings
    of the Fifth International APL Users' Conference*, Toronto,
    Canada, May 1973, pp. 0.1-0.2, (Chapter 15).

    A Generalized Learning Game, *Proceedings of the Sixth
    International APL Users' Conference*, Anaheim, May 1974,
    pp. 424-428.

Petersen, T. I., The Ecology Decision Game: Introduction,
    Report No. G320-2073, IBM Cambridge Scientific Center,
    Cambridge, Mass., Sept. 1971.

Polivka, R. and S. Pakin, *APL: The Language and Its Usage*, Prentice-Hall, 1975.

Prager, W., *An Introduction to APL*, Allyn and Bacon, 1970.

Proceedings of the International APL Users' Conference, annually since 1969.

Rault, J. C., An APL Bibliography, *APL Quote-Quad*, Vol. 6, No. 2, pp. 15-85, 1975.

Rose, A. J., *APL for Users of Basic*, Scientific Timesharing Corp., Washington, D. C., 1969.

Saal, H. J. and Z. Weiss, Some Properties of APL Programs, *Proceedings of the Seventh International APL Users' Conference*, Pisa, June 1975, pp. 292-297.

Smillie, K. W., *APL 360 with Statistical Examples*, Addison-Wesley Publishing Company, 1974.

Tava, P. A., The Financial Planning System-The Application of APL to Financial Modeling, *Proceedings of the Sixth International APL Users' Conference*, Anaheim, May 1974, pp. 487-498, (Chapter 12).

Taylor, A., APL-A Complex or Simple Language?, *Computerworld*, April 1, 1970.

Thanhouser, N., and L. Koeningsberg, A Graphics System for APL Users-APL/Graph-II, *Proceedings of the Sixth International APL Users' Conference*, Anaheim, May 1974, pp. 529-543, (Chapter 13).

Von Maydell, K. M. and K. W. Smillie, Two Methods of Using APL in the Teaching of Probability and Statistics, *Proceedings of the Seventh International APL Users' Conference*, Pisa, June 1975, pp. 244-248.

II. TEXTS AND ARTICLES ON COMPUTER PROGRAMMING AND APPLICATIONS

Andree, R. V., J. P. Andree, and D. D. Andree, *Computer Programming: Techniques, Analysis, and Mathematics*, Prentice-Hall, 1973, (Chapter 11).

Atkinson, R. C. and H. A. Wilson, *Computer-Assisted Instruction-- A Book of Readings*, Academic Press, 1969, (Chapter 15).

Awad, E. M., *Automatic Data Processing*, Prentice-Hall, 1970, (Chapter 14).

Dorf, R. C., *Introduction to Computers and Computer Science*, Boyd and Fraser, 1972.

Forkner, I. and R. McLeod, *Computerized Business Systems*, Wiley, 1973, (Chapter 14).

Forrester, J. W., World Dynamics, Wright-Allen Press, 1973, (Chapter 11).

Forsythe, A. I., T. A. Keenan, F. I. Org nick, and W. Stenberg, *Computer Science-A First Course*, Wiley, 1975 (Chapters 9, 10, 14).

Gear, C. W., *Introduction to Computer Science*, Science Research Associates, 1973, (Chapters 9, 10, 11).

Huntington II Project, Simulations, Digital Equipment Corporation, Maynard, Mass., (Chapter 12).

Knudth, D., *The Art of Computer Programming, Vol. 3, Sorting and Searching*, Addison-Wesley, 1973, (Chapters 9, 10).

Kochenburger, R. J. and C. J. Turcio, *Computers in Modern Society*, Hamilton, 1974, (Chapters 9, 11).

Margolin, J. B. and M. R. Misch, *Computers in the Classroom*, Spartan Books, 1970, (Chapter 15).

Martin, F. F., *Computer Modeling and Simulation*, Wiley, 1968, (Chapters 11, 12).

Ockene, A., Computer Simulation, *Computer Decisions*, January 1970, (Chapter 12).

Proceedings of the Conference of Computers in the Undergraduate Curricula, Annually since 1970, (Chapter 15).

Reichardt, J., *The Computer in Art*, Von Nostrand-Reinhold, 1971, (Chapter 13).

Rothman, S. and C. Mosmann, *Computers and Society*, Science Research Associates, 1972.

Sorting on Computers, Communications of the Association For Computing Machinery, Vol. 6, No. 5, 1963.

Walker, T. M., *Introduction to Computer Science*, Allyn and Bacon, 1972, (Chapters 9, 10, 11, 13, 14).

Solutions to Odd-Numbered Exercises

CHAPTER 2 -- SPECIFYING INFORMATION
EXERCISES -- PAGES 23 TO 26

EXERCISE 9
```
      CHARAC←' ¨¯<≤=≥>≠∨∧+−×÷◊$?ωερ~↑↓ιο*
←→─α⌈⌊_∇∆○''⎕[(])[}⊂⊃∩∪⊥⊤|,;.:/\∨∧⌸⊕Φ⊖⍕
∇⎕↓⍋Ω!α∇I↓≠'
      CHARAC
¨¯<≤=≥>≠∨∧+−×‡◊$?ωερ~↑↓ιο*←→─α⌈⌊_∇∆○''⎕[
   (])[}⊂⊃∩∪⊥⊤|,;.:/\∨∧⌸⊕Φ⊖⍕∇⎕↓⍋Ω!α∇I
   ↓≠
```
SOME OF THESE CHARACTERS MAY NOT BE
PRESENT ON YOUR SYSTEM. NOTE THE ENTRY
AND DISPLAY OF THE APOSTROPHE.

EXERCISE 11
```
      GRADES← 80 90 95 85
      GRADES
80 90 95 85
      OLDGRADES←GRADES
      GRADES← 85 80 95 100 90
      OLDGRADES
80 90 95 85
      GRADES
85 80 95 100 90
```


****

CHAPTER 3 -- ARITHMETIC FUNCTIONS
EXERCISES -- PAGES 40 TO 43

EXERCISE 5
```
      N← 1 2 3 4 5 6 7 8 9 10
      N*2
1 4 9 16 25 36 49 64 81 100
      N*3
1 8 27 64 125 216 343 512 729 1000
```

```
      N*0.5
1 1.414213562 1.732050808 2
   2.236067977 2.449489743
   2.645751311 2.828427125 3
   3.16227766
      M←÷3
      N*M
1 1.25992105 1.44224957 1.587401052
   1.709975947 1.817120593
   1.912931183 2 2.080083823
   2.15443469
```
NOTE THE ADVANTAGE OF STORING THE
INTEGERS IN THE VECTOR N.

EXERCISE 7
ON THE SYSTEM USED TO RUN THESE
EXERCISES 45*45 GIVES AN ALLOWABLE
RESULT WHILE 46*46 GIVES A DOMAIN ERROR.

EXERCISE 9
```
      X←12311.237
      N← 1000 10 0.1 0.01
      X←X÷N
      X←⌊X
      X×N
12000 12310 12311.2 12311.23
```

EXERCISE 11
```
      A← 15 2.5 3.99 1.99
      B← 16 2.75 3.89 1.19
      C← 14.89 2.25 3.99 1.19
      MAX←A⌈B
      MAX←MAX⌈C
      MIN←A⌊B
      MIN←MIN⌊C
      MAX−MIN
1.11 0.5 0.1 0.8
```

EXERCISE 13
```
      72÷10
7.2
      1000×(1+0.1)* 7 8
1948.7171 2143.58881
```
THE RULE IS INDEPENDENT OF THE INITIAL
AMOUNT.

CHAPTER 3 -- ARITHMETIC FUNCTIONS
EXERCISES -- PAGES 53 TO 57

EXERCISE 3
A) ⌊V↔APPLIES THE FLOOR FUNCTION TO
V GIVING FOR EACH ELEMENT IN V THE
LARGEST INTEGER NOT GREATER THAN V.
⌊/V↔THE MIN-REDUCTION OF V GIVING THE
SMALLEST ELEMENT IN V.
B) THE EXPRESSION ×V GIVES A VECTOR
CONTAINING THE SIGN OF EACH ELEMENT IN
V.
THE EXPRESSION ×/V GIVES THE
TIMES-REDUCTION, THE PRODUCT OF ALL
THE ELEMENTS IN V.
C) THE EXPRESSION V××V GIVES THE
ABSOLUTE VALUE OF THE ELEMENTS IN V.

EXERCISE 5
EXAMPLES C,I,AND J ARE ALWAYS
EQUIVALENT;PAIR B ARE EQUIVALENT ONLY
IF ALL ELEMENTS IN V ARE POSITIVE;PAIR
F ARE EQUIVALENT ONLY IF ALL ELEMENTS
IN V ARE NONZERO AND OF THE SAME
SIGN;PAIR G ARE EQUIVALENT AS LONG AS
0 DOES NOT APPEAR IN V .

EXERCISE 7
A)   N←? 10 10 10 10 10 10
      N
5 9 8 7 6 3
      MIN←⌊/N
      MIN
3
      MAX←⌈/N
      MAX
9
      MAX-MIN
6
B)   N← 1 2 3 4 5 6 7 8 9 10 11 12
      N←2×N
      +/N
156

EXERCISE 9
      N← 10 100 1000
      (1+÷N)*N
2.59374246 2.704813829 2.716923932
      *1
2.718281828
THE EXPRESSION (1+(1÷N))*N APPROACHES
THE VALUE OF 'E', THE BASE OF THE
NATURAL LOGARITHMS↔*1.

EXERCISE 11
      MIN← 1.5 2 3 3.5 5 7.5
      COST←70+20×0⌈¯3+⌈MIN
      COST
70 70 70 90 110 170

EXERCISE 13
      HI← 47 50 30 28 15
      LO← 12 18 16 5 ¯2
      DD←0⌈65-0.5×HI+LO
      DD
35.5 31 42 48.5 58.5

EXERCISE 15
      SHARES← 75 200 50 150 180
      COST← 125 117.5 280 98.5 212
      MKT← 121 137 250 98.5 216
      ⎕←COSTVALUE←SHARES×COST
9375 23500 14000 14775 38160
      ⎕←MKTVALUE←SHARES×MKT
9075 27400 12500 14775 38880
      ⎕←LOWERVALUE←SHARES×COST⌊MKT
9075 23500 12500 14775 38160
      ⎕←LOSS←COSTVALUE-LOWERVALUE
300 0 1500 0 0

EXERCISE 17
      A←30000
      N←20×12
      I← 7.5 8 8.5 ÷12
      T←(1+I)*N
      ⎕←P←A×I×T÷T-1
18750 20000 21250
      ⎕←P←A×I×((1+I)*N)÷¯1+(1+I)*N
18750 20000 21250
TWO ALTERNATIVE EXPRESSIONS ARE GIVEN
THE FIRST USING THE TEMPORARY VARIABLE
T TO STORE(1+I)*N, THE SECOND DOING
THE CALCULATION IN ONE STEP.

****

CHAPTER 4 -- COMPUTER PROGRAMS
EXERCISES -- PAGES 81 TO 85

EXERCISE 3
THE EXPRESSION X←⎕ CAUSES THE KEYBOARD
TO BE RELEASED FOR QUAD INPUT. ANY
TYPED EXPRESSION IS EVALUATED AND
ASSIGNED TO X AS THOUGH YOU HAD TYPED
X←FOLLOWED BY THE EXPRESSION.

EXERCISE 5
A,B,D,F,I AND J ARE VALID NAMES.

EXERCISE 7

```
    ∇ RECTANGLE
[1]    'ENTER THE BASE'
[2]    B←□
[3]    'ENTER THE HEIGHT'
[4]    H←□
[5]    'A RECTANGLE WITH BASE ';B;' AND H
       EIGHT ';H
[6]    'HAS AN AREA OF ';B×H;' AND A PERI
       METER OF ';2×B+H
    ∇
```

EXERCISE 9

```
LINES TO BE ADDED TO MORTGAGE ARE
[18]    TOTAL←TIME×PAY
[19]    'THE TOTAL OF ALL PAYMENTS IS
';TOTAL.
```

EXERCISE 11

```
    ∇ EMPLOYEE
[1]    'ENTER NAME'
[2]    NAME←□
[3]    'ENTER HOURS WORKED'
[4]    HOURS←□
[5]    'ENTER HOURLY PAY RATE'
[6]    RATE←□
[7]    ' '
[8]    NAME
[9]    ' '
[10]   REGULAR←RATE×35⌊HOURS
[11]   'REGULAR EARNINGS     ';REGULAR
[12]   OVERTIME←1.5×RATE×0⌈HOURS-35
[13]   'OVERTIME EARNINGS    ';OVERTIME
[14]   GROSS←REGULAR+OVERTIME
[15]   'GROSS EARNINGS       ';GROSS
[16]   NET←0.8×GROSS
[17]   'NET EARNINGS         ';NET
    ∇
```

EXERCISE 15

```
A) THE RESULT IS
10 15  17.
B) [10]'THE RESULT IS ';R
[11]
    ∇      (DELETE LINE[11])
[12] ∇.
C) [10.1]' '∇.
D) [11]   ' ';R∇.
```

EXERCISE 17

```
A) [16] IS DISPLAYED
B) [7□]
C) [5.1]N←□
D) [2]M←⌊M
E) [□10]∇
F) 'THE END'∇.
```

EXERCISE 19

```
A) TRYING TO ASSIGN A VALUE TO A
FUNCTION GIVES A SYNTAX ERROR.
B TRYING TO DEFINE A PROGRAM WITH THE
SAME NAME AS A VARIABLE GIVES A
DEFINITION ERROR.
```

****

CHAPTER 4 -- COMPUTER PROGRAMS
EXERCISES -- PAGES 116 TO 122

EXERCISE 3

```
A)  ARGUMENT VARIABLES ARE P AND R
B)  LOCAL VARIABLES ARE Z,P,R, AND S
C)  VALID EXECUTIONS ARE I., III., AND
IV.
D.)  THE FIRST VALID EXECUTION, 3 Q 2,
RETURNS 8.
E)  Z AND P GIVE VALUE ERRORS, R, S,
AND T GIVE 5, U GIVES 64.
```

EXERCISE 5

```
THE VARIABLE Y IS GLOBAL TO BOTH A1
AND A2 . WHEN A1 IS CALLED FROM B1 THE
VALUE USED FOR Y IS THE ARGUMENT TO B1
SINCE THIS 'SHADOWS' THE GLOBAL VALUE
OF Y . WHEN A2 IS CALLED FROM B2,THE
GLOBAL VALUE OF Y IS USED SINCE THE
ARGUMENT TO B2 IS CALLED W AND DOES
NOT SHADOW Y . A COMMON WAY OF
OVERCOMING SUCH DIFFICULTIES IS TO
ESTABLISH NAMING CONVENTIONS,FOR
EXAMPLE UNDERLINING THE FIRST LETTER
OF ALL GLOBAL VARIABLES .
```

EXERCISE 7

```
    ∇ Z←CONSTANT
[1]    Z←2*0.5
    ∇
```

EXERCISE 11

```
    ∇ A RTΔ B;C;P
[1]    'HYPOTENUSE= ';C←((A*2)+B*2)*0.5
[2]    'PERIMETER= ';P←A+B+C
[3]    'AREA= ';0.5×A×B
    ∇
```

****

CHAPTER 5 -- LOGICAL DATA
EXERCISES -- PAGES 137 TO 141

EXERCISE 5
≠IS EQUIVALENT TO THE 'EXCLUSIVE OR'
GIVING 1 ONLY IF ONE OF ITS ARGUMENTS
ARE 1 AND NOT THE OTHER .=IS THE
NEGATION OF≠.
× AND ⌊ ARE EQUIVALENT TO ∧ FOR
LOGICAL DATA
⌈ IS EQUIVALENT TO ∨ FOR LOGICAL DATA
<, ≤,≥, AND > ARE DISTINCT FROM THE
OTHER LOGICAL FUNCTIONS.

EXERCISE 7
∧/GRADE≥60.

EXERCISE 11
```
     ∇ C LOCATE TEXT
[1]    TEXT
[2]    (C=TEXT)\'↑'
     ∇
```

EXERCISE 13
```
     ∇ MONEY X
[1]  ⍝DOL = AMOUNT IN DOLLARS, L1 IS 1 I
       F THIS IS NOT 0
[2]    DOL←⌊X
[3]    L1←0≠DOL
[4]  ⍝CNTS = AMOUNT OF CENTS, L2 IS 1 IF
        THIS IS NOT 0
[5]    CNTS←100×1|X
[6]    L2←0≠CNTS
[7]    L1/DOL;L1/' DOLLARS ';(L1∧L2)/'AND
       ';L2/CNTS;L2/' CENTS'
     ∇
```

EXERCISE 15
```
       BILL← 123.75 89 32.12 54 23.14
       TIME← 4 3 1 2 2
       NUMBER← 10023 15012 45198 67342
73456
       (TIME>2)/BILL
123.75 89
       +/(TIME≥2)/BILL
289.89
       (TIME>3)/NUMBER
10023
```

****

CHAPTER 6 -- ADDITIONAL APL
             FUNCTIONS
EXERCISES -- PAGES 174 TO 179

EXERCISE 13
```
     ∇ HELLO
[1]    'HI! WHAT''S YOUR NAME?'
[2]    NAME←⎕
[3]    'HELLO ',(NAME⍳' ')↑NAME
[4]    'MY NAME IS APL,'
[5]    'BUT YOU CAN CALL ME APE!'
     ∇
```

EXERCISE 15
```
     ∇ Z←ASORT X;A;L;Y
[1]    A←'ABCDEFGHIJKLMNOPQRSTUVWXYZ'
[2]  ⍝EXTRACT NONALPHABETIC CHARACTERS F
       ROM X AND STORE IN Y
[3]    L←X∊A
[4]    Y←(~L)/X
[5]    X←L/X
[6]  ⍝FIND LOCATION IN ALPHABET OF LETTE
       RS IN X
[7]    X←A⍳X
[8]  ⍝SORT THE INDICES
[9]    X←X[⍋X]
[10] ⍝CONVERT TO A CHARACTER VECTOR
[11]   Z←A[X]
[12] ⍝ADD BACK NONALPHABETIC CHARACTERS
[13]   Z←Z,Y
     ∇
```

A MORE DIRECT APPROACH TO THE SOLUTION
IS GIVEN BY THE EXPRESSION
    Z←X[⍋A⍳X].

EXERCISE 17
```
A)    C←'STUDY THE VOWELS IN C'
      VOWELS←'AEIOU'
      +/C∊VOWELS
5
B)    +/VOWELS∊C
4
C)    (VOWELS∊C)/VOWELS
EIOU
D) LOCATE AL VOWELS
      LOC←(C∊VOWELS)/⍳⍴C
REPLACE BY ELEMENTS SELECTED FROM AEIOU
      C[LOC]←'AEIOU'[VOWELS⍳C[LOC]]
      C
STUDY THE VOWELS IN C
```

EXERCISE 19
```
      ∇ ANALYSIS PRICE;SALES;REVENUE;COSTS
      ;PROFIT
[1]   SALES←10000+400×(1⍵PRICE)÷0.01
[2]   REVENUE←SALES×PRICE
[3]   COSTS←SALES×0.6
[4]   PROFIT←REVENUE⍵COSTS
[5]   'PRICE ($)    ', 10 2 ⍒PRICE
[6]   'SALES(UNITS) ', 10 0 ⍒SALES
[7]   'REVENUE ($)  ', 10 2 ⍒REVENUE
[8]   'COSTS ($)    ', 10 2 ⍒COSTS
[9]   'PROFIT ($)   ', 10 2 ⍒PROFIT
    ∇
```

```
********************************************
```

```
     CHAPTER 7 -- TRANSFER STATEMENTS
                   AND BRANCHING
     EXERCISES -- PAGES 209 TO 215
```

EXERCISE 1
```
A)  →(EPSILON>|Δ)/0
B)  →(X<0)/NEG
C)  →(STOP=N←⎕)/0
D)  →(∧/'HELP'=4↑Y←⍞)/HLP
E)  →(N>ρY)/LP1
F)  →(MAX≥I←I+INC)/LOOP
G)  →(YES1,NO1,IN1)['YN'⍳1↑⍞]
H)  X←⍞
    →((4=ρ,X)∧∧/'STOP'=4↑X)/0∇.
```

EXERCISE 5
```
A)  ∇ PROGRAM;I;V;X
[1]   ⍝INITIALIZATION
[2]   I←0
[3]   V←⍳0
[4]   ⍝PROCESS
[5]   LP:'INPUT A VALUE'
[6]   X←⎕
[7]   V←V,X
[8]   ⍝INCREMENT
[9]   I←I+1
[10]  ⍝TEST
[11]  →(I<10)/LP
[12]  'X VALUES ';V
[13]  'THEIR SUM ';+/V
    ∇
```

```
B)  ∇ NEWPROGRAM;I;V;X
[1]   ⍝INITIALIZATION
[2]   I←1
[3]   V←⍳0
[4]   ⍝PROCESS
[5]   LP:'INPUT A VALUE'
```

```
[6]   X←⎕
[7]   V←V,X
[8]   ⍝TEST
[9]   →(I≥10)/OUT
[10]  ⍝INCREMENT
[11]  I←I+1
[12]  →LP
[13]  OUT:'X VALUES ';V
[14]  'THEIR SUM ';+/V
    ∇
```

ALSO NOTE THE DIFFERENT INITIALIZATION
USED IN NEWPROGRAM .

EXERCISE 7
CONVERT LINE[7] TO
```
[7]   →(M≥YEAR)/LOOP.
```

EXERCISE 9
```
B)  ∇ PROD MAX;COUNT;P
[1]   P←1
[2]   COUNT←1
[3]   LOOP:P←P×COUNT
[4]   COUNT←COUNT+1
[5]   →(MAX≥COUNT)/LOOP
[6]   'THE PRODUCT OF THE INTEGERS FROM
      1 TO ';MAX;' IS ';P
[7]   'THE GEOMETRIC MEAN IS ';P*÷MAX
    ∇
```

```
C)  ∇ APLPROD MAX;P
[1]   'THE PRODUCT OF THE INTEGERS FROM
      1 TO ';MAX;' IS ';P←×/⍳MAX
[2]   'THE GEOMETRIC MEAN IS ';P*÷MAX
    ∇
```

EXERCISE 11
```
      ∇ CHECKGRADES;GRADES;I
[1]   'ENTER A VECTOR OF GRADES'
[2]   GRADES←⎕
[3]   I←0
[4]   LP:→((ρGRADES)<I←I+1)ρ0
[5]   →(GRADES[I]<60)/FAIL
[6]   'PASSING ';GRADES[I]
[7]   →LP
[8]   FAIL:'FAILING ';GRADES[I]
[9]   →LP
    ∇
```

EXERCISE 13
```
      ∇ SQUAREROOTTABLE N
[1]   I←1
[2]   'VALUE  SQUARE ROOT'
[3]   LP: 5 0 13 5 ⍒I,I*0.5
[4]   →(N≥I←I+1)/LP
    ∇
```

EXERCISE 15
THE PROGRAM IN1 USES A COUNTER I WHICH
IS NOT LOCALIZED TO THAT PROGRAM .
WHEN IN1 IS CALLED BY OUT1 THE CHANGES
MADE TO THE COUNTER BY IN1 ARE CARRIED
TO THE COUNTER I USED IN OUT1,ALTERING
THE LOOP . THE COUNTER I IN IN2 IS
LOCALIZED AND DOES NOT AFFECT THE LOOP
IN OUT2 .

EXERCISE 17
```
     ∇ SALARYPLANS;I;WAGE1;WAGE2;CUM1;CUM
2;COMPARE
[1]   ⍝INITIALIZE COUNTER, WAGES, CUMULAT
      IVE
[2]   ⍝WAGES AND A COMPARISON VECTOR
[3]    I←1
[4]    WAGE1←WAGE2←500
[5]    CUM1←CUM2←0
[6]    COMPARE←⍳0
[7]  LP:CUM1←CUM1+WAGE1
[8]    CUM2←CUM2+WAGE2
[9]   ⍝ELEMENTS IN COMPARE ARE 1 IF THE C
      UMULATIVE
[10]  ⍝WAGES OF PLAN TWO ARE LESS THAN TH
      OSE OF PLAN 1
[11]   COMPARE←COMPARE,CUM2<CUM1
[12]   →(96≤I)/OUT
[13]  ⍝WAGE1 IS INCREASED BY 5 EVERY MONT
      H
[14]   WAGE1←WAGE1+5
[15]  ⍝WAGE2 IS INCREASED BY 80 EVERY YEA
      R
[16]   WAGE2←WAGE2+80×0=12|I
[17]   I←I+1
[18]   →LP
[19] OUT:'CUMULATIVE WAGES FOR PLAN 1 ='
      ;CUM1
[20]   'CUMULATIVE WAGES FOR PLAN 2 =';CU
      M2
[21]   'PLAN 1 EXCEEDS PLAN 2 IN MONTHS '
      ;COMPARE/⍳⍴COMPARE
[22]   'PLAN 2 EQUALS OR EXCEEDS PLAN 1 I
      N MONTHS ';(~COMPARE)/⍳⍴COMPARE
     ∇
```

EXERCISE 19
```
     ∇ CRAPS
[1]    ROLL←+/?2⍴6
[2]    'FIRST ROLL IS ';ROLL
[3]    →(ROLL∊ 7 11)/WIN
[4]    →(ROLL∊ 2 3 12)/LOSE
[5]    'THAT''S YOUR POINT'
[6]    POINT←ROLL
[7]  LP:ROLL←+/?2⍴6
[8]    'YOU ROLL ';ROLL
[9]    →(ROLL=POINT)/WIN
```

```
[10]   →(ROLL=7)/LOSE
[11]   →LP
[12] WIN:'YOU WIN'
[13]   →0
[14] LOSE:'YOU LOSE'
     ∇
```

EXERCISE 21
```
A)  ∇ Z←E SOLVE X
[1]   LP:Z←F X
[2]    →(E≥|(Z-X)÷Z)⍴0
[3]    X←Z
[4]    →LP
     ∇
```

```
B)  ∇ Z←F X
[1]   ⍝FUNCTION TO SOLVE 21.B
[2]    Z←10+(¯10÷X)-5÷X×X
     ∇
```

```
     1E¯12 SOLVE 3
8.798914063
```

****

CHAPTER 8 -- MATRICES
EXERCISES -- PAGES 249 TO 256

EXERCISE 5
```
     ∇ DATADESCRIBE X
[1]   ⍝DETERMINE THE RANK OF THE DATA
[2]    RANK←⍴⍴X
[3]   ⍝CONVERT TO A CHARACTER EXPRESSION
[4]    RANK←(3 6 ⍴'SCALARVECTORMATRIX')[R
      ANK+1;]
[5]   ⍝CALCULATED ABOVE RANK IS A 1 ROW M
      ATRIX.
[6]   ⍝  TURN IT INTO A VECTOR
[7]    RANK←,RANK
[8]   ⍝DETERMINE THE DATA TYPE
[9]    TYPE←' '=0\0/,X
[10]   TYPE←(TYPE/'CHARACTER'),(~TYPE)/'N
      UMERICAL'
[11]  ⍝DISPLAY RESULT
[12]   TYPE,' ',RANK
     ∇
```

EXERCISE 7
```
A)    ⎕←G← 3 5 ⍴ 17 18 20 18 27 16 19
20 19 18 21 20 19 19 17
 17 18 20 18 27
 16 19 20 19 18
 21 20 19 19 17
```

```
        (+/,G)÷×/ρG
19.2
B)   COMPUTE ROW AVERAGE
        ROWAV←(+/G)÷(ρG)[2]
DETERMINE ROW WITH LARGEST AVERAGE
        (ROWAV=⌈/ROWAV)/⍳ρROWAV
1
C)      ⎕←YOUNG←⌊/,G
16
        ⎕←OLD←⌈/,G
27
D)   THE FIRST PROCEDURE USES A LOGICAL
MATRIX.
        ⎕←YOUNG←G=YOUNG
 0 0 0 0 0
 1 0 0 0 0
 0 0 0 0 0

COMPUTE ROW POSITION
        ⎕←ROW←(∨/YOUNG)/⍳(ρYOUNG)[1]
2
SIMILARLY COMPUTE THE COLUMN POSITION
        ⎕←COL←(∨⌿YOUNG)/⍳(ρYOUNG)[2]
1

A SECOND USES THE POSITION IN THE
RAVELED MATRIX
        OLD←(,G)⍳OLD
        ⎕←ROW←⌈OLD÷(ρG)[2]
1
        ⎕←COL←1+(ρG)[2]|OLD-1
5


EXERCISE 9
A)      ⎕←SALES← 3 4 ρ 43775 46472 30064
55135 37055 27371 52899 32388 66035
43829 34100 52120
 43775 46472 30064 55135
 37055 27371 52899 32388
 66035 43829 34100 52120

        6 1 ▼PERCENT←100×SALES÷+/,SALES
    8.4    8.9    5.8   10.6
    7.1    5.3   10.1    6.2
   12.7    8.4    6.5   10.0

        +/,PERCENT
100
B)   COMPUTE MONTHLY SALES FOR EACH EMPLO
     YEE
        ⎕←MTHSALES←+/SALES
175446 149713 196084
        6 1 ▼PERCENT←100×SALES÷⍉(⌽ρSALES)ρ
MTHSALES
   25.0   26.5   17.1   31.4
   24.8   18.3   35.3   21.6
   33.7   22.4   17.4   26.6
```

```
        +/PERCENT
100 100 100
C)   COMPUTE TOTAL WEEKLY SALES
        ⎕←WKSALES←+⌿SALES
146865 117672 117063 139643
        6 1 ▼PERCENT←100×SALES÷(ρSALES)ρWK
SALES
   29.8   39.5   25.7   39.5
   25.2   23.3   45.2   23.2
   45.0   37.2   29.1   37.3

        +⌿PERCENT
100 100 100 100


EXERCISE 11
     ∇ CHESS;P1;P2;OFFSETS;ROOK;BISHOP
[1]    'INPUT ROW, COLUMN OF PIECE 1'
[2]    P1←⎕
[3]    'INPUT ROW, COLUMN OF PIECE 2'
[4]    P2←⎕
[5]    OFFSETS←|P1-P2
[6]    ⍝ROOKS CAN CAPTURE IF EITHER OFFSET
         EQUALS 0
[7]    ROOK←∨/OFFSETS=0
[8]    ⍝BISHOPS CAN CAPTURE IF THE OFFSETS
        ARE EQUAL
[9]    BISHOP←=/OFFSETS
[10]   'ROOKS CAN';(~ROOK)/'NOT';' CAPTUR
       E EACH OTHER.'
[11]   'BISHOPS CAN';(~BISHOP)/'NOT';' CA
       PTURE EACH OTHER.'
     ∇


EXERCISE 13
     ∇ Z←MAT MATINDEX A
[1]    A←(,MAT)⍳A
[2]    ⍝LOCATE THE ROW POSITIONS
[3]    Z←((ρA),1)ρ⌈A÷(ρMAT)[2]
[4]    ⍝LOCATE THE COLUMN POSITIONS
[5]    Z←Z,1+(ρMAT)[2]|A-1
     ∇

        ⎕←MAT← 3 4 ρ12?12
 9  7 12  3
 1  4  5  8
 6 10 11  2


        MAT MATINDEX 3 10
 1 4
 3 2


THE ABOVE FUNCTION SOLVES BOTH PARTS
A) AND B).
```

<u>EXERCISE</u> 15
A)   AND B)
         □←MAT← 1 ¯3 + 5 7 ρ0,ι31
   7 8 9 10
  14 15 16 17
  21 22 23 24
  28 29 30 31

         +/ 0 1 2 3 ⌽MAT
76 76 76 76
         +/,MAT[1 4 ; 1 4]
76
C)   , D) AND E)
CHOOSE A 3 BY 3 SUBMATRIX AT RANDOM
         □←MM←((ι4)ε3?4)/((ι4)ε3?4)≠MAT
  15 16 17
  22 23 2+
  29 30 31

         +/MM[2;]
69
         +/MM[;2]
69

<u>EXERCISE</u> 17
      ∇ Z←CHAR BOX1 MAT
[1]   Z←MAT,CHAR
[2]   Z←CHAR,[1] Z
[3]   Z←CHAR,Z
[4]   Z←Z,[1] CHAR
    ∇

      T∆BOX1←ι4
      '*' BOX1 2 3ρ'□'
BOX1[1]
□□□*
□□□*
BOX1[2]
****
□□□*
□□□*
BOX1[3]
*****
□□□
□□□
BOX1[4]
*****
□□□
□□□
□□□
*****.

<u>EXERCISE</u> 19
      A← 8 4 ρ'↑'
      B← 2 5 ρ'□'
      C← 4 3 ρ'o'
      D← 2 3 ρ'.'
      E← 6 2 ρ'ε'

      MAT←D,[1] C
      MAT←MAT,E
      MAT←B,[1] MAT
      □←MAT←A,MAT
↑↑↑↑□□□□□
↑↑↑↑□□□□□
↑↑↑↑...εε
↑↑↑↑...εε
↑↑↑↑oooεε
↑↑↑↑oooεε
↑↑↑↑oooεε
↑↑↑↑oooεε

<u>EXERCISE</u> 21
      ∇ Z←BOARD SIZE;SQ
[1]   ⍝SIZE[1]←→NO OF ROWS
[2]   ⍝SIZE[2]←→NO OF COLUMNS
[3]   ⍝ROUND SIZE UPWARDS TO A MULTIPLE O
      F 8
[4]   ⍝SQ←→SIZE OF A SINGLE SQUARE
[5]   SIZE←8×SQ←⌈SIZE÷8
[6]   ⍝CREATE MATRIX WITH VERTICAL COLUMN
      S
[7]   ⍝ HAVING THE WIDTH OF A SQUARE AND
      THE
[8]   ⍝ LENGTH OF THE BOARD
[9]   Z←SIZEρ(SQ[2]ρ'□'),SQ[2]ρ' '
[10] ⍝CREATE BOARD BY ROTATING SELECTED
      ROWS
[11]   Z←(SIZE[1]ρ(SQ[1]ρ0),SQ[1]ρSQ[2])⌽
      Z
    ∇

      BOARD 16 24
□□□   □□□   □□□   □□□
□□□   □□□   □□□   □□□
   □□□   □□□   □□□   □□□
   □□□   □□□   □□□   □□□
□□□   □□□   □□□   □□□
□□□   □□□   □□□   □□□
   □□□   □□□   □□□   □□□
   □□□   □□□   □□□   □□□
□□□   □□□   □□□   □□□
□□□   □□□   □□□   □□□
□□□   □□□   □□□   □□□
□□□   □□□   □□□   □□□
□□□   □□□   □□□   □□□
□□□   □□□   □□□   □□□
   □□□   □□□   □□□   □□□
   □□□   □□□   □□□   □□□

<u>EXERCISE</u> 23
A)   ∇ Z←X ELIM MAT
[1]   Z←X=MAT
[2]   Z←(~v/Z)≠(~v⌿Z)/MAT
    ∇

```
      □←Z← 4 5 ρ20?20
  7  8 20  4 15
 17 18  1 14  9
  2 10  6 16 11
  3 13  5 19 12

      16 ELIM Z
  7  8 20015
 17 18  1  9
  3 13  5 12
```

B) ∇ Z←X SUMELIM MAT
```
[1]    Z←|MAT
[2]    MAT←(X<+≠Z)/MAT
[3]    Z←(X<+/Z)≠MAT
    ∇
```

```
      40 SUMELIM Z
  8  4 15
 18 14  9
 10 16 11
 13 19 12
```

EXERCISE 25
```
      MAT← 2 3 ρ'□'
      SH←ρMAT
      □←MM←(SH+4)↑(-SH+2)↑MAT
```

```
□□□
□□□
```

```
      ρMM
6 7
      MM←(0 0 ,SH[1]≥ι2+SH[1])\MAT
      □←MM←(0 0 ,SH[2]≥ι2+SH[2])\MM
```

```
□□□
□□□
```

```
*******************************************
```

CHAPTER 9 -- SORTING DATA
EXERCISES -- PAGES 275 TO 275

EXERCISE 1
B) ∇ DESCEND N;I;J;L;LARGE
```
[1]    J←1
[2]    LPJ:LARGE←N[L←J]
[3]    I←L+1
[4]    LPI:→(LARGE≥N[I])/ENDI
[5]    LARGE←N[L←I]
[6]    ENDI:→((ρN)≥I←I+1)/LPI
[7]    N[L]←N[J]
[8]    N[J]←LARGE
[9]    →((ρN)>J←J+1)/LPJ
[10]   'THE ARRAY IN DESCENDING ORDER'
[11]   N
    ∇
```

C) ∇ DESCENDBUBBLE N;I;J
```
[1]    J←1
[2]    LPJ:J←J+1
[3]    ⍝TEST FOR END OF THE VECTOR
[4]    →((ρN)<J)/OUT
[5]    I←J
[6]    ⍝SEARCH BACKWARDS TO FIND PROPER LO
         CATION
[7]    LPI:I←I-1
[8]    ⍝CHECK FOR BEGINNING OF THE VECTOR
[9]    →(I=0)/LPJ
[10]   ⍝CHECK FOR PROPER POSITION
[11]   →(N[I+1]≤N[I])/LPJ
[12]   ⍝EXCHANGE N[I+1] AND N[I]
[13]   N[I+ 0 1]←N[I+ 1 0]
[14]   →LPI
[15]   OUT:'THE ARRAY IN SORTED ORDER'
[16]   N
    ∇
```

THE ONLY CHANGE REQUIRED IS IN
LINE[11] WHERE ≤ REPLACES ≥.

EXERCISE 3
```
      ∇ M ASCEND2 N;I;J;L;SMALL
[1]    ⍝VECTOR N IS SORTED AND DETERMINES
         THE ORDER OF THE RESULTS
[2]    ⍝VECTOR M UNDERGOES THE SAME CHANGE
         S AS N
[3]    J←1
[4]    LPJ:SMALL←N[L←J]
[5]    I←L+1
[6]    LPI:→(SMALL≤N[I])/ENDI
[7]    SMALL←N[L←I]
[8]    ENDI:→((ρN)≥I←I+1)/LPI
[9]    N[L]←N[J]
[10]   N[J]←SMALL
[11]   ⍝MAKE CORRESPONDING CHANGES IN M
[12]   SMALL←M[J]
[13]   M[J]←M[L]
[14]   M[L]←SMALL
[15]   →((ρN)>J←J+1)/LPJ
[16]   'THE ARRAYS IN ASCENDING ORDER'
[17]   N
[18]   M
    ∇
```

THE EXECUTION OF ASCEND2 IN THE FORM
<WAGE ASCEND2 SOC> WILL PROVIDE THE
DESIRED SOLUTION.

EXERCISE 5
```
      ∇ Z←INTERCHANGESORT X;N;J;JP;TEMP;LA
      ST
[1]   ⍝MAKE SURE X IS A VECTOR
[2]   →(1=ρρX)ρL1
[3]   'RANK ERROR'
[4]   →
[5]   ⍝N GIVES THE UPPER LIMIT ON THE SEA
      RCH FOR UNSORTED
[6]   ⍝ELEMENTS. BEYOND THIS ALL ELEMENTS
      ARE IN ORDER.
[7]   L1:N←ρX
[8]   ⍝J GIVES THE POSITION OF THE ELEMEN
      T CURRENTLY BEING CHECKED.
[9]   LP1:J←1
[10]  ⍝LAST GIVES THE POSITION OF THE LAS
      T ELEMENT SWITCHED. AFTER
[11]  ⍝ A COMPLETE SWEEP ALL THE ELEMENTS
      BEYOND LAST WILL BE IN ORDER.
[12]  LAST←0
[13]  LP2:→(N<JP←J+1)ρEND
[14]  ⍝TEST IF ELEMENTS ARE IN ORDER
[15]  →(X[JP]<TEMP←X[J])/SWITCH
[16]  ⍝IF ELEMENTS ARE IN ORDER INCREMENT
      COUNTER AND LOOP.
[17]  J←JP
[18]  →LP2
[19]  ⍝IF ELEMENTS ARE NOT IN ORDER INTER
      CHANGE
[20]  SWITCH:X[J]←X[JP]
[21]  X[JP]←TEMP
[22]  ⍝RECORD POSITION OF INTERCHANGE
[23]  LAST←J
[24]  J←JP
[25]  →LP2
[26]  ⍝TEST IF ANY INTERCHANGES MADE
[27]  END:→(LAST≤1)ρOUT
[28]  ⍝SET UPPER LIMIT TO SEARCH FOR UNSO
      RTED ELEMENTS.
[29]  N←LAST
[30]  ⍝RESET LAST
[31]  LAST←0
[32]  →LP1
[33]  OUT:Z←X
      ∇

      ⎕←X←20?20
19 20 17 6 13 3 12 7 8 1 5 10 11 18 14
   16 4 2 15 9
      INTERCHANGESORT X
1 2 3 4 5 6 7 8 9 10 11 12 13 14 15 16
   17 18 19 20
```

CHAPTER 10 -- SEARCHING DATA
EXERCISES -- PAGES 284 TO 285

EXERCISE 1
```
      ∇ Z←A DESCENDBINSRCH B;HIGH;LOW
[1]   →(1=ρρA)/OK
[2]   'LEFT ARGUMENT TO BINSRCH MUST BE
      A VECTOR'
[3]   →0
[4]   ⍝INITIALIZE HIGH AND LOW
[5]   OK:LOW←1
[6]   HIGH←ρA
[7]   ⍝B IS NOT PRESENT IN A IF LOW>HIGH
[8]   LP:→(LOW>HIGH)/OUT
[9]   ⍝CALCULATE THE MIDPOINT OF THE CURR
      ENT INTERVAL
[10]  Z←⌊0.5×LOW+HIGH
[11]  ⍝TEST FOR THE DESIRED VALUE
[12]  →(A[Z]=B)/0
[13]  →(A[Z]>B)/LW
[14]  ⍝IF A[Z]<B, RESPECIFY HIGH
[15]  HIGH←Z-1
[16]  →LP
[17]  ⍝IF A[Z]>B, RESPECIFY LOW
[18]  LW:LOW←Z+1
[19]  →LP
[20]  ⍝ASSIGN Z IF B IS NOT IN A
[21]  OUT:Z←1+ρA
      ∇


      ⎕←X←⌽⍳20
20 19 18 17 16 15 14 13 12 11 10 9 8 7
   6 5 4 3 2 1
      X⍳5
16
      X DESCENDBINSRCH 5
16
```

EXERCISE 3
```
      ∇ C←A EPSILONSRCH B;Z
[1]   →(1=ρρA)/OK
[2]   'LEFT ARGUMENT TO LINSRCH MUST BE
      A VECTOR'
[3]   →0
[4]   OK:Z←1
[5]   LP:→(Z>ρA)/0
[6]   ⍝THE VALUE OF C IS RETURNED AS 1 IF
      A MATCH IS FOUND, 0 OTHERWISE.
[7]   →(C←A[Z]=B)/0
[8]   Z←Z+1
[9]   →LP
      ∇
```

THE ONLY MODIFICATION REQUIRED IS TO
RETURN THE RESULT OF THE EQUALITY
TEST, HENCE THE NEW HEADER AND
LINE[7]. AN IDENTICAL MODIFICATION
APPLIES TO BINSRCH.
```
      A←ι10
      A EPSILONSRCH 3
1
      A EPSILONSRCH 12
0
```

EXERCISE 5
ON THE SYSTEM USED TO RUN THESE
EXERCISES, THE BREAK POINT WAS BETWEEN
20 TO 25. BELOW THIS LINSRCH WAS THE
FASTEST, ABOVE BINSRCH. THE BINSRCH
REQUIRED ROUGHLY A CONSTANT AMOUNT OF
TIME TO FIND ALL VALUES WHILE THE TIME
REQUIRED BY LINSRCH INCREASES LINEARLY
AS THE ELEMENT SEARCHED FOR MOVED
FURTHER OUT IN A .

EXERCISE 7
```
     ∇ Z←A NEWLINSRCH B;I;R
[1]   →(1=ρρA)/OK
[2]   'LEFT ARGUMENT TO LINSRCH MUST BE
       A VECTOR'
[3]   →0
[4]   ⍝STORE THE SHAPE OF B
[5]   OK:R←ρB
[6]   ⍝CONVERT B TO A VECTOR.
[7]   B←,B
[8]   ⍝I IS USED AS A COUNTER TO INDEX B
[9]   I←0
[10]  LP1:→((ρB)<I←I+1)ρOUT
[11]  Z←1
[12]  LP:→(Z>ρA)/END
[13]   →(A[Z]=B[I])/END
[14]  Z←Z+1
[15]  →LP
[16]  ⍝B ITSELF IS USED TO STORE THE POSI
       TIONS
[17] END:B[I]←Z
[18]  →LP1
[19]  ⍝RESHAPE B INTO ITS ORIGINAL SHAPE
[20] OUT:Z←⌊RρB
     ∇
```

THE VERSION GIVEN HERE WORKS FOR RIGHT
HAND ARGUMENTS OF ANY SHAPE. THE SHAPE
OF THE RIGHT HAND ARGUMENT IS THE SAME
AS THE SHAPE OF THE RESULT.
```
      A←ι20
      A NEWLINSRCH 12
12
```
THE ARGUMENT AND RESULT ARE SCALARS.

```
      ρρA NEWLINSRCH 12
0
      A NEWLINSRCH 0 5 10 15 20 25
21 5 10 15 20 21
      A NEWLINSRCH 2 2 ρ 2 5 8 11
  2  5
  8 11

      ρA NEWLINSRCH 2 2 ρ 2 5 8 11
2 2
```

****

CHAPTER 11 -- COMPUTER GENERATED
                RANDOM NUMBERS
EXERCISES --   PAGES 298 TO 301

EXERCISE 1
```
     ∇ CKRANDOM N;R
[1]   R←?Nρ20
[2]   'AVERAGE ';(+/R)÷N;' EXPECTED AVER
      AGE ';(+/ι20)÷20
[3]   'NO. OF VALUES ≤10 ';+/R≤10;' EXPE
      CTED ';0.5×N
[4]   'NO. OF ODD INTEGERS ';+/2|R;' EXP
      ECTED ';0.5×N
[5]   'NO. OF VALUES APPEARING TWICE IN
      SUCCESSION ';+/(¯1↓R)=1↓R
[6]   'EXPECTED ';(N⍪1)÷20
     ∇
```

EXERCISE 3
```
     ∇ EASYCARDS;N;PLAY;WIN
[1]   'ENTER THE NUMBER OF GAMES TO BE P
      LAYED'
[2]   N←⎕
[3]   PLAY←WIN←0
[4]   LP:WIN←WIN+1≥+/(ι52)=52?52
[5]   →(N>PLAY←PLAY+1)/LP
[6]   'ESTIMATE OF PROBABILITY OF WINNIN
      G'
[7]   WIN÷PLAY
     ∇
```

EXERCISE 5
```
     ∇ Z←NONRANDOM N
[1]   L1:Z←N?N
[2]   →((+/0=2|Z[2×ιⁿ⌊N÷2])<⌊N÷4)ρL1
     ∇
```

WINS WOULD BE TOO INFREQUENT SINCE
THERE WOULD BE AN INCREASED CHANCE OF
A MATCH. THE FUNCTION NONRANDOM MIMICS
SUCH A SITUATION BY REGENERATING 52
RANDOM VALUES UNTIL THERE ARE MORE
EVEN VALUES WITH EVEN INDICES THAN NOT.

```
EXERCISE 7
      X← 1 ¯1[?100ρ2]
      10↑X
¯1 ¯1 ¯1 1 1 1 ¯1 ¯1 ¯1 1
      +/X=1
47
      +/X=¯1
53
```

```
EXERCISE 9
      ∇ PICK
[1]   'SHELF ';((60ρ1),(13ρ2), 3 3)[?75]
      ∇
```

```
EXERCISE 11
C)  ∇ Z←DARTS;A;B
[1]   A←((10ρ1),(50ρ5),40ρ15)[?100]
[2]   B←+/((30ρ1),(65ρ5),5ρ15)[? 100 100
      ]
[3]   Z←(1↑(B>A)↓'AB'),' WINS'
      ∇
```

```
      DARTS
B WINS
      DARTS
B WINS
      DARTS
A WINS
D)  ∇ PLAYDARTS N;I;A
[1]   A←I←0
[2]   LP:→(N<I←I+1)ρEND
[3]   A←A+'A'=1↑DARTS
[4]   →LP
[5]   END:'PROBABILITY OF A WINNING IS ';
      A÷N
      ∇
```

```
EXERCISE 13
      ∇ H←HAND;SUIT;FACE
[1]   ⍝DEAL THE CARDS
[2]   H←13?52
[3]   ⍝ARRANGE IN ORDER
[4]   H←H[⍋H]
[5]   ⍝DETERMINE THE SUIT
[6]   SUIT← 4 5 ρ'CLUB DIAM HEARTSPADE'
[7]   SUIT←SUIT[⌈H÷13;]
[8]   ⍝DETERMINE THE FACE VALUE
[9]   FACE← 13 2 ρ' 2 3 4 5 6 7 8 910 J
      Q K A'
[10]  FACE←FACE[1+13|¯1+H;]
[11]  ⍝DISPLAY THE HAND
[12]  H←FACE,' ',SUIT
      ∇
```

```
      HAND
 5 CLUB
10 CLUB
 6 DIAM
10 DIAM
 A DIAM
```

```
 2 HEART
10 HEART
 Q HEART
 A HEART
 2 SPADE
 4 SPADE
 8 SPADE
10 SPADE
```

```
EXERCISE 17
      ∇ Z←JAR
[1]   ⍝DETERMINE THE NUMBER OF COINS DRAW
      N
[2]   Z←(8,(9ρ9),(15ρ10),(25ρ11),(25ρ12)
      ,(20ρ13),5ρ14)[?100]
[3]   ⍝DETERMINE THE VALUE OF THE COINS D
      RAWN
[4]   Z←+/(10 10 ,8ρ1)[?Zρ10]
      ∇
```

```
      JAR
30
      JAR
9
```

****

CHAPTER 12 -- A FINANCIAL MODEL
EXERCISES -- PAGES 311 TO 312

```
EXERCISE 1
      ∇ Z←ENTER Y
[1]   LP:→(∧/'END'=3↑X←⎕)/OUT
[2]   Y←Y,[1](ρY)[2]↑X
[3]   →LP
[4]   OUT:Z←Y
      ∇
```

```
EXERCISE 3
      ∇ FMT PRINT S;I;J
[1]   S←,S
[2]   I←0
[3]   LP:→((ρS)<I←I+1)/0
[4]   →(1 0 ¯1 =×J←S[I])/LPRT,SK,RPRT
[5]   LPRT:→(J>1000)/TITLE
[6]   '   ',LN[J;],FMT▼L[J;]
[7]   →LP
[8]   TITLE:J←J-1000
[9]   UNDERLINE T[J;]
[10]  →LP
[11]  SK:''
[12]  →LP
[13]  RPRT:J←|J
[14]  '        ',RN[J;],FMT▼R[J]
[15]  →LP
      ∇
```

EXERCISE 5
```
     ∇ MODEL5
[1]    ⍝INDUSTRY SALES FROM CURRENT SALES
       AND GROWTH RATE
[2]    L[1;]←P[1]×(1+P[2])* 0 1 2 3 4
[3]    ⍝HITECH MARKET SHARE
[4]    L[2;]←DS[1;]
[5]    ⍝HITECH SALES FROM INDUSTRY SALES A
       ND MARKET SHARE
[6]    L[3;]←L[1;]×L[2;]
[7]    ⍝AVERAGE SALES
[8]    R[1]←AVERAGE L[3;]
[9]    ⍝SALES REVENUE FROM SALES VOLUME AN
       D PRICE
[10]   L[4;]←P[3]×L[3;]
[11]   ⍝AVERAGE SALES REVENUE
[12]   R[2]←AVERAGE L[4;]
[13]   ⍝DEFECT RATE
[14]   L[5;]←DS[3;]
[15]   ⍝PRODUCTION VOLUME FROM SALES VOLUM
       E AND DEFECT RATE
[16]   L[6;]←L[3;]×1+L[5;]
[17]   ⍝PRODUCTION COSTS FROM VOLUME AND F
       IXED AND VARIABLE COSTS
[18]   L[7;]←P[5]+P[6]×L[6;]
[19]   ⍝MARKETING COSTS FROM NORMAL AND SP
       ECIAL COSTS
[20]   L[8;]←DS[2;]+P[4]×L[4;]
[21]   ⍝ADMINISTRATIVE COSTS
[22]   L[11;]←DS[4;]
[23]   ⍝TOTAL AND AVERAGE COSTS
[24]   L[9;]←L[7;]+L[8;]+L[11;]
[25]   R[3]←AVERAGE L[9;]
[26]   ⍝PROFIT FROM SALES REVENUE AND TOTA
       L COSTS
[27]   L[10;]←L[4;]-L[9;]
[28]   ⍝TOTAL AND AVERAGE PROFIT
[29]   R[4]←+/L[10;]
[30]   R[5]←AVERAGE L[10;]
     ∇
```

THE MODEL HAS BEEN MODIFIED BY THE
INCLUSION OF THE ADMINISTRATIVE COSTS.
THESE ARE STORED IN DS[4;] AND L[11;].
```
       DSN[4;], 6 1 ▼DS[4;]
ADMIN. COSTS              40.0  45.0  50.0
       55.0 60.0
```
THE TOTAL COSTS, LINE[24], NOW INCLUDE
ADMINISTRATIVE COSTS.

EXERCISE 7
```
     ∇ MODEL7
[1]    ⍝INDUSTRY SALES FROM CURRENT SALES
       AND GROWTH RATE
[2]    L[1;]←P[1]×(1+P[2])* 0 1 2 3 4
[3]    ⍝HITECH MARKET SHARE
[4]    L[2;]←DS[1;]
[5]    ⍝HITECH SALES FROM INDUSTRY SALES A
       ND MARKET SHARE
```

```
[6]    L[3;]←L[1;]×L[2;]
[7]    ⍝AVERAGE SALES
[8]    R[1]←AVERAGE L[3;]
[9]    ⍝SALES REVENUE FROM SALES VOLUME AN
       D PRICE
[10]   L[4;]←P[3]×L[3;]
[11]   ⍝AVERAGE SALES REVENUE
[12]   R[2]←AVERAGE L[4;]
[13]   ⍝PRODUCTION FOR INVENTORY, L[11;],
       CALCULATED FROM
[14]   ⍝     INVENTORY LEVEL AS PERCENT OF
       SALES VOLUME,
[15]   ⍝     P[7], AND SALES VOLUME, L[3;]
[16]   L[11;]←P[7]×L[3;]-¯1↓0,L[3;]
[17]   ⍝DEFECT RATE
[18]   L[5;]←DS[3;]
[19]   ⍝PRODUCTION VOLUME FROM SALES VOLUM
       E, INVENTORY
[20]   ⍝     PRODUCTION L[11;] AND DEFECT R
       ATE
[21]   L[6;]←(L[3;]+L[11;])×1+L[5;]
[22]   ⍝PRODUCTION COSTS FROM VOLUME AND F
       IXED AND VARIABLE COSTS
[23]   L[7;]←P[5]+P[6]×L[6;]
[24]   ⍝MARKETING COSTS FROM NORMAL AND SP
       ECIAL COSTS
[25]   L[8;]←DS[2;]+P[4]×L[4;]
[26]   ⍝TOTAL AND AVERAGE COSTS
[27]   L[9;]←L[7;]+L[8;]
[28]   R[3]←AVERAGE L[9;]
[29]   ⍝PROFIT FROM SALES REVENUE AND TOTA
       L COSTS
[30]   L[10;]←L[4;]-L[9;]
[31]   ⍝TOTAL AND AVERAGE PROFIT
[32]   R[4]←+/L[10;]
[33]   R[5]←AVERAGE L[10;]
     ∇
```

THE COMPUTATION PERFORMED IN
LINES[13~16] GIVES THE APPROPRIATE
FRACTION OF THE CHANGE IN SALES VOLUME.
EXERCISE 9
```
     ∇ MODEL9
[1]    ⍝INDUSTRY SALES FROM CURRENT SALES
       AND GROWTH RATE
[2]    L[1;]←P[1]×(1+P[2])* 0 1 2 3 4
[3]    ⍝HITECH MARKET SHARE
[4]    L[2;]←DS[1;]
[5]    ⍝HITECH SALES FROM INDUSTRY SALES A
       ND MARKET SHARE
[6]    L[3;]←L[1;]×L[2;]
[7]    ⍝AVERAGE SALES
[8]    R[1]←AVERAGE L[3;]
[9]    ⍝SALES REVENUE FROM SALES VOLUME AN
       D PRICE
[10]   L[4;]←P[3]×L[3;]
[11]   ⍝AVERAGE SALES REVENUE
[12]   R[2]←AVERAGE L[4;]
```

```
[13]  ⍝DEFECT RATE
[14]  L[5;]←DS[3;]
[15]  ⍝PRODUCTION VOLUME FROM SALES VOLUM
      E AND DEFECT RATE
[16]  L[6;]←L[3;]×1+L[5;]
[17]  ⍝PRODUCTION COSTS FROM VOLUME AND F
      IXED AND VARIABLE COSTS
[18]  L[7;]←P[5]+P[6]×L[6;]
[19]  ⍝MARKETING COSTS FROM NORMAL AND SP
      ECIAL COSTS
[20]  L[8;]←DS[2;]+P[4]×L[4;]
[21]  ⍝TOTAL AND AVERAGE COSTS
[22]  L[9;]←L[7;]+L[8;]
[23]  R[3]←AVERAGE L[9;]
[24]  ⍝PROFIT FROM SALES REVENUE AND TOTA
      L COSTS
[25]  L[10;]←L[4;]-L[9;]
[26]  ⍝COMPUTE PROFITS AFTER INTEREST EXP
      ENSES
[27]  L[11;]←0.11 LOANS L[10;]
[28]  ⍝COMPUTE INTEREST EXPENSE
[29]  L[12;]←L[10;]-L[11;]
[30]  ⍝TOTAL AND AVERAGE PROFIT
[31]  R[4]←+/L[11;]
[32]  R[5]←AVERAGE L[11;]
      ∇


      ∇ NEWPROF←RATE LOANS OLDPROF;LOAN;CA
        SH;PAY
[1]   ⍝INITIALIZE COUNTER AND PROFITS AFT
      ER INTEREST EXPENSES
[2]   NEWPROF←0×OLDPROF
[3]   I←1
[4]   ⍝INITIALIZE OUTSTANDING LOAN BALANC
      E
[5]   LOAN←0
[6]   ⍝INITIALIZE CASH BALANCE
[7]   CASH←0
[8]   ⍝COMPUTE INTEREST ON OUTSTANDING LO
      AN BALANCE
[9]   LP:INT←LOAN×RATE
[10]  ⍝COMPUTE PROFITS AFTER INTEREST EXP
      ENSE
[11]  NEWPROF[I]←OLDPROF[I]-INT
[12]  ⍝COMPUTE NEW CASH BALANCE BEFORE LO
      ANS
[13]  CASH←CASH+NEWPROF[I]
[14]  ⍝COMPUTE NEW LOAN BALANCE
[15]  LOAN←-0⌊CASH
[16]  →((⍴NEWPROF)≥I←I+1)/LP
      ∇
```

THE FUNCTION LOANS IS USED IN LINE[27]
TO COMPUTE THE AFTER INTEREST PROFITS
WHICH IS STORED IN L[11;].
INTEREST EXPENSES ARE STORED IN
LINE[12;].

CHAPTER 13 -- GRAPHICAL
                PRESENTATION OF DATA
EXERCISES -- PAGES 321 TO 321

EXERCISE 1

```
      ∇ LIM GRAPH DAT;NX;NY;M;I;X;Y;XINC;Y
        INC
[1]   ⍝INITIALIZE BLANK MATRIX
[2]   NX←60
[3]   NY←30
[4]   M←(NY,NX)⍴' '
[5]   ⍝CHECK VALIDITY OF INPUT DATA
[6]   →(2≠⍴⍴DAT)/ER
[7]   →(4≠⍴LIM)/ER
[8]   ⍝SEPARATE INDEPENDENT AND DEPENDENT
        VARIABLES
[9]   X←DAT[;1]
[10]  Y← 0 1 ↓DAT
[11]  ⍝COMPUTE X AND Y INCREMENTS
[12]  XINC←(LIM[2]-LIM[1])÷NX
[13]  YINC←(LIM[4]-LIM[3])÷NY
[14]  ⍝COMPUTE PLOT POSITIONS IN GRAPH
[15]  X←1⌈NX⌊⌈(X-LIM[1])÷XINC
[16]  Y←1⌈NY⌊⌈(LIM[4]-Y)÷YINC
[17]  ⍝SETUP HORIZONTAL AND VERTICAL AXES
[18]  M[1⌈NY⌊LIM[4]÷YINC;]←'-'
[19]  M[;1⌈NX⌊⌈-LIM[1]÷XINC]←'|'
[20]  ⍝PLOT DATA POINTS
[21]  I←1
[22]  PLOTVAR←,PLOTVAR
[23]  M←,M
[24]  LOOP:M[X+NX×Y[;I]-1]←PLOTVAR[I]
[25]  →((⍴Y)[2]≥I←I+1)/LOOP
[26]  M←(NY,NX)⍴M
[27]  ⍝DISPLAY PLOT AND KEY
[28]  M
[29]  'LOWER X LIMIT ';LIM[1]
[30]  'UPPER X LIMIT ';LIM[2]
[31]  'X INCREMENT   ';XINC
[32]  'LOWER Y LIMIT ';LIM[3]
[33]  'UPPER Y LIMIT ';LIM[4]
[34]  'Y INCREMENT   ';YINC
[35]  →0
[36]  ⍝DISPLAY ERROR MESSAGE IF INPUT DAT
      A IS INCORRECT
[37]  ER:'INCORRECT INPUT DATA'
      ∇
```

CHAPTER 13 -- EXERCISE 1, Continued

THE FUNCTION SHOWN HERE CONTAINS
MODIFICATIONS TO SOLVE EXERCISES 1,
4,5, AND 7.
SET UP THE INDEPENDENT VARIBLE
    X←¯32+2×ɩ31
THE FIRST DEPENDENT VARIABLE
    Y←(X+25)×(X+6)×X¯28
THE SECOND DEPENDENT VARIABLE
    Y1←¯2000+250×X
ARRANGE THE DATA INTO THE APPROPRIATE
MATRIX
    DAT←⍉ 3 31 ρX,Y,Y1
SET THE LIMITS AND THE PLOT VARIABLE
    LIM← ¯30 30 ¯11000 4000
    PLOTVAR←'*O'

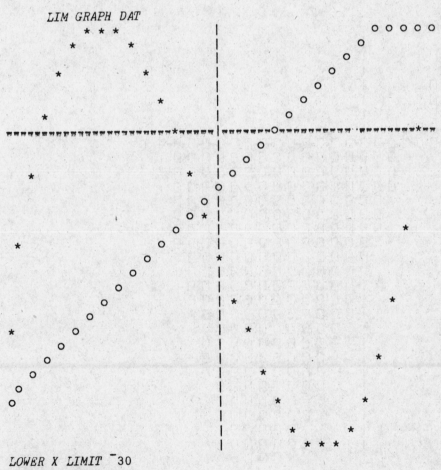

    LIM GRAPH DAT

LOWER X LIMIT ¯30
UPPER X LIMIT 30
X INCREMENT   1
LOWER Y LIMIT ¯11000
UPPER Y LIMIT 4000
Y INCREMENT   500

EXERCISE 9

```
      ∇ LIM HISTOGRAM DAT;NX;NY;M;I;X;Y;XI
        NC;YINC;LOC;XMARK
[1]     NX←60
[2]     NY←30
[3]     M←(NY,NX)ρ' '
[4]     →(0≠2|ρDAT)/ER
[5]     →(4≠ρLIM)/ER
[6]     I←(ρDAT)÷2
[7]     X←I↑DAT
[8]     Y←I↓DAT
[9]     XINC←(LIM[2]-LIM[1])÷NX
[10]    YINC←(LIM[4]-LIM[3])÷NY
[11]    X←1⌈NX⌊⌈(X-LIM[1])÷XINC
[12]    Y←1⌈NY⌊⌈(LIM[4]-Y)÷YINC
[13]    ⍝RETAIN THE POSITION OF THE X AXIS
[14]    XMARK←1⌈NY⌊⌈LIM[4]÷YINC
[15]    M[XMARK;]←'¬'
[16]    M[;1⌈NX⌊⌈-LIM[1]÷XINC]←'|'
[17]    I←1
[18]    LOOP:LOC←ιNY
[19]    LOC←(((XMARK⌊Y[I])≤LOC)∧(XMARK⌈Y[I
        ])≥LOC)/LOC
[20]    M[LOC;X[I]]←'▯'
[21]    →((ρX)≥I←I+1)/LOOP
[22]    M
[23]    'LOWER X LIMIT ';LIM[1]
[24]    'UPPER X LIMIT ';LIM[2]
[25]    'X INCREMENT   ';XINC
[26]    'LOWER Y LIMIT ';LIM[3]
[27]    'UPPER Y LIMIT ';LIM[4]
[28]    'Y INCREMENT   ';YINC
[29]    →0
[30]    ER:'INCORRECT INPUT DATA'
      ∇
```

```
      X←¯32+2×ι31
      Y←(X+25)×(X+6)×X-28
      LIM← ¯30 30 ¯11000 4000
```

```
      LIM HISTOGRAM X,Y
```

```
LOWER X LIMIT ¯30
UPPER X LIMIT 30
X INCREMENT    1
LOWER Y LIMIT ¯11000
UPPER Y LIMIT 4000
Y INCREMENT   500
```

CHAPTER 14 -- WEEKLY PAYROLL
EXERCISES -- PAGES 334 TO 335

EXERCISE 1
```
      ∇ TIME;END;ID;IDNOS;LOC;REC
[1]   END← ¯2*7
[2]   ⍝IDNOS CONTAINS ALL EMPLOYEE ID NUM
      BERS.
[3]   IDNOS←EMP[;1]
[4]   ⍝REC IS USED TO KEEP TRACK OF EMPLO
      YEES FOR WHO DATA IS ENTERED
[5]   ⍝   IT IS INITIALIZED TO ZERO FOR E
      ACH EMPLOYEE.
[6]   ⍝     AND SET TO ONE UPON ENTRY OF D
      ATA.
[7]   REC←(ρIDNOS)ρ0
[8]   IN:'ENTER ID NO:'
[9]   →(END=ID←⎕)/CK
[10]  →((ρEMP)[1]≥LOC←IDNOSιID)/OK
[11]  'INVALID ID'
[12]  →IN
[13] OK:'ENTER HOURS WORKED'
[14]  EMP[LOC;9]←INPUTHOURS
[15]  REC[LOC]←1
[16]  →IN
[17] CK:→(∧/REC)/CK1
[18]  'DATA FOR ';(~REC)/IDNOS;' NOT ENT
      ERED'
[19]  →IN
[20] CK1:'    IDNO     HOURS'
[21]  8 0 10 0 ▼EMP[; 1 9]
[22]  ''
[23]  'CORRECT? Y OR N'
[24]  →('Y'=1↑⎕)/0
[25]  →IN
      ∇
```

```
      ∇ Z←INPUTHOURS
[1]   L1:'ENTER HOURS WORKED'
[2]   Z←⎕
[3]   ⍝CHECK DATA
[4]   →((30≤Z)∧Z≤45)/0
[5]   Z;' ARE YOU SURE? Y OR N'
[6]   →('Y'=1↑⎕)/0
[7]   →L1
      ∇
```

THE ABOVE TIME FUNCTION CHECKS THAT
ALL DATA HAVE BEEN ENTERED. CHECKS
EACH HOURLY INPUT USING INPUTHOURS AND
DISPLAYS THE INPUT FOR REVIEW.

EXERCISE 3
```
      ∇ FED
[1]   ⍝CONTAINS A SCHEMATIC FORM OF AN AL
      TERNATIVE SCHEME
```

```
[2]   ⍝WAGES↔EMPLOYEE WAGES AFTER ALLOWA
      NCES
[3]   ⍝LIMITS↔LIMITS FOR EACH WAGE INTER
      VAL
[4]   ⍝PERCENT↔VECTOR OF PERCENTS FOR EA
      CH INTERVAL
[5]   ⍝BASE↔BASE AMOUNTS FOR EACH INTERV
      AL
[6]   TAX←(ρWAGES)ρ0
[7]   I←2
[8]   ⍝DETERMINE WAGES FALLING IN CURRENT
      INTERVAL
[9]   LP:IND←((LIMITS[I¯1]≤WAGES)∧WAGES<L
      IMITS[I])/ιρWAGES
[10]  TAX[IND]←BASE[I¯1]+PERCENT[I¯1]×WA
      GES[IND]¯LIMITS[I¯1]
[11]  →((ρLIMITS)≥I←I+1)ρLP
[12]  ⍝COMPUTE FOR LAST WAGE INTERVAL
[13]  IND←(LIMITS[I¯1]≤WAGES)/ιρWAGES
[14]  TAX[IND]←BASE[I¯1]+PERCENT[I¯1]×WA
      GES[IND]¯LIMITS[I¯1]
      ∇
```


EXERCISE 5
```
      ∇ TOTALSTODATE
[1]   ⍝MAXIMUM FICA INCOME
[2]   MAX←14100
[3]   ⍝FICA WITHOLDING RATE
[4]   RATE←0.0585
[5]   ⍝UNEMPLOYMENT WITHHOLDING RATE
[6]   URATE←0.03
[7]   '   ID NO.  REGULAR      O.T.  FED
      TAX  FICA   UNEMPL    NET PAY'
[8]   FMT← 10 0 ,12ρ 10 2
[9]   FMT▼EMP[;1],(¯/EMP[; 6 7]),EMP[; 7
      6 8],(RATE×MAX⌊EMP[;6]),URATE×EMP
      [;6]
      ∇
```

NOTE THAT THE PARAMETERS FOR FICA AND
UNEMPLOYMENT TAX ARE INCLUDED IN THIS
ROUTINE ALSO. NORMALLY SUCH PARAMETERS
WOULD BE STORED IN THE DATA BASE WHERE
THE COULD BE ACCESSED BY ALL FUNCTIONS
BUT WOULD REQUIRE ONLY A SINGLE CHANGE
WHEN REGULATIONS CHANGED.

EXERCISE 7
ADDITIONS TO OR DELETIONS FROM THE
PAYROLL REQUIRE THE EXPANSION OR
COMPRESSION OF THE MATRIX EMP AND
STORAGE IN SOME OTHER MATRIX OF LAPSED
RECORDS
NOTE ALSO THAT CUMULATIVE TOTALS IN
COMP ARE NOW NO LONGER THE REDUCTION
OF THE CORRESPONDING COLUMNS IN EMP IF
EMPLOYEES ARE DELETED.

CHAPTER 15 -- COMPUTER ASSISTED
                    INSTRUCTION
EXERCISES -- PAGES 344 TO 345

EXERCISE 1
```
     ∇ CHECK CANS;ANS
[1]  ⍝THIS VERSION REMOVES ALL BLANKS AN
     D CHECKS IF THE REMAINDER IS IDENT
     ICAL TO CANS
[2]  ANS←,⎕
[3]  ANS←(' '≠ANS)/ANS
[4]  →(((ρANS)=ρ,CANS)∧∧/ANS=(ρANS)↑CAN
     S)/CORR
[5]  'SORRY THE CORRECT ANSWER IS ',CAN
     S
[6]  →0
[7]  CORR:NCORR←NCORR+1
     ∇
```


EXERCISE 5
```
     ∇ MULTDRILL;STOP;NTRY;NCOR;A;B;C
[1]  'ENTER ''STOP'' TO END'
[2]  STOP←¯2*31
[3]  NTRY←0
[4]  NCOR←0
[5]  LP:A←49+?51
[6]  B←49+?51
[7]  A;' × ';B;' = ?'
[8]  C←⎕
[9]  →(STOP=C)/END
[10] NTRY←NTRY+1
[11] →(C≠A×B)/WRONG
[12] 'CORRECT'
[13] NCOR←NCOR+1
[14] →LP
[15] WRONG:'WRONG THE ANSWER IS ';A×B
[16] →LP
[17] END:' '
[18] 'YOU DID ';NCOR;' OUT OF ';NTRY;'
     CORRECTLY.'
     ∇
```


****

Index of Defined Functions

Subject Index